D1566870

The Americanization of Zionism, 1897–1948

The Americanization of Zionism, 1897–1948

Naomi W. Cohen

Brandeis University Press

PUBLISHED BY UNIVERSITY PRESS OF NEW ENGLAND

HANOVER AND LONDON

Brandeis University Press

Published by University Press of New England,

37 Lafayette Street, Lebanon, NH 03766

© 2003 by Brandeis University

This book was published with the generous support of the Lucius N. Litthauer Foundation, Inc.

Printed in the United States of America

5 4 3 2 1

Library of Congress Cataloguing-in-Publication Data
Cohen, Naomi Wiener, 1927–
The Americanization of Zionism, 1897–1948 / Naomi W. Cohen.
    p.   cm. — (Brandeis series in American Jewish history,
culture, and life)
Includes bibliographical references and index.
ISBN 1–58465–346–9 (alk. paper)
1. Zionism—United States—History. 2. Jews—Attitudes toward
Israel. 3. Jews—United States—Politics and government—20th
century. 4. Israel and the diaspora. I. Title. II. Series.
DS149.5.U6 C66 2003
320.54'095694'0973—dc22   2003018067

Brandeis Series in
American Jewish History, Culture, and Life

Jonathan D. Sarna, EDITOR
Sylvia Barack Fishman, ASSOCIATE EDITOR

To the memory of G.D.C.

Contents

Acknowledgments

I have studied and written about American Zionism ever since I was a graduate student at Columbia University. Along the way I have benefited from the wisdom and insights of teachers, colleagues, students, and friends. To all of them, beginning with my revered mentor, the late Professor Salo Wittmayer Baron, I am grateful. This book, which ties together segments of my research over many years, represents some of their contributions.

The libraries I have used are too numerous to thank individually, but the following librarians deserve special mention: Adina Feldstern of Hebrew Union College in Jerusalem, Cyma Horowitz of the American Jewish Committee, Kevin Proffitt of the American Jewish Archives, and Mira Levine of the Institute of Contemporary Jewry (Jerusalem).

Many friends and associates have contributed to the completion of this book in a variety of ways. Nor do I minimize their help when I single out only two to whom I am particularly indebted: Jonathan Sarna, professor at Brandeis University, who read the first draft of the manuscript and offered incisive and valuable suggestions, and Phyllis Deutsch, editor at the University Press of New England, whose investment of time and energy in my work helped me shape a more sharply focused book. I alone, however, am responsible for any inadequacies that remain. It is also a pleasure to give special thanks to my research assistant, Charlotte Bonelli, and to my children, Jeremy Cohen and Judith Rosen, for their unstinting aid and encouragement.

Some material that I published previously has been reworked for this book, and I wish to thank the original publishers for permission to include that material here:

Chapter 1: "Forging an American Zionism: The *Maccabaean*," from "The *Maccabaean*'s Message: A Study in American Zionism until World War I," *Jewish Social Studies* 18 (July 1956): 163–78.

Chapter 3: "Zionism in the Public Square," from "The Specter of Zionism: American Opinions, 1917–1922," in Melvin I. Urofsky, ed., *Essays in American Zionism* (*Herzl Year Book*, Volume 8) (New York: Herzl Press, 1978), pp. 95–116, and from *The Year after the Riots: American Responses to the Palestine Crisis of 1929–30* (Detroit: Wayne State University Press, 1988), ch. 3.

Chapter 8: "Out of Step with the Times: Rabbi Louis Finkelstein of the Jewish Theological Seminary," from "'Diaspora Plus Palestine, Religion Plus Nationalism': The Seminary and Zionism, 1903–1948," in Jack Wertheimer, ed., *Tradition Renewed: A History of the Jewish Theological Seminary,* vol. 2 (New York: The Jewish Theological Seminary of America, 1997), pp. 113–76.

The Americanization of Zionism, 1897–1948

Introduction

Writing a few years after the organization of the Zionist movement in 1897, Dr. Max Nordau, a prominent European Zionist leader and close associate of Theodor Herzl, said: "Zionism's only hope is the Jews of America."[1] In large measure he spoke correctly. But for the financial support and political pressure of American Jews, a group whose numbers and socioeconomic importance made them by midcentury the most powerful Jewish community in modern history, Israel might not have been born in 1948. Indeed, the American Jewish investment in the development and preservation of the Jewish state has continued to the present day. Nordau, however, could not have foreseen the compromises and vicissitudes, or the achievements and inadequacies, that molded the character of Zionism in the United States. The result was an American Zionism, one that differed markedly from Nordau's own interpretation of Jewish nationalism.

Much has been written on the subject of Zionism—its origins, leaders, ideology, and development. American Zionism, however, with features peculiarly its own, requires separate treatment. Like the Zionist movement worldwide, it went through several chronological phases before the founding of the state of Israel. But different from the movement in Europe, Zionism in the United States was shaped by its American context. In each of its phases it responded to the same elemental factors: the needs of Jews in America (as well as in Europe), the stand of the American government, and the demands of American public opinion. Nor could it ignore the forces operating within the American Jewish world—a passion for acculturation and acceptance, the struggle over communal leadership, and the impact of American antisemitism. On the Zionist leaders, therefore, devolved the task of accommodating their movement and its message to the realities of the American and American Jewish scenes. The product they created was an *Americanized* Zionism, a movement that was as much American as it was Zionist.

The process of building an American Zionism was fraught with weighty questions: Could or should Zionists mouth Herzlian rhetoric, predicated on the belief in an unrelenting, universal antisemitism that inescapably doomed the survival of world Jewry, at the same time that they considered themselves an integral part of American society? Wasn't it futile for political Zionists who despaired of the future of Jews and Judaism even in the Western world to engage in American politics? Was American antisemitism a nonissue or was it something to be feared? Were assimilation and total acceptance inevitable in the United States, or was the Jew always destined to be the alien or outsider in a Christian culture? Perhaps, as Saul Bellow wrote many years later: "As a Jew you are also an American, but somehow you are also not."[2]

The Americanization of Zionism is the theme that connects the following chapters. This study does not purport to be a synthetic history of American Zionism. Nor does it consider anew the persuasive interpretation of some historians of how Zionism in the United States, identifying with the ethos of America, held forth the vision of a more perfect social order for America, indeed for all humanity, as well as for a Jewish state.[3] Rather, my approach has been to concentrate on certain specific events, institutions, or persons that flesh out the American/Zionist nexus. Based for the most part on primary sources that are treated in depth, the chapters explore the strengths and weaknesses of the organized American movement and suggest certain significant subthemes—for example, how Zionism can serve as a barometer of the overall condition of the American Jewish minority in any given time period, and how Zionist activities provide an index of Jewish acculturation.

Overall, the book posits that Zionists and their opponents always measured the compatibility of Zionism with Americanism, and that during its first fifty years American Zionism constructed its own balance between American identity and Jewish particularism. The Americanization of Zionism may not have convinced all Americans of the rectitude of the Jewish nationalist cause—it failed, for example, to win the approbation of the American State Department—but it succeeded in making Zionism a familiar and legitimate issue in the political arena. It thereby contributed significantly in preparing American public opinion for the establishment of a Jewish state.

The roots of Zionism are embedded in traditional Jewish prayers and customs that express a yearning for a return to Zion. Phrases in prayers repeated generation after generation, "Next year in Jerusalem" or "From Zion shall come forth the Law," testify to a force that propelled Jews throughout the ages—idealists and dreamers, mystics and pseudomessiahs, as well as some ordinary people— to repair to the land ordained by God for their forefathers and for them. Inspired by the biblical promise of restoration, they believed that when the messiah came at the end of the days, Eretz Yisrael, the land of Israel and birthplace of the Torah, would again become a Jewish country. The theme of restoration has figured as well in Christian eschatology, which held that a Jewish return to

Palestine was a precondition of the second coming of Jesus. In both synagogue and church those motifs have lasted to the present.

Modern Zionism emerged in the last quarter of the nineteenth century as an offshoot of the resurgence of European nationalism. Nurtured by the failure of liberalism in Europe, which left millions of Jews unemancipated, and by the pervasiveness of a virulent antisemitism, Zionism developed a Jewish nationalist ideology. Many now defined the Jews as a discrete national group; like all those that populated the Continent yet apart from the others, the Jewish national group had its own religion, language, and culture. Jews, as Professor Hans Kohn pointed out in a seminal study of nationalism, also had a "national consciousness" and a "national aspiration" of long standing.[4] Despite denials from newly emancipated Jews in western Europe, the idea that Jews constituted a national group in the modern sense was axiomatic to the thinking of Jewish proto-Zionists in eastern Europe.

At the same time, Jewish nationalism shed its religious cast and became secularized. Modern nationalists looked for neither divine intervention nor a personal messiah to lead them back to Palestine. Jews themselves, responding in particular after 1870 to the new, racist antisemitism, would by their own efforts build a secure home in Palestine. In the last quarter of the nineteenth century Zionists banded together in small groups such as the *Chovevei Zion* (Lovers of Zion), and the first modern *aliyah* (ascent to Palestine) was initiated by a few idealists who set out to drain the swamps and cultivate the soil. Zionism became a *political* movement, however, only when an assimilated Western Jew, Theodor Herzl, convened the First Zionist Congress at Basel in 1897. Herzl's message was straightforward; he appealed for the creation of a democratic Jewish state in Palestine, to be achieved by Jewish political activity and to be underwritten by international fiat.

Although the modern Zionist movement retained a secularist bent, it should be noted that secularists too could not divorce themselves totally from Zionism's religious matrix. Whether religiously observant or not, they too carried the baggage of Jewish tradition with them and could well empathize with the sentiments of the traditionalists. One example is blatant: when England offered a piece of its territory in Africa to the Zionists in the first decade of the twentieth century, a majority of delegates at the Seventh Zionist Congress in 1905 turned down the idea. The persecuted Russian Jews were in desperate need of a refuge, but most Zionist leaders knew well that their movement could successfully appeal to their fellow Jews only if the end goal were Palestine.

Herzl died in 1904, but by then he had put political Zionism on the world's diplomatic agenda. In 1917 during the First World War, England issued the Balfour Declaration, expressing approval of a Jewish national home in Palestine and promising to facilitate its establishment. Written into the terms of the postwar mandate over Palestine, the declaration stamped political Zionism with the seal of respectability. With confidence, albeit misplaced, in the promise of the declaration and mandate, some believed that the political struggle for an internationally recognized Jewish homeland was over.

After the Great War, Zionism worldwide passed through new phases. During the 1920s and '30s, political Zionism stagnated, and under the leadership of Chaim Weizmann the movement shifted to Palestinianism, or the practical job of building up the land. A significant *aliyah* from the West never materialized, but Zionists repeatedly sparred with England, the mandatory power, over the right of Jews to enter Palestine. In the 1930s, the turbulent decade or third phase, the need of a refuge for those fleeing Hitler raised the debate on immigration to fever pitch. When World War II erupted, Jews worldwide became the captive allies of the nations fighting the Axis. Zionists, however, continued to press England and the United States on Jewish immigration to Palestine, even as they built up the infrastructure of what in 1948 became a Jewish state. Within a few years a more aggressive leadership of the World Zionist Organization (WZO) moved into the fourth phase, the resurrection of political Zionism and the demand for statehood.

The Formative Years of American Zionism

Far fewer Jews in America than in Europe were attracted to Herzlian Zionism. To be sure, religiously observant Jews affirmed the traditional belief in restoration, and a small handful of nineteenth-century Jews had been prepared to accept a man-led Jewish return or had joined American branches of the *Chovevei Zion*. But the realities of life in America and the immediate concerns of a largely immigrant community in the two decades preceding the war dictated other priorities. Thousands of Jewish immigrants were arriving annually from eastern Europe, and their primary focus was the need to find jobs, housing, and schooling for their children. Having chosen the United States as their refuge from czarist oppression, they had little personal interest in uprooting themselves once again, this time from a country comparatively free of antisemitism, to make their home in an undeveloped land in Asia Minor. Moreover, a movement built on Jewish separatism clashed with the immigrants' aim of acclimatizing rapidly to their American surroundings. Zionists like philosopher Horace Kallen and Rabbi Judah Magnes may have endorsed the theory of cultural pluralism, but had the new immigrants themselves been polled on the issue of melting-pot versus cultural pluralism, most would have opted for the former.

Despite the weak response to the Zionist cause, the period until World War I set the dominant patterns of American Zionism's first fifty years (chapter 1). While Zionist leaders were Americanizing their ideology in order to appeal successfully to the Jewish public, four Zionist organizations were founded. The most prominent was the English-speaking Federation of American Zionists (FAZ), the precursor of the Zionist Organization of America (ZOA). Although the rank and file were mostly eastern Europeans, the founders stemmed from the older stratum of western Europeans—Reform Jews like Stephen Wise and Gustav and Richard Gottheil.[5] Strains developed in a short time between the leadership and the members, coming to a head shortly after the war when the eastern Europeans gained control of the ZOA and replaced the dominant and the most Americanized faction under the leadership of Supreme Court Justice Louis Brandeis. Rivalry for control of the ZOA testified to the power of Americanization. The newer immigrants basked in the importance of Americanized leaders whose participation added social respectability and prestige to the movement, but as the newcomers themselves acculturated, they felt freer about substituting leaders of their own.

Parallel to the rise of the Zionist organizations was American Jewish opposition to political Zionism. The opponents included the *anti*-Zionists, those opposed to all aspects of the movement, and the *non*-Zionists, those who objected to a Jewish state and a separate Jewish nationalism but who, out of a concern for oppressed Jews seeking a refuge, willingly contributed to the upbuilding of Palestine. In the ranks of the "antis" stood Jewish labor, the powerful Jewish unions, which were committed to the universalist ideal of socialism and scorned the nationalist movement. Alongside them were those Orthodox Jews who, despite a faith in restoration, deplored a godless and secular nationalism.

More significant opposition came from the leaders and institutions of Reform Judaism (chapter 2). Born in Germany in the early nineteenth century, Reform flowered in the United States. American Reformers equated their philosophy with Americanism. Setting themselves up as *the* expositors of Judaism in the modern age, Reformers, with the exception of a few like the Gottheils and Wise, delivered impassioned tirades against Zionism—its medieval character, its immigrant constituency, and, in particular, its un-Americanism. The Reformers said repeatedly that Zionism, unlike Reform, was incompatible with patriotism and thereby exposed all Jews to the serious charge of dual allegiance. Since Reform paraded its opposition before the non-Jewish public, and since Reform was the oldest and best-organized English-speaking branch of American Judaism, it helped to cultivate anti-Zionism among Jewish and Christian Americans. Most non-Jews showed little interest in Herzl's movement until the Balfour Declaration of 1917, but if they did, they usually agreed with its opponents.

Reformers and other assimilationists dominated the Jewish Establishment—those Jews, self-appointed stewards, who took it upon themselves to handle the problems of the community at large and to guide its development. Powerful adversaries of political Zionism, these men, most of German origin, aroused Zionist wrath. In response American Zionism led a crusade against the Establishment and for a democratically run community. Not all democrats were Zionists, but the democratic impulse, articulated in an American idiom, strengthened the movement's popular appeal. The Zionist struggle to shift the locus of power to the masses cropped up repeatedly before 1948. Here too the issue reflected the process of Americanization. Earlier German Jewish immigrants had, as they assimilated, entrenched their leadership of American Jewry but the eastern Europeans, far stronger in numbers and also bent on acculturation, were rapidly catching up. By supporting democracy in Jewish communal life, the Zionists were able to argue that *they* were as much American as their opponents.

The most important product of the formative years was a "comfortable" American Zionism. Early political Zionists like Herzl and Nordau as well as the leaders of the FAZ were prepared to modify the function of American Jews in the Zionist design. They expected Americans to agitate for a Jewish homeland, but in appeals aimed at winning their approval, they saw the Americans primarily as financial supporters of the movement rather than as potential *olim* (those who embarked on *aliyah*). Even Herzl, who decried the stunted Jewish life of Diaspora Jewry, never expected all Jews to leave their homes for Palestine.

Some Zionists substituted a cultural and spiritual ideal for Herzl's political focus. They too favored a national Jewish center in Palestine, but men like Solomon Schechter of the Jewish Theological Seminary taught that the state of Judaism was more important than a Jewish state (chapter 2). The true objective of Zionism, they said, was the establishment of a vibrant religious center equipped to revitalize Judaism wherever Jews lived. American Zionists were obligated to support the creation of that center, but they were not required to do the physical building themselves. Rejecting Herzl's premise that Jews had no future as Jews outside Palestine, the spiritual-cultural Zionists made a major contribution to the Americanization of Zionism. They never called on fellow Jews to prepare for *aliyah* or to renounce their faith in American exceptionalism. Instead they offered an undemanding Zionism that freed American Jews from any serious personal commitment but served their needs both as Jews and as Americans.

As financial contributors to a refuge for oppressed Jews, or as proponents of a Jewish religious center in Palestine, American Jews could discharge their ethnic responsibilities without sacrificing the comforts of American life. True, Zionists of all stripes posited the existence of a separate Jewish national group and stressed a Jewish national consciousness—concepts that many Jewish and Christian Americans rejected out of hand. But as long as Jewish nationalism manifested itself as philanthropy or as a function of religion, and as long as Zionist propaganda for a Jewish homeland confined itself to those goals, it did not seriously jeopardize Jewish "at homeness" in America.

American Zionism scored the greatest triumph of its formative years when Louis D. Brandeis joined the movement (chapter 2). Brandeis, the "people's attorney" and a close adviser to Woodrow Wilson, headed the ZOA for a short time (1914–16) before his appointment to the Supreme Court, but both his term in office and his influence throughout the 1920s reinforced the patterns set during American Zionism's first phase. Most important for our purposes, Brandeis contributed significantly to the process of Americanization. Not only did he employ American imagery in describing Zionism and Zionists—"our Jewish Pilgrim Fathers" is how he referred to the pioneers in Palestine—but as a supporter of cultural pluralism, he defended Zionists against the charges of un-Americanism and dual loyalty. The Jewish mission in Palestine and elsewhere, he said, was to propagate the humanistic, American-like values of liberty and justice. That belief underlay his oft-quoted statement, "Every American Jew who aids in advancing the Jewish settlement in Palestine . . . will . . . be a better man and a better American for doing so."[6]

Discounting the need of *aliyah* from America, Brandeis viewed Zionism through the lens of an American Progressive. He likened it to the tide of American reform that had peaked before the war; a Jewish Palestine would be the social laboratory in which Zionists experimented with new forms of economic and political democracy. A proponent of communal democracy against the elitist Establishment, Brandeis also put the Zionists squarely behind the national campaign for a democratic American Jewish Congress (1918) to represent the Jews at the postwar peace conference. By such means he interpreted Zionism in American terms—it was essentially a Progressive movement led by men who resembled America's Founding Fathers—and he thereby made it more attractive and respectable for American Jews.

Although Brandeis participated in the negotiations with England leading to the Balfour Declaration, his primary focus after the war shifted from political to "pragmatic" or "practical" Zionism. Active behind the scenes and through his lieutenants throughout the decade, he encouraged American Jewish investment in the physical upbuilding of Palestine. That emphasis, also adopted by the ZOA, well suited the shift of world Zionism into its second phase, Palestinianism.

Palestinianism

Palestinianism, the substitute for Herzl's program, was a modified version of Jewish nationalism that lasted from 1917 until World War II. Precisely because it put statehood aside, thereby deradicalizing Zionism, Palestinianism brought certain advantages to the American Zionist movement. For one thing, it provided a needed cooling-off period for war-weary Americans to absorb the political implications of the Balfour Declaration without immediately confronting the potentially divisive issue of statehood. Furthermore, since Palestinianism made practical aid to the *yishuv* (the pre-state Jewish settlement in Palestine) its primary focus, it placated many critics.

The Balfour Declaration, tantamount to an announcement that Zionism was here to stay, did, however, generate heated discussions of Jewish nationalism by the American public. Non-Jewish opinion, which dictated the limits to which Jews could push their nationalist or indeed any objectives, now wielded greater influence over Zionist policy. Although a strong majority in Congress and the American press expressed approval of the declaration when it first appeared, popular opposition to the Zionist movement slowly increased.

One public debate immediately after the war disclosed the multifaceted opposition to Zionism (chapter 3). Jewish "diehard" Reformers, still fulminating against the Zionist "menace," were joined in those years by liberal and assimilationist Jewish intellectuals and by serious Christian critics. Liberals, disenchanted by a war and a peace treaty that seemed to mock the Wilsonian principles of internationalism, democracy, and anti-imperialism, saw no justification for a Jewish nation, which they saw as another product of British imperial interests and one at odds with the democratic rights of the Palestinian Arabs. In a decade that witnessed the wide circulation of the *Protocols of the Elders of Zion* and the popularity of the "Jew = Bolshevik" myth, Zionism, a "foreign" product that conflicted with the antiforeign mood in America, easily became a target for nativists and bigots. In some cases antisemites found in anti-Zionism a more respectable garb for purveying Jew-hatred. Zionists attempted to refute their opponents, but at times they found it more expedient to recoil. In the unfriendly setting of the 1920s, when discrimination against Jews reached new heights, Zionism had to give way to other priorities crowding the communal agenda.

Despite the Balfour Declaration, Zionists worldwide failed to capitalize on the momentum for Jewish statehood generated by the war and the peace conference. Since neither European nor American Jews bent on *aliyah* were storming the gates of Palestine, earlier Zionist expectations were dashed. Moreover, Jewish inaction not only gave England cause to retreat from its promise but vindicated those anti-Zionists who charged that Zionism was impractical and chimerical.

Nevertheless, the retreat to Palestinianism wasn't all bad. Coping with antisemitism, which increased in the 1920s, and with the grim conditions spawned by the Great Depression of the 1930s, American Jews dared not risk any major outbursts about Jewish statehood from their non-Jewish fellow Americans. Within American Jewish circles, Palestinianism, far less strident than political Zionism, permitted the spread of a "quiet" Zionism in synagogues and Jewish schools. It also made possible significant cooperation between Zionists and non-Zionists, which resulted in new economic, social, and cultural institutions in the *yishuv*. Perhaps the best example was the establishment in the 1920s of the Hebrew University in Jerusalem, which received significant funding from the American non-Zionist Felix Warburg. During this period the importance of American non-Zionists grew. Non-Zionism peaked in 1929 when the Zionists and the "nons" agreed to share control of the Jewish Agency, the body provided for in the terms of the mandate to formulate and administer policy for the WZO. For the most part the partnership was not a happy one, but the presence of prominent Western non-Zionists raised the status of the Agency in its dealings with England and the League of Nations. The middle road of Palestinianism and non-Zionism also thinned the ranks of the American anti-Zionists and permitted access to financial resources hitherto untapped on behalf of a Jewish homeland. Although many Reform laymen and rabbis remained vocal critics of Zionist objectives, the organization of Reform rabbis bowed to the appeal of non-Zionism and officially repudiated its anti-Zionist stand in the 1930s.

Above all, Palestinianism seemed eminently compatible with American requirements of the proper citizen. To outsiders, it was basically a philanthropy, and Americans admired philanthropy and philanthropists. Since the end goal of a Jewish state was at least temporarily shelved, Palestinianism as philanthropy shielded Jews against any charges of disloyalty or dual allegiance. Zionists still talked of a Jewish "home" or "religious center," but those were bland terms devoid of political meaning. In the eyes of many Americans, Jews who sought religious guidance from a restored Jewish center probably seemed little different from American Catholics whose spiritual center was the Vatican.

After the war, when more American Jews were visiting Palestine and judging for themselves how Zionism was shaping a Jewish nation in the making, talk of "cultural bridges" between American and Palestinian Jewries became more common. One variation of that theme emerged in the heyday of Palestinianism in discussions by spokesmen of Conservative Judaism on what American Jews could do for *Judaism* in Palestine. Beyond the all-important expertise and financial help to Palestinian Jews and institutions, American Jews could perhaps export their modern style of worship. The *yishuv* needed to revivify religion, and since traditional Orthodoxy by then was grossly inadequate for modern Jews, a modified traditionalism, or Conservatism, offered a possible answer. The basic question—could Judaism in its Conservative version take root in Palestine?—was daunting, but the very idea was exciting. Were it to succeed, the Diaspora and Palestine would be forging a symbiotic relationship whereby Palestinian religious life would take from and be enriched by the Diaspora (specifically America) in the building of a spiritual center. Just as America had shaped Conservative Judaism, so would the latter in turn endeavor to Americanize the religious dimension of life in the *yishuv*. An early attempt in the 1920s to build an American-like synagogue in Jerusalem failed (chapter 4), and the challenge of transplanting American Judaism (both Conservative and Reform) to Israel, with rights equal to those of the Orthodox, remains even today.

During the era of Palestinianism a prime factor in the American Zionist equation, the government's stand, took on significant meaning. Until then Washington, whose primary concern in the Near East was the protection of business interests and the powerful Protestant missionaries, was largely silent.

Nevertheless, several anti-Zionist forces—missionary influence, increasing business interest in Near Eastern investments, and Turkish apprehension about Zionist territorial aims—combined to plant a tradition of anti-Zionism in the State Department. That opposition, often flavored with rank antisemitism, became significantly more pronounced after the war. To be sure, the Zionists had fared well under Woodrow Wilson. The president sympathized with humanitarian diplomacy, or the right of the United States to intercede on behalf of victims of foreign oppression, and he called for ethnic self-determination in his Fourteen Points. Both principles could be harnessed for the Zionist cause, the first to validate the establishment of a refuge for eastern European Jewry, the second to endorse the legitimacy of Jewish nationalist aspirations. Most important, Wilson added his personal approval of the Balfour Declaration.

The State Department, however, thought differently. Secretary Robert Lansing, the incumbent during the war, and his successors during the 1920s wasted little sympathy on the Jewish nationalist movement even when it involved the interests of American citizens. Since the United States was now recognized as a major world power, its opinions carried more weight than ever before, but since the country was swept by a wave of isolationism, the department steered a course of noninvolvement in Palestine. Meanwhile, the middle managers of the department, the men who stayed in office and for all intents and purposes set policy regardless of the political party in power, ignored a pro-Zionist Congressional resolution of 1922 that approved the Balfour Declaration.

Colored by an anti-Jewish bias, the State Department's anti-Zionist and pro-Arab sympathies flowered at the end of the 1920s in the wake of the Arab riots, which left some Americans dead or injured. The United States was forced to take note of Zionism in Palestine, if only for the protection of its citizens, but despite Zionist pressure it refused to admit then or at any time before 1948 that its responsibility for the Balfour Declaration or for England's obligations under the mandate went any further.

The Turbulent Decade

The first decade of Palestinianism closed on a sorry note. The bloody Arab riots of 1929 followed by the MacDonald White Paper of 1930, which restricted Jewish immigration to Palestine, pointed up the *yishuv*'s vulnerability to Arab attacks and to British malfeasance. Both the colonial officials in Palestine and the Labor government in London preferred the Arabs to the *yishuv;* they disliked the Jewish settlers, and they feared that Arab unrest in Palestine might spread through Asia and rock the imperial boat. Given international endorsement of the Balfour Declaration and the mandate, England was in no position to dismiss the Zionist cause in one fell swoop, but within those broad and often ambiguous parameters it adopted pro-Arab rather than pro-*yishuv* policies.

The events of 1929–30 also triggered the second popular debate on Zionism in the United States (chapter 3). Although the focus this time was broader, encompassing as it did Zionist behavior in Palestine, it resembled the debate of 1917–22 in several ways. Antisemitic themes and imagery permeated much of the opposition to Zionism, and again the Zionists lost both Jewish and Christian liberal support.[7] Nonetheless, the anti-Zionism of liberalism, the ideology with which Western Jews had identified ever since the Enlightenment, failed to sway Jewish voters to a conservative posture in American politics. For a variety of reasons American Jews, including Zionists, remained loyal to liberalism and, beginning in the 1930s, to the New Deal and its legacy. As was their custom, they continued to rank their American interests above the needs of the Jewish homeland.

During the years of the mandate both Arabs and Jews agreed that the core issue dividing them was that of Jewish immigration to Palestine. England's contradictory wartime promises to the Zionists and the Arabs placed it, the mandatory for Palestine, in the unenviable position of having to juggle claims and counterclaims for the next thirty years. The Balfour Declaration notwithstanding, the British proceeded slowly to pare down the rights of the Jews. Emboldened by less than modest Jewish immigration in the immediate postwar years and by the fact that Zionists worldwide barely reacted to the closing of Transjordan to Jewish settlement or the initial curbs on immigration in the early 1920s, they deemed it more prudent to appease the troublesome Arabs. The Arab objective in the two decades before World War II was to curb if not end Jewish immigration and Jewish land purchase, and Arab riots in the 1920s and 1930s succeeded in alarming England.

On the issue of immigration, American non-Zionists usually sided with the Zionists. Although they still opposed statehood and the philosophy of Jewish nationalism and were prepared to compromise with the Arabs and with England on most matters, American non-Zionists stood firm on the right of Jews to enter Palestine. Using whatever personal clout they could muster with London and Washington, they even resorted to one-on-one diplomacy with British officials (chapter 5), and indeed they were far more palatable to the State Department and Whitehall than the Zionists. But alone they were too weak to effect a change in British policy. If anything, their failure served to discredit the myth of Jewish power.

When Arab opposition to Jewish immigration erupted in violence in the mid-1930s, England was again hard-pressed to find a compromise solution. At that time, however, the Zionist case took on a new urgency. Since European Jews increasingly tried to flee Nazi persecution, and since the United States and other Western lands kept their doors shut to refugees, Zionists pleaded with the mandatory to honor the promise of the Balfour Declaration. Chaim Weizmann and the Jewish Agency had no success with England, and neither did the

American Jews, Zionists or non-Zionists, who sought to convince the State Department to apply pressure on England. Washington took its cue on Palestine from the British, and in general wasted little sympathy for the Jewish refugees. The Department had not softened its stand on Zionism; like all its representatives despatched to Jerusalem, it favored the Arabs and lent a willing ear to Arab opinions. The ZOA brought Zionist demands to the Department's attention in a steady stream of representatives and memoranda, and its pressure for involving the United States directly in the Palestinian impasse intensified. But as long as the State Department knew that American Jews were divided on the issues of Jewish nationalism and statehood and that Jewish support for Roosevelt was unshakable, it refused to budge (chapter 6).

A few short months before the outbreak of World War II, England issued the notorious White Paper, which put a finite limit on Jewish immigration to Palestine. Although the Zionists had no recourse but to support England's war with Hitler, they refused to accept the White Paper without a struggle. A more bellicose tone against the British was heard in the *yishuv*, and it slowly spread to the United States. Finally, in 1942 American Zionists reverted to Herzlian ideology and resurrected the demand for a Jewish state.

The Struggle for Statehood

At a conference held at New York's Biltmore Hotel in May 1942, the major Zionist organizations in the United States called for control of immigration to Palestine by the Jewish Agency. More dramatically, the Biltmore platform committed the American Zionists to support the proposal that "Palestine be established as a Jewish Commonwealth integrated in the structure of the new democratic world."[8] Fifteen months later, after news of Hitler's extermination of the Jews first reached the public, the commonwealth resolution was overwhelmingly passed by the Zionist-controlled American Jewish Conference, a democratically elected assembly that represented more than two million affiliated American Jews (chapter 7). Primarily a response to the Holocaust, it was the first time since 1897 that American Jewry acting in unison endorsed the political aims of Theodor Herzl. Many of the delegates may not have understood the essence of Zionist ideology, but the need to "do something" in answer to the death camps drove many to the side of a Jewish state.

The organization of the American Jewish Conference signaled the emergence of a different type of Zionist leader. Rabbi Abba Hillel Silver,who took center stage in the direction of American Zionist affairs during World War II, was of the new breed. Like David Ben-Gurion in the *yishuv*, he injected an assertive if not aggressive note into the campaign for a Jewish state. Simultaneously, the conference, at least theoretically, brought an end to the earlier competition between the elitist anti-Zionists and the democratic Zionists over leadership of the Jewish community. How well it succeeded would, among other things, test the efficacy of representative democracy for the community at large. The conference lessened the power of the elitists, but the latter were never totally displaced. They felt impelled, however, to bow to the appeal of self-rule. For example, the American Jewish Committee (AJC), long the bastion of a small group of stewards, undertook to broaden its leadership base by organizing chapters. Over time, what had started as an exclusive club opened its doors to all strata of American Jewry.

The drive for an independent Jewish state between 1939 and 1948 erased the distinctions that heretofore had divided American Zionists. Cultural or spiritual Zionism, as opposed to political Zionism, and non-Zionism, or the doctrine of material aid to the *yishuv* that stopped short of political entanglement, lost their meaning. The *yishuv* was unconditionally committed to independence, and any sort of contribution from the outside—be it even by planting trees through the Jewish National Fund or by endowing a scholarship at the Hebrew University—was a contribution to the infrastructure of a state in the making. True, there were some notable holdouts on the issue of a political state instead of a religious or cultural center (chapter 8), but for the most part it boiled down to a single issue—one either favored or opposed a Jewish sovereign state.

Despite the need for communal unity, a new organization, the American Council for Judaism, founded in 1942 for the express purpose of preaching anti-Zionism, determinedly distanced itself from the main body of American Jews. Dedicated to the prevention of nationalist activity of any sort on the part of American Jews, it publicly fought the conference and lobbied with the government and the two major political parties against Jewish statehood. The council slowly lost ground during the early years of Israel's existence, and after the Six-Day War of 1967 the few remaining antistatists organized the American Jewish Alternatives to Zionism, a group that actively cooperated with anti-Israel Arab propaganda networks in the United States. Like the council, the organization failed to make a significant dent in Jewish and non-Jewish acceptance of the state of Israel. For all intents and purposes, vocal anti-Zionism within the American Jewish camp has become a relic of the past.

Events moved at a rapid pace during the trying days of the war and the Holocaust. American Zionists unleashed a massive public relations campaign for winning public approval of their efforts on behalf of Jewish statehood. They circulated innumerable information sheets and petitions; they staged mass rallies; and they nurtured cooperation with sympathetic Christian clerics and lay leaders. Avoiding the charge of dual allegiance, Zionists were careful to couch their appeals in an American idiom. They interpreted Zionism as a war aim of the United States; the Zionists, American patriots first and foremost, were "interested" in Palestine *"because Palestine is an important outpost in this indivisible war."* News of the Nazi death camps and the needs of the survivors injected the humanitarian issue into the Zionist cause even as it dramatically swelled the large sums of money raised to aid the *yishuv*.

In the immediate aftermath of the war, free immigration to Palestine, especially for Holocaust survivors and displaced European Jews, continued to generate support for Jewish statehood. Until the United Nations voted the partition of Palestine into an Arab and a Jewish state (1947), and until the *yishuv* declared its independence in May 1948, American Zionists incessantly lobbied their own government and England on the issue of free immigration and a Jewish commonwealth. Since England, however, held to a policy of stringent restrictions, many Jews openly supported the *yishuv's* efforts to bring in immigrants illegally. Because of the problems of displaced persons (DPs), the AJC, heretofore the most powerful non-Zionist organization, finally joined the Zionists on behalf of a Jewish state. (In 1946 Joseph M. Proskauer, then president of the AJC and long a confirmed non- or even anti-Zionist, indicated a readiness to modify his position. He explained: "The one great overwhelming objective is to get immediate substantial immigration into Palestine and . . . I don't care very much how I get it.")[10]

The same reason contributed to the support of statehood on the part of members of Congress as well as the president. Realizing in the end that the DP issue could not be separated from the issue of a state, Harry Truman rejected the State Department's advice and sided with the Zionists. Eleven minutes after Israel's independence took effect, the president recognized the Zionist state.

CHAPTER 1

Forging an American Zionism:
The Maccabaean

The Federation of American Zionists (FAZ), the most important organization of American Zionists, dutifully followed the policies set by the congresses and executive bodies of the World Zionist Organization (WZO). Until
Herzl's death in 1904 both European and American Zionists committed themselves to Herzlian or political Zionism, i.e., attempts at securing an internationally recognized charter for an autonomous Jewish state in Palestine before efforts at mass settlement. Different emphases precluded total unity within the
ranks; some Zionists argued the need of practical work in Palestine to precede
or at least operate alongside the political, and others stressed the development
of the cultural and religious dimensions of Jewish nationalism. But until 1905
when Israel Zangwill led a group of dissidents into the Jewish Territorial Organization (ITO), which was willing to accept any suitable land outside Palestine for Jewish settlement, the political Palestine-centered goal remained fixed.
Wrangling between the "practical" and "political" camps increased, and the
practical emphasis won out at the Tenth Zionist Congress in 1911. Instead of replacing the "political," however, the Congress merged the two in what was
termed "synthetic" Zionism."[1]

Four years after the First Zionist Congress at Basel (1897), the FAZ launched
its official monthly journal, the *Maccabaean*. The mirror and mouthpiece of its
parent organization, the journal pitched its message to American Zionists and
potential Zionists. Its task, to win acceptance of Zionism and the FAZ, was an
uphill battle. In 1901 Zionism was not yet a respectable movement in the United
States. The popular melting-pot theory was antithetical to the heart of the
Zionist message, and the new Jewish immigrants from eastern Europe, as the
journal itself explained, "resent the idea of [Jewish] national interests apart
from the general interests of the country." Within the Jewish community, the
3800 members who paid their shekel (a biblical word used for membership
dues to the constituent groups of the WZO) in 1900 were greatly outnumbered

by their opponents and by the apathetic. Within the larger society some non-Jews followed the lead of the assimilated Jewish anti-Zionists. Among most other Americans, general indifference to or ignorance of Zionism prevailed. In 1908 the *Maccabaean* proudly printed a letter from Dr. Lyman Abbott, editor of the influential weekly *Outlook*, in sympathy with Jewish nationalism even though Abbott confessed that he knew very little about Zionism.[2]

Less obvious but potentially powerful were the advantages that the FAZ enjoyed. Its enthusiastic officers and staff disseminated a convincing message precisely because they were genuine idealists. That message did not fall on totally deaf ears. Zionist leaders could count on some familiarity with Jewish tradition or at least nostalgic sentiment on the part of the eastern Europeans. Unencumbered by fixed habits and organizational machinery, Zionists were also able to serve as disinterested critics of the American-Jewish scene and, where advantageous for them, to capitalize on any disaffection with the prevailing system of communal organization. Finally, since the formative years of American Zionism coincided in time with the burgeoning Progressive movement, the FAZ could hope for sympathy from liberals who, as Professor Eric Goldman wrote many years ago, saw a similarity between "greater opportunity within the nation and minority nationalism."[3]

Since the *Maccabaean* appeared in English—a Yiddish supplement lasted for less than a year—its target was not the newest immigrants, those concerned with the bare necessities of life in the new country, but those who had at least mastered the language and had the wherewithal to purchase and peruse a monthly journal. On one occasion the editor noted that the FAZ was directed by professionals and supported by members of the middle class and upper proletariat.[4] The *Maccabaean* opened its pages to different shades of Zionist opinion—political, cultural, religious, philanthropic—and occasionally even to anti-Zionists. Its own views, however, were usually in accord with Herzl's prime objective for a legal charter.

The periodical offered a rich and varied menu. News on Zionism and features of the movement's leaders in the United States and Europe dominated its pages, and full coverage was given to local, national, and international congresses and conventions. Visits by prominent European Zionists to the United States were reported in detail, and so were the impressions of American visitors to Palestine. Openly propagandistic, the *Maccabaean* frequently appealed for new members. It urged its readers to circulate their copies of the periodical; it also advised: "When you see a Jew who is not a Zionist, hand him a Zionist pamphlet. If you haven't one with you, hand him an argument."[6] The journal welcomed articles that explained Zionist principles and those that dealt with some aspects of the *yishuv*'s development. For a limited time it ran a page for children or young adults. Most striking was the full literary portion in each issue. A large amount of space was allotted to fiction and poetry—both by past masters and by contemporary authors—as well as to serious articles on Jewish history and culture. With its eye on the Jewish and general press, the journal occasionally reprinted articles from other periodicals, and on occasion it presented a piece written by a non-Jew. If, as one rabbi said, many American Jews merely followed a periodical of their choice,[6] the FAZ entered the competition with a journal of quality.

A National Consciousness

When the Zionist movement was born, its marketability among Occidental Jews, i.e., those in western Europe and the United States, was virtually nil. Had Zionism not answered the needs of the eastern Europeans, mired in poverty and ever vulnerable to attack, it could never have survived. Nonetheless, the Westerners who gloried in their emancipation and joyfully chose to abandon Judaism for rapid assimilation could not be written off. If for nothing else, their wealth and any influence they had with the masses made them extremely desirable for the nationalist movement. To convert the Westerners thus became an important goal of Zionists worldwide.

Dr. Max Nordau, Theodor Herzl's closest disciple and counselor, set forth the problem in the first issue of the *Maccabaean*. He said that since Zionism required leaders of substance and stature, the culture of the Westerners and their experience with freedom made them ideal candidates. But, he added, it was impossible to reach the Occidental Jew by the use of reason. He imagined a dialogue between the Zionist (Z) and the Westerner (W) that in part went like this:

Z: Zionism is the only means for preserving Judaism.

W: That is the very fault we find with it. We do not want Judaism to be preserved; we want it to disappear.

Z: Zionism guarantees the Jewish race a future and dignity as a nation.

W: Nonsense. There is no Jewish nation; there is only a Jewish religion, and with that we don't concern ourselves. Our Jewish past and present is enough of an annoyance to us; what should we want with a Jewish future? No, thanks! National dignity? Is the old clothes trade to become an ideal occupation? Is the Jewish singsong to reach the aristocratic distinction of the military snarl? Are the splay foot and the hooked nose to be the models of manly beauty? We don't believe in such a shifting about of values, and we don't want to do it. . . .

Z: Zionism makes freemen and citizens of the [Jews].

W: Legally that's what we already are; and that's what we shall be socially, as well, when we have completely sloughed our Judaism, or hidden it so skillfully that even the antisemites cannot scent it out.

Nordau concluded, therefore, that Westerners could be converted only by appeals to idealism and sentiment.[7]

Even without Nordau's reminder, the founding fathers of the American Zionist movement knew that American Jews, different from their eastern European brethren, were unlikely to make an existentialist commitment to the core of Herzlian Zionism. Most had found their promised land in America, and in a country of freedom and equality Herzlian laws on the course of antisemitism appeared totally irrelevant. From the outset, therefore, the need to square Zionist theory with American reality and make it meaningful to the lives of American Jews remained the major task of the FAZ. Its leaders addressed that issue in the various roles they assumed—as propagators of Zionism among Jews and other Americans, as critics of American Jewish behavior, and as defenders of Jewish interests in the United States and foreign countries. Their arguments and interpretations were hammered out publicly and further refined in the pages of the *Maccabaean*, and their conclusions constituted an Americanized Zionism.

Until the Balfour Declaration of 1917 the editors of the *Maccabaean*, particularly Jacob De Haas, a longtime associate of Herzl, and Louis Lipsky, a journalist and writer of fiction, remained consistently loyal to the original political objective. They and many of the articles they printed were, like Herzl, harsh critics of other approaches. For example, they often said that the Lovers of Zion who stood for piecemeal colonization erred. Colonies without legal guaranties faced serious risks to their security, and they diverted resources away from the goal of statehood. The political thrust was all-important: "The mere adoption of a political attitude, independent of its success, means some enfranchisement for us as a people; it gives us strength and courage." Cultural Zionists who, under the influence of essayist Ahad Ha'am, focused not on a state but on a Jewish center that would vitalize Judaism throughout the world, were also wrong; since Jewish ideals could not survive if the people died, culture in itself was not an end. Philosopher Horace Kallen dismissed the theories of Ahad Ha'am as being only "an intensification of the status quo," and De Haas candidly wrote that they "belong to an unreal world and an unreal age." The worst wrongdoers were the philanthropists, including men like Baron Edmond de Rothschild, whose generosity notwithstanding cramped attempts at self-help and even self-sacrifice. In the words of Herzl: "A people cannot be helped by means of Philanthropy; it can only be helped by means of Politics."[8]

Nevertheless, political Zionists like Lipsky and De Haas had to compromise their personal convictions. They well understood that a successful Zionist appeal to American Jews could not rest exclusively or even primarily on the demand for a political charter. Acceptance of the need for Jewish statehood required the more gradual approach of indoctrination. Accordingly, the *Maccabaean* concentrated on another plank of the Basel program—"the strengthening of Jewish national sentiment and national consciousness." Stating that Zionism stood for "a rebirth of the Jewish folk [and] of the Jewish spirit,"[9] the journal posited that an awakened national consciousness had to precede political efforts for a Jewish state. That emphasis altered the order of Herzl's priorities. The latter had put a charter first; national consciousness-raising would follow or, at best, proceed concomitantly with political work. In the United States, however, early Zionist leaders made consciousness-raising the first and all-important objective. Political statehood would or would not be won—and the subject was never fully discussed by the *Maccabaean*—in the vague and distant future.

Writers for the *Maccabaean* rested the crusade for an aroused national consciousness on the premise that Jews were not only a religious body but a national group that shared a common history and common ideals. As a separate race or nation, they had made lasting cultural and spiritual contributions to world civilization, but since *galut* (exile from Palestine, or Diaspora) put them by definition in a hostile environment, such contributions could resume only when Jews developed their own talents, preferably in their own land. First, however, they needed to recover "their individuality as a people" or what Kallen called the "race-self." Before we have Zion, we must prepare the masses—"we must have the Jewish people"—and that necessitated a concentration on national consciousness. Like Nordau, the writers interpreted Zionism in arational or idealistic terms more relevant for the Western Jew.[10]

An aroused national consciousness, the *Maccabaean* explained further, would breed loyalty to the Jewish nation or race as well as feelings of Jewish unity and self-respect. It also signaled the rise of the New Jew—self-emancipated, proud, unafraid of non-Jewish opinion, physically strong, fearless as opposed to timid, independent, and confident. In that vein, Richard Gottheil, the first president of the FAZ, told how he was captivated by the assertive and dignified demeanor of the delegates to the Fifth Zionist Congress, who proudly asserted the individuality of the Jew and his right to a dignified existence. Only in a state of their own could Jews reach their full potential, both with respect to character traits and their gifts to mankind. Ranking Jewish nationalism above universalism, Zionists saw their movement as the "highest expression" of the life of the Jewish people.[11]

To be sure, the way in which a heightened Jewish national consciousness in America directly advanced political Zionism was never clearly spelled out. Perhaps it was assumed that Zionists and potential Zionists, after proper indoctrination, would make the necessary leap of faith and commit their resources as well as themselves to the goal of a Jewish state. In any event, immediate political statehood was not a serious objective of American Zionism until World War II.

In tandem with consciousness-raising, the *Maccabaean* presented a strong indictment of *galut*. Jewish life in the Diaspora was unavoidably abnormal—*luftmenschen* existed in place of productive men, the values of the Torah were neglected, and expressions of Jewish art were eccentric and bizarre. Since the taint of exile was all-pervasive, it was "impossible to attain permanent forms of

Jewish life." Most important, exile spelled the disintegration of Jewish ideals and dignity: it "attracts our people away from their own [and] it produces mean vices and common virtues."

On the subject of *galut*, Zionists desperately sought a compromise between Herzlian principles and American exceptionalism. They admitted that the burden of *galut* was less weighty in America, but nonetheless its inherent abnormality led to social evils like prostitution and crime in the immigrant ghettos. More significant, *galut* even in America augured total assimilation and dissolution of Jewry. In 1912 a review of *The Promised Land*, Mary Antin's autobiographical account of her adjustment to America, pointed out that the author's glory in Americanization was purchased at the price of drifting away from the Jewish people.[12] Yet although the *Maccabaean* hinted that unstunted American Jewish development, like Jewish development elsewhere, could not be ensured, it avoided the issue of *sh'lilat ha-golah* (negation of the *galut*, or the idea that Jewish life in the Diaspora was automatically doomed). The closest the journal ever came to introducing that idea was in one paper by Louis Lipsky. There Lipsky argued that a Jew couldn't be bound up emotionally with both America and Zionism; he had to decide where his destiny lay. But, Lipsky concluded, that sort of emotional allegiance was neither "censurable" nor dangerous to America. Neither he nor the *Maccabaean* ever brought it up again.[13]

Theoretically at least, the journal stood squarely behind Herzl with respect to the problem of antisemitism. The founder of Zionism had made antisemitism a prime mover of the Zionist scheme. His very definition of a nation, reprinted in the *Maccabaean*, had said it all: "The nation is a group of people of recognizable kinship kept together by a common enemy." The *Maccabaean* agreed; everywhere Jews were victims of at least a "silent" persecution. Reports of major antisemitic outbreaks throughout the world appeared in the journal, and never were they excused as aberrational or singular events. Rather, they were functions of the Jewish condition and applied to all Jews. Commenting on the famous ritual murder case of Mendel Beilis in Russia (1912–13), the *Maccabaean* was horrified that Jews, "the oldest monotheistic race, the People of the Book," were still charged with "religious cannibalism by men outside of a lunatic asylum. . . . Enough of the comical to make Satan roar with laughter; but the tragedy of it is ours!"[14]

Jews even in America were not immune to the eternal hatred, and the journal offered concrete examples—exclusion of Jews from clubs and vacation resorts, exaggerated charges of Jewish crime, antisemitic attitudes of university faculties, and unfounded taunts about Jewish wealth. Those instances as well as the mob attack on Jews at the funeral of New York City's Rabbi Jacob Joseph (1902) were not pogroms, but they were sufficiently alarming to justify the need of raising the Jewish national consciousness.[15] Moreover, and despite the attempts of assimilationists to shrug off talk of American antisemitism,

Jew-hatred cast doubt on the claim that Jews had reached their Zion in the United States.

Logic may have dictated that the one solution to bleak exile and ubiquitous antisemitism lay in a new Jewish life in Palestine. Rigid negators of the Diaspora might also have argued that it was futile to combat antisemitism; for example, why bother asking, the way the *Maccabaean* did, that the *Merchant of Venice* be banned from elementary schools if Jew-hatred was eternal?[16] The *Maccabaean*, however, stopped short of suggesting that the solution lay in Jewish statehood. In sum, its position was riddled with inconsistencies. On the one hand it preached that the evils of *galut*, specifically antisemitism, were fixed in the United States. On the other hand, its occasional advice on how to meliorate discrimination suggested that a secure future for American Jews (as opposed to Judaism) was perhaps attainable.

A focus on national consciousness without joining it to statehood accounted for such inconsistencies. Juggling Zionist principles with the Jewish faith in America, leaders came up with compromises that combined elements of both. The result, inconsistent or not, was an Americanized Zionism, a Zionism acceptable and beneficial to Jews *in* America. Aware that the majority would not opt for *aliyah* with or without a legally recognized Jewish homeland, the journal insisted that Zionism made for better Jews and better American citizens. It was the force that would invigorate American Jews, and by supplying that needed ferment and inspiration, it would undergird American Jewish survival. In the words of one writer: "To us American Jews Zionism will serve as moral support, as a spiritual adviser, [that] will elevate our social and political standing in the eyes of our [non-Jewish] neighbors." Sensitive to the limits of Herzl's logic and conclusions for America, American Zionism stipulated that America was different.[17]

Complicating the issue still further, the *Maccabaean* preached the political empowerment of Jews at the same time that it soft-pedaled statehood. History begins, the journal stated categorically, when the Jews have political power. Ideally that meant a Jewish state, but short of that it meant the liberation of Diaspora Jewry and the latter's full use of the rights that the law guaranteed. In the United States, one editorial stated, we need to wield our political power. Arguing that Jews were either too ignorant of their rights or too timid to use them, the journal pointed out the underrepresentation of Jews in appointive offices. The implication was clear: Jews had a ready weapon in the ballot box for registering their concerns, and their votes did make a difference. Challenging conservative Jewish leaders who had long argued the pitfalls of a "Jewish vote," the *Maccabaean* advised against denying or apologizing for separate Jewish political interests. Here too, where involvement in politics rested on faith in a secure future for American Jews, the journal's advice contradicted the principle of an antisemitic *galut*.[18]

Justification for a Zionism that ignored or at least questioned the relevance of Jewish statehood for Americans was provided in articles by Zionist leaders and other contributors to the journal. Rabbi Gustav Gottheil, a founder of the FAZ, claimed that Zionism never proposed to withdraw all Jews from their homes in the Diaspora. His son Richard admitted before a convention of the FAZ that Zionism meant more than political efforts for a Jewish homeland: Zionism means, "as it should mean, a return to Judaism as well as a return to a Jewish land." A lifelong political Zionist, he prudently deferred to American Jewish inclinations and assigned to national consciousness-raising a status at least equal to Herzl's goal. Another contributor to the *Maccabaean* quoted directly from Herzl where the Zionist leader himself acknowledged more than political objectives. For example, one of his sentences read: "Zionism is the rehabilitation of Judaism before the return to the Jewish Land." Again, an emphasis on a strong national consciousness not tied necessarily to a separate Jewish state was an American-inspired modification of the pursuit of immediate statehood. American Zionists scored twice thereby. They neither alienated American Jews, nor did they renounce their right to engage in American and American Jewish affairs. Some also took comfort in the thought that practical work added a dimension to the viability of political work.[19]

The amended reading of American Zionism grew more pronounced when Dr. Harry Friedenwald, a prominent ophthalmologist of Baltimore, served as president of the FAZ (1904–11).[20] His public addresses to Zionist audiences that appeared in the *Maccabaean* reflected the sentiments of a cultural-religious Zionist. A member of the board of the Jewish Theological Seminary, Friedenwald's opinions may have also been influenced by the Seminary's president, Solomon Schechter. The doctor's favorite phrases, repeated time and again, were "national consciousness," "spiritual center," and "Jewish idealism." Friedenwald claimed that Zionism was far more than a response to antisemitism or a concern for persecuted Jews. Rather, it aimed at forging a spiritual unity among Jews that would lead to the creation in Palestine of a spiritual Jewish center. Taking a page from Ahad Ha'am but adding a religious dimension, he believed that the center would inspire a vibrant Judaism in the Diaspora built on traditional ideals. A political state was not crucial; after all, the Jews in Palestine during the Second Commonwealth influenced Diaspora Jewry even though the latter outnumbered the former. On the other hand, a national consciousness was essential. It raised Jewish dignity and self-respect at the same time that it made the Jew a "complete" person.

More important for our discussion, Friedenwald gave a non-Herzlian purpose to national consciousness. Unlike the political Zionists who preached about a national consciousness leading to a state, he stressed a national consciousness for *American* Jews. "The work of Zionism," he said, "lies not only in Palestine, not only in Russia, but everywhere and *especially here in America*" (emphasis his). To guard against assimilation and to keep the American Jew Jewish was the task of Zionism, and Friedenwald repeatedly urged that national consciousness suffuse Jewish education, libraries, clubs, and literature. Jews had prospered in America, and now, for the preservation of the Jewish people and Jewish idealism, they needed to develop as loyal Jews. That loyalty embraced Palestine too, and Friedenwald called on his fellow Jews to develop and support institutions in the *yishuv*. In no way, however, did his Zionism impinge on American patriotism, and Friedenwald never doubted that American Jews would remain in America.

Coincidentally, the *Maccabaean* published an article by Professor Ralph Barton Perry of Harvard during Friedenwald's incumbency. Under the title "Jewish Ideals," Perry wrote of his sympathy with Zionism. His conclusion well suited Friedenwald's interpretation of national consciousness: the Jew "will be the man who is a good American, possibly a better American than anyone has seen, because he has the courage of the Judaism which is within him."[21]

Zionism and Americanism

The *Maccabaean* understood that talk of Zionist principles as well as criticism from opponents of Zionism demanded an answer to the question "Is Zionism compatible with Americanism?" While the bogey of dual allegiance fast became a major weapon in the arsenal of Jewish anti-Zionists, the problem was made easier just because American Zionists concentrated on the development of a national consciousness in place of Jewish statehood. Since they had modified Herzl's end goal of working for an immediate political state, American Jews were enabled thereby to hold on to their good life in *galut* while simultaneously satisfying their collective ethnic urge. Nor were they forced to admit to any contradiction between their amended Zionism and their loyalty to America. From that vantage point the journal strove to disarm opponents and to convince unaffiliated Jews that Zionism would not compromise their position in the larger society.

Some commentators on the problem of compatibility explained that belief in a separate Jewish nationality in no way contradicted Americanism because the nation was a composite of nationalities. Not only did the Irish and the Germans retain their distinctive (and tolerated) group interests, but America's composite makeup and the manifold contributions of its different national groups accounted for the success of the country. Americanization would proceed naturally even if not deliberately fostered. For those reasons the journal was highly critical of Israel Zangwill's popular play "The Melting Pot" and its message of assimilation.[22] Interestingly, however, most Americans disagreed. While the *Maccabaean* was developing an early version of cultural pluralism on behalf of the new immigrants, the latter, both Jews and non-Jews, preferred the path of the melting pot, or conformity to the established Anglo-Saxon mold.

Writers for the journal liked to point out the similarities of the American and Zionist ideologies. Democratic Zionism, they said, ran parallel to the impulse of the Pilgrim Fathers and the American Revolution, and loyalty to Zionism, because it never mandated political allegiance to a Jewish state, suited the American concept of patriotism. Seeking to reassure those whose fear of gentile disapproval and nonacceptance was paramount, Harry Friedenwald once explained: "This land demands our complete loyalty. . . . But it does not demand that we shall be recreant to any duty, whether it be to our family, to our kin, to our people, here or elsewhere." Judah Magnes added that American citizenship did not require national or religious suicide.[23] Nor was *aliyah* seriously discussed by the *Maccabaean*. Only once, in connection with the writings of an eighteenth-century rabbi who favored settlement in the Holy Land, did the journal ask "Why not live in Palestine?" It also mentioned a speech by Magnes calling on Jewish youth to prepare for *aliyah*. For the most part it kept silent on the *chalutz* (pioneer) movement then inflaming Zionist youth in eastern Europe.[24]

Lengthier pieces on the compatibility of Zionism with Americanism were featured in the journal. One was a statement allegedly written by Theodor Herzl on Zionism and patriotism that had not been published before. In answer to a question from America, the Zionist leader said that Zionism would not separate the nationalist Jew from his compatriots. Calling Zionism the only humane and practical solution for persecuted Jews, he alluded to the traditional American ideal of aid to the oppressed: "American Jews aid their beloved fatherland [the United States] when they aid an unhappy people from whom they spring. That is not disloyalty . . . but a double measure of loyalty."[25]

The *Maccabaean* reprinted statements on the issue of compatibility from three individuals well known in the American Jewish world—Israel Zangwill, Cyrus L. Sulzberger, and Josephine Lazarus. None of the three preached extremism, nor did they belabor the issue of Jewish statehood. The longest piece was that by Lazarus, sister of the more famous Emma and herself a writer. She discussed in detail the idealism of Zionism and its intrinsic resemblance to American ideals. Just as America taught the gospel of "freedom and light," so in a new Jerusalem would the Jews again be the great religious teachers of the world, the preachers of true liberty. A "prophetic" movement, "Zionism like Americanism is not a matter of creed or custom or local 'habitat.' The Zionist may remain an American, even as the American may be transplanted to the Philippines, or to Palestine, and yet remain an American. . . . Zionism is the soul, the spirit of the Jewish people to-day, coming into its own again, coming into self-consciousness, self-manifestation, self-realization, in a word spiritual autonomy." Like Americans, Zionists were a composite of peoples from different lands determined to create a "spiritual democracy": "Zionism, like Americanism, is an emancipation, a release from enforced limitations and legislation, from a narrow . . . tribal polity of life . . . and from old-world prejudice and caste. Like Americanism, it is a sifting of the nations of the globe, among all of whom our people are to be found, and the recasting of them into a new mold . . . with more exalted and more fearless ideals of freedom, and a more assured conviction of the inherent dignity of the race and the individual." Lazarus added a new twist when she said that Zionism idealism could enrich America, because it offered an idealism for countering the materialistic race of the times.[26]

The strongest weapon of those who defended the compatibility of Zionism with Americanism was the claim that the essence of Zionism was democracy. (The claim began with Herzl; when his scheme for a Jewish state was initially turned down by Barons Maurice de Hirsch and Edmond de Rothschild, the Zionist leader called for a democratic movement and looked for support from the Jewish masses.) Zionism, they said, was a movement of the people; it stood for democracy within the American Jewish community, and it was the base for the intended Jewish state. Statements like the following were frequently aired in the *Maccabaean:* "Zionism stands for a democracy of the Jewish people"; "Zionism has everything in common with the needs of a democracy"; "Zionism in America has become the first triumph of a Jewish democracy."[27] Since democracy was a built-in feature, how could Zionism not be compatible with Americanism?

Jewish Culture and Religion

Convinced that a national consciousness could not be propagated in a cultural vacuum, the *Maccabaean* filled its pages with scholarly and popular articles on Jewish history, art and philosophy, translations from Yiddish and Hebrew classics and original stories and poems in English. A perennial favorite was the great Hebrew poet of medieval Spain, Yehudah ha-Levi, who dreamed of Eretz Yisrael and moved there at the end of his life.[29] To further an appreciation of Jewish culture, the journal often included "think pieces," book reviews, and guidelines for study circles. It even planned a model Jewish library for its readers.[29] The varied content was directed not only at subscribers but also at neutral, unaffiliated, and indifferent Jews. Unfortunately, the scholarly and educational emphases dulled over time, and the later volumes dealt primarily with contemporary developments in the Zionist world and information on the *yishuv.*

A topic treated repeatedly by contributors and by the editors was the need to properly educate the children. As Louis Lipsky put it, "A people which has passed through centuries bearing the burden of Christian hatred, persecuted in common, reading a common literature, hoping for a common freedom, and living the same life for centuries and centuries . . . must retain a peculiar psychology which demands a peculiar education." Since, according to the

Maccabaean, the Reform Sunday school and the "ossified" old-world Orthodox classroom were inadequate to the task of instilling a full appreciation of the Jewish heritage and of counteracting the neglect of the "Jewish spirit," the journal was entering what was still virgin territory. The early Zionists did not organize schools of their own, but at conventions and in the pages of the *Maccabaean* they debated ideas of improved educational programs. All agreed that a proper education would preserve Judaism in America and would inculcate a national consciousness. A consensus also emerged on language; Hebrew and not Yiddish was preferred.[30] None, however, suggested the replacement of American public schools by Jewish day schools.

Simultaneously, the *Maccabaean* encouraged Jewish cultural activity in the United States. It applauded the efforts of the young Jewish Publication Society, "a valuable auxiliary to Zionist propaganda," to disseminate serious works in religion, history, and literature, and it took pride in current literary activity. The establishment by banker Jacob Schiff of the Semitics Museum at Harvard was also praised. (Schiff hoped thereby to show how the ancient period in Jewish history contributed to world civilization and to inculcate an appreciation of the Jewish heritage among Jews and non-Jews.)[31] As in the case of education, the emphasis on an American Jewish culture was a Zionist investment in the preservation of a Jewish future *in the United States.*

Contributors to the *Maccabaean* claimed that only a grounding in nationalism could erase the indifference of Jews to the riches of their heritage. Religion alone did not suffice. Aware, however, that most American Jews and non-Jews held religion to be the most natural and legitimate expression of Jewishness, the journal never assumed the secularist stance of so many Zionist activists in Europe. On rare occasions it even printed articles by, or made mention of, religious leaders who urged the observance of the Sabbath. In one editorial De Haas called the substitution of Sunday for Saturday services by some rabbis a betrayal of Jewish religious and historic causes. But although it carefully refrained from disparaging religious faith, the *Maccabaean* claimed that "the Jewish nation cannot . . . be maintained in the religious form. It must re-establish itself on its own territory [and] re-assume its normal national life." Only a restoration to Palestine, it continued, could safeguard religious values: "As exiles, we are always in danger of neglecting the values contained in the Torah. Only as citizens in our own land can the Torah be surrounded by the faithful."[32]

The *Maccabaean* was far more biting in its treatment of religious anti-Zionists. It accused those among the ultra-Orthodox, who objected to the very concept of a manmade restoration to Palestine and who were scandalized by the godlessness of the Zionist platform, of formalism and rigidity and of driving American Jews to assimilation by their outmoded and inadequate educational facilities. The journal predicted only a brief future for Orthodoxy in *galut,* and it advised traditionalists to adapt their Judaism to modern conditions.[33] Reform Judaism, led mostly by earlier German immigrants, aroused more serious attacks. Recent scholarship has shown that although Reform institutions remained officially anti-Zionist, early Zionism gained more than a few adherents among Reformers.[34] Nonetheless, the opinions of the small if influential minority were eclipsed by the intense, at times near-hysterical, statements of the anti-Zionists and their press. Well organized, affluent, and at home in Christian America, Reformers bitterly fought Zionism on theological and political grounds. (Reform's anti-Zionism is fully discussed below in chapter 2.) Copying Reform's method of attack from pulpits, institutions, and the press, the *Maccabaean* lashed back: By its rejection of Jewish nationalism, Reform was only present-minded and deficient in "sincerity, genuine piety, and manliness." (The periodical, to be sure, was not overly concerned about piety, for it conceded that had Reform accepted the concept of Jewish national life, it would have condoned even Reform's repudiation of the Torah.) As for those Reformers who feared that Zionism could alienate Christian good will, the journal called them "weak-minded, half-hearted Jews" without self-respect. Since Zionists were unafraid of public opinion, it proved that they, who relied on the fundamental liberty of freedom of expression, had more faith in democratic America than their opponents.[35] Hardly a single issue of the journal appeared without some dissection and/or ridicule of Reform's principles or of individual Reformers who preached against Jewish nationalism. For several months the *Maccabaean* traded insults with Reform in a separate page under the heading "Among the Mission-Jews." Our enemies help us in one way, Richard Gottheil wryly remarked, for they keep us from making any false moves.[36]

In the drawn out conflict between Reform and Zionism, mudslinging and *ad hominem* diatribes by both sides glossed over significant facts. Reform may have encouraged rapid acculturation, but it stemmed the wave of complete assimilation and conversion. In the United States it offered a religious anchor for Jews racing to keep up with a rapidly changing environment. More important, in an age when Americans expected some sort of religious affiliation but frowned upon group separatism on other than religious grounds, Reform fashioned Judaism into a respectable religious denomination. It failed to recognize, however, that the peculiar condition of eastern European Jewry had bred a Jewish nationalist enlightenment; nor did it grasp the Eastern Jew's identification of Zionism with liberty. For its part, Zionism concealed its true colors when it criticized Reform on religious grounds. Although it built on the traditional yearning for a return to Palestine, Zionism was basically a secular movement, a child of nineteenth-century nationalism. Like Reform it offered emancipated Jews a compromise formula between modernity and Jewish loyalty. At bottom, the issue between the two movements was secularist nationalism versus universalist religion.

Although they charged that Reform had betrayed the essence of Judaism, the Zionists did not lose hope of converting them. Occasionally they reported that Reform leaders were indeed modifying their views of Zionism. The journal's confidence also rose as Zionists observed that the day of the German Jew was fast giving way to the day of the Russian Jew.[37] Increasingly outnumbered by the nationalist-minded eastern Europeans, Reformers by 1917 had the option of digging in their heels on the issue of Zionism or swimming with the nationalist current.

Jewish Leadership and American Jewish Politics

The focus of American Zionist leaders on national consciousness-raising legitimated the *Maccabaean's* concern with the American Jewish scene. A rigid Herzlian Zionist might have decided that his purview included only matters pertaining to political Zionism, or that his interest did not encompass a Diaspora unable to nurture Jewish continuity. But national consciousness without immediate statehood permitted a wider latitude because it could be linked with any feature of the contemporary Jewish scene. The first editors of the *Maccabaean,* who never personally disavowed Herzl's objective, may have been illogical or inconsistent, but as previously mentioned, the course they chose better suited the realities of American Jewish life.

The *Maccabaean* kept an eye on important American Jewish personalities and institutions. Its primary focus, however, was the lack of a democratic communal structure and the concentration of leadership in relatively few hands, usually those of German Jews who were non- or anti-Zionists. The Zionists had more in mind than merely replacing the incumbents with men of their own. Herzl had posited that Zionism was a democratic movement standing for the political empowerment of the Jewish masses. Furthermore, a democratic community was theoretically more compatible with the essence of Americanism. Accordingly, the journal lashed out time and again at the unrepresentative and undemocratic character of the major defense and philanthropic organizations, such as B'nai B'rith and the American Jewish Committee (AJC).

The AJC was the periodical's *bête noire:* "The American Jewish Committee is an instrument of a party of worthy gentlemen, who disdain to be accountable to the Jewish people for what they do; they conduct their sessions in secrecy, refuse to admit the Jewish press, and make no public statement of their income and disbursements." Paraphrasing a line in a popular poem by Bret Harte, the journal added: "Our American Jewish Committee, like the Heathen Chinee, works in ways that are dark and peculiar." Whereas the AJC stood for stewardship, or *shtadlanut* and *hofjudenthum* (the ways by which "Court Jews" interceded with pre-Emancipation governments), the Zionists championed democracy. Adopting the watchword "benevolent despotism is out of date," they claimed to have fashioned the most democratic Jewish organization in America. An editorial further explained that control by a few stewards could not awaken national consciousness: "The Jewish people must emancipate themselves. They must . . . solve their own problems. . . . The success of Zionism depends upon our success in creating a Jewish democracy."[38] The same criticism applied to the major Jewish organizations in Europe, like the French Alliance Israélite Universelle and the German Hilfsverein der deutschen Juden, as well as to ideas of coordinated activities through an international elitist committee.[39]

In the formative years of American Zionism, even when eastern European Jewry required all the non-Jewish help it could get, the *Maccabaean* harshly criticized those organizations or prominent individuals who took it upon themselves to intervene with the American government on behalf of the oppressed. In 1902, largely under prodding by three leading Jews—Oscar Straus, Jacob Schiff, and Lucius Littauer—Secretary of State John Hay circulated a note among the powers protesting Romanian persecutions. The journal opposed the move, arguing first that Jewish diplomacy that aimed at coercing one government through the intervention of other governments was doomed to failure. Second, America's kindness was appreciated, but Jews had to help themselves. A year later the *Maccabaean* more vehemently objected to the Kishinev petition, a protest against the recent pogrom (a "holocaust," the journal called it) drawn up and circulated by B'nai B'rith and dispatched to Russia through State Department channels. The petition did not receive the sanction of the Jewish people or their responsible representatives, the Zionists said, and it risked a worsening of the Russian situation. Again, in 1905, the Zionists supported the Jewish Self-Defense Association, an organization for arming Russian Jews in case of pogroms, instead of the stewards' relief campaign, the National Committee for Relief of Sufferers by Russian Massacres (NCRSRM). The *Maccabaean* had this to say about two of the officers of the NCRSRM: "We should be only too glad to see Mr. Schiff and Mr. Oscar Straus elected to carry out a Jewish policy—but it must be a policy that has the sanction of the people who elect them to carry their messages to the nations." For similar reasons, the Zionists foresaw only failure when a small Jewish delegation appealed to Sergius Witte of Russia, then in the United States to negotiate a peace treaty concluding the Russo-Japanese war, for the emancipation of Russian Jews. The delegates may have meant well, but they should have first consulted with American and Russian Jews. Furthermore, the meeting injured more than it helped, because the unrepresentative delegation, acting as the guardian of its eastern European wards, left the impression of Jewish helplessness.[40] Constantly decrying oligarchical rule at the expense of self-help, the Zionists urged the convocation of congresses that would enable Jews of all countries to express their will on problems of foreign Jewries.[41]

Only when the AJC orchestrated a national campaign in 1911 to have Congress abrogate the Russo-American treaty of 1832 did it win the *Maccabaean's* approval. Russia was refusing visas to American Jews, and the committee, as well as the Zionists, rightly interpreted the practice—to which the United States under the treaty was a partner—as an infringement of American Jewish equality. The committee at first applied quiet pressure on political leaders to force an end to Russian discrimination, and the *Maccabaean* as usual criticized its methods. But since quiet pressure proved unsuccessful, the AJC went public in order to rally the community to its side. At that point the journal applauded the stewards and their change of policy; not only had the committee abandoned its "backstairs" habits and appropriated the straightforward Zionist approach, but an appeal directly to the people was in fact a show of political power. Hadn't the Zionists always said that the methods of the *shtadlanim* "who were afraid to speak in the name of justice but appealed to the sentiment of charity, must be replaced by a new method, breathing the spirit of freedom and self-help"?[42]

The Zionists deserve a large measure of credit for the decline of stewardship in America. Nevertheless, the picture of *shtadlanut* painted by the *Maccabaean* was incomplete. Admittedly, *shtadlanut* was inherently undemocratic. For a few men to arrogate to themselves the right to bargain for the community without the community's consent or even awareness bespoke a belief in their own superiority. Given the wide social gap between the stewards and the rank and file, and the deferential treatment they received from non-Jews as well as Jews because of their socioeconomic status, they were in a position to mold the community as they alone saw fit. Rarely were the stewards constrained by the masses. *Shtadlanut* also meant cautiousness to the point of timidity; it implied excessive fear of official disfavor or popular antisemitism, which, the stewards thought, could be sparked by loud agitation or public demonstrations.

The Zionists ignored the impressive record of the *shtadlanim*—how they labored to avert antisemitic outbreaks abroad and restrictive immigration legislation at home, and how they provided financial relief for needy European Jews. Not only did American officials approached by the *shtadlanim* prefer behind-the-scenes pressure to noisy agitation, but the *Maccabaean* itself, despite its criticism of the stewards, and despite its protestations of Zionist fearlessness, rarely risked alienating the government or public opinion. Finally, it was most unlikely that the hopelessly divided American Jewish community at the beginning of the century could have been organized democratically to deal with the same problems. As history would show, the Zionists too indulged in behind-the-scenes negotiations when they became a respectable lobby in America.

In a veritable crusade for democratizing the communal structure, the *Maccabaean* also charged that the major Jewish charities were undemocratic and therefore estranged from the community. Dealing principally with the seemingly endless flow of immigrants, the charities, according to the journal, were unable to cope properly with the material and educational needs of the newcomers. The Baron de Hirsch Fund, controlled by nine prominent philanthropists and saddled with problems of immediate relief, economic rehabilitation, and Americanization, was called an agency that crushed Jewish life "into the mold of prejudiced theories," and the Educational Alliance of New York City, a settlement house supported by the fund, was a place where "the American spirit is so rampant, at the expense of Jewish instruction."[43]

The fund as well as other organizations also aroused criticism for attempts to uproot Jews from the congested ghettos on the eastern seaboard and ship them to points farther west. The sponsors of distribution sought thereby to accelerate the process of Americanization and to defuse the mounting alarm of immigration restrictionists. The *Maccabaean,* however, which roundly condemned distribution for its destructive impact on Jewish cohesiveness, prophesied the failure of their plans. Although it did approve of schemes to settle Jews on farms, it observed that it was natural for immigrants to herd together in the cities and equally natural for them to ignore directives from above that paid no attention to their personal preferences. Besides, inner-city congestion was not a problem for which Jews alone could be blamed, especially at a time when a general exodus from the American countryside to the cities was under way. Schemes of distribution, the *Maccabaean* concluded, only validated the charges of antisemitic restrictionists who held the new immigrants responsible for the evils of rapid urbanization. (It is quite likely that the Zionists also realized that densely settled urban enclaves enhanced the influence of the Jewish vote in local and national elections.) In short, just as it measured individual Jews, so did it judge communal institutions by their loyalty to Judaism as a national and cohesive force.[44]

The *Maccabaean*'s concern for a heightened Jewish national consciousness enabled it to discuss American as well as American Jewish issues. On grounds of Jewish interest, it supported separation of church and state, denounced Sunday laws, and criticized the prejudiced and what it called the anti-American immigration restrictionists. Denying that it was a political journal that freely commented on political developments and parties, or boasted a political agenda for the country, or advised Jews how to vote, the journal found it easy enough to relate most events to Jewish interests.[45] Here too the question of consistency arose; as long as they posited an unfriendly if not destructive Diaspora, it would have been quite logical for political Zionists to stand aloof from all American issues. But at the same time the special position of American Jewry, who had neither a physical need of, or personal desire for, a Jewish state, and whose passion for acceptance as Americans by Americans was paramount, was not forgotten by Zionist leaders. Since America was recognized as different, the solution was not clear-cut. Flitting back and forth between engagement and nonengagement in current American affairs, the journal never fixed on any firm line that delimited Jewish from non-Jewish interests.

Two examples point up the halfway compromises settled on by the *Maccabaean.* One instance: When New Yorkers prepared to choose a new mayor in 1901, prostitution in the Jewish ghetto on the city's Lower East Side became a major focal point of the anti-Tammany party. Although Jewish leaders joined the reformers' campaign, and although they made special efforts appealing to Jewish voters, the journal refrained from advising Jews how to vote. A month later, however, Richard Gottheil used the journal to attack the Jewish press. The recent election concerned a moral issue, he wrote, but not one Yiddish or Hebrew newspaper supported the antiprostitution ticket. [46] Jewish interests were unquestionably involved, but if so, why had the journal ignored the issue until after the election?

A second example concerns the *Maccabaean*'s approach to the subject of immigration restriction. During the formative years of American Zionism, pressure for limiting the seemingly endless flow of immigrants increased significantly. Although popular opinion was not specifically antisemitic, it did single out the Jews as among the most undesirable groups. The *Maccabaean* reported the successive attempts in Congress at framing restrictive legislation, and repeatedly it registered its opposition. True, as Jewish life in eastern Europe continued to worsen, free immigration was very much a Jewish interest. But instead of concentrating on Jewish needs, the journal spent more time arguing how restriction worked against the country's democratic tradition and the promise of America.[47] It may have been a wiser political choice to rest the case on American rather than Jewish grounds, but the entire subject appeared somewhat out of place in a Zionist journal. How logical was it to press for free immigration to the United States if Zionism looked upon a Jewish Palestine as the optimal refuge? One might have sooner expected a campaign encouraging would-be Jewish immigrants to make their goal Palestine, where their labors would redound both to their own security and to the establishment of a Jewish state. Here again the treatment of immigration shows that the guidelines for what was within the *Maccabaean*'s purview were neither hard nor fast.

The World War

The outbreak of World War I injected a new tone into the *Maccabaean*. To be sure, some subjects were rehashed as before—the errors of the anti-Zionists, the undemocratic AJC, the need of continued support for the *yishuv,* and the internal problems of the FAZ. But in the swift course of events on the war and home fronts, a sense of imminent radical change pervaded the journal. Despite the untold atrocities and suffering that accompanied military action, the journal usually presented an optimistic face, confident that postwar gains would accrue to the Jews and to humanity at large. Caught up in the wave of Americanization that swept the country, the Zionists also used the war years to prove how American they and their movement were.

Before 1914 the *Maccabaean* had paid scant attention to foreign affairs. Except for news of Zionist developments, the only two countries of concern were

Turkey and Russia—the former because it ruled Palestine, the latter because of recurring pogroms. In light of the violent waves of anti-Jewish outbreaks in the czarist regime, the journal showed little confidence in the prewar revolutionary ferment in Russia, and despite the calling of the Duma in 1905, Zionists did not expect the emancipation of their fellow Jews.[48] On the other hand, the Young Turk revolt of 1908, which the journal consistently applauded, generated much optimism. Whether the new constitution would help Zionism, what the Young Turks thought about Zionist efforts in Palestine, and whether the time had come to renew Herzl's earlier negotiations with Turkey became favorite topics for articles and editorials. Judah Magnes wondered whether Zionists ought to reformulate their objective. Was it necessary to insist on an autonomous Jewish state or was settlement under a free government sufficient? In answer to such comments, Max Nordau explained that it was premature to reopen Herzl-like diplomatic negotiations; it was necessary first to ascertain Turkish opinion on Zionism and to strengthen the movement. Even if the Turks were to offer concessions for Jewish settlement, Nordau said, there was no need to alter the Basel program. In 1913, Zionists hailed Woodrow Wilson's appointment of Henry Morgenthau as ambassador to Constantinople, and the *Maccabaean* was confident, although its confidence proved to be misplaced, that he sympathized with their cause. When the war broke out less than a year later, the Zionists aligned themselves with Turkey in opposition to any intervention by Europe. Banking on Turkish friendship, the *Maccabaean* said that any move against Turkish territorial integrity was a move against Zionism.[49]

Never had the prewar issues of the journal seriously suggested the form that a Jewish state would take. Herzl had offered several pointers in *Der Judenstaat*, but like other statements by the Zionist leader, they were not developed in detail by his supporters. Aside from very occasional remarks—that Zionism was "radically progressive," that it would be not enslaved by laissez-faire or laws of private property—and aside from denunciations of the widespread charge that Jews couldn't govern themselves, writers for the *Maccabaean* usually ignored the subject.[50] (An interesting exception: The writer of one article posited that a Jewish state would not be like all the nations. An exemplar of justice and morality, it had to be better than the others.)[51] Only during the war years, when England was considering a pro-Zionist move to win Jewish support, did thoughts turn to the future of a Jewish homeland in Palestine.

The closest attempt to define the nature of the Jewish state was Herzl's novel, *Altneuland,* which was serialized in the journal. Employing the genre of the late-nineteenth-century utopian novel, Herzl wrote that he meant the novel to be a fairy tale with a moral. The story begins with a visit to Palestine by two young disillusioned western Europeans, one Jewish and one Christian. The Palestine they find at the end of 1902 is a land of decay. Twenty years later the two visitors return, this time to a land transformed, a Jewish utopia. The introduction of technology and electrical power has modernized industry and agriculture, cities and commerce. The prevailing economic system is neither individualism nor collectivism but is rather one of cooperatives. Cooperatives also distinguish a reformed social order that deals successfully with matters like education and treatment of prisoners. The rights of women are guaranteed and so is religious freedom; Jew and Arab live side by side in a spirit of brotherhood. Despite the rosy aura that was projected, the *Maccabaean* never discussed *Altneuland*. Modern Zionists took to heart only the motto coined by Herzl for the novel: "Wenn Ihr vollt, ist es kein Märchen." (If you will it, it is no fairy tale.)

From the onset of the war, Zionist opinion supported Wilson. Sounding no different from the established Jewish organizations, the *Maccabaean* aimed at proving the patriotism of American Jews. The journal came out strongly in favor of the president's early efforts at mediation as well as his call for strict neutrality. Neutrality was a sticky issue for Jews; whereas Americans in general showed greater sympathy for the Triple Entente, many Jews opposed any alliance in which czarist Russia was a partner. The *Maccabaean*'s tone smacked of anti-Russian sentiment, but the periodical itself, careful not to take sides openly, criticized Richard Gottheil for a public statement in support of the Allies.[53] When Wilson broke off relations with Germany, the journal announced its full accord. "The Zionist movement runs parallel with the idealism of this land," it said. Agreeing with the president's idealistic talk of a world safe for democracy, the Zionists added a note of self-interest: the war was for democracy *and* for the rights of small nationalities. "Since nations do not disappear," one article asked, "why should we?" America's entry into the war in April 1917 prompted further patriotic declarations. Identifying America's cause as "our" cause, the *Maccabaean* spoke against Jewish pacifists and urged Jews to enlist in the war effort. Military service was not only the duty of the citizen, but necessary to dispel a popular view of the Jews as draft dodgers.[54]

American Zionism underwent a radical upheaval upon the outbreak of the war. Since it was now impossible for the *Actions Comité*, the executive of the WZO, to coordinate activity in Europe, a substitute body in the United States, the Provisional Zionist Committee (PZC), was established for the duration under the chairmanship of Louis Brandeis. Since the hub of WZO which administered financial affairs was transferred temporarily to the United States, the shift automatically elevated the status of American Zionism. Until now we were only a "distant contributor" in the upbuilding of Palestine, one statement in the *Maccabaean* said, but now we are asked for our personal services, our expertise, and our abilities in state-building. The journal asserted with great confidence that since "the future of Zionism lies in America," American Jews would rise to the challenge.[55] More significant for the future of American Zionism was the assumption of leadership by Brandeis, a close adviser to the president and a reformer of national repute.

The PZC eclipsed the FAZ, and for all practical purposes, as Professor Melvin Urofsky has written, the FAZ existed during the war in name only. The PZC immediately turned its attention to the problems of Jewish wartime relief. It faced a dilemma: Should it respond first to the needs of the *yishuv* or the needs of European Jews? In the end it undertook both. The Allies had imposed a blockade upon Turkish ports, and economic life in Palestine, dependent upon export of its citrus crop, ground to a virtual halt. In central and eastern Europe, more than three million Jews lived directly in the path of the contending armies and suffered atrocities at the hands of both sides. Despite their military service in the various countries, the *Maccabaean* commented bitterly, Jews were still regarded universally as aliens. On behalf of the *yishuv* and with the help of the American government, Zionists in cooperation with the AJC contributed to the despatch of a relief ship with necessary foodstuffs and other supplies. They also raised funds for the direct relief of Jewish victims in Palestine and Europe and for keeping alive the Jewish institutions in Palestine. Unable to compete financially with the wealthy steward-led American Jewish Relief Committee, the Zionists nonetheless kept their multipronged relief campaign before the readers of the *Maccabaean*.[56]

Zionists took particular pride in their newly created Transfer Department, which serviced both Palestine and Europe. With the approval of the American government they introduced a way for relatives to send money to victims in different battle zones. The money was transmitted by the PZC to the State Department, which in turn relayed the funds to American representatives abroad for distribution to the designees. One statement in 1916 reported that about $1000 was transmitted daily. Available also to non-Jews and to people of all groups at home and abroad, the Transfer Department earned Washington's commendation, and it functioned as long as the United States remained neutral. Zionists basked in the praise; they thought their prestige had risen just because people now saw the Jew as a humanitarian.[57]

Relief work brought another benefit. According to Brandeis, aid and support from the American government to Zionist wartime ventures showed yet again that Zionist ideals were in essence American. He elaborated in broad terms: "It is democracy that Zionism represents. It is full and complete liberty which Zionism represents, and every bit of that is the American ideal of the Twentieth Century."[58]

Of all their wartime activities the Zionists were proudest of their campaign for an American Jewish Congress. The oft-told story[59] of the movement for a congress began at the very onset of the war. Attention turned to the issue of guaranteeing Jewish rights in Europe, and the notion of a democratically elected congress, representative of the community, that would formulate and present the Jewish case to the peacemakers rapidly caught on. The Zionists favored the idea for two reasons. First, the congress planned to ask for Jewish national rights in postwar countries—success would mean international sanction of the concept of a Jewish nationality, the heart of the Zionist brief. Second and more compelling, a democratically elected congress promised to shift communal leadership away from the established Jews into the hands of the Zionist-led majority.

The fight over a congress, which raged between 1914 and 1917, pitted the Zionists against their old adversary, the AJC. Since much of Zionist invective was directed at the committee, the latter bitterly contested the Zionists and their supporters. It had assumed that it alone would handle postwar negotiations; later, in light of communal pressure, it grudgingly agreed to a conference of delegates of national organizations, still a far cry from a democratic congress elected by the masses. Fearful of noisy agitation directed by nationalist Jews, the AJC believed that its very life was at stake. Long drawn-out negotiations between the Zionists and the committee and between their leaders—Cyrus Adler, president of the AJC, and Louis Brandeis, chairman of the PZC—publicly exposed the bitterness between the two sides. The committee was finally compelled to capitulate. It managed, however, to win on two matters: the leaders of the congress movement promised that the congress would not become a permanent organization, and bowing to the government's suggestion, they agreed to defer the congress until after the war. In the end, there was a congress and a congressional delegation to Versailles, but it was Louis Marshall of the AJC, and not the Zionists, who formulated the American Jewish demands and led Jewish negotiations at the peace conference.

Understandably the *Maccabaean*, ever the champion of communal democracy, cheered on the congress supporters in its very full reportage of developments. Claiming an increased interest in Zionism brought about by the war, the journal stated that the very idea of a national and democratic congress would further activate that interest. The AJC, it said, was unworthy of serving as the people's representative, because it didn't even pretend to care about public opinion.[60] In the summer of 1916 a conference to resolve the differences was held at the Hotel Astor. There, according to Zionist reports, the committee appeared particularly high-handed and belligerent in an interchange with the Zionists. Its blatant insults, the *Maccabaean* charged, forced Brandeis to resign from the congress organization committee. Peace was finally reached; the committee accepted a congress with the stipulations mentioned above.[61]

The *Maccabaean* was ecstatic. The congress, it said, marked a new era of self-emancipation and self-help, a virtual "revolution," in American Jewish life. It was the Jewish Parliament, "the organ of Jewish national aspiration"; and "the first step in the direction of distributing the responsibilities, as well as the privileges, connected with Jewish citizenship." The Zionists were responsible, the *Maccabaean* concluded, for having democratized the American Jewish community.[62] For our purposes it should be noted that the victory of communal democracy, like the wartime patriotism of American Jews, proved yet again how Zionist leaders made use of American principles on which to base their activities.

Zionism scored its first major triumph when England issued the Balfour Declaration. In a letter dated November 2, 1917, from Arthur James Balfour, the British foreign secretary, to Baron Lionel Rothschild, it was announced that "His Majesty's Government view with favor the settlement in Palestine of a national home for the Jewish people, and will use their best endeavors to facilitate the achievement of this object." A wartime measure, the declaration had been in the making ever since Turkey had entered the war on the side of Germany and Austria-Hungary. Its immediate object was to capture Jewish sympathy, especially in the United States, for the Allies and to shore up England's strategic interests in the Near East. Pushed by leading Zionists in England and by Brandeis, who intervened with President Wilson, the declaration, which was eventually recognized internationally, put the seal of legitimacy on political Zionism. Twenty years after the first congress at Basel, Herzl's goal had been achieved.

A mood of exhileration gripped American Zionists. Those who shared their sentiments with the *Maccabaean* lavished much praise on England. They talked exuberantly of the Jewish Magna Carta, the "happiest epoch" in Jewish history, and the first ray of light for eastern European Jewry. An editorial in the *Maccabaean* summed up the Zionist hopes: "Zionism was. Zion is about to be."[63]

Overall, American Zionist leaders were satisfied with the progress they had made during the first twenty years of the FAZ. As early as 1910 they demanded that European Zionists not limit the role of the Americans to philanthropy; they wanted greater European attention to the American situation and a greater share for themselves in Zionist policymaking.[64] To be sure, as the *Maccabaean* reported, the leaders frequently bemoaned the paucity of members— twelve thousand in 1914, an increase of only eight thousand since 1900—a condition that changed dramatically only under the leadership of the charismatic Brandeis.[65] Troubled throughout the years by lack of funds, they realized too that their type of organization, a loose federation, bred problems of inefficiency and disunity. Nevertheless, at least according to the *Maccabaean*, they had successfully injected heightened idealism and self-confidence into the evolving mold of American Jewish life, and their movement had contributed to a palpable diminution of Reform's intense opposition to a Jewish homeland in Palestine.

Inconsistencies and compromises notwithstanding, the *Maccabaean* took pride in its contributions to Zionism and to American Jewish life. Louis Lipsky wrote on the journal's tenth anniversary:

The *Maccabaean* has contributed something to the fabric of Jewish life in America. It has contributed the silver threads of a proud Jewish consciousness.... The *Maccabaean* has brought into the literature which the American Jewish youth will read something more than the apologetics that have belittled Jewish life. It . . . has interpreted the positive movements in Jewish life abroad, and has aided materially in preventing the isolation of American Jewry by compelling it . . . to give attention and thought to the larger interests of the Jewish people.[66]

Nor were Lipsky's claims unfounded. A dignified pride in Jewish culture and history, which was conspicuously absent from other Anglo-Jewish periodicals, made the *Maccabaean* a serious literary journal. Without apologetics, a common characteristic of the Jewish minority, it encouraged the development of an American Jewish literature.

How successful the *Maccabaean* and its parent organization were in building a strong American Zionist movement was quite another matter. Undeniably they planted Zionism in American soil, never to be uprooted. Their ability to win the support of a man like Brandeis testified to the attractiveness of their message and, like their campaigns for heightened self-respect and communal democracy, was a notable achievement.

Some Zionist weaknesses, however, lasted as long as Zionism itself. Despite the creation of an Americanized Zionism, the leaders of the FAZ failed to define adequately the differences that Zionism would make in the life of the average American Jew. Their answers to questions about American antisemitism, Jewish activity in American politics, and the limits to acceptance in Christian America were neither firm nor entirely convincing. Most American Jews, including enrolled Zionists, neither regarded America as *galut* nor disengaged themselves from participation in American affairs. The very idea of an aroused national consciousness was doubtless lost on the vast numbers who consciously or unconsciously preferred the path of assimilation. For them Zionism was at best another philanthropy dedicated to the needs of Jewish refugees.

Other weaknesses marred the progress of the formative years. Just as the FAZ and the *Maccabaean* neglected the concerns of Jewish labor, so did they keep aloof from the social and economic problems of needy Jews. The ferment of Progressive reform left them untouched. Despite a vague identification with liberal forces in general, they never actively sought out allies within the political parties. Alone, their arguments were unable to stand up to the American nativist forces of the postwar decade. More disturbing, American Zionism during its first twenty years failed to impart to Jewish youth the enthusiasm of the European *chalutz* (pioneer) movement or the idealism of *aliyah*. Zionists preached the need of a Jewishly educated community, but they provided neither schools nor specific guidelines of their own. Consequently, their message was unable to attract or make sense to the next generation, the children of the eastern Europeans, who in increasing numbers were lured away from things Jewish by secular studies at American colleges and universities. After the glorious days of Louis Brandeis, American Zionism remained little more than a comfortable Zionism, one that was eminently fitted to the oncoming era of Palestinianism.

CHAPTER 2

A Clash of Ideologies:
Reform Judaism vs. Zionism

The most formidable opposition to American Zionism during its formative years came from Reform Judaism. Indeed, Reform's anti-Zionism was in place long before there was a Zionist movement. From its very beginnings Reform had fused its theological precepts with American principles, and the resultant compound was the base from which it derived its anti-Zionism. At the heart of its controversy with Zionism lay the issue of two antithetical ideologies and two contradictory assessments of the compatibility, or incompatibility, of Zionism with Americanism. By Americanizing its religious principles—or, the obverse, by cloaking Americanism in religious garb—Reform's leaders became the most vehement critics of Jewish nationalism in the United States. Just as Zionists worked to depict their cause in terms familiar and acceptable to other Americans, so did Reformers Americanize anti-Zionism.[1]

The argument that Reform because of its American dimension could not tolerate Jewish nationalism was heard in some Reform circles well into the twentieth century. In 1944 Rabbi Solomon Freehof, then president of Reform's Central Conference of American Rabbis (CCAR), explained that long-lived theme:

All American Jews love America . . . but the love of America among Reform Jews is to this extent different, that it is virtually part of their religion. . . . Judaism and Americanism are so inextricably intertwined that any doctrine which carries the slightest implication of any other national allegiance arouses their instantaneous opposition. Nothing is gained by describing this feeling in deprecatory terms as an inferiority complex. . . . The fact is, this Americanism is a living and integral part of the *religious* feeling of the average Reform layman. He dislikes the word "national" in connection with the word "Jewish" because it instantly implies to him that he is asked to have some national allegiance other than the one which he so proudly holds in his heart and mind for America.

These sentiments, deep-rooted and pervasive, have not been the result of indoctrination. They were, in some form, part of the conviction of the first Reform laymen long before the rabbis even participated in the Reform movement.[2]

Classical Reformers fashioned their religion into an American creed *par excellence*. In their eyes, should political Zionism ever succeed, it would signal the bankruptcy of their faith.

Reform put American Zionism on the defensive and forced the young nationalist movement to find answers to the incessant criticism. Although the contenders fought for the same prize, i.e., public acceptance, they were in no way equals. In manpower, material assets, and social status Reformers outstripped the Zionists by far. Nor did the Zionists begin to enjoy the influence that Reformers wielded with non-Jews. All told, the wonder is that Zionism did not collapse under Reform's onslaught. But for the counterchallenges to Reform's anti-Zionism—notably by those Reform rabbis who supported Zionism and by Solomon Schechter and Louis Brandeis—the American Zionist movement might well have succumbed to its archenemy.

Reform's Religious Principles

With roots going back to the seventeenth century, the idea of a "reformed" Judaism was given a significant boost by the climate of the French Revolution. Freedom was in the air, and European Jews dreamed of emancipation from the servitude and degradation they had so long endured. Intellectuals among them, having imbibed the optimistic teachings of the Enlightenment, latched onto the ideas of rationalism, liberalism and individualism, universalism and progress, and turned their backs on the "anachronistic" Judaism of the now-despised ghetto. Understanding that the modern state would not tolerate separatism of a nationalist nature within its borders, they defined themselves solely as a religious group. In a few cases government prompting led to public denials of Jewish nationalism and the excision of prayers for a return to Palestine. Although many Jews left the faith entirely, some thinkers who desired to retain their religion, albeit in modern dress, experimented with reform—changes in substance as well as form in the local synagogues and Jewish schools. Underlying those experiments was the quest for civic equality and social acceptance; implicit in them was the promise to conform, as Jews, to the practices of the countries in which they lived. Those pioneers well understood that only by reconciling the Jewish faith with modernity could they hope to keep their fellow Jews within the fold. The experiments spread, and by the 1840s, when German rabbis held three conferences for outlining their emendations of Jewish law and ceremonials, Reform had become a movement. For our purposes it is especially important to note that the repudiation of the "national" dimension of rabbinic

Judaism—including laws and customs connected with Palestine—had by the middle of the nineteenth century become a norm of the new faith.[3]

Reform continued to develop in Germany, but it came to fruition in the United States. Without the medieval baggage of ghettos, feudalism and caste, monarchy and established church, America, a land of liberty and promise, attracted wave after wave of European immigrants. Early Reformers saw a country that offered freedom of religion, a commitment to the separation of church and state, and noninterference in rifts between Reform Jews and traditionalists—in short, a land destined for the fulfillment of their religion.[4]

Rabbis first arrived in the new country after 1840, but the stirrings of Reform, influenced by the German experience, had begun earlier.[5] In 1824, members of Charleston's Beth Elohim congregation petitioned for a revision of the traditional beliefs and customs of their synagogue. When their requests were rejected, they seceded from the congregation and organized the Reformed Society of Israelites. Their intellectual leader, Isaac Harby, called for shrugging off the yoke of rabbinic Judaism and substituting a rational faith that was relevant to American sentiments. Among other things, he taught that if the country lived up to its ideals, American Jews had no need of Palestine ("some stony desert") in place of "this happy land." Harby co-authored a new prayer book for the Society, and, not surprisingly, references to a return to Zion were omitted. The Reformed Society failed within a short time, but the arrival from Germany of rabbinic leaders like Isaac Mayer Wise, David Einhorn, Kaufmann Kohler, Samuel Adler, and Samuel Hirsch speeded up the pace of Reform's growth in the United States. The revolt of the rabbis against Mosaic laws and Talmudic precepts proceeded, and also high on their list of recommended changes in beliefs and liturgy was the rejection of the traditional longing for restoration to Palestine, replete with Temple, priests, and sacrificial system.

After the Civil War, attempts were made to unite the moderate and radical Reform rabbis and to formulate a common creed. The first successful conference was held in 1869 in Philadelphia. There the assembled rabbis adopted resolutions that summed up the repudiation of restoration: the destruction of the Second Temple was providential; the institutions of sacrifices and priesthood were "consigned to the past"; the messianic era no longer meant restoration and Jewish statehood. Reformers repeated those principles along with their definition of Israel's mission and Jewish exile in the Pittsburgh Platform of 1885, the official creed of Reform rabbis for more than half a century. In Pittsburgh the rabbis explicitly stated: "We consider ourselves no longer a nation, but a religious community, and therefore expect neither a return to Palestine, nor a sacrificial worship under the sons of Aaron, nor the restoration of any of the laws concerning the Jewish state."[6] A few years later, a firm denial of a restoration to Palestine was included in the *Union Prayer Book,* which serviced American Reform congregations for almost fifty years. In 1890, at its first annual convention, the CCAR incorporated into its proceedings the resolutions passed by the conferences in Germany and at Philadelphia and Pittsburgh, saying that those precedents constituted the basis on which the CCAR built.[7] Opposition to Jewish nationalism and to the hope of restoration thus became keystones of the American Reform creed.

The American Reform movement was well entrenched by 1897. Its tripartite structure—an organization of rabbis, an organization of congregational lay leaders, and a rabbinical seminary—governed a network of congregations, usually the more affluent in a city or state, which were spread throughout the land. By 1917 the number of congregations had risen to two hundred, with a membership of twenty-three thousand. At the same time, Reformers dominated the Jewish Establishment; their rabbis and laymen headed the major charitable and defense agencies and for the most part set policy for the community. The national religious census of 1890, the only one to distinguish between Reform and Orthodox Jews, revealed that the former outdistanced the latter in membership and in the value of synagogal property.[8] To be sure, the numbers of the traditionalists, from whose ranks most of the Zionists came, rose rapidly with the mass immigration of eastern Europeans. But they were as yet too foreign, too poor, and too divided—hardly a match for the acculturated Reformers.

After the publication of Theodor Herzl's *Der Judenstaat (The Jewish State)* in 1896 and the calling of the First Zionist Congress a year later, Reform vigorously renewed its antinationalist stand. To begin with, the secular cast of the Zionist movement alienated religious leaders and traditionalists of all stripes as well as Reformers. On the premise that nationalism by definition was secular, critics leveled charges against Zionism. "There is nothing religious . . . about the whole scheme," and their "very use of the name of Zion is a profanation and abuse," said one Reformer. Agnostics and infidels, Zionists lacked "a spark of religiosity in their soul," ranted another.[9] But unlike the spokesmen for traditionalists, Reformers more frequently sparred with Zionists on theological grounds. Since the time and energy expended on that effort seems excessive in light of the small number of enrolled Zionists, it is not unfair to assume that Reform's anti-Zionist crusade was directed at a larger audience, i.e., the general public as well as the undecided Jews. Doubtless non-Jews learned more about Zionism from Reform statements than from Zionist sources.

In 1897 the CCAR passed an anti-Zionist resolution that was reaffirmed time and again by American Reform institutions and Reform press:

Resolved, That we totally disapprove of any attempt for the establishment of a Jewish state. Such attempts show a misunderstanding of Israel's mission, which from the narrow political and national field has been expanded to the promotion among the whole human race of the broad and universalistic religion first proclaimed by the Jewish prophets. . . .

We reaffirm that the object of Judaism is not political nor national, but spiritual, and addresses itself to the continuous growth of peace, justice and love in the human race, to a messianic time when all men will recognize that they form "one great brotherhood" for the establishment of God's kingdom on earth.[10]

The resolution touched on the key ideological precepts of Reform—the mission of Israel, Jewish exile, and the messianic age. Since those beliefs readily lent themselves to denunciations of political Zionism, an explanation of each is in order:

1. *Israel's mission.* Reform taught that Jews constituted a unique *religious* community, preserved by religion and bound together only by religious ties. As the chosen priest-people of the Almighty, theirs was a universal mission to propagate the religion preached by the Prophets—the knowledge of Israel's one God and the loving-kindness of man to his fellow man throughout the world. Borne by past, present, and future generations of Jews, the mission was "for all times and places." But for that mission, Jews had no claim to a separate existence. When the prophetic ethical message was realized worldwide, Jews would become part of a common humanity and the messianic era would have arrived.[11]

The mission idea was sufficient to damn political Zionism and Zionists. In Kaufmann Kohler's words, "the underlying idea, the *fundamental principle* of Reform Judaism to be accentuated more than any other, is that Judaism is *no more a national religion* than its God is a tribal God." Zionism, reactionary and pessimistic because it reverted to narrow and particularistic nationalism, denied the promise of the oncoming universal messianic age. Its "negation of the best hope . . . of Judaism" made its message one of despair. It was destined to fail, confident Reformers agreed, and bound to add yet another "disillusionment" to the "tragedies of the ghetto." Failing to recognize the universal character of Judaism and its mission, which transcended the confines of a political state, Zionism preached a false philosophy.[12]

2. *Israel's exile.* A logical derivative of the ideas of universal religion and mission was Reform's interpretation of Israel's exile. Repudiating traditional beliefs and flying in the face of Jewish history, Reformers had reached a consensus as early as 1869 on the concept of Jewish dispersion among the nations. At Philadelphia they affirmed the following:

We look upon the destruction of the second Jewish commonwealth not as a punishment for the sinfulness of Israel, but as a result of the divine purpose revealed to Abraham which, as has become ever clearer in the course of the world's history, consists in the dispersion of the Jews to all parts of the earth for the realization of their high priestly mission, to lead the nations to the true knowledge and worship of God.

A few years later Rabbi Emil Hirsch wrote in a similar vein that Israel had left Palestine not longing for restoration but "as a missionary, to suffer and sigh, live and die for the truth entrusted to him."[13]

With the advent of political Zionism, Reformers expatiated on the concept of exile. The dispersion of the Jews after the destruction of the Second Temple, they reiterated time and again, was a positive blessing, for exile from Palestine was the first step toward the fulfillment of the Jewish mission. Therefore, it was wrong to mourn the destruction of the Temple. Turning rabbinic tradition on its head, some Reformers even taught that Tisha b'Av, the traditional day of mourning the destruction, should be commemorated as a joyous occasion: "Our Judaism is . . . not a widow mourning for Zion and Jerusalem, but a bride adorned for the wedding with humanity." Modern Jews needed no separate homeland of their own, Reformers insisted, since the Torah was not bound to any particular soil and the center of Judaism was the "universal kingdom of righteousness to be established on earth."[14] It followed that Zionism, based on the "ingathering of exiles" into a Palestinian Jewish center, home, or state, was unacceptable.

3. *The messianic age.* Substitution of a messianic "age" in place of a personal messiah had been discussed by Reformers since the early nineteenth century. The creed of the Reformed Society in Charleston, for example, omitted mention of a messiah. At the German conferences in the 1840s rabbis spoke against both a messiah and a national restoration to Palestine and statehood. The thrust of those pioneers was to spiritualize eschatological beliefs, to interpret the end of the days as the golden age dominated by "light, truth, and peace." Whereas rabbinic tradition spoke of redemption from exile when the messiah came, Reform defined redemption as deliverance from physical and spiritual evil. Restoration had no part within history or the messianic age.[15] Since Zionism was but a pseudo-messianism, its teachings were at least as false as those of rabbinic Judaism.

Reformers did not omit entirely the mention of Palestine in the liturgy. Palestine deserved a place in Jewish memory just because it was the birthplace of Judaism, the "cradle of our people" and the setting of the Prophets and the psalmists. Nevertheless, it had no purpose as a home for the modern American Jew: "Do not weep for Zion. Jerusalem is not our tomorrow. It was our yesterday." Jewish nationality and statehood belonged to a closed chapter of the past, one that served merely as a training period to prepare the Jews for their future mission. The Zionists cried "backward," Reformers taunted, while Reform's path was "forward" to the "promised and certain future."[16]

The theology of classical Reform in the formative years of American Zionism clearly set forth the essential differences between the two movements. As Rabbi David Philipson wrote, they were "incompatible" and "irreconcilable": "Reform Judaism is spiritual, Zionism is political; Reform Judaism is universal,

Zionism is particularistic; Reform Judaism looks to the future, Zionism to the past; the outlook of Reform Judaism is the world, the outlook of Zionism is a corner of Western Asia."[17]

Reform and Americanism

The teachings of the Age of Reason resonate throughout the writings and speeches of Reformers. The Reform movement was a child of the eighteenth-century Enlightenment, and it remained fixed in that time warp long after the Age of Reason had given way to Romanticism and heightened nationalism. American Reform stayed true to its roots. Not only did it shape its theology according to the philosophy of the Age of Reason, but it found in the Enlightenment the connective link between Americanism and the Reform faith. It could thereby claim a shared parentage with the American creed.

Reform's identification with Americanism had a mathematical precision about it. Given: Reform was grounded in the philosophy of the Enlightenment, and the American creed was grounded in the philosophy of the Enlightenment. Thus, if "a" (Reform) = "c" (a product of the Enlightenment) and "b" (the American creed) = "c," then "a" = "b." On those scales Reform confidently equated American ideals with its own religious beliefs. It followed first, that if Zionism was at odds with Reform theology, it was simultaneously un-American, and second, that if Zionism appeared to be un-American, it was also a contradiction of the Reform faith.

Buttressing the American connection still further, Reformers found support in the mission concept of the early Puritans. The latter, calling themselves the children of Israel, drew heavily from the Pentateuch and the books of the Prophets in their quest to establish a new Zion on the American continent. When Reformers became aware of the Puritan legacy, they embraced the similarities to their beliefs. Like the Puritans, they too consigned the Israelites of biblical times to the past, and they too proclaimed a mission to create a spiritual Zion. Their Zion, again like the Puritans', was in the United States, the Holy Land, the new land of milk and honey. One Reform Jew and amateur historian, Oscar S. Straus, advanced the theme of a common heritage still further. His book, *The Origin of Republican Form of Government in the United States of America,* showed how the biblical commonwealth, frequently cited in early American sermons and political tracts, served as the model for the colonists during the Revolution and the establishment of a democratic government. Like his fellow Reform Jews, Straus reduced both Judaism and Americanism to the common denominator of liberty.[18]

Talk of an American mission persisted in the postcolonial era. In many cases, interpreters posited that America was destined to be the exemplar of universal liberty. As Benjamin Franklin had said during the Revolution: "Our cause is *the Cause of all Mankind*, and . . . we are fighting for their Liberty in defending our own." A national mission of freedom was also invoked during the era of manifest destiny; since America was destined to spread the blessings of liberty, its expansion into new territories was entirely justified. Reformers extolled the American mission; along with the values of justice, equality, and righteousness, the American mission echoed themes in the Old Testament. The biblical verse "Zion shall be redeemed with righteousness" (Isaiah 1.27), one Reformer said, clearly referred to America, since only in that land was there a hope for righteousness. Kaufmann Kohler, the leading theologian of American Reform at the turn of the century, was moved to write:

> We perceive in the jubilant tocsin peals of American liberty the mighty resonance of Sinai's thunder. We recognize in the Fourth of July the offspring of the Sixth of Sivan [the traditional date marking God's grant of the Torah to Israel]. We behold in the glorious sway of man's sovereignty throughout this blessed land the foundation stone for the splendid temple of humanity we hope and pray for.[19]

Like the statement of Rabbi Freehof quoted above, Kohler's message underscored the American content that permeated the Reform faith. A loyal Reform Jew was thereby a loyal American and one whose feelings for America evoked a religious-like passion that transcended mere patriotism. Untroubled by the seeming contradiction between intense nationalism and their universalist message, classical Reformers believed that Reform could soonest come to full bloom in the United States.

During the formative years of American Zionism (1897–1917) Reform rabbis and lay leaders preached incessantly on America as the religiously sanctioned promised land. The Union of American Hebrew Congregations (UAHC), the lay organization of Reform congregations, resolved in 1898 that "America is our Zion. Here, in the home of religious liberty, we have aided in founding this new Zion, the fruition of the beginning laid in the old."[20] Used principally against Zionism, the theme well fit the upsurge of hypernationalism in the United States during the same twenty years. With arguments acceptable to both non-Jews and Jews, Reform's anti-Zionism was far more than a Jewish in-house squabble. Throughout the first period of American Zionism, Reform served as the most articulate and best-known critic of the Jewish nationalist movement.

With the average Reform layman in mind, we may assume that the American element of the Reform creed was of greater pragmatic value to the anti-Zionists than the theological. Members of a Reform temple were usually those who enjoyed or aspired to social status within the community and whose religious needs were filled by truncated prayers in English conducted by Americanized rabbis in a Protestant-like setting. Since full acceptance as Americans by the larger society was their aim, they could well relate to Reform's charges against the un-Americanism of Zionism even if they didn't understand Reform's theology.

According to Reform leaders, Zionism contradicted Americanism in extra-ideological ways as well. To begin with, its origin was foreign—it was brought into the country by recent refugees fleeing eastern European antisemitism—and it stood for Jewish separatism and clannishness. Rabbi Isaac Mayer Wise, the master builder of the American Reform movement, feared what he called the "Russification" of the American Jew. As pernicious as hyphenated nationalism and the retention of Yiddish and other abominable ghetto habits, Zionism was a movement alien to the United States and to all Americans. No decent native American Jew countenanced Zionism, Wise's *American Israelite*, the leading Reform periodical, wrote, except for "a very few young visionaries and impractical college professors." The solution, which meant stripping Zionism of its appeal, lay in rapid and total Americanization, or the casting of the immigrant Jews into the mold fixed by the Reformers.[21]

Reform preached the need of assimilation to the masses of eastern European immigrants who were then seeking refuge in the United States. Even if Reformers didn't actively encourage the growing sentiment for immigration restriction, they very likely contributed to nativist prejudice against the separatist Jewish arrivals. Positioning themselves as the virtuous champions of Americanization and hence the acceptable Jews, Reformers spoke with the support of American tradition. Hadn't John Quincy Adams demanded of immigrants as early as 1819: "They must cast off the[ir] European skin, never to resume it. They must look forward to their posterity rather than backward to their ancestors"? The anti-Zionists found backing in Jewish tradition too, and like the prophet Jeremiah, who counseled the first exiles from Jerusalem to Babylon, they advised the new immigrants to " 'seek the welfare of the city to which I have exiled you and pray to the Lord in its behalf, for in its prosperity you shall prosper' (Jeremiah 29.7)."[22]

Reformers protested repeatedly that American Jews were at home in their new land, that they neither required nor desired any other. Content to identify with the United States, and sharing the same values and interests as other Americans, they rejoiced in the honor and successes of the nation. In light of Jewish loyalty and love of country, it would be "lunacy to ask us to give up our glorious birthright here for a mess of pottage elsewhere." America was *not* exile (with the traditional nuances of suffering), and to suggest as much was "little short of treason."[23]

Thus disposing of the Zionists' political dream for American Jews, Reformers also trained their arguments on cultural Zionism, or the concept that Jews worldwide needed a spiritual center for the salvation of Judaism itself. Reform, however, countered that assimilation, a characteristic of the modern age, did not presage the extinction of Judaism. Weren't the greatest Jewish cultural achievements products of lands outside Palestine where Jews enjoyed the environment of their neighbors? Only cross-fertilization with elements of foreign civilizations enriched Jewish culture and ensured the vibrancy of the Jewish faith. Conversely, in a land of their own, which would amount to a new ghetto, culture and religion were bound to stagnate. Implied was the assurance that Judaism and Jewish culture could live and thrive in the United States. Indeed, if, as Reform posited, America was the one true homeland of American Jews, the culture created in a Jewish state would not be their culture.[24]

Reformers found answers to Herzl's emphasis on the threat of antisemitism to a viable Jewish existence outside their own homeland. Not only did they minimize European antisemitism—and this at a time when pogroms raged in czarist Russia—but they also claimed that the constant noise about the wrongs suffered by Jews abroad had become wearisome to American non-Jews. After all, the popular wave of antisemitism in Paris in response to the Dreyfus affair was merely a minor outburst by juveniles and loafers! "If antisemitism sets the brain of Dr. Herzl on fire," Rabbi Kohler fumed, "must we act as madmen, too?" As for the charge of American antisemitism, that was only "reckless exaggeration" on the part of the Zionists. In truth, there was no "Jewish Question" in the United States. The significant rise in social discrimination in the last quarter of the century was similarly dismissed. Any anti-Jewish feeling that did exist, like exclusion of Jews from some hotels and clubs, was too insignificant to warrant protest.[25]

Far worse according to Reformers was the fact that Zionist ideology promoted antisemitism. By postulating that Jews were homeless and that they constituted a separate alien national group within the larger society, Zionism fed the streams of bigotry and fanaticism. Rabbi Joseph Stolz put it this way in his presidential address to the CCAR in 1906:

> Should we make anything else than our religion the line of cleavage from our non-Jewish fellow-citizens, we would be putting into the mouths of others an excuse for Antisemitism and would be giving our enemies an opportunity to charge us with an unwillingness to assimilate and to impute unto us the desire of creating a state within a state.

Zionism thereby was tantamount to treason against the Jews. Moreover, should Zionists ever achieve a separate Jewish homeland, the United States and all Western countries would close their doors to Jewish immigrants.[26]

The accusations heaped by Reform on the un-American character of Zionism—its foreign origins, its secular nationalist character, its threat to Jewish "at-homeness" in America, its promotion of antisemitism—added up to the ugly charge of dual allegiance. Years before the rise of political Zionism, Reformers had sworn their primary allegiance to the United States: "First Americans and then Jews," Rabbi Max Lilienthal had said in 1870. But then along came Zionism and threatened to undo all that had been achieved to convince Americans of unalloyed Jewish patriotism.[27] Arguing that Zionism and its emphasis on loyalty to Jewish nationalism compromised the single, total, and unqualifed allegiance demanded of its citizens by the United States, Reformers sounded the alarm of "dual allegiance."

The very phrase "dual allegiance" had a strong impact on both Jews and non-Jews. It troubled most Jews; in an environment where Americanism was a monolith and acceptance of pluralism had not yet taken root, the fear of "what will the Gentiles say" was still widespread. Zionists worried too about arousing popular disapproval, and that fed a determination to express their interests in terms of American tastes and standards. As for non-Jews, the charge of dual allegiance was one that even those who were otherwise ignorant of Zionism could well understand. Doubtless many felt that it was hard enough to tolerate the Jews in general let alone those whose loyalty was suspect.

By the end of the First World War, the word *Zionist*, with connotations of disloyalty and incompatibility with Americanism, had entered the vocabulary of American antisemites. The phrase "dual allegiance" was still in use after the state of Israel was established. David Ben-Gurion, Israel's first prime minister, tried to reassure a prominent American Jew, Jacob Blaustein: "Dear Yaacov," he wrote, "don't be afraid of dual loyalty. Every human being must have many loyalties."[28]

Despite the abuse and ridicule they suffered at the hands of Reform rabbis and the Reform press, Zionists slowly built up their strength. In the clash of ideologies average Zionists did not dispute the theological principles of Reform theology, but they refused to accept the underlying premise that Jews constituted no more than a religious group. The eastern Europeans, whether believers or nonbelievers, knew that Jewish tradition and history proved the inseparability of faith from peoplehood. Moreover, most had came from the empires of Russia and Austria-Hungary, where people were commonly divided into national groups. Like the Reformers who had rejected restoration even before the Zionist movement began, many eastern Europeans, who had been acquainted in Europe with the antecedents of Herzl, actively or passively supported the nascent Zionist movement before the first congress at Basel. Building on that rapidly expanding base, Zionists in the United States established four organizations before the war, the English speaking Federation of American Zionists (FAZ) and Hadassah, as well as two groups of European origin, one founded by labor (Poale Zion) and the other by the Orthodox (Mizrachi). Those groups boasted their own journals, and full coverage of Zionist affairs, if not endorsement, also came from the influential Yiddish press. More and more, knowledge of the Zionist movement permeated the Jewish community.

Challenges to Reform

Zionism stood to gain when forces both internal and external attacked or weakened Reform. Such was the case during the formative years of American

Zionism, when serious social and intellectual influences compelled classical Reform to review and perhaps amend its cardinal antinationalist beliefs.

Despite its numbers and material assets as attested to by the census of 1890, Reform was showing signs of slippage.[29] Challenges to its resources and hegemony coalesced in the last two decades of the nineteenth century and intensified before the First World War. In that era of heightened nationalism, American Jews, including Reformers, were called upon to press for the amelioration of the Jewish plight in eastern Europe and to raise massive sums for the relief of the hordes who sought refuge on American shores. (Unlikely candidates for affiliation with Reform, the new immigrants were not warmly welcomed, but despite Reform's crusade against Jewish ethnicity, a sense of responsibility for fellow Jews remained.) Simultaneously, discrimination against Jews in the United States, now bolstered by racism, was also on the rise. All those issues not only taxed Reform's institutions, but, more important for our purposes, they made a shambles of Reform's optimistic beliefs in the decline of antisemitism and the inevitability of universal progress.

Meanwhile, Reform's internal problems were gnawing away at its very essence.[30] As a result of the forces of industrialization and secularization, defections from the synagogue, particularly among the youth, multiplied. Many married non-Jews; some were attracted to the Ethical Culture and Christian Science movements; others followed the "great infidel," Robert Ingersoll; some, out of sheer ignorance, advised a merger of Reform with liberal Christianity. Those who retained synagogue affiliation were largely apathetic. Little wonder that sermons on the need to "rekindle" the spark of religious faith became more popular.

At the same time, the older generation of Reform rabbis had largely died out, and their successors lacked the zeal of the earlier pioneers. Faced with the inroads of materialism and secularism, which increasingly characterized American society, they were ill-suited to shore up Reform's beliefs or to revive the spirituality of their congregants. The average Reform layman had little interest in Reform's concepts of mission, Jewish exile, and universalism. When Jews, like other middle-class Americans, were won over to the popular faith in science and scientific research—including the currents of Darwinism and biblical criticism—Reform Judaism was badly hit. Why bother with religious teachings of any sort, many wondered, if science advanced contradictory answers? If, as Reform said, the national element in Judaism was irrelevant, and if, as the biblical critics said, the religious corpus of Judaism was anachronistic or downright false, was there any meaning left in Judaism for the modern Jew? (One possible answer, the synagogue's involvement in the movement for social justice, the Jewish equivalent of the Christian social gospel movement, compensated to some degree for Reform's spiritual inadequacies.)

Reformers accepted the new currents of thought like evolution and biblical criticism, but most rabbis who ministered to congregations lacked both the knowledge and the ability to engage in critical scholarship or theological creativity. There were, however, two notable exceptions, Kaufmann Kohler and Emil G. Hirsch. Those two prominent men (each a son-in-law of Reform pioneer David Einhorn) probed deeply into the shortcomings of Reform in the new intellectual climate. In effect, they admitted that the ideas of the Enlightenment were at odds with the temper of the times. Looking back at the philosophical roots of their own movement, they now criticized total acceptance of the Enlightenment's belief in rationalism. Hirsch maintained that the "old liberalism" of the Age of Reason had outlived its purposes. It had spawned "shallow" or "insipid" liberalism as well as materialism and even nihilism. Early Reformers had needed rationalism to free Judaism from fossilization and to gain toleration from Christians, but the task of their successors was to teach a vibrant human religion. Kohler similarly indicted rationalism for having impaired Jewish reverence, and he too saw the need to fire and sustain Jewish idealism: "Reform theology, when based on sole reason as fundamental principle, is, or was, built on sand and quagmire. Reason, which often ends in doubt and anarchy, is a *corrective*, not a *constructive* force of humanity." According to Kohler, spirituality did not exclude reason, but only a balance between intellect and spirit—and here he also stressed the importance of Jewish rituals—would allow Reform to propagate its mission with renewed vigor. Their criticisms of reason and "old liberalism" notwithstanding, neither man dared to attack the Enlightenment foundations of the American creed.

Despite their critique of the early Reformers, neither Hirsch nor Kohler relinquished the concept of mission. Influenced by the work of Moritz Lazarus on the psychology of nations, they now grounded the Jewish mission in the concept of "national consciousness." The Enlightenment's dream of a single humanity was illusory; nationalism was the reality. Positing that Jews, like other peoples, had a distinct "soul" (*Volkseele*), that it was not merely a religion like all others, the two rabbis now freely used terms like "Jewish race" and "national genius." The mission to teach the true monotheism remained, but only a Jewish *collectivity*—a people, or nation, or race—committed to the observance of Jewish rituals and ceremonials could effectively carry out that mission. By emphasizing the legitimacy of Jewish group survival, Hirsch and Kohler adjusted Reform theology to fit the nationalist spirit of the age. That might have been the cue for Zionism to push its answers to the meaning of Judaism, but the young movement lacked the knowledge and ability to missionize among the disaffected Reformers.

In the end, both Hirsch and Kohler, whose theories of ethnic psychology antedated the appearance of Herzl's *Der Judenstaat,* had little success in converting their followers to their way of thinking. Although a few rabbis wrestled with the need to defend their faith against further onslaughts and to restore the attractiveness of their beliefs, Reform's institutions, the CCAR and UAHC, before the 1920s were content with both classical Reform and anti-Zionism. Hirsch and Kohler themselves remained ardent anti-Zionists.

The fact that Zionism had defenders *within* the Reform camp was of greater aid to the nationalist cause. Indeed, some leading Reformers identified with Zionism from the very beginnings of the movement. One active Zionist was the venerable Bernhard Felsenthal, a pioneer Reform rabbi in Chicago. A believer in Jewish "racial" unity—a word used interchangeably at that time with "ethnic" or "national"—he supported Jewish colonization in Palestine before Herzl and the Basel program. His enthusiasm for the Zionist cause increased during the last years of his life; he participated in local Zionist meetings, and he served on the *Actions Comité* of the World Zionist Organization and as a vice-president of the FAZ. During that period he argued against the mission concept of classical Reform. As he saw it, the Jewish mission was simply "to work as one nation among many to further the ends of humanity." He wrote repeatedly that "from Palestine, from a Jewish *Mutterstaat*, our so-called 'mission' can best be fulfilled." The Reform creed, on the other hand, would result in the absorption "of Israel by other nations and gradual dying of Judaism." Too old to attend the Second Zionist Congress in 1898, he sent a warm message to the delegates via Richard Gottheil: "Extend my greetings to them, and tell them that on the shore of distant Lake Michigan there is an old man who longs for the blessed fulfillment of their hopes."[31]

Among Felsenthal's younger colleagues the most prominent of the Reform Zionists were Max Heller, Stephen Wise, and the Gottheils (Rabbi Gustav of New York's prestigious Temple Emanu-El and his son, Professor Richard). Only a small minority, they nevertheless made their voices heard to the Jewish and non-Jewish public through the FAZ, at sessions of the CCAR, and through the pulpit and the press. In a statement printed by the *New York Times,* Gustav Gottheil dismissed the very possibility of anti-Zionist Jews: "There is no such thing as an anti-Zionist. . . . [H]ow can anyone in whose veins flows Jewish blood oppose the movement?"[32] Never did he or his colleagues contemplate a rupture with Reform, nor did they differ from other Reformers on issues like Americanization.

Aiming to prove the compatibility of Reform with Zionism, the Reform Zionists worked on the premise that Zionism was the most effective instrument for preventing the extinction of the Jews and Judaism. They defined the Jews as more than a religious group; Jewish history, they said, testified to the everlasting link between Jewish religion and Jewish nationality. Since Reform substituted universalism for Jewish nationalism, they claimed that it had more in common with Unitarianism and Christian theism than with Judaism. More important to the Reform Zionists, however, were the fallacies they found surrounding the mission concept. They didn't renounce the mission idea, but they took exception to the conditions outlined by Reform for its fulfillment, particularly the need of a dispersed Jewry. Some men argued that a Jewish national homeland would actually facilitate the propagation of the mission.

The one who most cogently criticized Reform's anti-Zionist ideology was Richard Gottheil, professor of Semitic languages at Columbia University and president of the FAZ from 1898 to 1904. Before the war Gottheil wrote a pamphlet for the FAZ called *The Aims of Zionism*, a comprehensive survey of Zionism for the *Jewish Encyclopedia*, and the first full-length history in English of the movement.[33] His writings discussed the problems facing the modern Jew in the aftermath of Emancipation: the breakdown of Jewish unity, the loss of a common language and customs, and, as a result, the "deadening of Jewish consciousness." At the same time and despite the rosy optimism of the Reformers, the "ravages" of antisemitism and social discrimination compounded those problems. The best solution, he wrote, lay in the establishment of a Jewish center in Palestine, one that would infuse Diaspora Jewry with moral and religious strength and thereby keep them loyal to the faith.

Gottheil focused special attention on Reform's concept of mission. He could not deny the noble objective of the mission, but he charged that the Reformers had ignored a vital prerequisite. National unity came first, and despite the "doctrinal sublimity" assigned by Reform to dispersion, unity was essential in order to guard against the extinction of the Jews in emancipated nations: "The first mission of a people is to live its life as a member of the great family of nations the world over; and in so far as it lives that life worthily and contributes to the moral uplifting of society, it is fulfilling its first and primary mission." Only then could it turn to its "higher" mission. Furthermore, Reformers had failed to stir modern Jews to engage in mission activity, and to think otherwise was merely self-deceptive. "Are the pitiful denizens of our eastern ghettos preaching actively a gospel in the world? Or are the well-fed dwellers in our golden western ghettos more actively engaged in this messianic propaganda?" While defending a Jewish center in Palestine, Gottheil attempted to reconcile Reform to the nationalist idea. He maintained that Reform too would benefit, because the center in Palestine would provide a stimulus for spreading the mission: "The closer Jews are kept within the fold, the greater their interest in Jewish life and Jewish thought, the more propagators there will be for that mission."

Gottheil's analysis gave short shrift to Reform's argument of dual allegiance. A country could demand services of its citizens, but—and here he was the pluralist—it could not require any group to give up "its historic associations [or] its connection with other[s] of the same race or of the same religion living elsewhere." Didn't other non-Jewish ethnic groups in Europe and the United States retain bonds with the countries of their birth at the same time that they were loyal to their adopted lands? Emancipation had left Western Jews with a certain "nervousness," he explained, which was played out in "an exaggerated nationalist ardor for the country of their adoption." Zionism, on the other hand, instilled the Jews with confidence. Gottheil also affirmed that American Zionism neither demanded nor expected an existential commitment from its followers that they give up on America and move to Palestine. We are not asking you to go, he said; "we are striving for a Jewish home and a safe political condition for those Jews who have no such home, and a Jewish environment for those who feel that they need such."

Gottheil weighed the principles of classical Reform on the Zionist scale and found them wanting. Although his writings were addressed to all Western Jews, *The Aims of Zionism* had particular relevance for Americans. As historian Arthur Hertzberg has pointed out, in that first pamphlet published by the FAZ (1899), Gottheil confronted the major problems that acculturated American Jews had with Zionism. Not only did he exempt them from *aliyah,* but he recognized the fears attending the subject of dual loyalties and reassured them with a reminder about the ethnic ties of the Germans and the Irish in America to their homelands. Implicit in his discussion was the suggestion that the country itself was less extreme about rapid Americanization and assimilation than the Jewish anti-Zionists. We also know that Gottheil, who corresponded with Herzl on American affairs, cautioned the European Zionist leaders, as yet unfamiliar with the American scene, against injecting the subject of Jewish nationalism into American politics.[34] He could thereby show his fellow American Jews that Zionism in no way compromised the demands on their civic behavior. In time Gottheil's views on ethnic separatism and the caveat against political action became outdated. Americans grew more resentful of "hyphenates," and Zionists in time did turn to political action. But at the turn of the century his opinions served to familiarize world Zionist leaders with the special concerns of American Jews and to assure the Americans that those concerns were addressed in Zionist policymaking. By seeking to adjust the nationalist movement to the tastes of American Jews, Gottheil contributed to the Americanization of Zionism.

The prominent Reform Zionists were of important propaganda value. Their main contribution was to teach the meaning of Zionism to the English-speaking public and thereby counter the influence of the anti-Zionists. By virtue of their position in the Jewish "aristocracy," they made Zionism less foreign and more respectable to the Jewish upper class, the new immigrants, and the non-Jews. Furthermore, the fact that these Americanized Jews met the newer arrivals under a Zionist banner helped to bridge the chasm that separated the established German Jews from the "lowly" eastern Europeans. In practical terms the first Reform Zionists, like Felsenthal and the Gottheils, were too few in number to undo the edge that Reform enjoyed over the nationalists; of the same socioeconomic class as the leading Reformers, they had too little in common with most Zionists and would-be Zionists. But the sentiments of that socially secure and Americanized minority were of great psychological value to the average Zionist. If men like the Gottheils were unafraid to support Zionism publicly, then the same applied to the immigrants. In the case of two young charismatic rabbis in New York, Stephen Wise and Judah Magnes, involvement in Zionist affairs brought them closer to the newcomers from eastern Europe. (Wise later wrote that the Zionist movement changed his opinions of the eastern Europeans; at the Second Zionist Congress of 1898 he met Jews who "were not victims, nor refugees, nor beggars, but educated men, dreaming, planning, toiling for their people.")[35] Understandably, the new immigrants responded with pride and admiration.

At times Reformers exacted a price of the Zionists within their ranks. Not unlike the subjects of the Protestant heresy trials that swept churches and seminaries at the end of the nineteenth century, some were tested and found guilty of flouting the principles of their creed. Reform Zionists, who by definition strayed from accepted Reform theology, became the Jewish heretics. One well-known episode involved Stephen Wise, an applicant for the position at Temple Emanu-El in 1905. Negotiations broke down, however, on Wise's condition of a "free," unmuzzled pulpit. Louis Marshall of the temple's board informed him in no uncertain terms that the pulpit was subject to the board's control and that certain matters, like Zionism, could not be discussed in sermons. Wise defended the concept of a free pulpit, an issue admittedly broader than Zionism, but doubtless the board found his nationalist sympathies as distasteful as his involvement in politics. Whatever the importance of Zionism in their calculations, the trustees proceeded to reject Wise's candidacy.[36]

Less than two years later, Zionists were angered by the resignations of three of their supporters from the faculty of Hebrew Union College (HUC).[37] It seemed clear to them that Professors Henry Malter, Max Margolis, and Max Schloessinger were victimized by the president of HUC, Kaufmann Kohler, the anti-Zionist Torquemada. Not only was their academic freedom curtailed, but as the Zionists told it, Kohler persecuted them precisely because of their Zionism.[38] Some Zionists expected a formal response from the FAZ; we know, Judah Magnes wrote to Harry Friedenwald, president of that organization, that "these men are after all giving up their positions because of Zionism."

HUC had been committed to an anti-Zionist stand ever since the First Zionist Congress. Isaac Mayer Wise, the first president of the college, affirmed in 1897: "We want teachers of Judaism. Judaism, we say, and not nationalism, Judaism and not Zionism, Judaism and not Messiahism of any kind; that eternal Judaism which is not tied down to a certain piece of land . . . or to . . . peculiar laws and institutions." Wise himself bent the law at least on one occasion; he permitted a known Zionist, Caspar Levias, to remain on the faculty. When Kohler succeeded to the presidency in 1903, he told the Board of Governors that he wished to make the school completely American and thereby prove the Americanism of his fellow Jews. The Judaism he advocated "stands for American thought and American spirit, and not for Zionistic neo-Hebraism or the language of the Jewish ghetto." The laymen who ran the college may not have understood the fine points of theology, but it sufficed for them to believe that Zionism was un-American. Between 1903 and 1905 two Zionist instructors (including Levias) were forced to resign.

HUC drew its anti-Zionist lines tighter in the 1907 case of the three professors. Malter, a stauch nationalist, had written five articles for the *Hebrew Union College Journal* before 1907 in which he criticized Reform's theology and advocated a revival of the Jewish national idea. But the sixth article, in which he was to give his solution to the Jewish question, was refused publication. Schloessinger, a Zionist since his student days in Germany, also published an article attempting to refute the claim that Reform theology was incompatible with Zionism. Margolis had at first been an anti-Zionist, but by 1907 was an active worker for the cause. Discounting Malter, who explained his resignation on the grounds of salary and tenure—although those problems might have stemmed as well from his Zionist sympathies—we are left with the more complicated stories of Schloessinger and Margolis.

An examination of relevant documents pertaining to the case discloses that reasons other than Zionism were doubtless involved. The strained personal relations between Kohler and each of the men were significant, and so were the charges and countercharges of *lehrfreiheit* and insubordination. The board also figured in the chain of events; a resolution adopted two weeks before the resignations that vigorously reaffirmed the college's anti-Zionist stand fueled the controversy further. Understandably, a crucial issue was whether a theological institution could tolerate "heretical" opinions. From other sources we learn that Kohler, at exactly the same time, was impressed by a scandal in Berlin surrounding the forced resignation of a Zionist rabbi who had held the post of preacher and teacher. Aware therefore of how the pernicious teachings of Zionism could split a community, Kohler was not likely to be moved by accounts of the professors' martyrdom.

Early in 1907 Schloessinger requested Kohler's permission to attend a Zionist banquet in New York. Kohler refused, but the professor took his leave nonetheless. On his return the president pressed charges of insubordination. Schloessinger answered that Kohler would have permitted the leave for any other but Zionist purposes, and that the president was denying him the freedom of personal opinion that was guaranteed by faculty regulations. The matter was brought before the board, and Schloessinger's resignation, which followed shortly thereafter, was accepted unanimously.

Within the walls of the college, the Margolis case commanded most attention. The incident immediately preceding his resignation concerned a Zionist sermon that he had delivered in the chapel of the school. A public scene ensued, and Kohler went away enraged. He met with the professor and, according to Margolis, said that "the College was not an academic institution where mooted questions might be freely discussed and the students trained to think for themselves and arrive at their own conclusions." Referring to Margolis's controversial articles that had appeared in the Jewish press, he declared that "had I informed him of the nature of my sermon, he would not have allowed me to preach it." "Dr. Kohler further stated," Margolis added, "that as a Zionist I could not be entrusted with the teaching of Biblical Exegesis at the College."

In his own defense the professor claimed that two years before the sermon Kohler had assured him that his theological opinions could be freely expressed. Moreover, faculty regulations provided specifically for academic freedom; an instructor could not be criticized before students, nor could his personal opinions be questioned as long as those that conflicted with the purpose of the school were not introduced into the classroom. On all those grounds Kohler was the transgressor. Margolis added that he had never discussed Zionism in class—a statement that was corroborated by the students before the board—and that Kohler, who had used the pulpit for his own partisan views, denied his *lehrfreiheit* only because of Zionism.

Margolis submitted a letter of resignation to the board, but in light of its consistent anti-Zionist policy, there was virtually no chance that the board would decide against Kohler. The latter, however, wrote formal statements in answer to the professor. He charged Margolis with misrepresentation of facts and distortion of his, Kohler's, words. Furthermore, Margolis approached the Bible with "a preconceived partisan opinion detrimental to the principles of American Reform Judaism, inducing him . . . to falsify facts and willfully misrepresent the position of Reform theology." Never at any time in the college's history was complete *lehrfreiheit* guaranteed, and Margolis was disseminating ideas "subversive" of Reform principles in his teachings and articles. While narrowing the definition of academic freedom to fit the needs of a theological college, Kohler also intimated that Margolis's actions reflected the professor's personal animus against the president, an animus that bred disrespect and disloyalty. He asked the board, however, to disregard his personal differences with Margolis and discuss the professor's resignation solely on the grounds of his opposition to Reform. Despite counterefforts on the part of students and some alumni to prevent positive action by the board, Margolis's resignation, like that of Schloessinger, was finally accepted in May.

The episode of the three resignations damaged Reform's public image. To the Jewish public the issue appeared to be one of academic freedom and blatant discrimination against Zionism. Kohler himself contributed to that interpretation. In statements to the Jewish press he argued that a seminary could not tolerate unrestricted academic freedom. He insisted that since the aim of the college was to inculcate the specific religious views of Reform, it was necessary to prevent a Zionist professor "from twisting and distorting the grand universal teachings of the prophets and sages of Israel or of the Pentateuch with the view of turning them into crude and nationalistic utterances." Kohler, however, could not maintain total unity within the college; two members of the board voted not to accept Margolis's resignation, two rabbinical students resigned, and the alumni divided. Besides the turmoil within HUC surrounding the resignations, the episode may have encouraged another rift between Zionists and Reformers, when but a few months later Jacob Schiff opened a public debate with Solomon Schechter, the president of the Jewish Theological Seminary (Conservative), on the dangers of Zionism.[39]

While Reformers licked their wounds and called Zionism a power for evil, Zionists gleefully pounced on the opportunity to criticize their opponents. The *Maccabaean*, the journal of the FAZ, talked of unethical behavior and persecution by HUC and warned that Kohler might, among other things, withhold the rabbinical degree from Zionist-inclined students. Linking the president's behavior to its long indictment of Reform generally, the Zionist journal happily announced that Reform had been exposed and had destroyed itself.[40]

Solomon Schechter and Louis Brandeis

American Reformers were dealt a major blow when Solomon Schechter joined the FAZ in 1905. Schechter was then president of the Jewish Theological Seminary (JTS), the Conservative rabbinical school and competitor of Reform's Hebrew Union College. He preached the Conservative message of traditionalism adapted for modernity, an ideology that had its greatest appeal in America to the rapidly acculturating eastern Europeans and their children. From its faint beginnings in the nineteenth century, the movement stood squarely behind a restoration to Palestine. Some of its early leaders opposed a Jewish state, but all supported the upbuilding of Palestine.[41] It was Schechter, however, who made Zionism an integral component of Conservative Judaism and Conservative Jewry an integral component of the American Zionist movement.

Schechter championed Zionism[42] partly out of a bitter opposition to Reform theology. In his anti-Reform brief, which began even before he left England for the United States, he consistently fought Reform's divorce of a Jewish national consciousness from Jewish religion. That consciousness, he maintained, had kept Jews and Judaism alive through the centuries, and therefore "the rebirth of Israel's national consciousness, and the revival of Israel's religion . . . are inseparable." Sniping time and again at Reform's catch phrases, such as "prophetic Judaism," "universalism," and "progress," he disputed the concept of a religious mission separate from nationhood. He claimed that such antinationalist ideas approximated theological antisemitism, and he warned that Judaism stripped of its national features would lead inevitably to tragic results—i.e., the very extinction of the Jewish faith and the drift of Jews to Christianity. Zionism, on the other hand, was the bulwark against Reform's destructive tendencies.

A religious and cultural Zionist, Schechter believed in a Jewish center in Palestine whose influence would radiate throughout the Diaspora, a center that would generate a vibrant Jewish religion and culture for Jews worldwide. A center in Palestine did not preclude Jewish centers elsewhere—and he accepted the ongoing existence of multiple centers—but Diaspora Judaism would depend upon the Palestinian center for a meaningful existence. Although he rejected Herzl's premise that Jews as Jews had no future in the Diaspora, the Conservative leader, unlike Reformers, never considered Jewish dispersion providential or *galut* less than a tragedy. More concerned about the exile of the "Jewish soul" than the exile of Jews, he maintained that the Jewish soul required a center in Palestine for its sustenance. Until the soul was redeemed, any talk of a Jewish mission was premature and meaningless. Only then, just as a Jewish Palestine had given birth to the Bible, might Jews resume their mission for the benefit of humanity: "Israel will be the chosen instrument of God for [a] new . . . mission; but . . . Israel must first effect its own redemption and live again its own life, and be Israel again." Schechter's views added significantly to the Americanization of Zionism. Speaking primarily as a religious Jew who criticized the secular cast of Zionism—on those grounds he opposed an American Jewish Congress under Zionist sponsorship—he conformed to the American preference for religion over secularism. Even the importance of a Jewish national consciousness was predicated on the needs of the Jewish religion. Nor did he agree that his interpretation of Zionism, any more than the traditional belief in a Jewish restoration to Palestine at the end of the days, conjured up any hint of dual loyalty. Most important, Schechter's Zionism freed the American Jew from any personal sacrifices like *aliyah*. Palestine as the Jewish religious center never questioned the legitimacy of Jewish survival in America, nor did it deny the right of Jews to share in the American dream. It was a comfortable Zionism that Schechter bequeathed to the students at the JTS, and they in turn to their congregations. The typical Conservative parishioner welcomed the way that he, a loyal American, could satisfy his ethnic urges as a Jew at a cost no greater than that of any other philanthropy. Doubtless for many, Zionism under the rubric of the synagogue became a surrogate for the religion of the synagogue.

Louis D. Brandeis's affiliation with the Zionist movement compounded the challenges to Reform. Raised in a liberal agnostic home in Kentucky, Brandeis was a star pupil at Harvard Law School and went on to establish a successful and profitable law practice in Boston. His Jewish consciousness, which he interpreted as a belief in the morality of Judaism and its mission of morality, had been awakened by members of his family, but in no way observant, he was connected only peripherally with the American Jewish world. Not until he turned fifty did he acknowledge his Jewishness publicly. Meanwhile, he found ways to express his liberal political principles through his legal cases and his meetings with social reformers in industry, labor, politics, and social work. The Jews among those reformers contributed in turn to the development of his Jewish consciousness. The oft-cited example in that connection concerned the 1910 strike by the garment workers (largely Jewish) in New York, which Brandeis mediated. He was impressed, he recalled, by the idealism of Jewish labor; their commitment to democracy and social justice made for exemplary American citizenship and proved to him that the ideals of America "had been the age-old ideals of the Jews." By preserving and disseminating those ideals, which constituted the Jewish mission, Jews could best contribute to the welfare of the country. Indeed, that mission would come to fruition in the United States.

A few years after he articulated his interpretation of the American-centered Jewish mission, Brandeis added to it the elements of a Jewish nationality and a Jewish state. In 1910 he announced his sympathy and respect for the Zionist movement, but he saw a Jewish state as ancillary to the Jewish moral mission, whose principal focus would remain in America. Essentially, a Jewish Palestine of courageous and idealistic settlers, living according to time-honored Jewish values, would serve as a laboratory for testing new principles of economic and social organization that could be applied equally in Palestine and the United States. For those like Brandeis, Jonathan Sarna explained, "Zion became . . . a utopian extension of the American dream, a Jewish refuge where freedom, liberty, and social justice would reign supreme."[43]

On a path by which he constructed a nexus between Americanism and Zionism, Brandeis gained fame as a spokesman for political democracy and a champion of socioeconomic reform. Leaving his practice to fight social issues through litigation, the "people's attorney" became an architect of sociological jurisprudence. In 1910 he joined the Progressives, who sought to destroy the power of the conservative Republicans, and in 1912 he served as adviser to the Democratic contender for the presidency, Woodrow Wilson. That same year he met Aaron Aaronsohn, a Palestinian agronomist known for his experiments with wild wheat. According to one biographer, Brandeis was won over by Aaronsohn's descriptions of Jewish Palestine, which appeared to embody the attributes he so admired—democracy, morality, experimentation, industry, and smallness. The *yishuv* appeared to replicate his beloved New England, and the Zionist pioneers were the new Puritans: "Zionism is the Pilgrim inspiration and impulse over again; the descendants of the Pilgrim Fathers should not find it hard to understand and sympathize with it.

Although *aliyah* was unnecessary, American Jews had a duty to support the creation of a Jewish nation to further the development of the Jewish mission: "Every American Jew who aids in advancing the Jewish settlement in Palestine, though he feels that neither he nor his descendants will ever live there, will . . . be a better man and a better American for doing so." Since Americanism and Jewish national creativity were one and the same, the issue of dual allegiance was totally irrelevant. As Brandeis explained:

There is no inconsistency between loyalty to America and loyalty to Jewry. The Jewish spirit, the product of our religion and experiences, is essentially modern and essentially American. Not since the destruction of the Temple have the Jews in spirit and in ideals been so fully in harmony with the noblest aspirations of the country in which they lived.[45]

The "Brandeisian synthesis" the term used by Melvin Urofsky, welded American Progressive ideals to those of Zionism. Brandeis may not have understood the emotional and religious baggage that underlay the movement, but he fired American Zionism with renewed idealism. By making Zionism a tool for constructing a better America, and by adding to the comfortable Zionism of Schechter and the cultural Zionists, he brought the Americanization of Zionism to a dramatic high. Many Jews were impressed by his idealistic and well-circulated pronouncements and, above all, by his political prominence. The first Jew to be appointed to the Supreme Court (1916), his appeal was magnified, and after he assumed leadership of the American movement in 1914, the number of affiliated Zionists rose rapidly.[46]

Opposition Is Moderated

Despite the gains that accrued to Zionism before the war, a majority of Reform leaders continued to denounce the aims for a Jewish state. On the appearance of the Balfour Declaration in 1917, Reform institutions dredged up the arguments used over twenty years to express their opposition. The CCAR passed a resolution that said in part:

> We are opposed to the idea that Palestine should be considered the home-land of the Jews. . . . The ideal of the Jew is not the establishment of a Jewish state—not the reassertion of Jewish nationality which has long been outgrown. We believe that our survival as a people is dependent upon the assertion and the maintenance of our historic religious role. . . . The mission of the Jew is to witness to God all over the world.

Equal rights for Jews all over the world and not a Jewish homeland was the solution to anti-Jewish sentiments.[47] Reform laymen in the UAHC concurred. Repeating its anti-Zionist resolution of 1898, the union added that Jews must, for their own welfare, heed their religious mission and that Israel must spurn "any aspiration for the revival of a Jewish nationality or the foundation of a Jewish state."[48]

Responding to what they saw as the danger in the Balfour Declaration, some Reform Jews attempted more extreme ways of distancing Reform from Zionism. One layman, Isaac W. Bernheim of Louisville, Kentucky, called for the formation of a "Reform Church of American Israelites" made up of "100 percent Americans." His object was to sharpen the differences between Zionists with their divided loyalties and Reform Jews who believed that "here is our Palestine, and we know no other." Since Zionists used the word "Jewry" to signify a separate national group, Bernheim suggested substituting the name "Israel" for "Jews" and the word "church" for "synagogue" or "temple." Neither his project nor one by Rabbi David Philipson at the end of the war, to convene a conference for the sole purpose of combating Zionism, made any serious headway. Both plans showed, however, how deeply rooted Reform's prewar anti-Zionism was.[49]

Nevertheless, American Reform was inching its way to a new position on Zionism. Its very tone had changed; the vitriol and ridicule that characterized its early denunciations of Herzlian Zionism slowly gave way to more serious and even respectful appraisals. The same CCAR that expressed its opposition to a Jewish homeland in Palestine in answer to the Balfour Declaration also noted the issuance of the declaration "with grateful appreciation." Even the *American Israelite,* long a sharp critic of a Jewish center in Palestine, now printed statements supporting a Jewish Palestine as a safe haven for refugees. Finally, when England received the mandate for Palestine after the war, Reformers joined wholeheartedly in projects for the rehabilitation of the land.[50] Political Zionism, no, but Palestinianism, yes.

A combination of reasons accounted for Reform's gradual change. For one thing, Zionism had grown increasingly respectable during its first twenty years and could no longer be dismissed as a passing and foolhardy fad. Abroad, Theodor Herzl had negotiated with heads of state; in the United States, Reform Zionists and leaders like Solomon Schechter and Louis Brandeis were by no means a deranged extremists but rather men who wielded significant influence within the Jewish and non-Jewish communities. The Balfour Declaration added the final touch. International support of the declaration and mandate at home and abroad, including American public opinion, legitimated Zionism and quieted the fears of many anti-Zionists. Second, American Reform felt less secure in 1917 than it had in 1897. The shortcomings of its theology had been exposed; the Conservative movement under Schechter's leadership was fast becoming a serious competitor; and it is likely that the younger generation of Reform rabbis began to realize the inadequacy of Judaism shorn of its national component. Finally, and at least of equal significance, the nationalist-minded eastern European immigrants were maturing rapidly. The more they acculturated and the higher they rose on the economic ladder the more reluctant they were to heed the strictures of the Reformers about political Zionism. Vastly outnumbering the German Reformers of the Jewish Establishment, they were on the way to assuming the leadership of American Jewry.

Reform's dramatic shift on Zionism came only in the 1930s. Confronted by the worsening condition of the Jews under Nazi rule, Reformers, if for no other reason, looked more favorably on the right of Jews to enter Palestine. In 1935, exactly fifty years after the Pittsburgh platform, the CCAR resolved to leave the acceptance or rejection of Zionism to the determination of the individual rabbis. Two years later, in the famous Columbus platform, the rabbis officially bound the membership of the CCAR to the Zionist cause: "We affirm the obligation of all Jewry to aid in [Palestine's] upbuilding as a Jewish homeland by endeavoring to make it not only a haven of refuge for the oppressed but also a center of Jewish culture and spiritual life." (Because the opposition to Zionism was stronger among Reform laymen, the UAHC lagged behind the rabbis.)[51] A hard core of anti-Zionists, both rabbis and laymen, remained opposed to Jewish nationalism, and from their ranks came the rabidly anti-Zionist American Council for Judaism in 1943. Through that organization the anti-Zionism of classical Reform, albeit significantly reduced, lived on.

CHAPTER 3

Zionism in the Public Square

Until the Balfour Declaration of 1917, Zionism in the United States was for the most part an in-house affair. Zionist ideology divided the Jewish community, but non-Jews did not actively participate in struggles that usually pitted Reform anti-Zionists alongside the steward-led communal agencies like the American Jewish Committee against the Jewish nationalists. Nor did the general press or prominent non-Jews customarily take a stand on the Zionist movement or pass judgment on the contending factions. The Balfour Declaration changed all that. Since the British move legitimated Zionism, raising it in effect to an Allied war aim, the American government and the public became very much involved. And, since the war catapulted the United States to the position of a leading world power, the course of Zionism and especially of American Zionism, from then until the establishment of Israel some thirty years later, was significantly shaped by American opinion.

Like all American Jews, ever sensitive to the attitude of the government and the general public on all sorts of Jewish matters, from Sabbath observance to crime in the ghetto, Zionists could not close their eyes to public opinion. In every major step they took, they factored that element into their equation. They had Americanized Zionism to accommodate the Jews, and after the Balfour Declaration they had to Americanize it further by consciously shaping their goals and demands to accommodate the larger society. In two major public debates on Zionism's compatibility with Americanism, 1917–22 and 1929–30, Zionists were hard-pressed to prove to Jewish and non-Jewish assimilationists and liberals, to religious spokesmen and journalists, how American-like their movement was.[1]

The First Debate

The year 1917 stands out as one in which the course of Jewish history was permanently altered. First, England issued the Balfour Declaration, a statement of policy sanctioned by the other Western powers, that raised Herzlian Zionism out of the realm of fantasy and into the world of *realpolitik*. Secondly, the Bolsheviks in Russia swept into power. Jewish sympathizers had hoped that the Russian Revolution would bring about the long-awaited freedom of more than five million Jews, but it resulted instead in a new kind of tyranny. More immediately, the two events called forth new expressions of anti-Jewish sentiment in the United States and Europe. The Balfour Declaration aroused supporters of disgruntled Arabs, Protestant missionaries, and Jewish assimilationists to mount a campaign with worldwide reverberations against Zionism. Opponents of the new regime in Russia seized upon the participation of Jews in the revolution to accuse them of engineering the Bolshevik takeover. Judeophobes in different parts of the world had no qualms about finding parallels between Zionism and Bolshevism. Their task was facilitated by the spread of the *Protocols of the Elders of Zion* between 1919 and 1922. Elaborating on the conspiracies of the alleged Elders of Zion to attain world dominion, propagators of the *Protocols* cited both Zionism and Bolshevism as proof of the nefarious designs of an international Jewry. From then on, "Zionist" and "Bolshevik" enriched the vocabulary of antisemites. As Zionist or as Bolshevik, or as both at the same time, the Jew was the quintessential menace to Christian civilization.

In the United States not all antisemites were outspokenly anti-Zionist, nor all anti-Zionists antisemites. The two, however, were connected in the first debate. To be sure, neither anti-Zionism nor antisemitism was foreign to the United States, and even before the Balfour Declaration many Jews who criticized Jewish nationalism, like the Reformers, had called it a cause of Jew-hatred.[2] But only with the Balfour Declaration and the postwar mandate did the menace of political Zionism appear more serious. In turn, criticisms by opponents, if not intrinsically antisemitic, played directly into the hands of Jew-baiters.

Americans who spoke out against political Zionism usually made two assumptions about the Balfour Declaration. In the first place, they claimed that the declaration implicated *all* Jews, Zionist and anti-Zionist alike. Although the British statement promised that "nothing shall be done which may prejudice ... the rights and political status enjoyed by Jews in any other country," the taint of Jewish nationalism rubbed off on the entire group. Second, like the political Zionists, anti-Zionists interpreted the declaration to be the license for Jewish statehood and not merely the right to a "homeland." Some critics insisted that they did not oppose colonization in Palestine or the need to make that country a refuge for oppressed Jews. But the distinct possibility of a Jewish state, or at least the expectation that statehood was the next logical goal of organized Zionists, aroused their bitterness.

This reading of the Balfour Declaration may not have led to so vehement an opposition had it not emerged during the war and immediate postwar years. The intense Americanism generated by a "crusade against the Hun," which sparked concentrated drives to Americanize the immigrant and which read hyphenate groups like the German-Americans and Irish-Americans outside the pale of a loyal citizenry, spilled over into the post-Armistice period. The war had been advertised to Americans as the way to make the world safe for democracy, but the shocks of readjusting to a peacetime economy and the collapse of Woodrow Wilson's design for an effective League of Nations raised American antagonism toward the outside world. The unspent hatred of the Germans was channeled into a hatred of the foreigner generally and into an hysterical Red Scare. In the postwar period as during the war itself, loyalty meant Anglo-conformity, a monolithic concept of Americanism that earmarked any display of political or ethnic separatism as an outright danger.

Jewish opponents of Zionism included many liberals—prominent academics, journalists, government officeholders, and Reform spokesmen. Popular essayists Ralph Boas and Gilbert Seldes raised the specter of dual allegiance. They argued the dire consequences of Zionism, which branded American Jews as a hyphenated group. "Certain as the day follows the night," Professor Morris Jastrow similarly wrote, Jews would be considered a foreign group, or temporary sojourners with separate political interests, for whom their enemies would advocate an exodus to Palestine. Rejecting Brandeis's oft-hailed statement that Zionism made for better Americans, Jastrow added: "The State has a right to demand, especially under the modern conception, that all its citizens should be 100 per cent citizens—not 50-50, or even 70-30, but full 100 percent." Therefore, "it was impossible to belong to two countries. . . . 'Allegiance must be perfect—cannot be divided. Either a Palestinian or an American.'" When the *New Republic* of October 5, 1918, supported the idea of a Jewish state on the grounds that Jews could not contribute to mankind generally as long as "they dwell as aliens among more or less friendly peoples," Jastrow blamed the Zionists for inciting the public to put the label of "aliens" on American Jews.[3]

Two men known for their government service added their criticisms. Congressman Julius Kahn of California used words reminiscent of the antisemitic image of the Wandering Jew, the Jew who sojourned in different lands never sinking permanent roots but merely skimming off the benefits of those lands: "One of the great dangers of Zionism is the fact that the non-Jew will begin to look upon the American Jew as having a lurking desire always to return to the so-called Jewish homeland—that the Jew will be accused by the non-Jew of being merely a sojourner in the United States, using the benefits, opportunities, and advantages that he can get by residence here with the ultimate object of becoming . . . a resident of the Jewish State."[4] Henry Morgenthau, Wilson's ambassador to Turkey and later the head of the government's investigative mission to Poland, wrote an article for *World's Work* in 1921 that developed the theme "Zionism is the most stupendous fallacy in Jewish history." Lambasting Jewish nationalism while it glorified the "spiritual" Americanism of anti-Zionist Jews, the article caused quite a stir in the secular press. Like Jastrow's statements, it supplied material for Christian writers who joined the attack against Zionism.[5]

Other Jewish anti-Zionists charged that Zionism sought to turn the clock back on the desirable process of assimilation. By choosing self-ghettoization, as well as by trampling on the rights of Palestinian Arabs, Zionism was alien to the American spirit of democracy and progress. In that vein, the renowned liberal philosopher Morris Raphael Cohen formulated the equations "liberalism = Americanism = good" and "Zionism = tribalism = evil." He claimed that Zionism rejected the American ideals of individual freedoms in favor of group rights:

> Nationalistic Zionism demands not complete individual liberty for the Jew, but group autonomy. . . . Indeed, how could a Jewish Palestine allow complete religious freedom, freedom of intermarriage and free non-Jewish immigration, without soon losing its very reason for existence? A national Jewish Palestine must necessarily mean a state founded on a peculiar race, a tribal religion and a mystic belief in a peculiar soil, whereas liberal America stands for separation of church and state, the free mixing of races, and the fact that men can change their habitation and language and still advance the process of civilization.

Because Zionists opposed the path of assimilation, Cohen charged, they feared the American ideal of freedom. Parenthetically he added another dig by likening their readiness to ignore the rights of the native Palestinian Arabs to Prussian oppression.[6]

American Jews whose loyalty to nineteenth-century liberalism fueled their attack on Zionism were caught in a logical trap. Defenders of assimilation and internationalism, they denounced Zionism, the child of darkness and reaction. Yet wasn't it equally reactionary to tout American chauvinistic nationalism if the road to progress lay through internationalism? Anti-Zionist Jews, however, sidestepped the issue. They tailored their liberalism to fit the American temper, indicating thereby a greater concern for their security and a desire to demonstrate an unquestionable patriotism.

Leaders of Reform Jewry and their institutions joined the secular liberal chorus. As discussed above, Reform's ardor in combating Zionism had cooled somewhat by 1917, but the unyielding antinationalists had a new burst of energy with the appearance of the Balfour Declaration. Laymen joined rabbis when Jastrow, Max Senior, and Rabbi Henry Berkowitz drew up a petition against Zionism in 1919 that was signed by 299 Americans and presented by Congressman Kahn to President Wilson. Announcing that it was speaking for the majority of American Jews, the petition revived the bogey of dual allegiance in all its intensity. It added that if Jews were to leave for Palestine, those left behind would suffer increased prejudice and hostility, which would impede their attempts at assimilation.[7] The petition was meant not only for the American government but for the nations engaged in peacemaking at Versailles.

In 1922, when Congress considered the Lodge-Fish resolution, which expressed American satisfaction with the proposed mandate for Palestine—the terms of the mandate incorporated the Balfour Declaration—Reform anti-Zionists were particularly upset. This time they faced the challenge of countering a commitment by the American *government* to a Jewish homeland. To prevent any official endorsement of Zionism, Rabbis David Philipson and Isaac Landman summed up Reform's position in testimony to the House Committee on Foreign Affairs. Adding to the usual litany, Philipson said, "I know that ever since political Zionism has been in the limelight the troubles of the Jews in the world have largely increased." The only solution to the Jewish problem, he said, would be the grant of full freedom for the Jews everywhere. The rabbis charged that the resolution itself was un-American, since it appealed to the Jewish vote, a concept whose existence and very legitimacy was denied by Reform. Philipson, consistently among the most rabid of the anti-Zionists, also criticized the resolution for deviating from the nation's traditional policy of nonentanglement in Old World affairs. Landman fought the resolution outside the committee's rooms too. Editor of the *American Hebrew,* he printed numerous opinions against congressional action and the un-American character of Zionism.[8]

More than ever before, Reform felt threatened by political Zionism. Should Zionists succeed in capturing the loyalty of the Jewish majority or, even worse, acceptance by the American public, Reform would lose the predominant position it had held since the 1870s in Jewish religious and secular institutions. Zionists had scored one major victory when they swayed American Jews to the idea of a democratic American Jewish Congress, and Reform had admitted then that the Jewish nationalists had the ear of the masses.[9] If after the Balfour Declaration that pattern persisted, the power of Reform in determining the allocation of communal resources as well as the very path that the community chose to follow for the future would be largely eroded.

Some of the Christian opinion molders and academics who contributed to the public critique of Zionism followed the line of Professor Albert Bushnell Hart of Harvard. Hart announced upon the appearance of the Balfour Declaration that Jews now had to fish or cut bait, to choose which country and nationality claimed their loyalty.[10] Thomas Nixon Carver, a sociologist and colleague of Hart, agreed that the Jew could not divide his allegiance. At bottom, he said, Jews had two diametrically opposed alternatives: territorial separatism through Zionism or complete amalgamation with other peoples and disappearance as a distinctive group. If Diaspora Jews chose separatism, they had to be prepared to pay the price—racial hostility on the part of their conationals.[11] Paul

Mowrer, foreign correspondent for a Chicago newspaper, wrote that Jewish resistance to assimilation—that the Jews constituted "a body persistently and willfully foreign"—was the root of antisemitism throughout history. Jews ought to discard certain religious practices—even be ready, he specified, to intermarry with non-Jews—in order to be accepted fully in the United States. Those who could not prove their undivided allegiance in this fashion should make their way to Palestine.[12]

A professor of international law at Princeton, Philip Marshall Brown, began with the premise that the Jew was the eternal alien in Western society: "The Jew is restless, and by nature detached from most nationalistic interests because of his sense of racial solidarity that militates against his taking deep root in any community. . . . This thing we term Christian civilization is something alien to him." Brown called racial solidarity the driving force behind Zionism, and he suggested that the prominence of Jews in the Socialist and Bolshevik movements derived from the same matrix. Although he denied that Jews joined those movements out of sinister motives, his choice of analogies was unfortunate. In the years 1917–22 Bolshevism was anathema to proper Americans; if Zionism drew from the same source, it was inherently evil.[13]

Doubtless very few of those who argued the either-or position on Jewish versus American nationalism considered their opinions antisemitic. It was not the Jew they disliked, they said, as much as Jewish group distinctiveness. To many well-meaning Christians in the United States, Jewish separatism had always been the major stumbling block to harmonious relations with Gentiles and was responsible, more than Christian prejudice, for anti-Jewish discrimination.[14] For their own good, some advised, Jews had to look beyond the Jewish community and show their readiness to participate on multiple levels of civic activity. Accordingly, Zionism was an unwise course, for it merely reinforced clannishness and in turn the barriers between Jew and Christian.[15]

Although responsible Christian criticism usually stopped short of attacking Zionists directly—it was Zion*ism* that caused the Jewish problem[16]—Dr. Herbert Adams Gibbons was as harsh as the Jewish liberals who denounced the "un-American" Zionists. Differentiating between Zionists and other Jews, he said openly: "We do not hold in abhorrence the Jews, but we do hold in abhorrence the Jewish nation." According to Gibbons, a Presbyterian minister who had taught at a missionary college in Turkey, "the Zionist movement tends to emphasize in the immigrant what makes him unfit for American citizenship." The immigrant had to submerge himself in American interests and build his life around American ideals, in short to copy the biblical example of Ruth, who merged her identity with Naomi's people. But a Jewish immigrant who brought with him the belief that he was part of a closely knit international community with an attachment to a cultural center in Zion would always be an unwelcome alien. "Many of my dearest friends are Jews," Gibbons protested, but because of the Zionists who undermined Jewish loyalty to the United States and weakened

American unity, antisemitism could well flourish. Therefore, it behooved the anti-Zionists within the Jewish community to fight the nationalists.[17]

The distinction between the good antinationalist Jew and the bad Zionist quickly took root. In 1919 the prestigious liberal weekly the *Independent* printed an editorial summarizing the pros and cons of Zionism. What purported to be an objective account of the two opposing views concluded with the *Independent*'s own value-ridden statement:

> On the whole the conservative Jews, who desire above all things to maintain the old Jewish faith and the Talmudic tradition, incline to be Zionists. The progressive Jews, the men who deprecate race distinction and hostilities . . . would prefer to see Jews intermarry and amalgamate with their Gentile fellow citizens in Europe and America and are disposed to discourage the Zionist experiment. Yet the Zionist movement has also attracted the support of many of the radical Jews who see in it an opportunity to found a semi-socialistic state.[18]

With "progressive," "race hostilities," and "radical" as clues, it took little wisdom to tell the good from the bad.

Unlike the Jewish opponents of Zionism, Christian critics concentrated more on depicting the evils of the Zionist movement in Palestine. Those who had lived in the Near East, such as the missionaries, journalists, and former government officials, were the most outspoken. They agreed that Zionism, the attempt of a minority in the country to gain complete control over Palestine, would incite the justified hostility of Muslim and Christian inhabitants, who had their own histories and aspirations, and they predicted pogroms, religious strife, and even war between the "white" and "brown" races. The Zionists in Palestine were imperialistic, conniving with their British protectors, trumpeting an aggressive and bombastic propaganda line, and always seeking more land. Ruthless exploiters of the natives, the Jews pursued an undemocratic program. Since they rejected the principle of self-determination for the Arabs, they denied the latter their rightful share of political power. Although a small minority in Palestine, Jews in a state of their own would wield absolute power. A Zionist state would also mean a Jewish theocracy, offensive to Muslims, Christians, and secular democrats. Furthermore, Zionists made their settlements exclusively Jewish and thereby created a gulf between themselves and the non-Jews. All told, the native Palestinians understandably preferred the tyranny of their former overlords, the Turks, to the tyranny of the Zionists.[19]

Not all critiques confined the specter of Zionism to Palestine alone. Some charged that Zionism was a child of international Jewry, financed by Jewish money from around the world and protected by a powerful Jewish press, which carefully doctored the news. Edward Reed of Yale interpreted Zionism as a vast international Jewish conspiracy when he testified against the Lodge-

Fish resolution of 1922. The Balfour Declaration, he said, was a secret document framed by British and American Zionists, who kept some of its details hidden from the public. Hinting at Zionist influence in American government circles, he talked of the Zionists' inordinately strong position at the Versailles peace conference, where they succeeded in drawing up the very favorable provisions of the mandate and made plans for assuming control over the land of Palestine. Although Reed was the most extreme, other critics, including American consuls in the Near East, struck equally ominous notes by linking Zionism with Bolshevism. That connection would make the Jewish "materialistic" and "atheistic" state the center for the spread of international revolutionary propaganda.[20]

The long brief against the effects of Zionism in the *yishuv* evoked images well calculated to turn war-weary Americans against the Jewish nationalist movement. Alien to American ways, Zionism betrayed the American war aims of universal democracy, self-determination, and impartial justice. Most important, after "the war to end all wars," Zionism jeopardized world peace. Imperialistic and Prussian-like by nature, a Zionist-controlled Palestine that aroused Arab opposition could only be maintained by armed force. If the United States was not dragged into a war begun by Zionist-generated hostility, it might be forced into supporting a Jewish state by military means. Still another scenario suggested that America and Britain would be compelled to use stringent measures to counter Bolshevism in Palestine before it infected the entire Near East.[21] Thus, the apprehensive American would understandably shudder at the thought of a Jewish state, which threatened his own security. He might also direct his resentment and suspicions against his American Jewish neighbor, who, even if not a Zionist, was somehow related to the troublemaking Zionists in Palestine.

The indictment of Zionism by non-Jewish critics clearly illuminated the interrelatedness of anti-Zionism and antisemitism. Like the picture of the good Jew versus the bad Jew, the popular charges resembled the antisemite's brief against Jews in general: the international Jew was clannish, materialistic, manipulative, exploitative, separatist, and radically anti-Gentile. When the anti-Zionist adopted those readymade images, he intentionally or unintentionally found a respectable rubric for any latent Jew-hatred he may have harbored. He may have opposed Zionism for objective reasons, and like Dr. Gibbons many of his best friends may have been Jews, but his indiscriminate use of adjectives about the Zionists made him in the last analysis indistinguishable from the antisemite. From then on to the present, anti-Zionism became more often than not a synonym for antisemitism.

The Jewish liberals, the Reform critics, and the Christian anti-Zionists found nothing qualitatively new in the theory of political Zionism. They all agreed on its alleged dangers, which stood in the way of the assimilation and social acceptance of American Jews and disrupted the postwar order. All three relied on traditional images of the undesirable Jew, for even the Jewish liberals structured their arguments on the basis of the alien and clannish Jew. What aroused their concentrated opposition at this time was the fact that the world powers at Versailles had shown that they took Zionism seriously.

Basic differences, however, precluded the possibility that the several groups could ever consciously band together in a fight against a Jewish state. In the eyes of the Jewish critics, the ones who would suffer most because of Zionism were the American Jews themselves. The Christian commentators agreed that Jewish security was endangered, but they added warnings about Zionist (and Bolshevik) threats in Palestine and to world peace. Only Jewish liberals really believed that Jews could change their behavior and obliterate the unfavorable images reflected in Zionism. As for some of the moderate Christian critics, their use of anti-Jewish imagery suggests that they expected nothing different from Jews.

The linkage between anti-Zionism and traditional antisemitism had two important corollaries. First, it meant that Zionists were less likely to convince opponents of the merits of their case, no matter how effective a countercampaign they mounted. Second, since American Jews were frightened by the increasing Judeophobia and overt discrimination of the 1920s, which led among other things to barriers against Jewish immigrants as well as Jews in white-collar jobs and in higher education, the anti-Zionist attacks drove many in the Jewish community away from the cause of political Zionism.[22] Nevertheless, American Zionists had no choice but to defend their movement. They, like their Reform counterparts, were fighting for control of the community, and it seemed more prudent to answer their opponents than to maintain silence. Under Brandeis's leadership their prestige and power had soared; they could point to the Balfour Declaration and the organization of the American Jewish Congress as notable victories. But challenged after 1917 by a wide and militant opposition and by serious internal rifts, their movement, especially if undefended, could easily revert to a weaker position.

In 1906 Zionist leader Richard Gottheil had stated that only Jews and not Christians worried about Jewish nationalism. An exaggeration even then, his claim was hardly relevant after the Balfour Declaration. However, much as they felt the need of non-Jewish support, Zionists reasoned that it would have done little good to contest those who spun their anti-Zionism out of a deep-seated Jew-hatred.[23] In the immediate postwar period they focused principally on Jewish critics like Cohen, Jastrow, Morgenthau, and Philipson. Resorting frequently to ridicule and contempt, they denounced those men for creating dissension within the community and thus aiding the Jew-haters. They fumed especially at the rabbis who had testified against the Lodge-Fish resolution, calling them traitors and Benedict Arnolds. Their charge that Zionism conflicted with Americanism, the Zionist witnesses at the hearings said, was totally groundless. How could Zionism be called un-American when it numbered among its supporters prominent government officials and civic leaders like

Brandeis and Julian W. Mack, and Jewish soldiers who had fought in the American army? Since the Allies gave their support to Jewish national self-determination, Zionism had become one with American patriotism.[24]

Widely respected Zionist leaders in particular took pains to defuse their Jewish critics. Several, usually toning down Zionist demands, wrote for the *Menorah Journal*, a bimonthly published by the Intercollegiate Menorah Association that appealed to Jewish intellectuals. For example, Julian Mack, federal judge and onetime president of the ZOA, asserted categorically that "we do not want an independent State for the Jewish people in Palestine *at this time* [emphasis his] . . . because at this time the Jews form only one-sixth of the population, and an independent State under such conditions would be both impracticable and undesirable." Until such time, Zionists were content with a mandate held by England that would lay the foundation for a state. When Jews became a majority under British administration, they would be ready for statehood. During that transitional period, American Jews could not in good conscience hold aloof from aid to the *yishuv*. Nor would a Jewish state when established hurt them in any way: "We are Americans politically, and nothing but American. There is no dual nationality in any political sense; there can be none. We look to Palestine for nothing. We look to America for everything."

Another contributor to the *Menorah Journal*, law professor Felix Frankfurter of Harvard, discussed the obligations of American Jews to a Jewish state. A state did not mean, he said, "that we should desire to go there or that we should be forced to go there." European Jews living in undemocratic lands needed Palestine, and on American Jews rested only the duty to help them, financially and intellectually, to build a free and healthy life. In Frankfurter's essay, American Zionism boiled down to a philanthropy dedicated to the creation of a Jewish state for other Jews.[25]

Two younger Zionist intellectuals probed more deeply into the nature of Judaism, nationalism, and assimilation. Elisha Friedman, an economist who worked for the government during the war, discussed the beneficent effects of Zionism and a Jewish state. The better-known professor of philosophy, Horace Kallen, addressed the issue of assimilation. Privately, he and Friedman, followers of Brandeis, labored in 1917–18 at converting a leading non-Zionist, Jacob Schiff, to the Zionist cause.[26]

Other Zionists also replied to the prominent critics. Law professor David Amram answered Morris Jastrow; attorney Samuel Untermyer took on Henry Morgenthau; Louis Lipsky, then head of the ZOA, rebutted David Philipson at the committee hearings in 1922.[27] The most profound interchange pitted two respected philosophers, Morris Raphael Cohen and Horace Kallen, against each other. Cohen's article in the *New Republic*, in which he equated Zionism with tribalism and Prussianism, triggered the clash. Kallen's rejoinder, appearing in the same journal a month later, laced into Cohen's impassioned denunciation of Jewish nationalism and called it erroneous, slanderous, irresponsible, and downright false. Different from the extremist Teutonism and Slavism to which Cohen had likened it, Zionism, Kallen said, was not a challenge to liberalism but rather a product of a liberalism derived from the bonding of democracy and nationalism. It stood neither for a tribal religion nor despotic rule over Palestinian non-Jews. The core of the article—and here the reader recognizes Kallen, the expositor of cultural pluralism—was the defense of group freedoms. In Kallen's words, Zionist ideology was "an extension of the assumptions of liberalism from the individual to the group." With only slight modification, it resembled the Declaration of Independence: "All nationalities are created equal and endowed with certain inalienable rights; among their rights are life, liberty and the pursuit of happiness." Every individual was shaped by the nationality in which he was born; those nationalities were "the essential reservoirs of individuality" and "the prerequisite to the liberation of the individual." The nation too would be enriched by the free development of various nationalities. A return to Zion, which in turn would lead to continued Jewish contributions to civilization, was predicated on the acknowledgment of the rights of the Jewish nationality.[28] Even if Kallen didn't change Cohen's mind, his article reached more readers than those that appeared in Jewish periodicals.

Along with taunts and slurs against anti-Zionists, the *New Palestine*, the weekly newspaper of the ZOA and successor to the *Maccabaean*, took on the *New York Times*. That prestigious daily was solidly entrenched in the anti-Zionist camp. A prominent non-Jewish writer once suggested in the *Nation* that the *Times*, perhaps just because it was known as a Jewish newspaper, did not readily plead the cause of Jews on any issue. But, as reflected in its news coverage and editorials, the *Times* was more exercised than usual about Zionism. Why, for example, the *New Palestine* pointedly asked, was it the only New York publication that failed to mention, let alone quote, Untermyer's response to Morgenthau? In the spring of 1922 *Times* publisher Adolph Ochs visited Palestine. Since he commented favorably on the Jewish settlements he had seen, the *New Palestine* was eminently gratified. Despite Ochs's reservations about a Jewish homeland—it could lead to friction with the Arabs, and it posed possible dangers to Christian holy sites—he was seen as a non-Zionist rather than an anti-Zionist. A few weeks later, however, the *Times* strongly criticized the Lodge-Fish resolution. A long editorial said that the resolution appealed to the "Jewish vote" and that by injecting religion into politics, it would arouse anti-Jewish prejudice. True, the *Times* shifted the blame to Congress, but it cautioned Jews who "unthinkingly" supported the resolution not to endorse a move that divided them from their fellow Americans. At this point the *New Palestine* switched gears. Ignoring Ochs entirely, it pulled apart the "muddled" editorial: "There is a flavor in[it] that reminds us of [Rabbi David] Philipson. It seems to be written by a Jewish anti-Zionist pen, that at the same time wanted to appear as if it were just a plain *goyish* pen."[29]

Throughout the public debate on a possible Jewish state, American Zionists were on the defensive. To be sure, there were some prominent non-Jewish supporters of the Balfour Declaration, but the stature of the liberal critics and Christian opinion molders arrayed in opposition to Jewish nationalism, plus the renewed vigor of Reform anti-Zionists, endowed the "antis" with greater authority and influence. Most important, since the debate itself was caught up in the antisemitism unleashed by the Red Scare and the popularization of the *Protocols*, the antistatists enjoyed a decided advantage.[30] The embattled Zionists, confronting intense Judeophobia as well as anti-Zionism, were left with two options. They could have asserted that America was no different from other countries with respect to antisemitism, thereby directing their movement closer to Herzl's initial premises. Or, they could have watered down American Zionism to make it more palatable to the critics. Opting for the latter course, the movement neither abandoned the principles set in its formative years, nor did it doubt that Jews had a secure future in the United States. Zionists continued to insist that America was different and that a personal commitment by American Jews to a Jewish Palestine was unnecessary. Along the lines of the article by Frankfurter, they said that American Jews supported Zionism on behalf of oppressed Jews elsewhere. Further trimming their movement down to a philanthropy, Zionists tacitly admitted that the regnant concept of a monolithic American loyalty was both unimpeachable and too difficult to combat. By accommodating to public opinion they took another step in the Americanization of Zionism.

In the end, it mattered little that in November 1917 the initial American response to the Balfour Declaration was favorable. The negative criticism of the immediate postwar period held fast, reemerging with new intensity at the end of the decade in the wake of Arab riots in Palestine. Jewish and non-Jewish anti-Zionism also served to strengthen the State Department's opposition to a Jewish state during the 1920s and 1930s. Meanwhile, American Zionists recoiled. The enthusiasm of the Brandeis era leading up to the declaration rapidly dissipated; membership in the ZOA, which stood at 149,000 in 1918, shrank to 18,500 in 1922.[31] In the United States and elsewhere Palestinianism replaced Zionism, and the evolution of a Jewish state out of the British mandate, which Zionists had confidently predicted, appeared less and less certain.

The Second Debate

In August 1929 the Arabs went on a weeklong rampage against Jews and Jewish settlements in the *yishuv*. Native unrest, which was fueled by claims that England had reneged on its wartime pledges to the Arabs and had made conflicting promises to the Jews in the Balfour Declaration, had been simmering since the end of the World War. It erupted more furiously in 1929, amounting to a veritable spree of killings and destruction of property, which went uncontained by British officials. Among the brutally massacred victims were six young students, all citizens of the United States, at a yeshivah in Hebron. If for no other reason, the reaction of the American government and American public opinion to the riots was immediately involved.

Technically the headache over the mandate was England's alone, but because England looked to America after the war to shore up British interests in the Pacific as well as the Atlantic, it trod warily with its strongest ally even as it sought to balance the conflicting Arab and Jewish claims. But the United States and American public opinion posed no serious obstacles, and London chose to appease the Arabs, a path that received encouragement from the anti-Zionist American consul in Palestine and from the anti-Zionist State Department. His Majesty's Government (HMG) found a temporary solution to the problem in the Passfield White Paper of October 1930, which followed the reports of two British commissions of inquiry. Unsatisfactory to both sides, it failed to settle the Arab-Jewish controversy, which dragged on through the 1930s and World War II.[32]

A. THE ISSUES

The second debate on Zionism, in 1929–30, was more than a reprise of the first. To be sure, Jewish and Christian liberals as well as the press again led the anti-Zionists, and criticisms of Zionism laced with antisemitism again depicted the Jewish oppressor and the Arab victim. But since the Arabs had taken up arms against the *yishuv*, the same charges rang with greater intensity. Seen as a vindication of those who had argued that the Balfour Declaration set the Arabs and the Jews on a collision course, the riots appeared to justify the claims that Zionism, a threat to world peace, could be maintained only by force.

All American parties concerned in the aftermath of the riots openly acknowledged the importance of public opinion, both Jewish and non-Jewish, in the resolution of the Palestine question. The government carefully assessed that opinion; Arabs and Zionists tried to capture it. The end result was never really in doubt. Barely had the ink dried on public statements in sympathy with the victims or in condemnation of the rioters when the public's concentration shifted. Americans knew *who* the killers and looters were, but they set about questioning *why* the rioters had so acted. The pro-Arab answers they formulated derived from evaluations of the Arab and Jewish cases as well as of Arabs and Jews in general. Thus, both sides had their work cut out for them— the Arabs to play upon and nurture American support, the Jews to dig beneath the riots and defend the beliefs and behavior of their nationalist movement.

Jewish defense spelled retrogression. Challenging the legitimacy of political Zionism, the public focus on Arab rights set back Zionist efforts to prove the similarities of their program to American democratic principles. In essence, Zionists were forced to reargue the terms of a twelve-year-old contract (the Balfour Declaration) that had been signed by England, sealed by international approval, and acclaimed by Americans.

During the months between the riots and the Passfield White Paper, the Jewish and non-Jewish anti-Zionists targeted Zionism in general and the policies of the Jewish Agency in particular. (The Agency was a body created under the terms of the mandate to cooperate with the British in the development of a Jewish national home. Consisting at first of members of the WZO, it was enlarged to include non-Zionists only days before the riots.) Ostensibly, any defense of Zionism and the Agency devolved on the three American Jewish factions most concerned about the *yishuv* : the ZOA, now headed by Louis Lipsky and always loyal to Chaim Weizmann, president of the Agency; the non-Zionists, the new participants in the Agency under the leadership of banker Felix Warburg; and the independent and influential Brandeis group, the justice and his close associates who, although without office in the ZOA or Agency, were committed Zionists and fully immersed in Palestinian affairs. Together, theirs was the task of creating a climate of opinion supportive of Zionism.

Various reasons, however, crippled the possibility of a joint effort at defense from the very outset. Even the bare essentials that united the Zionists and non-Zionists—a commitment to the *yishuv*, a partnership with England, and an acceptance of Weizmann's leadership—could not produce a united response. For one thing, the mood of the 1920s militated against public support of the nationalist aspirations of a beleaguered minority; for another, the defenders faced formidable adversaries of all stripes—liberal and conservative, capitalist and worker, religious and secular—whose combined numbers and influence made their position virtually unassailable. In the end, however, the failure of the three factions to mount a joint campaign, thereby dooming any chance of an effective defense at all, stemmed primarily from their inability to rise above personal rivalries and unite the American Jewish community.[33]

It is arguable that had the discussion been limited to the failure of England to encourage and protect the upbuilding of the *yishuv,* the Jews would have been in a stronger position. Circumstances, however, precluded that option. In light of the country's recoil from political involvement abroad, and in light of the strong Anglo-Saxonist current within American society, the public shied away from an indictment of England. Moreover, the leaders of the Agency in London, all loyal Englishmen, had warned American Jews against raising an anti-British cry. The Agency itself recommended the removal of incompetent colonial officials but refrained from faulting London's policies. Zionist leader Chaim Weizmann sought to impress upon Prime Minister

Ramsay MacDonald the mutuality of Zionist and British aims in Palestine and how he, Weizmann, had encouraged Jewish trust in England. If that confidence, particularly among American Jews, were betrayed, he was prepared to resign.[34]

Neither the ZOA and the Brandeis group nor the non-Zionists contemplated a rupture with Great Britain. Their gratitude for the Balfour Declaration, and their hope that England would thereby become the guardian of a developing Jewish homeland, had been fixed since 1917. The Jewish community at large followed suit; a mass rally of more than twenty-five thousand Zionist sympathizers at Madison Square Garden on August 29 affirmed Jewish confidence in England's honor and good faith. More important, faith in England accorded with American diplomatic policy. Hadn't President Herbert Hoover made it known that although he opposed anti-British attacks, it would not be inappropriate to blame the colonial officials? Therefore, the position chosen by the Jews not to fault the Labor government was eminently American.[35] The coincidence of American and Zionist diplomatic aims, another facet of the Americanization of Zionism, took root and continued to flourish long after the birth of the Jewish state.

The months passed, and the issue of England's obligation to live up to the Balfour Declaration, which was incorporated in the text of the mandate, drew increasingly less attention. Since the Agency agreed to the two British investigative commissions, the first led by Sir Walter Shaw and the second by Sir John Hope Simpson, any sharp criticism was put on hold until the final reports were submitted. Reassured that Jewish acquiescence if not cooperation was beyond doubt, England felt freer about appeasing the Arabs. As events turned out, any Zionist reliance on British honor or sense of "fair play" was misplaced.[36]

B. JEWISH CRITICS

The fragmented nature of the Jewish community precluded the emergence of any one Jewish point of view. The outpouring of relief funds aside, American Jews broke ranks and spoke in many tongues. On the fringe of the opponents to mainstream Zionism stood the Revisionists, the militant faction that had broken away from the movement and opposed Weizmann, the British government, and Louis Lipsky. Charging Weizmann with tiptoeing around the British, they called for his ouster and that of his henchman Lipsky. A different type of response came from a small group of young Jewish intellectuals who wrote for the *Menorah Journal*. One of them, Lionel Trilling, recalled years later: "We were inclined to be skeptical about Zionism and even opposed to it, and during the violence that flared up in 1929 some of us were on principle pro-Arab."[37]

Outnumbering the Revisionists and the intellectuals by far, the Jewish Left also withheld its support. The Communists knuckled under to Moscow's line and explained the riots in Marxist terms: the Zionists were the bourgeois capitalists, the Arabs the heroic and rebellious proletariat, and the Grand Mufti the people's liberator.[38] Unlike the Communists, the Jewish Socialists had long been divided on the issue of a Jewish national home in Palestine. The minority who believed in a reconciliation of economic class with nationalism had joined the Poale Zion (Workers of Zion) party. As for the powerful Jewish unions, the leadership was neutral if not opposed to Zionism, and although the rank and file, the more recent immigrants, were more sympathetic, the leaders went unchallenged.[39]

Immediate circumstances also contributed to Socialist disaffection. Since the Socialists were enchanted by the rule of the Labor party in England, they were reluctant to embarrass MacDonald's government. Socialist leader Norman Thomas, at best lukewarm toward Zionism, called the riots tragic, but he saw the tragedy primarily as a setback to world peace. Idealistic Zionists would agree, he said, that Jewish nationalism could not be imposed by military means on an unwilling majority. Thomas denounced the Balfour Declaration, an expression of England's imperial motives, at the same time that he urged trust in the Labor government.[40]

The American partners in the enlarged Agency paid scant attention to the individual anti-Zionist Jewish groups. There were no high-level conciliation meetings and no appeals for united responses to the crisis. The measure of communal unity that had marked the successful relief drive for victims in the *yishuv* quickly evaporated. Efficient machinery nourished by public outrage had assured the successful collection of funds, but it was dismantled after a short campaign. Protest meetings organized locally in August and September were exploited neither as an opening wedge for public rallies nor for a network of active local committees. When the American Jewish Congress suggested a national Jewish conference, both Weizmann and Warburg objected.[41] In short, no one advanced a sound strategy for the education and mobilization of the community at large.

The obstacles to American Jewish unity were compounded by the plan for an Arab-Jewish binational state put forth in November 1929 by American rabbi Judah Magnes, chancellor of the Hebrew University.[42] Explaining his program in Jerusalem, Magnes said that despite the riots a "spiritual pressure" within Jews required them to find an answer to the Palestinian problem, even if that meant Jewish concessions to the Arabs. A moral peace was the only proper foundation for a Jewish homeland: "If we cannot find ways of peace and understanding, if the only way of establishing the Jewish National Home is upon the bayonets of some Empire, our whole enterprise is not worth while." The plan drew from Magnes's background—a Progressive and a pacifist, a Reform rabbi seeking to harmonize universalist beliefs with Jewish particularism—and from ideas being circulated in 1929 by a former British official and adviser to Arab leaders.

It mattered little to Magnes, still calling himself a Zionist, and to his follow-ers that his suggestion of a legislature based on population spelled total surren-der by the Zionists to the Arab majority. In his eyes the Balfour Declaration and mandate were products of imperialistic machinations and international politics that denied democracy and self-determination to the Arabs. He urged that Jews act in accordance with the Jewish ethical tradition, and he called for an "act of faith" from both sides showing that they could rise above their passions and weaknesses. His projected binational government, he said, recognized the claims of the Arabs and would lead them and the Jews to a mutual acceptance of each other's rights. Nevertheless, given the realities of both the Palestinian and inter-national scenes, the plan was as naive as it was idealistic. But Magnes persisted. He preferred, he observed, to renounce a Jewish national home and return Jews to the ghetto than to compromise Jewish spiritual integrity. Magnes may not have aimed to prove the democratic American-like features of Zionism, but that consideration was precisely what captivated his supporters in the United States.

Magnes's pronouncements brought on a fierce attack from loyal American Zionists—periodicals, individuals, and organizations. The plan and Magnes's "Jesus-like" homilies were at best untimely; the irresponsibility of the man, in no way a representative of the Agency, was appalling. The militants went fur-ther. Shouting treason, the American veterans of the Jewish Legion (those who had fought on the side of England during the war) called for his resignation from the chancellorship of the Hebrew University; the Revisionists asked the university and the WZO for disciplinary action. Prominent non-Zionists fa-vored his ideas, but Warburg, now an Agency official, faulted the chancellor for bypassing Weizmann and the Agency. For its part, the Brandeis group dis-missed the ill-advised plan. One friend candidly wrote Magnes: "There has been such a barrage of criticism that I would require the lamp of a Diogenes to find people—excepting certain Reform rabbis and anti-Zionists—who would speak with enthusiastic approval of your [program]."

Magnes put the Zionists even more on the defensive. To prove that they, like him, aimed to neither fight nor exploit their fellow countrymen in Palestine, they felt impelled to reiterate time and again how the *yishuv* shared its educa-tional and welfare institutions with the Arabs. With respect to Arab-Jewish re-lations, however, they failed to come up with a unified opinion. Some said to negotiate "in time"; others said to wait until the Arabs were better prepared for democracy or the Jews equalled the Arabs numerically. On the deeper issue of Magnes's challenge to their long-voiced protestations of the democratic char-acter of Zionism, they kept silent. Meantime, outright defections to the Magnes side as well as various approaches on how to handle him sapped the ZOA of energy and concerted direction. Communal solidarity appeared ever more elusive.

The Jewish reactions laid bare the underlying chasm between Zionists and non-Zionists. Despite representation in the enlarged Agency, the latter were acutely apprehensive about anything more than a vague, nonpolitical Zionism. Magnes, a respected rabbi, social reformer, and friend, articulated their underlying fears; so long as Jews engaged in political nationalist activity that contradicted America's liberal ideology, their security was tenuous. More important, Magnes backed up his words with a seemingly reasonable program. Moralistic and universalistic, it promised a democratic Palestine under majority rule and a safe Palestine where Jews and Arabs would live in harmony. The plan repudiated European imperialism and militarism, concepts that disillusioned Americans in the 1920s found particularly odious. One of Felix Warburg's sons confided that Magnes was "the one person who has expressed the ideal which the forward-looking youth of America can follow." Admittedly, the result would not be an autonomous Jewish homeland, but that was a small price to pay if Jews, living in accordance with their own as well as America's ethical tradition, would find peace and security.

C. THE PRESS AND THE LIBERALS

In the first short-lived round of public reaction to the riots, non-Jewish sympathy for the *yishuv* ran high. Leading newspapers expressed their horror over the bloodshed and demanded that England safeguard the rights of Jews in Palestine. Congressmen, governors, and public figures of all persuasions and geographical sections joined the Zionist chorus. In messages relayed to the British Colonial Office they added their concern for American lives and property and demanded reparations for the losses. Louis Lipsky reported that the "almost unanimous expression of sympathy"—and in particular the messages from Hoover and Senator William Borah, chairman of the Foreign Relations Committee—had made a profound impression in London.[43]

As the diplomatic correspondence reveals, the Zionists wrongly assessed London's reaction. England shuddered at neither Hoover's nor Borah's words. Within a few weeks, more ominous signals were heard: accounts of Jewish culpability for the riots, reports that Arab violence had been exaggerated, descriptions of the scandalous conditions in Palestinian Jewish relief operations. One contemporary analysis noted early on that the American press revealed "a strong undercurrent of feeling . . . against the Jewish nationalist aims in the Holy Land, and a tendency in some circles ordinarily favorable to Jews to regard the Arab as the true underdog."[44]

Coolness in the press toward political Zionism showed that attention had shifted to the deeper issue underlying the riots: "Should the bloodshed be viewed as just another pogrom, or as the genesis of a national uprising, with Jews as the victims merely because they had planted themselves in the Arab path to freedom?" By the end of September Lipsky reluctantly changed his mind, admitting that "there is a tremendous amount of public opinion against us."[45] Almost overnight the American Jewish task was transformed. Instead of merely collecting statements that would prove to England the depth of America's commitment to the Zionist movement, the Jews first had to convince the public of the justice of their cause.

The critiques of Zionism and Zionists in secular periodicals came mostly from journalists and interested scholars. Many claimed an expertise based on visits to Palestine. One influential critic, whose reportage of events for the *New York Times* coincided with the anti-Zionist views of publisher Adolph Ochs, was Joseph Levy. A man who worked closely with Magnes, Levy faulted the Jews as much as the Arabs for provoking the riots.[46] Another reporter who made a personal crusade out of anti-Zionism was Vincent Sheean. Falling under the influence of Arab sympathizers in Palestine, the antisemitic Sheean viciously attacked the Zionists and their animus toward the Arabs. The Zionist mind typified, he said, "how idealism goes hand in hand with the most terrific cynicism. . . . how they are Fascists in their own affairs, with regard to Palestine, and internationalists in everything else." Sheean cooperated with the anti-Zionist American consul in Jerusalem, and when he returned to the United States he spread his anti-Zionist views while on an extensive lecture tour.[47]

Since modern Jews had traditionally looked for liberal allies after Emancipation, the loss of liberal support in 1929–30, or betrayal as the Zionists called it, was especially troubling. In the United States two prestigious liberal periodicals, the *Nation* and the *New Republic*, had responded positively to the Balfour Declaration in 1917. After the riots, however, they adopted the Arab cause and judged the Palestine situation through the lenses of anti-imperialism, pacifism, and a majority's right to self-rule. Zionism tied to British imperialism and ignoring the wishes of the majority was out of place. Predicated on the use of force at a time when the Western world was riding the crest of naval disarmament and the Kellogg-Briand Peace Pact, Zionism contradicted the spirit of the times. The *Nation* concluded that Zionists, imbued with "war-time psychology," wrongly looked to the "Joshua" instead of the "Isaiah" method of progress. The periodical latched on to Magnes's plan, saying that it exemplified the best in Jewish tradition.[48]

Individual Zionists wrote letters to the *Nation* and the *New Republic*, but editorial policy remained fixed. The managing editor of the *Nation* explained privately to Magnes that the journal's opinion reflected no lack of sympathy for Jews and for the apolitical Zionist work in Palestine:

> With entire approval of the great cultural and economic task on which you and your [Zionist] associates have so finely embarked, we have felt . . . that the political exaggeration of the Balfour Declaration was likely to lead into a very difficult and dangerous situation. . . . If, in trying to express that judgment . . . we have failed to do justice to the reasonable hopes and aspirations of our Zionist friends, it has not been from any lack of desire to see full justice done to the Jews and to

see full opportunity given them for making their contributions to that international life in which they have already played so large and honorable a part.[49]

Other American liberals and pacifists joined in congratulations to Magnes on his quasi-prophetic utterances. They failed to see why he aroused Zionist antagonism. John Haynes Holmes, a liberal minister in New York who thought of himself as a Zionist supporter, declaimed that "once again as in ancient times, the prophets are stoned and slain," and Roger Baldwin of the American Civil Liberties Union commented, "Tolerance seems to be a stony road even for Jews." The *Nation*'s editor reported directly to Magnes: "We have certainly been having a hot time with our Jewish friends . . . and I have been greatly distressed to see the apparent failure to understand your position which seemed to me so nobly and characteristically taken." But, "those of us who went through the fires of 1917 and 1918 do not need popular approval for the positions that we have become honestly convinced are right."[50]

Editorials and articles the *New Palestine* attempted to rebut the liberal critics.[51] Since its readership was limited primarily to the faithful, it doubtless feared that the opinions of liberals might lead Zionists themselves to defect. Indeed, Jews could reasonably argue that a breach with American liberals over Palestine could be hazardous if it left the Jewish community isolated and bereft of allies on other issues. An article in the *New Palestine* by non-Zionist James Marshall assumed that Jews had no choice but to yield to liberal pressure. Marshall urged Zionists to correct the misguided behavior that had alienated the liberals and led them to back the Magnes plan. To swim with the current, which ultimately would decide the fate of the Balfour Declaration and the mandate, Zionists had to backtrack. "The picture of British guns forcing foreign rule upon the majority of the population so that a minority may achieve political, economic and cultural privileges," Marshall wrote, "does not accord with the conscience of people bred in America and western Europe to the principles of free self-government." It behooved Zionists to show the world that their movement was only cultural and spiritual and that it harbored no aggressive intentions toward the Arabs. "We neither need nor want a *Judenstaat*" (a reference to Herzl's book but in its Germanic form a hint of hated Prussianism). Since the mandate looked forward to the establishment of self-rule for Palestine, it was incumbent upon the Jews, and not England or the League, to come up with a workable scheme. "For our own spiritual sake, for our own chance to grow, as well as to earn the support of the impartial people of the world . . . , we must present a plan for self-government in Palestine." Jewish rights under an Arab majority could be guaranteed under League supervision, but in any event that issue was not a valid reason for denying the Arabs self-government.

Tackling Marshall's premise that liberals were right, writer Maurice Samuel published a stinging reply that simultaneously defended the Jewish right to a normal existence. Why did the Jews, as Marshall and Magnes thought, have to prove their good intentions and assure the world that they were "nicer" than any other nation? Their right to Palestine transcended international promises: "We are made sick, distorted, unnatural; we are stunted in our natural spiritual development; we are made the heir of a genuine national inferiority complex—all for the reason that *organically* Palestine and we are one; and physically Palestine has been taken from us. *This is the foundation of our right to a Homeland in Palestine.*" To rectify that condition, liberals had applied the formula *"Give the people its rights"* twelve years earlier and supported the Balfour Declaration. Now, after the riots and independently of Jewish behavior, the liberals found another cause, the rights of the Arabs, and they promptly forgot the Jews. "Liberals," Samuel sneered, "do not seem to be capable of carrying two principles simultaneously in their heads." He said that the worst error in Marshall's article was the implication that Zionists harbored thoughts about Arab displacement or subordination. From such misassumptions liberals deduced that Jews should be deprived of justice lest they abuse it! "Of no other people in the world would we dare to speak thus."[52] The Marshall-Samuel interchange proved the inability of the non-Zionists to plumb the depths of Jewish ethnic yearning for a Jewish homeland. Yet, Marshall's basic premise was irrefutable. Fair or not, public opinion could well decide the resolution of the Palestine impasse.

In London Chaim Weizmann worried about the failure of American Jews to effectively rebut the liberal arguments. He turned to Wise, Brandeis, and Frankfurter, the Jews most closely identified with liberal circles, requesting that they attack the "sentimental nonsense" being aired about Arab self-determination. Weizmann claimed that in England even left-wing Socialists knew that Arab democracy was "a mere farce and fake." Unfortunately, however, the popular formulas were "against us." The Zionist leader could only conclude from the absence of Zionist counterpropaganda that "the Jews in America are getting cold feet."[53]

As the months went by, a composite[54] and highly unflattering picture of Zionism emerged from the nation's leading journals. Incorporating the liberal argument and adding others, it eclipsed the few pro-Zionist articles that found their way into print. It drew sustenance from the bogeys that haunted the nation in the postwar decade. Americans who now spurned foreign entanglement and militarism, superpatriots who feared immigration and the specter of atheistic communism, and average citizens who may have been impressed by the "revelations" of Henry Ford and the *Protocols of the Elders of Zion* could well relate to the following anti-Zionist charges:

1. Zionism was undemocratic. Zionists had settled in an Arab land and although overwhelmingly outnumbered by the native population demanded political domination. The Balfour Declaration never promised a Jewish state, and Chaim Weizmann's phrase about making Palestine as Jewish as England was English was both unwarranted and unattainable. A Jewish *home* in Palestine under Arab benevolent rule was acceptable, but to press for more was undemo-

cratic and hence un-American. True, the Zionists had modernized the country and raised the Arab standard of living, but irrigation and health clinics did not allay Arab fear or invalidate Arab rights. Writer H. W. Nevinson put it this way: "The Arab is a camel; the Jew is a motorcar, bumping him off the road."[55]

2. Zionism spawned by British imperialism depended for its existence on military force. Since Arabs were prepared to fight a holy war in defense of their just rights, only a garrison state could prevent further bloodshed. Zionists, however, refused to yield. "Jews have been massacred by the best people in history for centuries, and Arab pogroms are hardly big-time stuff," one Zionist allegedly told reporter John Gunther.[56] Violence in turn would doubtless draw in other nations, including the United States.

3. Zionism was a disruptive social force. Modernization had destroyed the natural primitive charm of Palestine's landscape and the harmony of a rural economy. Zionist settlers on the land had dispossessed the Arabs (although admittedly the latter had been paid well), and the majority of Jews, drawn to the cities, had captured the country's wholesale and retail trade. On the land and in the cities, the new Jews lived according to social standards unseen before in Palestine and certainly incomprehensible to the average Arab. They spoke Hebrew, their women wore trousers, and their theater testified to Slavic antecedents and behavior. Their center, Tel Aviv, was "vulgarly" Levantine after the commonplace fashion of Beirut and Alexandria; in comportment, the place might be a seaside resort on the Black Sea." In the experimental "communistic" *kibbutz*, the Zionists were secularists or agnostics whose principles involved "the breaking down of the ordinarily accepted standards of family life." As a result, the harmony of Arab-Jewish relations in the pre-Zionist era had been permanently destroyed.[57]

4. Zionism was an artificial contrivance of international Jewry. Sustained by an "unholy alliance" between Western military power and limitless "Jewish gold," Zionism was unable to succeed on its own. The influx of Jewish immigrants into Palestine had overtaxed the country's economic absorptive capacity; there was neither sufficient land for cultivation nor proper outlets for urban employment. Economically and politically Zionism was a failure: "God promised . . . Moses, and Balfour promised . . . Weizmann; and all four have failed to make [Zionism] work."[58] However, the stream of Jewish money and a "worldwide Jewish organization and its access to the press" kept the movement alive and underwrote an aggressively nationalistic propaganda. The powerful international network closed ranks on Palestine and prevented a full hearing of the Arab side. Anytime Zionists imagined an infringement of their rights, "immediately there is a mass meeting in Chicago, a deputation waits upon the Prime Minister in London, and a letter is written to the *Melbourne Times*."[59]

Not all journalists and essayists leveled every charge, nor were they all equally vindictive. They pointed out the faults of the Zionists in Palestine—arrogant, pushy, irreligious, short on idealism—but in different terms. Some, to avoid the charge of antisemitism, took pains to distinguish between "good" indigenous Palestinian Jews and the "bad" Zionists. Most correlated Zionism with outside financial resources, but only the jurist Pierre Crabites was so obsessed that he could hardly write the word *Jew* without immediately linking it to an image of money. Overall, however, the major charges were repeated time and again.

From the least biased to the most vicious, the critiques revealed how closely the anti-Zionist vocabulary conformed to antisemitic stereotypes. Whether deliberate or not, allusions could trigger automatic responses, and Americans who may not have understood the Palestine situation could more easily grasp the equivalencies: the Zionist settler who dispossessed the Arabs was the Jewish Shylock; the Zionist who cornered business and commerce was the Jew as economic parasite; the *kibbutz* dweller was the Jew as Bolshevik; Zionist financial resources validated the image "as rich as a Jew"; world Jewish support proved that Jews were a clannish and separate international enclave; Zionists who disrupted the social order in Palestine were the alien race unassimilable to its surroundings. One critic also used the antisemitic image of the physically stunted Jew, who left the fighting to others, to prophesy the inevitable collapse of Zionism.[60] In the fusion of anti-Zionism with antisemitism, each of the two components was strengthened.

Virtually all of the solutions advanced to solve the Palestinian impasse claimed that their objective was an Arab-Jewish peace. Toward that end some called for limiting Zionist ambitions to a cultural and spiritual center in Palestine, or the internationalization of the Holy Land, or the adoption of Magnes's scheme for a binational state. Others recommended the rescission of the Balfour Declaration or that Zionists cut their ties to British imperialism. None of those ideas involved concessions from the Arabs.

The nagging questions persist. Why, if the choice was between the fundamental rights of the Jews and the fundamental rights of the Arabs, did the Jews have to yield? Why, as Maurice Samuel asked, did the Jews have to be "nicer" than other peoples even when some anti-Zionists admitted the Jewish historic and organic right to a homeland in Palestine? As Jews observed even then, anti-Jewish sentiment explained a good deal, and Jews were always a convenient scapegoat. But more than general dislike of the Jew was involved. In the 1920s a double standard of behavior still prevailed in America; in manners and conduct a Jew had to be better than a Gentile to be as good. The code still held fast in universities, professions, and corporate executive suites. Just as harsher requirements were imposed on the individual Jew, so could they be demanded of the collective group.

A variant of that theme was the argument that Jews, because of their noble tradition, were morally obligated to abide by their ethical values and deal more than evenly with the less advanced Arabs. Those who were wronged should not seek vengeance, the *Nation* piously intoned. In the *Atlantic Monthly,* Hallen

Viney wrote that on the Jew rested the responsibility to love his enemies: "Can he rise to the spiritual vision of Deutero-Isaiah, or will he keep to the nationalism of [the prophet] Haggai? Can he build up the character of the Arab by example?"[61] The possible eventualities were left unsaid. If in the process Jewish interests were crushed, well, that was the fate of the "suffering people." In any event, Jews would have had the satisfaction of self-sacrifice!

Articles and editorials in the most prominent Protestant and Catholic journals repeated many of the arguments that appeared in the secular press. Writers emphasized the rights of the Arabs and blamed the Balfour Declaration and political Zionism for Arab-Jewish friction; they too agreed that Zionism was sustained by world Jewish gold and that it depended on the use of British force for its existence. Again like the secular journals, leading Christian papers propagated an image of Zionism and Zionists—conniving, arrogant, separatist, communistic, atheistic—that was tinted by antisemitic imagery. In a letter to the *Christian Century* one Jewish writer called a particularly vicious article "worthy of [Henry Ford's] *Dearborn Independent* of five years ago, not of a liberal Christian journal."[62]

The roots of religious anti-Zionism, however, were different. The strong ties forged by the missionaries with the Arabs and the long-standing Christian conversionary efforts in the Near East contributed to a pro-Arab and anti-Zionist position. Visits by Christian Americans to Palestine, where they were exposed to the influence of missionaries, Christian Arabs, and the anti-Zionist American Colony, also turned them against Zionism. In October 1929 the editor of the *National Methodist Press,* reporting on his visit to Palestine, explained his pro-Arab sympathies to both the State Department and Prime Minister MacDonald. To the latter he said that the Grand Mufti, a man of culture and an inspiration to the Arabs, held liberal principles much like those of MacDonald himself.[63]

Mixing religious with practical objections, the Christian press raised two points different from the secular critique. They charged that the Jews were plotting to seize control of Christian as well as Muslim holy sites and to found a theocratic state in Palestine. They also raised the theme of the universal Jew, the Jew whose religious development was stunted by the forces of reaction and who longed to be absorbed within society. Once emancipated, the Jew did not and should not want a separate land but should again apply his religious talents to all mankind. The possession of Palestine, the *Christian Century* concluded, was unnecessary to "any . . . moral and religious leadership." Heeding the Christian theological view of the Jew in history, the Christian press flatly rejected Jewish nationalism. The issue was not nationalism *per se*, as the defense of Arab national rights proved, but rather the fact that Jews had forfeited their right to a normal national existence. They had lost control over their destiny—"the scepter had departed from Judah"—and be it as converts, or heralds of the

Second Coming, or pioneers in religion and ethics, their fate ultimately rested on the purposes of the Christian world.[64]

Small wonder that religious Christians enthusiastically supported Magnes's ideas. Zionism purely as a cultural or spiritual force was quite palatable, and, after all, Magnes thought also of Christians when he spoke for the internationalization of religious sites. Moreover, the rabbi supplied the means for cloaking opposition to political Zionism in moral and religious terms that could in no way evoke charges of antisemitism. "Magnes's word," Stephen Wise bitterly commented, "made it possible for Jews and Christians alike to speak up for the Arabs and against the Jewish position as they would not have dared to do but for that word." Even John Haynes Holmes, despite his personal ties to Zionists, congratulated Magnes for "one of the noblest utterances that I have ever read" and confided that he, Holmes, had tried to say the same thing in his book on Palestine.[65]

A warmer response to the objectives of the *yishuv* and Zionism, especially in the immediate aftermath of the riots, came from a few Christian quarters. The Federal Council of the Churches of Christ was sympathetic, and so was the Good Will Union, an organization that worked to foster greater understanding between Christians and Jews. Samuel Cavert, general secretary of the Federal Council, lavishly praised the revival of Jewish culture and other accomplishments of the Zionists in Palestine, and the Good Will Union convened a mass meeting of Catholics and Protestants at which it endorsed the Balfour Declaration and called on England to fulfill the provisions of the mandate. Zionist journals played up those sympathetic statements, but they failed to see that the Christian friends ascribed a purpose to Zionism that transcended Jewish yearnings for self-fulfillment. Palestine would become a laboratory, the Christians hoped, for resolving interreligious antipathies and creating "a model to all the nations of good will in action." It would restore Jewish consciousness of their prophetic mission to draw the world in the paths of peace.[66]

D. THE ZIONIST RESPONSE

The Zionists and their partners understood the importance of American public opinion, both Jewish and non-Jewish, in any attempt to influence negotiations between England and the Jewish Agency. As one important official in the ZOA stated, "In the last analysis American public opinion is almost our last card and the strongest weapon that the Jewish people have today."[67] Winning that opinion, however, grew increasingly elusive. It may have been impossible to convert those whose opinions rested on religious doctrine or blatant antisemitism, but no sustained strategy was followed to counter the general skepticism and hostility that Zionism evoked.

The obstacles to changing the tenor of public criticism were formidable.

The followers of the Agency could point neither to a united Jewish point of view with which to impress Christians nor to significant Christian support for influencing uncommitted or antipathetic Jews. Having failed with the liberals and Christians, they witnessed the use of articles from the *Nation* and the *Christian Century* by Arab lobbyists. Even Gentile friends of long standing required special persuasion. Julian Mack confided that if not for modifications that he and Stephen Wise had urged upon John Haynes Holmes, and the fact that Holmes was "such a fine fellow," his book would have been highly critical of Zionism. Another attempt by the Brandeis group, this time to brief Elizabeth MacCallum of the Foreign Policy Association (FPA), who was planning a pamphlet on the Palestine conflict, ended in total failure. Despite the time invested, her pamphlet turned out to be only a detached account of the interests of the Jews, Arabs, and British.[68]

The MacCallum episode, which involved only the Brandeis faction, typified the Zionists' unsuccessful forays into the field of public relations. Crippled by interorganizational disunity, none of the three groups, acting separately, had the means or desire to assume the tasks of an ongoing campaign. Brandeis and his associates enjoyed valuable contacts in the world of opinion-molders—the FPA, Walter Lippmann, the *New Republic, Survey* magazine, the Scripps-Howard newspaper chain. In recognition of the urgent need to sway public opinion, they toyed with various ideas. Brandeis talked vaguely of a corps of writers to answer critiques of Zionism as they appeared in the press, and he and Frankfurter recommended the publicization of the welfare measures of the *yishuv* that benefited Arabs. For the legal aspects of the situation, Frankfurter advocated a pamphlet or sourcebook that would contain, among other things, the Faisal-Frankfurter correspondence of 1919. The interchange between the Arab prince, later king of Iraq, and the American Jew contained a warm welcome and an offer of cooperation with the Zionists in Palestine.[69]

Nevertheless, Brandeis and his chief lieutenants preferred to use their influence behind the scenes and not to work openly in a public relations campaign. They rationalized that should they be called for high-level consultations, they needed to abstain from public statements that could prejudice their position with American and British policymakers and the Jewish Agency. Brandeis broke his silence only once, when he felt the need to counter Magnes. Frankfurter similarly declined to argue the Zionist case in the *Nation* or the *New Republic* or in a debate with an Arab spokesman. He was by far the most capable person to discuss the correspondence with Faisal, but he left the task to others. Not until the Passfield White Paper in October 1930 did Frankfurter enter the public arena.[70]

Waiting to be tapped for diplomatic negotiations may have been an honest motive, but it betrayed an arrogance and unwillingness to debate with "commoners" at a time when the Zionist cause desperately needed the talents of astute public defenders. In the case of Frankfurter, who had those talents and

who had insisted that *how* demands were couched was as important as the demands themselves,[71] nonparticipation in the public discussion of Zionism was
a clear abdication of responsibility. Only when the Brandeis group recaptured
leadership of the ZOA in the summer of 1930 did they become more outspoken, but by that time public opinion had been lost.[72]

The second group, Felix Warburg and the non-Zionists, had the money to
mount a public relations campaign, but they lacked the machinery and the
willingness. Their customary inclination to shy away from publicity was manifested in their opposition to Jewish rallies and to open controversy with non-
Jews. The non-Zionist leader suggested the formation of a committee on public relations but only with the limited function of issuing statements to the
government or to other bodies that were deemed necessary by the Agency's
London committee on diplomatic relations. Moreover, Warburg's distaste for
Louis Lipsky led him to dismiss the Zionists' plea for funds to underwrite the
public relations work of the ZOA. Semiticist Cyrus Adler, the most knowledgeable of the non-Zionists, also refused to get involved. He could have well answered the accounts of Jewish atrocities that appeared in Arabic newspapers
but he refused, and he also turned down a request from *Current History* to
comment on an article by the venomous anti-Zionist Pierre Crabites. The
American Hebrew, traditionally the mouthpiece of the non-Zionists, was of no
help at all. It had turned to anti-Zionism under the editorship of Rabbi Isaac
Landman and preferred to find fault with political Zionism rather than to defend the Jewish Agency.[73]

Of the three American Jewish groups only the ZOA laid plans for a
systematic campaign to earn non-Jewish as well as Jewish support. The executive appointed a Committee on Public Information (CPI), which came up
with elaborate suggestions: formation of a Pro-Palestine Committee of leading Christians; a series of pamphlets summarizing all angles of the Jewish position in Palestine, to be distributed to government officials, editors of all newspapers and journals, and public figures in every important community; articles
signed by prominent Jews for the most important periodicals; several radio
broadcasts by eminent Jewish and non-Jewish speakers; a special conference of
newspaper reporters and other representatives of the press to answer anti-
Zionist charges on an informal basis.[74] Ambitious and costly, the plans were
carefully conceived. They covered all nerve centers of public opinion, and by
focusing on Christian allies they were designed to prove that Zionists were not
an isolated and friendless minority. Unfortunately for the cause, most of the
plans fell through before they could be implemented. The Zionists had access
to competent writers and organizational machinery through its chapters, but
Zionist headquarters in London provided neither money nor cooperation.[75]
Time was another major hurdle. The unexpected attacks from the liberals had
caught the Zionists unprepared and had given their critics a crucial six-week
advantage. A concentrated, high-pressure counterattack might have permitted

the ZOA to catch up, but in light of the interfactional rivalry, the likelihood of capturing the initiative was unreal.

Although the combined assets of the three factions with respect to talent, contacts, organizational network, and money could have permitted a respectable Jewish campaign, none of the groups was prepared to consolidate forces. Left on its own, the ZOA watched helplessly as its initial blueprint disintegrated. All that was salvaged from the drawing board were plans to distribute an article by Meyer Weisgal of the ZOA from *Current History*, MacCallum's report for the FPA, and Maurice Samuel's book, *What Happened in Palestine*. Of the three only Weisgal's was an in-house product.[76]

To be sure, those pieces, like the occasional sympathetic articles that appeared in the national press,[77] outlined the major themes for the defense: 1) the elemental need of Jews and the Jewish people for a national homeland; 2) the Jews' historic right to Palestine, which was recognized in the Balfour Declaration and mandate and approved even by the Arabs (i.e., in the Faisal-Frankfurter correspondence); 3) Zionist accomplishments in Palestine that raised the Arab standard of living; 4) the absorptive capacity of the land, which could support continued Jewish immigration; 5) no intention on the part of the Zionists to violate Arab rights but rather a desire to live together amicably. Some elaborated on the theme of Arab-Jewish friendship, distinguishing between the Arab peasant and his real oppressor, the effendi, and Maurice Samuel stressed instances of Arab help to Jews during the riots. Most of the writers, however, shied away from the two questions of paramount importance to Americans: How could the democratic principle of majority rule be dismissed in the case of Palestine? And, in light of an intransigent Arab nationalism, could a Zionist state be sustained without the use of force?[78]

Too few and far between, the handful of articles made no perceptible dent in American public opinion. Nor did speeches by foreign dignitaries—General Jan Smuts of South Africa and Major Daniel Hopkin of the British Parliament—who were hosted by the ZOA. Their remarks were featured in the Jewish press, but the Zionists never packaged them for use as propaganda weapons within the larger community. The *New Palestine* also garnered statements of support from prominent Englishmen, including Winston Churchill, but since the journal spoke to a limited audience that needed little convincing, such ammunition was wasted.[79]

The inadequacies of the Zionist public relations efforts cannot be attributed solely to outside obstacles. The ZOA almost as much as the Warburg and Brandeis groups hardly put up a fight. They failed to call upon experts in public relations, they devoted more time and energy to partisan issues, they never tapped their regional chapters for help in reaching the public, and the CPI preferred to talk about diplomacy and politics. An aura of drift and an inability to persevere overlay their activity. After a few months of planning and discussion the CPI discontinued its meetings. At the beginning of 1930, when the Lipsky administration locked horns with the Brandeis-Mack faction in anticipation of the upcoming ZOA convention, any semblance of an ongoing public relations campaign was abandoned.

The poor showing of the Jews in the public debate was of inestimable help to the Arab-American lobbyists. The Arab nationalist movement in the United States had emerged in 1918 in response to the Balfour Declaration and the preparations for the Paris Peace Conference. In a religious and cultural as well as political sense anti-Zionism united Christian and Muslim Arabs. Wilson's support of national self-determination became their *leitmotif* and Christian missionaries and anti-Zionist Reform Jews their respected allies. In 1929, following the enlargement of the Agency and the riots, Arab-American nationalist forces were reinvigorated. Now an active lobby, they sent letters to statesmen and delegations to the State Department, in which they indicted British imperialism and wealthy American Jewish supporters of the Agency and put forth their demands for scrapping the Balfour Declaration and revising the mandate. Enjoying two advantages their Jewish opponents lacked, unity and the support of the liberals, they spread their message through their newspapers and in free lectures for clubs, college groups, the YMCA, and the FPA. They courted uncommitted Jews by talk of cultural Zionism and by playing up the Magnes plan.[80]

An Arab delegation despatched by the Arab Executive Committee in April 1930 sounded a more bellicose note. Only the outright repeal of the Balfour Declaration could lead to an understanding between Jews and Arabs; Zionists were a "foreign political power" in Palestine, and no fundamental difference separated the militant anti-Arab Revisionists from Weizmann; even the Orthodox Jews whose settlement in Palestine antedated the Zionists were suspect. The proper solution for Palestine was a parliamentary government representing both Arabs and Jews, but without faith in the Zionists, the Arabs were not prepared to open direct negotiations.[81]

The most prominent of the Arab propagandists during the year after the riots was Ameen Rihani, a Lebanese-born poet and man of letters who projected the romantic image of a moderate working for the spiritual union of Western and Arab cultures. Tireless in his efforts to generate sympathy for Arab nationalism, he met with Secretary of State Henry Stimson, lectured across the country, and wrote articles for the national press on the dangers of Zionism to the Arabs and the entire world. Meyer Weisgal of the ZOA, who met Rihani privately, reported that the Arab was a pacifist as well as a strong nationalist. Weisgal suggested a public discussion between Zionist representatives and Rihani. It would indicate, Weisgal thought, the sincerity of Zionist intentions to resolve the impasse with the Arabs.[82]

The ZOA steered clear of any organizational contact with Rihani, but in private capacity, leading Zionists crossed swords with him in debates sponsored by the FPA. At several debates Jacob De Haas represented the Zionists. Unofficial accounts of one such contest dwelt on Rihani's skills; he was "fluent, persuasive and . . . unscrupulous." Playing to the emotions of the crowd, the Arab called for the burning of the Balfour Declaration. If the Palestine stalemate was not broken, he warned of pan-Islamic uprisings in the Middle East and India. Because his audience included missionaries as well as Arabs and their sympathizers, even a brilliant Zionist performance, which DeHaas did not give, would not have defeated him. Observers also commented on the palpable antagonism and antisemitism of the audience. "Never before in my life," one said, "have I felt or seen antisemitism in mass." At several debates the British point of view was also represented, and where the Englishman sided with the Arabs, the Zionist case was totally crushed.[83]

Bested on all fronts in the contest for public support, Zionist and non-Zionist activities grew less and less impressive. In May 1930 they protested England's ban on Jewish immigration into Palestine, but again they failed to direct or channel the local wildcat outbursts of American Jewish communities. Shortly thereafter, when Jews and Arabs all over the world lobbied the Permanent Mandates Commission of the League of Nations during its deliberations on the Palestine question, the voice of organized American Jewry was conspicuously silent.[84] As a result of factors that had been operating since September 1929, the debate over Zionism was never much of a debate at all, and the wherewithal to pressure the British and American governments on behalf of Zionism failed to materialize.

Failure in the 1929 debate underscored the fact that the Jewish nationalist movement in the United States had reached an extremely low point. Although American Zionists had been ever-ready to accommodate to American opinions and Americanize their movement, the debate focused on Arab rights and had comparatively little to do with the compatibility of Zionism and loyalty to America. Indeed, since Zionism had faded by then into philanthropic Palestinianism, there wasn't very much left in its ideology to Americanize. True, the Zionists persisted and did what they could. They abandoned talk of a state, and they denied that the *yishuv*'s behavior was either immoral or undemocratic. Such denials, however, often redounded merely to a "they said/we said" interchange and had little effect. The sad truth was that Zionism, regardless of how much it had been Americanized, was still unacceptable to many Americans. Only a crisis of the magnitude of the Holocaust would effectively silence the majority of vocal anti-Zionists.

Exactly a year after the riots and less than three years before Hitler assumed office, Zionist sympathizer Pierre Van Paassen lamented American Jewish neglect of public opinion. He wrote: "We saw before our very eyes how the great wave of moral indignation which swept America . . . was not seized and held and that instead public opinion was dangerously allowed to swing . . . in a totally different direction." He predicted more accurately than he knew: "Other storms may arise for Israel some day somewhere in the world. In that day there must also be non-Jewish voices heard in defense of Israel."[85]

CHAPTER 4

A Modern Synagogue in Jerusalem[1]

Throughout the ages Western visitors to Jerusalem found a city whose very streets and stones bore the weight of Jewish history. The presence of Christians, Muslims, and their holy places was, moreover, a constant reminder of the centuries-old interplay among the three major faiths. Visitors in the early 1920s also saw a city of contrasts, in Rabbi Judah Magnes's words "a country of extremes," "the contact of old and new civilizations," "frontier life and dress-suit life." Specific contrasts were blatant: narrow streets where donkeys and camels competed for right of way with the occasional automobile; abject poverty and disease among the natives, many of whom were homeless and dependent on the alms they received from well-fed, well-clad tourists; nuns and monks in religious garb rubbing shoulders with *chasidic* rabbis dressed in caftans and *streimels* (fur hats adapted from eighteenth-century Polish garb); yeshiva students with long coats and ear locks alongside male and female *chalutzim* in shorts and blouses; a cacophony of sounds—municipal bells, chimes of churches and monasteries, and calls to prayer from Arab minarets.[2]

The city, however, was on a path of modernization. Although the population, around eighty thousand on the eve of World War I, had declined significantly during the war years, immigration and urbanization were raising the number once again. Jerusalem was fast spreading into newly built neighborhoods with modern residences, stores, hospitals, and cultural facilities. But in that city of contrasts traditional Jewish religious services went unchallenged. The city abounded with synagogues, both Sephardic and Ashkenazic, as well as those of various *chasidic* sects, but all camps were light years away from the "liberalization" of Judaism in the Western sense.[3] Dr. David Yellin, a prominent educator in the *yishuv* who was then deputy mayor of Jerusalem, summed it up in an interview with the *United Synagogue Recorder*: "Jerusalem has 300 Synagogues and yet has no Synagogue. That sounds paradoxical, but this is what I mean: it has no Synagogue which is inspiring—no Synagogue where the service is decorous and dignified."[4]

During the mandate period, religiously observant Americans who visited

Jerusalem were sharply critical of the religious condition in Palestine, where the Jewish population was polarized between the old-fashioned Orthodox and the modern secularists. Some reasoned that by planting a modern religious movement between the two antithetical poles, they could best provide a needed alternative. Since political wrangling over the future of a Jewish state had reached a plateau with the Balfour Declaration and the mandate, the time seemed right for concentrating on internal matters. Vast sums were still required for building the physical infrastructure of the *yishuv*, and American Zionists continued to contribute a goodly share, but the more they gave the more they believed that they had earned the right of direct intervention. In this instance they planned to export an American product for use in the *yishuv*. Although their focus was on religion, they were in effect setting the Americanization of Zionism on a new course. Zionism in the United States had been tailored to meet American standards, and now the object was to impose an American feature on the developing society in Palestine, i.e., to shape religion in the *yishuv* in the mold of American Judaism.

For a short time during the 1920s an attempt was made to establish a modern Western-like synagogue in Jerusalem. Given Reform's rejection of Zionism, a Reform synagogue at that time was unthinkable, but some thought that there might be a chance for traditionalism in modern dress, or what we today would call Conservatism.* The push came from a few Americans Jews in Palestine who were joined by several others from England and Canada. Although this group of "Anglos" was small in number, it included people of influence and distinction—Rabbi Judah Magnes, soon to be appointed first chancellor of Hebrew University; Henrietta Szold, the founder of Hadassah, and her friends, Norman Bentwich, the attorney general of the mandatory government in Palestine, and noted academicians. A common language drew these people together, and so did a similarity of cultural and intellectual backgrounds; all were familiar with the modern religious movements of Reform and Conservatism. An informal and fluid group, the members were brought together in various social and recreational activities of the *yishuv*. They explored the country together, entertained and were entertained together, and

---

*I use the word *Conservative* to denote a middle-of-the-road position between traditional Orthodoxy and Reform. In the United States of the 1920s a Conservative union of congregations did exist, but the movement itself was amorphous, including congregants who preferred traditional Orthodox worship as well as those whose tastes were closer to Reform. All agreed that religious services required modernization, but as Jonathan Sarna convincingly shows,[5] the boundaries between denominations at that time were permeable rather than rigid, and overall guidelines for Conservative beliefs and practices had yet to be fixed. The same range of opinions applied to the group I discuss here, and although they didn't refer to themselves as Conservative, I use the term for the group for want of a more precise label.

together attended the same lectures and concerts. Age made little difference where commonalities of background obtained, and young Western students mixed comfortably with their socially prominent elders. Not all of the group were committed to settling permanently in Palestine, but since they hoped for Jewish creativity in a Jewish national home and for means to satisfy their personal religious needs, they labored even as noncitizens to break the Orthodox monopoly over Jewish worship.

The following pages trace the first steps toward Conservative-like services in Jerusalem. It discusses the *Chevra* (group) led by Magnes, who designed an altered ritual for traditional synagogue services. The story continues with the involvement of the *Chevra* with another attempt at Westernization, that by the founders of the Yeshurun congregation. Within a very short time the Magnes group failed, both as an independent force and as a determining influence on Yeshurun. The essay concludes with an account of the "adoption" of Yeshurun by the United Synagogue of America (the organization of Conservative synagogues). A seemingly insignificant episode in and of itself, the failure of a modernized Judaism to take root in Jerusalem between the two world wars reflected problems that continue even today to militate against attempts at establishing a meaningful Conservative presence in Israel.

Magnes and the Chevra

The master planner of a modern form of worship was Judah Magnes (1877–1948).[6] A native of California, Magnes was ordained at Hebrew Union College in Cincinnati. Despite his Reform training, he soon emerged as an ardent Zionist, and, earning a reputation as a gifted orator, he preached Jewish political and cultural nationalism in the two Reform pulpits he filled in New York. Falling under the influence of Solomon Schechter, president of the Jewish Theological Seminary, he became an ardent disciple of the Conservative leader, who taught spiritual Zionism and "historic Judaism," i.e., a Judaism that sought to blend traditionalism with modernity. At Temple Emanu-El, the prestigious Reform "cathedral" in New York, Magnes's Zionism as well as his attempts to instill tradition into synagogue practices alienated his elitist congregation, and he was forced to resign. A year at New York City's leading Conservative synagogue, B'nai Jeshurun, where he labored to build a synagogue-center along more traditional lines, also ended in failure.

Meantime, the rabbi had developed a strong following among the newly arrived immigrants. His behavior abounded with contradictions—a sympathetic biographer called him a dissenter and nonconformist. He was at one and the same time a close friend of the Jewish patrician leaders and a champion of the masses who fought for democratic organization of the community, a spokesman for cultural pluralism in an age when the melting-pot philosophy predominated, a rabbi constantly wrestling internally with questions of theology who nevertheless worked with secularist radicals and Socialists, and a pacifist when America entered World War I. During the war Magnes recoiled from political Zionism—he called the Balfour Declaration a product of British imperialism—and at odds with Zionist leaders Chaim Weizmann and Louis Brandeis, he soon became an ardent supporter of a binational state in Palestine.

Ultimately distanced from both "uptown" and "downtown" New York Jews, Magnes left the active rabbinate and his native land in 1922 when he, his wife, and his three young sons set sail for Palestine. Jerusalem held out the promise of intellectual growth and spiritual fulfillment, but without a position awaiting him in Jerusalem (he was first tapped to head the newly created Hebrew University in 1924), he was unsure whether he would stay. Adjustment was difficult, but it was eased by his association with scholars and planners for the university, government officials, and especially two other disciples of Schechter, Henrietta Szold and Norman Bentwich.[7]

Among other topics that Magnes and his friends discussed was the organization of a modern religious service. Like other Westerners, they probably regarded the Sephardic style as a curiosity and *chasidic* services as interesting displays of fervent piety, but neither one could fulfill their personal needs. On the other hand, the Ashkenazic style as it existed was also unpalatable. To be sure, it was familiar to them; it was the Judaism of their ancestors in central and eastern Europe, which their fathers and they, the first generations of Reform and Conservative Jews in the Western world, had labored to alter along Western lines. Moreover, precisely because of its familiarity, it exuded neither the charm nor the emotional pull of the Sephardic or *chasidic* practices. In Jerusalem in the 1920s the same features of Ashkenazic services to which the original devotees of change had objected—squalid premises, a lack of decorum, raucous prayers, little if no congregational participation in the service, and what was regarded as a total lack of dignity—aroused the Westerners' distaste. (Henrietta Szold said that the situation created a "spiritual homesickness.")[8] Unlike the vast majority in Jerusalem, the Westerners were comfortable only with a modernized form of prayers. But theirs was a Judaism that spoke to neither wing in the *yishuv*, the Orthodox or the secularists. Those secularists who had come directly to Palestine from eastern Europe were not drawn to the Westernized style. Discarding the one type of Judaism that they knew, Orthodoxy, they had no understanding of or use for Conservatism or Reform. Strange as it seems, the Orthodoxy they had abandoned remained in their eyes the one authentic Judaism. Magnes and his friends could count, therefore, on the support of only a very small number.

Some two years before Magnes came on the scene, an informal Conservative-like Shabbat service had been instituted by Henrietta Szold. One of her biographers explained: "Finding the available ultra-orthodox synagogue services, in which women were completely segregated, not to her taste, she gathered a group who held their own services which were conducted along the conservative lines of her father's [Rabbi Benjamin Szold's] service in Oheb Shalom Synagogue in Baltimore. They were held in the home of Jessie Sampter, the poetess and Henrietta's dear friend."[9] One of the participants, Professor Alexander Dushkin, a prominent educator trained in the United States, recalled that the core group consisted of himself and his future wife, Szold and several of her friends, and Bentwich and his two sisters. Dushkin recounted that "the service was not traditionally complete—but it did include a *d'var Torah* [lesson on the Torah reading] and discussion on the portion of the week or some current problem, given by a member of the group." Szold herself told a little about the service in a letter to a friend: "At present we are reading the Mosaic lesson, the prophetical portion, and we are studying Jeremiah." But she was not optimistic about the group's progress: "We are still holding on. . . . But we are not creating even the smallest germ of anything vital."[10] Upon those modest beginnings Magnes endeavored to build a new congregation.

Barely four months after his arrival, the American rabbi was giving serious thought to the creation of a modern synagogue. At first he considered building a synagogue via a Jewish center. His scheme, far more ambitious than Szold's, required financial assistance unavailable in Jerusalem. Magnes therefore turned first to several non-Zionist Jewish patricians in New York. Not only had he mixed with them socially, but he had frequently been their link to Palestinian affairs. In Jerusalem he served as their guide when they visited the country, and he labored to cultivate a sympathy on their part for the *yishuv* and for projects relating to the upbuilding of the land. When banker and philanthropist Arthur Lehman, for example, spent a week in Palestine, the Magneses were the ones who awakened his enthusiasm for the country.[11] Since political Zionism was no longer a real issue after the Balfour Declaration, Zionists and non-Zionists (like Lehman) were able to cooperate in the physical and cultural development of the country.

A short time later the rabbi acted upon his idea of a center in Jerusalem. He wrote to Arthur Lehman's brother Irving, a justice of the New York Supreme Court, asking whether the Jewish Welfare Board, of which Lehman was director, had any funds for the erection of a Jewish center. Not only did a center derive from Magnes's belief that Judaism pervaded all Jewish activity, extrasynagogal as well as synagogal, but as he explained in a similar appeal to Louis Marshall, the influential president of the American Jewish Committee, Jerusalem needed a center *before* a synagogue: "Here, if anywhere, the Temple will have to be approached through many a vestibule, and a Jewish Center might do great things for the religious life." Hoping that a center might serve as the means of attracting those alienated from traditional Judaism back to religion, he explained his ideas more fully in a long letter to the powerful American Jewish banker and non-Zionist Felix Warburg:

Every group and community here has a central building with the exception of the Jews. Some of the structures are very beautiful. . . . If you see a fine building you can be sure it is not Jewish. This has a peculiar effect upon visitors and tourists, who either despise the Jews for their neglect of the Holy City or pass through in blissful ignorance of what the Jews are trying to do here. Whatever be my views of Palestine, it is not possible to forget that Jerusalem is the Holy City of three great religions and that thousands come here every year. What is done or not done here by the Jews must reflect upon the whole Jewish people one way or another.

But what is of the utmost importance is that the Jews of Jerusalem, particularly the young men and women, have no place where they can gather for religious, educational and social work. A Jewish Center here would be the first step towards attaching to the Synagogue many who are unable to go to the existing old [synagogues]. This is true of the increasing number of Americans and Europeans of education and spiritual refinement. A Jewish Center here would also serve as a place—the only place in the whole community Jew or Gentile—where lectures, concerts, conferences, congresses could be held under proper auspices. . . . This is a project about which everyone could unite, whatever his political or religious views. . . . This is an opportunity for many persons who are not Zionists to do something of value not only for Jerusalem, but for Judaism generally.

Magnes chose his words carefully. His appeal to Warburg was calculated to jibe with the religious and universalist sentiments of the non-Zionist. He talked about a center, not exclusively for Zionist activities but one that would do credit to "the Holy City of three great religions." His emphasis was on the spiritual and religious—"centers of spiritual life," a place for people of "spiritual refinement," a project that could unite every Jew "whatever his political or religious views."[12] Finally, Magnes's stress on the need to enhance the image of Jews and Judaism was a consideration that always aroused the sensitivities of American Jewish leaders.

Magnes's plan for a Jewish center, in which a synagogue would be just one component, was not new. While serving in the rabbinate he had toyed with the idea of a "People's Synagogue" that could appeal to the masses. He had also hoped to create a center out of B'nai Jeshurun. Other leading rabbis, like Mordecai Kaplan and Stephen Wise, were on a similar track. The center idea became increasingly popular with Conservative rabbis after the war, when their synagogues were spreading into new suburban areas. Although some believed that a center failed to augment synagogue attendance, or that a center's extra-synagogal activities were in fact secularizing the synagogue, the concept of integrating Jewish activities under the all-encompassing umbrella of a synagogue-center held sway in the 1920s.[13]

Warburg visited Jerusalem for a few days in the winter of 1923–24, and under the influence of Magnes and Chaim Weizmann his attitude toward Palestine grew more positive. A major donor to the Hebrew University, he sounded very much like Magnes when he said that "while Christian and Moslem institutions abounded, Jerusalem, the spiritual center of the three main religions, had few institutions to inspire the Jews." He also told Cyrus Adler, Schechter's successor at the Seminary, that Jerusalem lacked any dignified synagogue. Adler suggested that the Conservative congregations in America under the aegis of the United Synagogue might provide for such a synagogue, but nothing immediate resulted.[14]

The Szold-Magnes group now turned exclusively to the idea of a synagogue. In 1923 they held their own services on the High Holy Days. On Rosh Hashanah, in what he called "lively" services, Magnes was the Torah reader, and Bentwich read the *haftarah* (portion from the Prophets). At the Yom Kippur services, which Sir Herbert Samuel, British high commissioner for Palestine, also attended, Magnes and Bentwich both preached. Bentwich publicly announced that the group was preparing for regular Sabbath services after the holiday season and that Magnes "has promised his assistance." Indeed, the rabbi devoted many hours to thought and discussions with the other group members on the form and organization of a congregation. Given the influence of the Orthodox rabbinate and the pervasiveness of popular loyalty to Orthodox ideas, if not Orthodox practices, he came to realize that any significant change regarding prayer or ritual would require a long and arduous struggle.[15]

A few days after the holidays Magnes formulated the "General Principles" and "Regulations for the Services" for organizing the *Chevra*.[16] The statements drew from the input of the entire group, but Magnes was the dominant influence. The "democratization" of the services and the emphasis on universal brotherhood and social justice (see text below) were clearly his contributions. Nor did Magnes the nonconformist hesitate to suggest practices that American Conservative synagogues, or for that matter Reform temples, had not yet adopted. Seemingly inoffensive to the casual reader, the proposed innovations were quite radical in the eyes of the traditionalists.

The text of the "General Principles," as edited and amended by the group, enumerated the objectives:

1. Respect for, and as far as possible, adherence to the Jewish tradition as to religious services. The *Chevra* will, however, give its own emphasis to this or that part of the Service. [In his first draft Magnes was more extreme, stipulating that "the *Chevra* will, however, when occasion arises, use the traditional material and refashion it, or give it an emphasis acceptable to modern men and women."]

2. The complete conduct of the Services is to be in the hands of members of the *Chevra,* and is not to be entrusted to professional readers, singers, or preachers.

3. The active participation of the whole congregation in the Services is to be sought, i.e. in the congregational singing, in alternate responses, and in their freedom to say prayers with complete devotion and enthusiasm.

4. Fostering among the members a love of Torah, by encouraging the members

to read their own Torah portions, by discourses on the *Sedra* [Torah portion] of the day, and perhaps through study groups.

5. The complete equality of the sexes. This is to be expressed as far as possible within the tradition, but also in ways that the tradition has not provided for.

6. The Hebrew language shall be the language of the Services and of the discourses. Exceptions may be made by the *Chevra*. . . . The general rule shall be: Better a poor Hebrew than none.

7. The *Chevra* will endeavor to point out the present day implications of the teachings of social justice and human brotherhood as inculcated by the Torah, the Prophets and the history of the Jewish People.

8. In order to emphasize the brotherhood of Israel with all of humankind, appropriate selections (in harmony with the Jewish spirit) from the religious literature of other peoples and religions shall find an appropriate place in a Hebrew translation either before or during or after the discourse.

"Regulations for the Service" elaborated on or amended the "General Principles." The most interesting for a so-called Conservative congregation at that time concerned the *shacharit* (first section of morning prayers),Torah reading, and the place of women. The provision on *shacharit* stated: "The *Shacharit* is to be emphasized as the main part of the service and not the *Musaf* [second section of morning prayers], as is the present custom. At the end of the *Shacharit* . . . there is to be a pause, to enable the Congregation to leave either for the *Kotel Maaravi* [Western Wall] or for home. Those wishing to remain for *Musaf* may; but the *Musaf* is not to be a chief element of the service. It is merely a *Musaf*— an appendage, an addendum."

With respect to Torah reading, the "Regulations" fleshed out the "Principles": "Each person [with certain exceptions] called to the Torah is to read his own portion, with or without the *Niggun* [special chant]." As for the rights of women, which apparently raised most discussion within the group, the following modification was made: "Women shall be eligible for participation in all parts of the service on the same conditions as men. Men shall sit on one side and women on the other side of the congregation." Equal participation, contradicted immediately by the provision for separate seating (albeit without the physical barrier employed by the Orthodox), was not defined. This "Regulation" was a far cry from Magnes's original "Principles," which had hinted at a more sweeping change of tradition. At the end of the "Regulations," Magnes appended a note designed to protect the independence of the group, perhaps from the Orthodox rabbinate. It read: "A *Chevra* is a membership society organized primarily to meet the needs of the membership. . . . [It]organizes for a specific purpose, gets a membership, and goes ahead without asking too many questions of persons outside the membership."

The "Principles" and "Regulations" bore the stamp of a Reform rabbi turned Conservative who ventured beyond the typically moderate Conservative practices. Magnes did not hesitate to change either the order of the prayers or the accepted roles of women and of the cantor and preacher. He explained in his journal that "the Western Synagogue must be in the tradition, and in Hebrew, but it must above all things seek to accommodate itself in *thought* to the best Western mind." Eastern customs and traditions could remain, but *"ideas* must be the first consideration." His Reform background underlay his explanation of the *Musaf* prayer: "The *Musaf* is a substitute for the sacrifices. But Westerners do not really believe in the restoration of sacrifices. So why pray for them? Something, ancient or modern in its wording, on sacrifice can be substituted."[17]

The input of Magnes's associates, far less radical than the American rabbi's, was also discernible. It seems clear, for example, that Bentwich worked closely with Magnes on the drafts of the statements. Others were also consulted, and, as in the United States, differences of opinion obtained. At no point does the evidence suggest that Magnes resisted amendments offered by the group; he even accepted changes that distinctly curbed his crusading bent. Nevertheless, he soon realized that his advanced ideas stood little chance of acceptance: "Tell Bentwich," he wrote in his journal, that "I think we must give up all ideas of any 'reforms' in Prayer Book and Service, because neither he nor I will stay to fight for them, and it will not do to quarrel over little things."[18]

The Chevra *and Yeshurun*

At this point the story of the *Chevra* took a decided turn. Apparently, there was another small group in Jerusalem that was seeking a "modern" synagogue. The organizer was one Louis Lober, a young American then residing in Jerusalem, who worked as a clerk for the government. Arriving in Jerusalem in the fall of 1920, he recalled more than fifty years later: "I . . . felt keenly the absence of a modern traditional central synagogue outside the walls of the[Old] City, which would be especially appealing to youth. I discussed my idea with other residents and friends, who agreed that there was a crying need for a synagogue in Jerusalem with true decorum and congregational singing. While all people I talked to thought it was a great idea, most of them tried to discourage me, saying Jerusalem was not ready for this so called 'revolutionary' idea and it was doomed to failure. With much persistence I finally succeeded in getting a small group of young men interested in this project, all between the ages of 20 to 26. The action was slow and no urgency was felt; a real impetus to get started was lacking."[19]

Shortly after the High Holy Days of 1923, Lober's group learned of the *Chevra* and its plans "to start a Reform Service." (Like the average American Jew of the day, Lober apparently thought that any deviation from Orthodox custom was Reform.) Magnes explained the *Chevra* 's purpose to Lober, and the latter suggested that perhaps the two groups could organize "a traditional service and pray together in an atmosphere of reverence and decorum, which would preclude the need of a Reform service." Indeed, an agreement with the *Chevra* would have been a feather in Lober's cap, for his group could not boast of members with equal social status and prestige. Bentwich for one was amenable to Lober's idea. He told Magnes privately that Lober and his associates were "almost pathetically anxious to combine with us." He advised that if the *Chevra* won the necessary endorsement of the rabbinate, it would be well to join with Lober. If the rabbis did not approve, "then we can take a more independent line, but let us make an effort to keep within the *tzibur* [community]."[20]

When the two groups met, the *Chevra* proposed the adoption of the "Regulations." Both sides had thought that a merger might be possible, but because of the *Chevra's* stand on women's rights there was no agreement. Just as that group insisted on equal participation, so Lober's group refused to accept it. The *Chevra* promised to think over Lober's suggestion that the matter be referred to chief rabbi Abraham Isaac Kook for a decision, but in the end, without further consultations either with the other group or with the chief rabbi, the *Chevra* decided against compromise and to go its own way. On the first Shabbat of the Hebrew new year, the group held its first formal service.[21]

Lober responded by calling a meeting of his group, and he convinced them that in light of the new "Reform" *Chevra*, the need to begin their own service was of the utmost urgency. Organization proceeded rapidly; space was secured for religious services at a school, and one member contributed a Torah scroll. A second scroll presented a bit of a problem until Lober turned directly to the chief rabbi. Lober recalled that "Chief Rabbi Kook was very much impressed with our plans, which also had a special goal of attracting the youth. Appreciating our dilemma, the Chief Rabbi unceremoniously went to his *aron kodesh* [holy ark] and took out his own Sefer Torah, wrapped it in a silk cloth and handed it to me with his blessing." Thus equipped, weekly services of Lober's group were inaugurated shortly after those of the *Chevra*.[22]

Ironically, they—those who according to Bentwich were "pathetically anxious" to join the *Chevra*—succeeded while the latter failed. Lober recounted the sequence of events in a piece that he wrote fifty years later:

> We started our [services] on Shabbat, parashat Noah [chapter Noah in Genesis], 5624 [1923]. As our membership consisted of both Ashkenazim and Sephardim, and even though the form of prayer was to be essentially *nussach Ashkenaz* [Ashkenazic rite], we introduced the revolutionary innovation of reading all the prayers and the Torah in the Sephardic pronunciation, or as it is now universally accepted, as the "mifta Israeli" [Israeli pronunciation]. We introduced congregational singing from the start, with melodies from various Sephardic and Ashkenazic communities in different parts of the world. Many of those tunes are being

sung by the members of our congregation to this day. There was no professional
hazzan [cantor], and members officiated each Sabbath in turn. . . .

As the congregational singing in the synagogue was heard by passers-by, it attracted many people who came in to see, and many of them joined us. Our reputation spread so rapidly, that it also brought a visit of a committee from the Reform group. They too enjoyed the service and were so impressed that, within two
months the Reform group disbanded and most of their members joined us,
which proved that there was no need for a Reform Service in Jerusalem. Dr.
Magnes immediately became an active member, and said that his sons would be
Bar Mitzvah in our synagogue. Among the first women from this group to join
us, was Miss Henrietta Szold . . . with her secretary Emma Ehrlich. Miss Szold attended services regularly, although she protested against being seated behind a
mechitzah [a divider between the men's and women's sections]. Other prominent
women who prayed in our synagogue were the famous Miss Annie Landau, the
Head Mistress of the Evelina de Rothschild School for Girls and her deputy, Mrs.
Moss Levy. [Both women were English and had had connections with the *Chevra*.
Landau, as opposed to Szold, supported separate seating.] The Sabbath attendance grew so rapidly that within one month of its existence we had over one
hundred worshipers, which proved the crying need for this type of synagogue in
the new developing section of Jerusalem. . . .

It is interesting to note that our synagogue was the only one that had the blessing of both Chief Rabbi Kook and Rabbi Sonnenfeld of the [right-wing] Agudat
Israel. . . .

The group formally organized a congregation—which American Jews would
have called modern Orthodox—and came up with the name Yeshurun. According to Lober, "a constitution was drawn up with a preamble stating that
'the purpose of Yeshurun is to foster unity among Jerusalem Jewry in accordance with Traditional Judaism and National Aspirations,' by means of: a. well
organized religious services with congregational singing; b. study circles and a
library; c. cultural and social activities; d. youth activities; e. social service. . . ."
Lober concluded his account with the claim that Yeshurun had served as the
model for other synagogues in the *yishuv* that introduced congregational singing and adopted Sephardic pronunciation in an Ashkenazic ritual.[23]

Because of the dearth of documents, details of the *Chevra*'s last days remain
unknown. Why did the group give up after a short existence of two months?
Did it vote as a unit to affiliate with Yeshurun? Did Magnes continue to call the
signals? One source, the diary of Simon Greenberg for 1924, a year after the
Chevra began, ignored the *Chevra* entirely but mentioned Magnes's presence in
Yeshurun. Greenberg, who was then a young rabbinical student at the Jewish
Theological Seminary spending his last year of study in Jerusalem, told how he
struck up a close friendship with Lober. Greenberg wrote that on Yom Kippur
eve, "I . . . went to pray at the synagogue of which Lober is president. It is the

'modern' synagogue of Jerusalem, because they don't shout at will during the prayers, and because decorum is preserved. In Jerusalem that is considered modernity in religion. All of the high officials of the government pray here." Greenberg said about Magnes, "It was interesting to watch Magnes, the one time Temple Emanu-El Rabbi—praying now as the most Orthodox of Jews."[24]

In retrospect it is not difficult to understand why the *Chevra* failed and Yeshurun succeeded. The two groups replicated each other in some ways; both emphasized congregational participation and decorum, and neither employed a professional cantor or rabbi. But the differences transcended the similarities. For Yeshurun, and also for Jerusalem at that time, other changes in the services were too radical. Most observant Jews did not reason as Magnes did that *musaf* was merely an appendage. They neither saw any reason to change the order of prayers nor, above all, were they prepared to accept equal rights for women. If American Conservative congregations had made little progress on those issues, it was totally unrealistic to expect more in Jerusalem. Worshipers at Yeshurun, unconcerned by what their neighbors thought of their synagogue and its style—which for Conservatism in the United States was a weighty considera-tion—found the services sufficiently modern and attractive by the inclusion of congregational singing, Palestinian pronunciation, and decorum.

Nor was it politic for the *Chevra* to compete with Yeshurun. The chief rabbi had given Yeshurun his approval along with his Torah, but without rabbinical acceptance, the *Chevra* and its members individually were beyond the pale of respectability. Furthermore, Yeshurun had attracted the younger element in Je-rusalem or the same group desired by the *Chevra*. Lacking that, the *Chevra* would be left merely with a handful of "Anglos," some of whom were not plan-ning on permanent residence. Magnes, who as noted above had despaired of serious change early on, may have felt that it was wiser to join Yeshurun and at-tempt to influence policy from within. But any effort along those lines also failed. According to Bentwich's biography of Magnes: "The 'Yeshurun' Congre-gation . . . belied his [Magnes's] and others' hopes as regards the form of ser-vice; and he did not remain for long on its Board."[25]

On a deeper level, the *Chevra*'s program was doubtless too cerebral for the average layman in the *yishuv*, who like Lober probably didn't know the ideology of Reform or Conservatism. Perhaps if Magnes and his associates had started first with small study groups for teaching principles of Conservatism, they might have scored greater success. They who had enjoyed some connection with the Jewish Theological Seminary or Solomon Schechter rationally ac-cepted "tradition and change," but they failed to raise and answer questions on Conservatism and *halakhah* (Jewish law), particularly on matters of individual beliefs and praxis for the modern Jew.

At bottom, precisely because it was an *American* product, Conservatism was too alien for the *yishuv*. Born of the desires of the eastern European immi-grants and their children to acculturate rapidly to American modernity and

non-Jewish tastes, it mirrored a society where the conditions for popular acceptance were totally different from those of the Jewish homeland. Whereas
American Jews strove for a "respectable" religious style that discarded "outlandish" Orthodox practices but yet permitted the retention of ethnic loyalties,
Jews in a Jewish homeland never felt the same pressures. The early *olim* to Palestine and the eastern Europeans in America may have shared the same grand-
parents, but the country to which each group immigrated determined how they
shaped their religion.

The United Synagogue and Yeshurun

During the 1920s, when Zionism in America became Palestinianism, concentration shifted from the political aims of the movement to the economic needs
of a Jewish Palestine. On those grounds non-Zionists united with Zionists in
working for a Jewish *home* rather than a Jewish *state*. Conservative leaders in
America concentrated specifically on yet another element, the need to develop
the cultural and religious resources of the *yishuv*. President Cyrus Adler of the
Jewish Theological Seminary had suggested to Felix Warburg that the United
Synagogue might provide for an "appropriate synagogue" in Jerusalem, and the
project appealed as well to the two arms of the Conservative movement, the
United Synagogue and the Rabbinical Assembly. "We must not forget," an early
editorial in the *United Synagogue Recorder* declared, "that the soul of the Jew is
his religion. Whether in Palestine or in the Diaspora; therein lies his inspiration, his strength, his hope."[26] Insisting that contributions to Palestine did not
end with planting trees or building hydroelectric sites, Conservative spokesmen
said that Jews in the United States could and should contribute to the building
of institutions like synagogues, community centers, and the Hebrew University. More than before the rabbis preached about a Jewish Palestine, not one of
secular Zionism, but one that would serve as the spiritual and cultural center of
Jews throughout the Diaspora. Not only did the cause of spiritual Zionism fit
their very *raison d'être* as ministers of religion, but it aimed to forge an
American-*yishuv* partnership whereby each center would contribute meaning-
fully to the other. Just as Jewish life in America was strengthened by a Jewish
home in Palestine, so could the *yishuv* benefit by American input on religious
and cultural matters.

   An emphasis on the religious and cultural also enriched American Zionism,
by injecting a new enthusiasm, at least for the religious minded, into a movement that had lost much of the glamour and attractiveness of the Brandeis era.
In the pursuit of their goal, none of the Conservative leaders disputed the right
of American Jews to meddle in the affairs of the *yishuv* or attempt to influence
its religious character. Rabbi Max Drob, president of the Rabbinical Assembly
in 1927, stated bluntly: Since our men bear the brunt of the United Palestine

Appeal (an American national fund-raising agency for Palestine), "we are therefore justified in demanding that the upbuilding of Palestine should be spiritual as well as economic."[27]

The idea of a cultural-religious enterprise undertaken by their movement was pushed by Conservative Jews who visited Palestine. For example, Sarah Kussy, a member of the Women's League of the United Synagogue, recorded her impressions of religious life in Palestine in 1923 for the express purpose of having the United Synagogue undertake its own project in Jerusalem. After describing the abominable features, especially for female worshipers, of the city's Orthodox synagogues, she stressed the importance of modern religious services and religious education for adults and children. A modernized form of worship, she said, might even appeal to the secularist and agnostic *olim* from eastern Europe. At least as important were the needs of the Western "Anglos." Referring specifically to the Szold-Magnes group, she saw the members as "the nucleus for what will probably become a modern congregation, the first in Jerusalem," and she advised the United Synagogue to stay in touch with them. Kussy also pressed strongly for a YMHA or a community center in Jerusalem that would attract "modern young people" and would protect them from the blandishments of the active Christian proselytizers. At present, she concluded, no organization except the United Synagogue was in a position to make a religious contribution to the *yishuv*.[28]

Kussy's essay touched several important themes, which were picked up and developed by those who followed. First, unlike the Szold-Magnes group and more like Magnes's original notion, the focus shifted to something larger than a synagogue—i.e., to a community center or a synagogue-center. Second, the concerned American Jews stressed the needs of the "Anglos," especially their fellow Jews who had left the United States for Palestine. (However understandable, that reason stemmed from the mistaken belief that a significant American *aliyah* was under way. Actually, at the end of the decade there were only some two thousand Americans residing in all of Palestine.)[29] Third, the desire to protect Jewish youth in Jerusalem from the missionaries also found a receptive audience. Kussy herself warned of the danger a few years later. The YM/YWCA didn't discriminate against Jews, she said, but *"neither do the missionaries."* Finally, the idea of building on the Yeshurun congregation, which had swallowed up the Szold-Magnes group by the time Kussy wrote, had taken root.[30]

The theme of underwriting the Yeshurun congregation seemed eminently logical. (It was understood from the beginning that the contribution of the United Synagogue would be a *gift* to the *yishuv* and hardly an effort to establish its own synagogue.) The United Synagogue could not easily run a synagogue-center from New York,[31] and Yeshurun appeared to be a successful and ongoing venture, albeit without its own building. Its modernized style and plans for expanding into a social and cultural center made it very much akin to an American Conservative synagogue-center of the 1920s. Furthermore, in light of the traditionalist bent of most Conservative synagogues in the United States at that time, worshipers at those synagogues would find little distasteful in Yeshurun's traditionally Orthodox services.

But in effect, the decision to cooperate with Yeshurun was an admission of the weakness of Conservatism and the United Synagogue. The Conservative union was organized in 1913, but no consensus had emerged on what Conservatism meant. Yeshurun was entrenching itself as an Orthodox synagogue—modern perhaps in style but nonetheless Orthodox—and one that, as Magnes had learned through personal experience, was resistant to further innovations. The Americans doubtless knew of the *Chevra's* unsuccessful endeavors to launch a less-traditional prayer group, but that failure did not motivate them to try again. What is most striking about the United Synagogue's venture was the fact that Conservatism as a viable or desirable alternative to any form of Orthodox worship in Jerusalem never even figured in the American discussions. The Americans stressed the benefits for the "Anglos" and for Jerusalem youth, but other than an insistence on modernization, which was never really defined, nothing in the records indicates any attention to the matter of planting the Conservative movement in Palestine. Nor did the United Synagogue plan on "converting" Yeshurun. It may have decided on the basis of Magnes's attempts that it was wiser to proceed slowly, but that too was never debated. Just as the *Chevra* had bowed out in favor of Yeshurun, the very decision to adopt Yeshurun meant a further capitulation to Orthodoxy.

In the summer of 1924 Rabbi Samuel Cohen, executive director of the United Synagogue, visited Palestine. He interviewed numerous civic, religious, and educational leaders in Palestine, as well as Magnes, for the purpose of ascertaining what the United Synagogue could do to further the "spiritual development of our Homeland." He concluded that the first step toward developing a vibrant religious life in Palestine was to strengthen Yeshurun. That modern congregation needed a synagogue-center, and proper physical facilities would enable it to expand as well as to serve as a model for other congregations.[32]

A second visitor to Palestine the following spring was Israel Levinthal, the Conservative rabbi of the Brooklyn Jewish Center. Committed to the United Synagogue's project, he stated that the Jews who had settled in Palestine sought a "spiritual" as well as secure life. Although they faced the same religious problems that American Jews faced, "the youth . . . want to do something to keep themselves and their younger brothers and sisters within the influence of their ancient faith." The rabbi gathered enthusiastic endorsements from Chaim Weizmann and from prominent Jews in the *yishuv,* including Chief Rabbi Kook, for the synagogue-center idea, and he undertook negotiations with Yeshurun. Louis Lober of Yeshurun reported that Levinthal had come to Jerusalem to investigate the advisability of "presenting" Yeshurun with a building along the lines of an American Jewish center. Lober also arranged for the rabbi to meet Sir Herbert Samuel, and the latter added his warm approval. Yeshurun impressed Levinthal personally: "No finer or more inspiring picture can greet the visitor in Jerusalem than the religious services conducted by the Yeshurun Organization. . . . Never shall I forget the fervor and devotion of their service, the dignity, the decorum, the sanctity with which these young people participated in it." The rabbi later told how, on the eve of his departure from Jerusalem, a group of young men, including some from the United States, gave him a message for American Jews: We ask them for "an understanding of our spiritual needs. They have helped to give new life to the soil of Palestine. Will they not do something to keep alive the soul of the Palestinian Jew?" Nothing in Levinthal's words revealed that he was a Conservative rather than an Orthodox rabbi, and like Samuel Cohen he never talked of exporting Conservatism.[33]

Meantime, the United Synagogue had appointed a Committee on Palestine. At its first meeting in December 1924, the committee considered Cohen's report and recommended that a movement be launched for the erection of a synagogue-center, which they called the immediate need of Jerusalem youth. For the present, some wanted to postpone the idea of a synagogue; in due course, they said, an appeal "will go forth to the Jewry of the world for the greater and more imposing task of building the Great Synagogue of Catholic Israel." Nevertheless, the idea of a synagogue along with a center became the formal objective, and the Committee on Palestine went on record in support of a "Recreational and Religious Building" to be located in Rechavia, a new section of Jerusalem.[34]

Under the sponsorship of prominent Conservative rabbis, a national campaign for the synagogue-center was launched in October 1925.[35] Endorsed by the Rabbinical Assembly, the undertaking was also welcomed by leaders of the *yishuv*. Dr. David Yellin, who was then in the United States, sounded much like Sarah Kussy when he too emphasized the need of a synagogue appropriate for the thousands of visitors from America and other places and for those Americans and British who had settled in Jerusalem. Since the United Synagogue had announced that the synagogue was to serve world Jewry as well as the *yishuv*, individual Jews in Holland, Egypt, and South Africa also expressed their support.[36]

The campaign itself was directed by a committee under the chairmanship of Levinthal and the vice-chairmanship of Henrietta Szold.[37] A second committee, on which an American representative served, was set up in Jerusalem to assist in planning and administration. The initial plans divided the major tasks among the United Synagogue and its two branches, the Women's League and the Young People's League; the men would pay for the site and construction, the women were to furnish the synagogue, and the young people were responsible for furnishing the center. The funds required for building the center—estimated first at $150,000 but soon revised upward to $300,000—were to come from the member synagogues affiliated with the United Synagogue. (The cooperation of Orthodox synagogues was not solicited.) It was assumed that contributions from Jerusalem would help defray the costs.[38]

Levinthal summed up the ambitious plans, on which both committees agreed, while the United Synagogue was negotiating with architects. Filling the spiritual, cultural, and social aspirations of the *yishuv*, the rabbi reported, the synagogue-center would provide classrooms, conference rooms, stage facilities, a dance hall, a gymnasium, and a restaurant. But, "the central feature of this building is to be a Synagogue of such dignity and character as would be worthy of the city in which it will stand and the people whom it would serve."[39] As the plans took shape, the American committee yielded to Orthodox sentiments without any reservations. For one thing, it was agreed that the United Synagogue would not dictate the form of the services. Secondly, they adopted the idea of *several* buildings, because they realized that the Orthodox in Palestine would oppose combining secular and religious activities under the same roof. Clearly, the fear of alienating Jerusalem's Orthodox took precedence over any desire to service Conservatism.[40]

The campaign took off auspiciously. Within a few months the United Synagogue raised more than $86,000 in pledges, and the Women's League raised almost $25,000. In 1926 the Americans purchased a site on King George V Avenue, a block reputed at that time to have "one of the most beautiful views over Jerusalem." Construction was begun, but until its completion the Yeshurun congregation was permitted to erect temporary huts on the land for its activities.[42] The momentum of the first year, however, could not be sustained. Despite genuine enthusiasm at the beginning, the passing years brought no significant progress; building was at best sporadic, and in the next decade the project slowly petered out.[42]

Many factors contributed to the failure of the venture. The separate vested interests of the various participants compounded by poor coordination doomed hopes for speedy results. Serious controversy, for example, divided the United Synagogue and the Women's League. The bulk of the women's fund was loaned to the men for the purchase of the site, but the men, who had promised full recognition of the women's efforts, ignored the fact that the money was a loan that they had promised to repay. The two groups also quarreled on when to send payments to Jerusalem, even as costs were escalating annually. Differences arose too between Jerusalem and New York on monies promised by the former as well as on debts that the Jerusalem committee had incurred. Finally, a proper relationship with Yeshurun, whose cooperation was the keystone of the whole plan, was at best only casually established. (When Cyrus Adler visited Palestine in 1929, he was asked to confer with Yeshurun, but nothing further developed from that interchange.)[43] Meanwhile, external conditions—the Great Depression in the United States, Arab riots in Palestine in 1929 and the '30s, and the worsening of the Jewish condition under Nazi Germany—deflected attention and resources from the synagogue-center.

In the end the United Synagogue, forced to admit that it could proceed no further, ceded the land and the unfinished synagogue to the *yishuv*. Dashing the hopes of its supporters, its record was far from impressive. One Conservative rabbi who visited Yeshurun in 1948 was shocked by the yet-unfinished building and the ignominious end of a noble effort. "Is this the best . . . the United Synagogue could do?" he asked bitterly. The United Synagogue's contribution to religious life in the Jewish homeland amounted merely to another, in this case unfinished, gift from American Jews. Yeshurun lived on as an Orthodox congregation, and any hope of a more Conservative-like synagogue in prestate Jerusalem rapidly faded.[44] For all intents and purposes, the experience of the original *Chevra*, now but a dim memory, became a relic in the annals of history.

CHAPTER 5

The Social Worker and the Diplomat:
Maurice B. Hexter and
Sir John Hope Simpson

From its formative years to the 1920s American Zionism had consistently labored to fashion a product acceptable to Americans. Zionists heeded the
cues of public opinion, but the actual Americanization of their message was
their own work: they downplayed the relevance of Herzlian ideology for
American Jews, they latched onto cultural and religious Zionism in place of
Jewish statism, they were content after the war with a watered-down Palestinianism, and they unhesitatingly followed the guidelines of American foreign
policy. By the time of the 1929 riots, there was very little left in the Zionist design to Americanize.

In 1929, however, the American non-Zionists, now recognized as equal partners in the enlarged Jewish Agency, attempted to sharpen still further the
American features of the Zionist program. Major differences still separated
them from mainstream Zionism, and, influenced by the anti-Zionism of respected liberals and by Judah Magnes's plan for a binational Arab-Jewish state,
they openly expressed their opposition to Jewish political nationalism. Like the
liberals and Magnes, they questioned the rectitude of a Jewish Palestine where
the population was predominantly Arab. They too held that a Palestine without
Arab rights was undemocratic and hence un-American. Were they to sway the
Agency to their side on the Arab question, they could perhaps impress their fellow Americans by underscoring how American the Jewish interest in Palestine
really was. Increased non-Zionist input into Agency policy would also be a step
toward the Americanization of Zionism worldwide.

The leader of the American non-Zionists and chairman of the Agency's
Administrative Committee was banker Felix Warburg. Warburg, who sought
a larger role for himself in Zionist policymaking, bypassed the Agency and
his partners in the Zionist Organization of America (ZOA) by appointing a

personal emissary, social worker Maurice Hexter, to represent him and the non-Zionist position on all issues before the Agency after the 1929 riots. When Hexter's duties were expanded to include direct negotiations with the British on the Palestine impasse, he became the first American Jew to negotiate unofficially over a period of many months with a representative of a foreign power.

Warburg vs. Weizmann

The death of Louis Marshall only days after the riots of 1929 made Warburg the predominant American non-Zionist in the enlarged Jewish Agency. Unfortunately for the Agency, the new alliance of Zionists and non-Zionists began to unravel almost immediately. The close friendship between the Warburgs and Chaim Weizmann notwithstanding, Felix was jealous of the powers exercised by Weizmann, president of the Agency, and the Zionist members of its executive. As chairman of the Administrative Committee, he claimed that Weizmann and his associates kept him uninformed about developments in the *yishuv* and about Anglo-Zionist relations. According to Warburg, they did not consult him about policies and strategy that they devised, thus usurping powers that rightfully belonged to him and his committee. The banker also found fault with Weizmann for his "inept" leadership of the numerous Zionist factions and for his inability, or lack of desire, to control the ZOA.[1] Warburg's wealth, his easy access to American officials, including the president, and his ties to other monied non-Zionists assured him the right to criticize even as they forced Weizmann, despite his resentment, to preserve a show of amity. Louis Marshall, far more astute than either Warburg or Weizmann, might have been able to reconcile the personal differences between the two, but in his absence the rift between the American and the European reached a critical point soon after the riots.

Deeper issues underlay the tension. The banker and his close associates—important figures in American Jewish public life like Cyrus Adler, James Marshall, and James Rosenberg—had little patience for Zionists and Zionism. They regarded the ZOA as a troublesome lot; loud and quarrelsome, its aggressive nationalist propaganda endangered the welfare of American Jews. Nor did Warburg's men understand the ethnic sentiments that explained Jewish support of Zionism. True, a Jewish center in Palestine could serve as the refuge for persecuted European Jews—and they as good philanthropists contributed to the physical growth of the *yishuv*—but, like the negative assessment of Zionism by the press and the liberals, they held that a Jewish *state* was undesirable and impractical. Not all went so far as to urge the scrapping of the Balfour Declaration, but they focused not on England's promise of a homeland but on a qualifying clause in the declaration that read: "it being clearly understood that nothing shall be done which may prejudice the civil and religious rights of exist-

The Americanization of Zionism, 1897–1948

ing non-Jewish communities in Palestine." If the British promise clashed with Arab rights, the American non-Zionists preferred to whittle down Zionist goals. In short, they prescribed the same behavior for the Agency that they expected of American Jews: accommodationist toward the government and majority opinion, and unswerving in loyalty to political democracy.

Warburg's circle wanted the Agency to concentrate on economic and cultural projects of benefit to both Jews and non-Jews. Warburg for one saw Palestine as the spiritual center of Muslims and Christians as well as Jews, and he talked of interreligious committees to bridge the gaps that separated the different faiths. In light of such views as well as the social prominence of the non-Zionists, England carefully cultivated their friendship. For example, when Prime Minister Ramsay MacDonald visited the United States in the fall of 1929, he spent a weekend with the Warburgs on their summer estate.[2]

Differences over ideology and tactics made the Warburg-Weizmann rift virtually impossible to heal. Both men tried to ignore ideology while they quarreled, understanding that the modus vivendi between Zionists and non-Zionists that had been hammered out in the summer of 1929 was at stake, but tempers grew short. More than ever, Warburg wanted an American representative of his own choosing in Jerusalem, who would also be in close contact with the Agency's headquarters in London. His first appointments for posts in Jerusalem went to social worker Maurice Hexter and Tammany lawyer Jonah Goldstein. Goldstein, who arrived first, was assigned the task of bringing order into the chaotic relief program for the victims of the riots.[3]

Acting under Warburg's directive to keep the banker informed on all matters, Goldstein was inevitably drawn into the politics of the *yishuv* and its relations with England. He made his opinions known to prominent Zionists and to British officials in Jerusalem, but his arrogant and pushy manner alienated important people. He was discredited further when a story circulated about his alleged remark to the high commissioner that bribery of the Arabs was more effective than an English commission of inquiry.[4] Goldstein left Palestine before he had a chance to work alongside Hexter, but his performance made Hexter's task more difficult.

Meantime, Warburg attempted to build up his influence in other ways. Since non-Zionists did not constitute an organized group, he cultivated individual European and American non-Zionists, and he brought a few men with whom he was working on the Joint Distribution Committee (JDC) into his camp. He also corresponded over Weizmann's head with prominent Europeans engaged in Palestine affairs, such as England's Alfred Mond (Lord Melchett) and Sir Osmond d'Avigdor-Goldsmid and France's Baron Edmond de Rothschild. Whether Zionist or non-Zionist, such men were bound by the ties of wealth or banking, a relationship that often transcended loyalty to Weizmann and the Agency. To all whose support he desired, Warburg confided the same complaints about Weizmann, the Agency (whose middle management, he said, was made up of "little people" who talked too much[5]), and the ZOA. More daring were his independent forays into diplomacy, again made possible by his wealth and international connections and by the contacts he established with Prime Minister Ramsay MacDonald and other British officials. Indeed, he liked to think of himself as the "liaison officer" between the Agency and the British Colonial Office.[6]

Warburg found a representative more suitable than Goldstein in Maurice Hexter. Born in Cincinnati to lower-middle-class German parents, Hexter was ambitious and resourceful even as a young boy. Upon his completion of a doctorate in statistics at Harvard, he chose the field of social work, in which he rapidly advanced. As director of several large federations, he developed administrative skills as well as the ability to draw up budgets, allocate resources, and raise funds. Federation work and important service in the JDC after the First World War opened up a wider world. His cleverness, diligence, and fine sense of humor earned Hexter the recognition and respect of the lay leaders of the American Jewish community, wealthy men who sat on the boards of federations and devoted time and money to the needs of their fellow Jews. Among them was Felix Warburg, whose friendship Hexter enjoyed from 1924 until the banker's death in 1937. Many years later Hexter wrote that Warburg had been one of the two "most fascinating and shrewdest men of my time" (the other was David Ben-Gurion).[7]

Hexter's contacts led to an appointment in 1927 to the Joint Palestine Survey Commission, a group of experts despatched to Palestine shortly before the enlargement of the Jewish Agency to assess the economic needs of the land. The work of the commission taught Hexter much about the different Zionist organizations, and, at the same time, widened his acquaintanceship with leading Jews from England and the Continent. Warburg and Louis Marshall then sent him to Zurich, where, in 1929, he was nominated to be one of the American non-Zionists on the Agency's executive. Now drawn into Palestinian and Agency affairs, he kept in very close touch with Warburg, and in the aftermath of the riots it was quite natural for the banker to tap him for a Palestine post.

Warburg's offer was enticing. Hexter would become the secretary of the Agency's Administrative Committee as well as Warburg's "mouthpiece and earphone" in Jerusalem. The thirty-eight-year-old social worker was eager to set forth on what he called this "high adventure." Although the abrupt change in career was a gamble, Hexter doubtless calculated that he had little to lose. The job could only add to his professional experience and sophistication, and service for Warburg, especially if it proved successful, virtually guaranteed him any desirable post in the American Jewish world upon his return from Jerusalem. Well aware of the difficulties awaiting him in Jerusalem in the fall of 1929, Hexter commented, "I was an outsider—a non-Zionist—in a world of true believers."[8]

For his part, Warburg spoke glowingly about Hexter to Chaim Weizmann: "He is so delightfully orderly in his thinking apparatus that I really hope I will get a fuller picture, after he has seen you and after he has reached Palestine, than I am getting now." Warburg wanted Hexter to take charge of the distribution of relief funds, but with complete trust in his choice, he gave Hexter the open-ended power of committing him, Warburg, on any matter. Within a matter of weeks Hexter was relaying significant news to Warburg about Weizmann, Judah Magnes, and British and Arab opinion. Despite his efforts, however, he failed to resolve the impasse between Warburg and Weizmann on the distribution of powers within the Agency.[9]

To ensure Zionist respect for his representative, the banker made Hexter a non-Zionist member of the Agency's executive. Weizmann had suggested that Hexter first serve at least temporarily as secretary of the executive, but Warburg objected. He said that Hexter deserved the position because he had held administrative jobs superior to other Agency executives. Weizmann accepted the decision with good grace, reasoning that since Hexter was Warburg's alter ego, he could function "as a very valuable liaison between the PZE [Palestine Zionist Executive] and America." Although some Zionists justifiably complained that Warburg showed his suspicions of the executive by his special relationship with Hexter, Europeans and Americans in Warburg's circle soon corresponded directly with Hexter.[10] Nor did it take long before Weizmann, appreciative of Hexter's cooperation, confided in him too.

Goldstein had made little progress on the relief situation, but using his training and experience in Jewish social work, Hexter handled the job with despatch and efficiency. Under his direction a relief committee, the Emergency Fund, was organized to examine claims and decide on disbursements. In his new Packard, a gift from Warburg, he drove around the country three days weekly, assessing the havoc wrought by the riots and visiting settlements and sites that needed rebuilding or new facilities. When the immediate relief tasks ended, his committee went on to devise plans for overall reconstruction. In detailed cables (mostly in code) to a satisfied Warburg, Hexter kept the banker well informed about the work and the costs of various projects.[11]

Hexter had not yet entered the world of diplomacy, but his diplomatic abilities were already evident. His work with the boards of federations had demanded such skills, which, over the years, he had honed to a fine art. Before he reached Palestine, Warburg added to his experience, despatching him to Washington to consult with Justice Louis Brandeis on Palestinian affairs, to London, where he worked out details of the Emergency Fund with Melchett and Avigdor-Goldsmid, and to Berlin to establish communication with Felix's brother Max.[12] Once in Jerusalem, Hexter's abilities were again apparent in the way he placated relief applicants.

The very task of working so closely with Warburg also called for diplomacy. Hexter never fawned upon the banker, but he scrupulously asked for instructions, even when not absolutely necessary, and he generally was quick to identify with Warburg's opinions. For the most part such reactions came easily, because the non-Zionist Hexter shared his chief's views—support of England, sympathy for the plight of the Arabs, and opposition to Jewish statehood. If he differed with Warburg or suggested something that the latter had overlooked, he made it seem as if he had taken his cue from what the banker had intimated or had meant to say. The fact that Hexter became the confidential messenger between Warburg and Weizmann, implicitly entrusted by each with information for the other, proved his skill at handling two sensitive men so often at loggerheads.

Hexter was quickly drawn into myriad subjects other than relief. The conditions he coped with, however, had grown more grim—a deepening world depression that cut off funds for Palestine, divisiveness in Jewish ranks caused by Magnes, an animosity between Zionists and anti-Zionists that appeared to intensify by the week. He made frequent trips to London and the Continent for visits to prominent men and to attend Agency committee meetings. As his role expanded, he became a well-known figure in the *yishuv*. On a visit to Palestine, American Zionist leader Julian Mack heard that Hexter had made himself beloved and respected by all Jews; for his part, Warburg told an Agency committee that Hexter, "a perfect soldier in our camp," had brought commitment and enthusiasm to *yishuv* affairs.[13]

Warburg felt more in control by the beginning of 1930. His handpicked team was in place and functioning well. He was in close contact with Agency officials Oskar Wassermann and Bernard Flexner,[14] and he developed an ongoing and satisfying correspondence with Melchett and Avigdor-Goldsmid of England. He also appointed Werner Senator, formerly of the European JDC, to be treasurer of the Jewish Agency and his personal representative in Jerusalem alongside Hexter. Another former executive of the JDC, Joseph Hyman, became his assistant in New York, dealing largely with Palestinian affairs. The appointments of Senator and Hyman were not for lack of confidence in Hexter—indeed, the Warburg/Hexter connection was growing stronger. Although no sharp division of functions was formulated, Senator's concentration was on the economic affairs of the Agency other than relief.

To be sure, Warburg's complaints against the Agency and the fractious Zionists continued, and so did the divisiveness caused by Judah Magnes, but his network compensated at least partially. It permitted his representatives to disseminate his opinions more widely as well as to activate non-Zionists in both Europe and the United States with an eye toward achieving a more equitable balance with the Zionists in Agency affairs. The banker's quarrels with the ZOA persisted, but he was building up a countervailing force by efforts at cooperation with the Brandeis group. If he still was unable to move Weizmann to his point of view, at least he made sure that the Zionist leader was taking the non-Zionists, and the funds they controlled, more seriously. In all these efforts Warburg enjoyed Hexter's unqualified support.

Hexter too had rapidly grown in self-confidence. His achievements with respect to the organization of relief activities, as well as his style, had won recognition and praise from his associates, from British officials and the American consul general, and from the *yishuv* at large. Speaking softly and treading circumspectly with the leaders of the Agency, he gained the confidence of Weizmann and leading Zionists. His natural astuteness and a readiness to cooperate gained their respect and blunted their criticism of "Warburg's boy." His frequent shuttles to and from London and the Continent further enhanced his reputation as a trustworthy conduit of information. The more he was relied on, both by Warburg's circle and by the Zionists, the more independent and secure he felt. At the end of December 1929 he told Warburg that he had constructed a "suitable apparatus" for handling relief problems and that only the details needed to be hammered out. A few days later he wrote, unsolicitedly, that it was "essential" that Warburg consult him, Hexter, before making appointments to the Agency executive.[15] All signs indicated that Hexter felt ready for more delicate assignments.

Hope Simpson Prepares a Report

His opportunity came in the spring and summer of 1930, when the troubled relations between the British and the Agency cast him into the tangled diplomatic web. Tension had been mounting steadily in the *yishuv* since the appearance in March of the Shaw Commission's report.[16] The report had exposed England's pro-Arab bias and had generated acrimonious debate in London and Jerusalem. At a secret meeting with Weizmann, Warburg, and Lord Reading, Prime Minister MacDonald also admitted that the report was "bad and unpleasant." "No one who had not Palestine in his bones could grasp the whole breadth of the problem," he reportedly said. It was agreed that England would send another investigator to Palestine to reexamine the situation, and the prime minister promised to appoint General Jan Christian Smuts of South Africa, a Zionist supporter who was the choice of the Jews. A few days later, however, at a private luncheon with the prime minister, Warburg and Hexter learned that the appointment had gone to Sir John Hope Simpson, a man whose experience lay not in Middle Eastern but in Indian and Turco-Greek affairs, and who was a friend of Lord Passfield (Sidney Webb), the secretary of state for the colonies. His assignment was to assess the economic conditions and potentials of Palestine, a task that included the matters of Jewish immigration and Jewish land purchase. MacDonald reassured his visitors about Hope Simpson, but he offered no explanation as to why Smuts had not been chosen. When Weizmann approached Passfield, who was known to the Jews as a confirmed anti-Zionist, the latter agreed to arrange a meeting between Weizmann and Hope Simpson, but that promise was also broken.[17]

It became evident that Hope Simpson's appointment did not augur well for the Zionists. The Englishman knew virtually nothing about Palestine and understood less about the Zionist cause. In Jerusalem he lived with the high commissioner, Sir John Chancellor, and quickly identified with his anti-Jewish point of view. He liked the Arab fellah, with whom he could sympathize, but he found the Zionist attitude "repellent." The Zionist argument that cultivable land in Palestine could absorb many more settlers in addition to the Arab owners drew the following response: "I have a house in Wales with ten rooms in which I only occupy two; do you suggest that other people have a right to enter the eight empty rooms?"[18]

Nor did the *yishuv* welcome the Englishman. Still smarting under the Shaw report, it had grown increasingly resentful of London and the British administration in Palestine. The weak position of the Jews was compounded by a lack of unity. Magnes and his followers kept up their attack on the Agency and its policies with respect to the Arabs, and the American non-Zionists were leaning toward the rabbi's plan. To make matters worse, only days before Hope Simpson's scheduled arrival, England chose to suspend Jewish immigration into Palestine at least temporarily. Weizmann, who believed that the situation had reached a critical low and was barely on speaking terms with the prime minister, shared his pessimistic views with a convenient go-between, MacDonald's son. "It seems to me a terrible tragedy," Weizmann wrote, "that the whole fate of the Jewish National Home should in a measure depend upon what Hope Simpson may or may not say." The Englishman knew very little about the "moral and political implications" of London's policy. "After we have worked there for fifty years," Weizmann expostulated, "he is to tell us whether we can go on with our work or not. It seems a grotesque position, and is certainly intolerable to us."

On the matter of immigration, even the American non-Zionists were shaken. Indeed, the ban on immigration more than anything else drew the non-Zionists closer to their Zionist partners. Joining the latter, Warburg also protested, albeit mildly, to the British ambassador in Washington. Hexter too was indignant. To be sure, as a non-Zionist and like Warburg a critic of Agency policy, he was interested in peace with the Arabs and a revamped Agency structure in which the non-Zionists commanded a greater say. But, he declared, nine months had passed since the riots, and no progress at all had been made toward peace. Nevertheless, both he and Warburg confidently believed that Hope Simpson might yet be reached by a friendly attitude, and they urged cooperation with the Englishman.[19]

When Hope Simpson reached Jerusalem at the beginning of June, he met with the Agency's executive, but he sought out Hexter for private one-on-one discussions. He knew that Hexter was Warburg's close associate and that the former social worker agreed with the major points of Warburg's position: commutation of the death sentence for the Arab rioters, support of the Magnes plan, immediate bilateral negotiations between the Arabs and the Jews, and a comprehensive peace that joined the Agency, the British, and the Arabs. Those opinions, he realized, were closer to the British than to the Zionist position. For his part, Hexter optimistically awaited his meetings with Hope Simpson. Even the *yishuv,* he cabled Warburg, was reacting more positively: "*Yishuv* fears but hopeful. [Hope Simpson] has favourably impressed those he has already met with knowledge and capacity though [they] may suspect has secret instruction."[20] (The matter of Hope Simpson's secret instructions is discussed below.) Reporting to Warburg once or twice daily, Hexter recorded his impressions of the Englishman and the range of subjects they addressed. The accounts show that he did more than listen; he offered suggestions to Hope Simpson, and, at least so he thought, he successfully influenced the Englishman.

The following are excerpts from Hexter's cables and letters in the Warburg and Hexter Papers that detail developments. For the most part the tone is upbeat:

From a letter of June 5: "After a very interesting session with Sir John Hope Simpson which the Executive as a whole had, I got the impression of eminent fairness and a desire to serve the situation. . . . After I had presented the non-Zionist viewpoint, especially yours, he asked me to come and see him . . . at an early date."

From a second cable of June 5: "Successful conference with special commissioner. Convinced we shall get square deal."

From a cable of June 6: "Long satisfactory private conversation special commissioner. Inform you confidential information—think succeeded convincing him high desirability lifting restriction immigration when protests cease."

From a letter of June 7: "[Hope Simpson] is a very astute man and I am quite sure an honest one. I am, moreover, absolutely certain that a man of his capacity and stature would never have accepted a mission with any secret instructions. . . . He is greatly disturbed over the acquisition of land by the Keren Kayemeth [Jewish National Fund] removing it permanently from sale, and fears the re-creation of the old danger of mortmain. I told him in the first place that the proportion of the land held by the Keren Kayemeth is small as compared with the private Jewish holdings and certainly extremely modest when compared with the total tillable area. In the second place I told him that certainly as far as one can calculate, these lands would always be cultivated by small land owners so that the medieval danger of latifundia does not exist. . . . Another question which is going through his mind is that the Keren Kayemeth already has a reserve of land which should be used for colonization purposes before acquiring additional land. I am quite certain that this will be one of his recommendations, although I told him that the delays in acquiring lands in Palestine made it necessary to have a reserve of land; and secondly a reserve of land was necessary in order to keep the prices of land down. This point I believe he saw.

"He then asked me what I though about the advisability of providing agricultural education for the Fellaheen. I told him that this in my opinion was greatly to be desired and constituted only one of the things which we, as Jews, would like to be seen done for the entire population. I assured him that not alone were we desirous of having this done but that within our powers we would be prepared to cooperate because we were most anxious to build up the entire country with fairness to all. This statement I believe impressed him very much. . . .

"Concerning immigration, . . . I believe that when the furor subsides, he is prepared to make a preliminary recommendation along these lines." [See cable of June 6.]

From a letter of June 9: "Hope Simpson's plan is, and I write it to you in strictest confidence, to prepare two reports; one a private report for Lord Passfield and another, a report which probably will be published. . . .

"[On] the cessation of immigration . . . I told him that a grave psychological blunder had been made and that the Government might find it desirable in connection with whatever measures they felt impelled to make, to consider the method of communicating it to us and the impact which it would occasion; I told him that I thought this had not been done in most instances. He quite agreed . . . , [blaming] the shifting policy of the Government. . . . I believe that if the hue and cry subsides, he is prepared to do something [i.e., toward a rescission of the ban on immigration]. If all goes well, towards the 10th of July we might reasonably anticipate some action. . . .

"Sir John was quite frank in telling me that he believed Sir Herbert Samuel and Lord Plumer [two former high commissioners] had paid no attention whatsoever to the oppressed [Arabs] who, he said, suffer from the unequal competition of the Jewish colonists who have at their disposal a relatively large sum of money, expert advice, and Western knowledge. I replied that this was an inevitable consequence of people who are entering Palestine with a Western culture; but that I believed, with the ebb and flow of time, the differing standards of living . . . would inevitably approximate each other somewhere in between the present points; that I hoped that the Jewish standard would not need to fall very far but that rather the Arab standard would rise. To this he replied that he was quite in agreement."

Hexter summarized the gist of his conversations with Hope Simpson two weeks later in a report to the Agency's Political Committee. There he added that according to the Englishman, the cessation of immigration had been done without his knowledge and "had embarrassed him a great deal." Hexter also claimed that Hope Simpson seemed to have accepted, at least in part, the Zionist emphasis on the need for immigration and labor. In conclusion Hexter said that it was difficult to predict the content of Hope Simpson's report. "One thing was clear: he did not see the Palestine problem as they saw it, but the report would be that of a man who tried to see his task honestly."[21]

The talks with Hope Simpson were supplemented with meetings between Hexter and High Commissioner Chancellor, who worked closely with the special envoy. Hexter never mentioned any instance when his opinions were specifically contradicted, and he claimed that he enjoyed a good rapport with both men. As he cabled Warburg after the first joint meeting, "Extremely successful with both last night." No doubt it was eminently gratifying that in the course of the meetings he became less Warburg's mouthpiece and more an independent strategist who just happened to be the banker's appointee to the Jerusalem executive. He boasted in particular of the "entente cordiale" he had established with Hope Simpson, and he was pleased that the latter had invited him to Athens to help finalize the report two months later. In his opinion, his personal foray into diplomatic negotiations with the British had been successful.[22] Had Warburg been in Hexter's place, he might not have done as well. Hexter's style differed from Warburg's and was more suited to diplomatic negotiations. Whereas the banker was highly emotional, politically naive, and prone to fawning on and identifying with government leaders, Hexter was calmer, more knowledgeable, more skillful at logical analysis, and better able to express his views in hardheaded fashion.

Hexter would have been less sanguine had he taken seriously the rumors flying around Jerusalem of Hope Simpson's secret agenda. The Zionists were hinting darkly that England had compromised the emissary's mission from the start. They charged that London was out to make use of the factional rifts within the *yishuv* and the Agency, specifically to drive a wedge between the Zionists and non-Zionists. Under the influence of the anti-Zionist high commissioner, Hope Simpson would, they said, write a pro-Arab report that would appease the Arabs and capitalize on the disaffection of the non-Zionists. Since the scheme held out the chance of weaning the latter away from the policies of Weizmann and the Zionists, England anticipated the likely collapse of the enlarged Agency.[23]

The story has since been verified by a study of British manuscript sources.[24] It shows that the Colonial Office, swayed by an earlier anti-Zionist memorandum from Sir John Chancellor, had decided on the lines of Hope Simpson's report even before he set foot in Palestine. The strategy called for him to investigate the questions of immigration and land settlement with the aim of helping the Arabs. Since the non-Zionists were not overly disturbed at the prospect of whittling down Zionist political goals, the British would involve them in the actual formulation of Hope Simpson's conclusions. Sensitive to Diaspora Jewish opinion, they hoped thereby to ward off a united Jewish protest against the report and, more important, to cut off the economic aid from wealthy American non-Zionists to the *yishuv*. Hexter, who wrote Warburg on June 7 that he doubted the existence of secret instructions to Hope Simpson, was pivotal to the plan. How better to begin the wedge-driving process than by working on Warburg's confidant and through him on the American circle?

The Hexter–Hope Simpson talks appeared to have closely followed the British scenario; both Chancellor and Hope Simpson played their assigned roles with consummate skill. Nor did Hope Simpson conceal the two major points that concerned him, aid for the fellaheen and the inequities of Jewish land purchases. Although Hexter was neither stupid nor naive, he seems to have been taken in by the Englishman's "fairness." He also erred badly by believing that the final report drawn up by Hope Simpson could change England's predetermined policy. But even though his associates in the Agency suspected him of "intrigues," Hexter was less tractable than London expected. True, he gave Hope Simpson a secret document on the Histadrut (labor federation of the yishuv),[25] but at least according to his written accounts, he made no special case for the non-Zionists, nor did he criticize Weizmann and the Zionists. Sounding rather as if he spoke for the entire yishuv, Hexter reported regularly to Weizmann and the Agency.

Despite the suspicions, Hexter and Warburg persisted. The conspiracy charge was as yet unproved, and if there was the slightest chance of influencing Hope Simpson, it should not be dismissed. Warburg confidently wrote Weizmann a few days after the Hexter/Hope Simpson talks: "I do not think that the sending of Sir John was anything else but the carrying out of the plans which we discussed with the Prime Minister and I regret exceedingly that an excitable Jewish public has been, in this case as in other cases, too ready to put the most unfavorable construction upon every step which was taken." Since Brandeis also commended Hexter's efforts, Weizmann dared not repudiate the social worker or openly attack his venture into diplomacy.[26]

During the summer of 1930 the mood of the Jewish Agency was one of disappointment and despair. The Agency feared a disastrous report by Hope Simpson, and repeated meetings between leading Zionists and a consistently hostile Lord Passfield added to the gloom. As one Zionist official put it," The forces now working against us are of such a magnitude [and] our resources to combat them [are] so hopelessly inadequate." Weizmann, who hinted to associates that he might resign, found no cause for optimism in Hexter's talks with Hope Simpson. The latter met once with Werner Senator, another Warburg appointee, but that proved even less promising. Senator reported that he too thought the Englishman was honest, but that he was misinformed about Jewish work in Palestine.[27] Meantime, Hexter was spending the summer in the United States. In preparation for the next round of talks with Hope Simpson, he met with Brandeis and two of the justice's coworkers, Julian Mack and Felix Frankfurter.[28]

Hexter was called to Athens to meet Hope Simpson in mid-August. Despite his rapport with the Englishman, the American seemed more on his guard and more defensive of the yishuv than he had been in June. He still did not believe that England was trying to drive a wedge between the Zionists and non-Zionists, but those charges had made him more cautious. He made it clear at the outset to Hope Simpson that he was no one's representative: "I think it is due you to say, what I am sure you already know, that I have no mandate, official or otherwise, to negotiate any part of the recommendations you are going to make. I came in a personal capacity because all of us are interested in securing a genuine constructive report for Palestine." Both he and Hope Simpson understood, however, that Hexter would relay a full report to the Agency and to Warburg, which in turn would influence Jewish negotiations with the His Majesty's Government (HMG).

In the course of thirteen hours of discussion, Hexter listened to Hope Simpson's conclusions and was quick to criticize where he disagreed.[29] The heart of the draft report was Hope Simpson's idea of a development commission, a three-man body (one Jew, one Arab, and a British national as chairman) appointed by the League of Nations that would undertake intensive agricultural cultivation of Palestine and thereby make more land available for settlement. Although intensive agriculture could benefit the Jews too, the Englishman was out primarily to improve the conditions of the Arab fellaheen. Hence, he recommended that the commission control the transfer of all land. In effect, that would have put an end to private Jewish purchases from the Arabs as well as the ownership of land by the Jewish National Fund. Sounding more like a representative of the Zionist-dominated Agency than of Warburg, Hexter called the plan discriminatory; if Jewish land purchases were so drastically limited, the very survival and growth of the *yishuv* was threatened. Didn't the express terms of the mandate call for the "close settlement" of Jews on the land? The *yishuv* was not opposed to raising the Arab standard of living, but, in Hexter's words: "The Mandate never contemplated improving [the fellah's] lot *before and at the expense of* doing something under the 'close settlement' clause." Implying that strict control by England over land transfers was unnecessary, Hexter said that Jewish settlers on their own were able to workout a modus vivendi with the fellaheen.

Hexter also questioned Hope Simpson's assumption that Jewish settlement caused Arab unemployment. Well prepared with relevant facts and figures, he contended rather that Jewish immigration, capital, and economic progress also benefited the Arabs. Furthermore, as he told Warburg, "I repeated Brandeis' statement 'we did not come to Palestine to lift up the Fellah but to save ourselves,' but if I know anything of economics, the development of a country helps all within it." Hope Simpson said he agreed, and he promised to rewrite the section on unemployment in his report.

When the American charged that Hope Simpson's estimates of the Arab and Jewish portions of land or financial aid were based on political rather than economic considerations—and hence beyond his jurisdiction—the Englishman again said he agreed. (The criticism, however, made no difference in his written report.) He also accepted minor modifications of the development plan along lines suggested by Hexter. If Hope Simpson had no intention of changing the report but was merely placating Hexter to avoid a major rift with the Agency, he succeeded very well.

The new round of talks dashed Hexter's hopes for lifting the ban on immigration. When the Englishman said that the high number of unemployed warranted restriction, Hexter countered that since the ban affected the image of the government, vacillation on England's part would interrupt the flow of capital from abroad on which the *yishuv* depended. Hope Simpson "was convinced," he said, but he refused to recommend a change. He shifted the blame to the prime minister, explaining that the immigration order had been instituted because MacDonald, "who wants popularity and is vain," had nothing else to give the Arabs.

The Englishman did not divulge the text of his report, but he maintained that he wrote it free of political pressure. At the talks he seemed open to reason and counterarguments, and it appeared that he genuinely liked Hexter. Perhaps to allay the American's suspicions and to prove his own good intentions, he freely criticized both MacDonald and the British administration in Palestine. He concluded his report, he told Hexter, with a challenge to London — adopt the plan for a development commission or renounce the mandate. According to Hexter, Hope Simpson injected another radically new note: "H.S. threw out the hint and I inferred it was to see how far we would go [i.e., whether the Jews would agree], that the Mandate might be dropped and Italy or France take it." Hexter answered merely that England would permit neither of those two powers to assume control. The talks ended with Hope Simpson's statement that he had persuaded Passfield to meet with Warburg and Hexter. A week later in Geneva, Hexter talked with Hope Simpson again, but nothing new was discussed.[30]

Despite the defeats on land transfers and immigration, Hexter saw certain advantages in Hope Simpson's report. As he told Weizmann four days later, intensive agriculture to be underwritten by HMG was one, and the strong criticism of MacDonald's administration was another. Nor were all the Zionists prepared to denounce Hexter or his diplomatic efforts. Weizmann was still suspicious of British moves but was reserving judgment; Brandeis believed that "distinct progress" had been made. To one Agency official who again raised the charge that London was playing up to the non-Zionists, Hexter gave a curt reply: "I told him that Americans were not entirely stupid and that there was a different interpretation possible with respect to the British flirtation with us; namely, they merely wanted to try a different telephone line and we should give them the chance. . . . I also told him we should as far as possible make a fresh start with the government and that I believed his profound distrust, hatred and contempt of the administration did not permit him to view proposals on their merit."[31]

The American, however, was far less optimistic than he had been in June. Even if Hope Simpson was truly independent, and even if Hexter had succeeded in convincing him of the *yishuv*'s needs, the Colonial Office still had the final say. A week after the talks in Athens, Hexter accompanied Warburg to a meeting with Passfield. The invitation, which Hope Simpson had promised them, showed that in London's eyes Hexter was a key player in negotiations. Since the colonial secretary was on his best behavior with the banker, the tone of the conversation, so different from that of the Zionists with the Colonial Office, was amicable. Nevertheless, the Americans scored no positive gain. Sounding much like Hope Simpson on the subjects of land development, labor and unemployment, and immigration, Passfield divulged neither Hope Simpson's report nor the government's reaction to his findings. He too was interested primarily in the fellah, and he too looked askance upon the practices of the Jewish National Fund and the Histadrut. Warburg and Hexter repeated the arguments that the latter had raised with Hope Simpson, but Passfield resorted to platitudes and refused to indicate whether he agreed. When Warburg asked for a positive message on immigration that he could deliver at the upcoming meeting of the Agency's Administrative Committee, Passfield sidestepped the question. More discouraging even than Hope Simpson, he answered vaguely that he anticipated only a slow trickle of immigrants in the future. Hinting that the government was prepared to allocate money for Palestine development, the colonial secretary promised that "we are going to put our back into the job." Warburg had come to the meeting wanting to be reassured, and despite the lack of substantive progress, those few words did reassure him. Still trusting in Hope Simpson and in Hexter's negotiations, he appeared optimistic a short time later at a meeting of the Administrative Committee.[32]

The Agency wasn't shown Hope Simpson's report, but Weizmann knew that it dealt with land purchases, immigration, and Arab settlements—all slanted against the Jews. During September he and other top Zionists had meeting after meeting with government officials and with leading British Jews. The purpose was to ascertain the contents of Hope Simpson's report and the government's statement of policy to be embodied in a white paper; where possible they hoped to do some last-minute lobbying. At the brink of despair, Weizmann reported that Passfield was playing for time, that he changed his mind from meeting to meeting, and that he turned down Weizmann's suggestion for a roundtable conference before the white paper was issued. At this time the Zionist leader observed that what he heard in London did not accord with Hexter's reports on the Hope Simpson talks.[33]

Still in the diplomatic loop, Hexter met briefly with Sir T. Drummond Shiels, a high official in the Colonial Office, and with High Commissioner Chancellor. From the latter he learned that the government had adopted Hope Simpson's report in principle but that it would reduce the amount of funds the Englishman had proposed for Palestine. Hexter spoke again with Hope Simpson, who told him that neither Arabs nor Jews would be consulted before the white paper was issued. The American gave no indication either of his own impressions or of his part in those conversations. Meantime, he continued to enjoy easy access to British officials. When Julian Mack, now the president of the ZOA, desired to meet Chancellor, he turned to Hexter to arrange the meeting.

Despite his doubts, Weizmann too expanded Hexter's diplomatic role. He gave the American permission to meet informally with Arab leaders, provided they knew that Hexter had no power to negotiate for the Agency. Excited at the prospect, Hexter visited the Bedouin tribes in the Jordan Valley in October 1930, and he planned additional "study trips" for the winter.[34] The social worker had become a seasoned observer and negotiator within a year.

The Passfield White Paper

The simultaneous appearance of the Hope Simpson report and the Passfield White Paper in October confirmed the *yishuv*'s fears. On the subject of economic development the White Paper closely followed Hope Simpson's conclusions; it put limits on Jewish land purchases and settlement, it restricted Jewish immigration by linking it to the question of Arab unemployment, and it recommended a government policy of agricultural improvement for the almost exclusive benefit of the Arabs. It did not specifically provide for a development commission, a project that Hexter and Hope Simpson discussed in detail and one that might have been of benefit to Jews too. That omission along with continued restrictions on immigration as well as a biased and hostile tone made the White Paper the more objectionable of the two documents. Even Weizmann said that at least Hope Simpson's report had suggested possibilities on which to build.

The Jewish Agency rose up in protest against HMG's repudiation of the promises of the Balfour Declaration and the mandate. Any expectation that London may have had of dividing the non-Zionists from the Zionists had failed miserably, for the two factions were now united as never before. Charges were hurled against England's breach of faith, deceit, and betrayal, and three leaders of the Agency—Weizmann, Warburg, and Melchett—immediately resigned. Melchett summed up the prevailing bitterness over England's "detrimental" policies: "We can no longer pursue our objectives or spend our money on the quicksands of compromise."[35] Warburg too was angered. He received a long, handwritten letter from Passfield in defense of his actions, but the banker, usually an easy mark for attention and flattery, was unmoved. At the same time, Prime Minister MacDonald attempted to shrug off the belief that England was purposely undercutting a Jewish national home by insisting to one American Jew that the policy statement did not signify any change in the country's objectives. Nevertheless, in response to public opposition and to criticism from Labor's political opponents, he invited Weizmann and others of the Agency to confer with a special cabinet committee.[36]

Hexter had personal reasons to feel betrayed. First, Hope Simpson's report omitted several of his suggestions that the Englishman had promised to include, and second, on the surface at least, the report vindicated those critics who claimed that England had used Hexter in an attempt to wreak chaos within the ranks of the Agency. But although he insisted that he hadn't accepted all of Hope Simpson's arguments, Hexter refused to admit that he had been duped. He told Warburg that he wasn't at all embarrassed. Yet, in a letter to the banker, he sounded a defensive note when he dissected the report, pointing out the good points as well as the bad. There he argued that "we" (i.e., the non-Zionists) could indeed sympathize with some of Hope Simpson's criticisms of the *yishuv*'s practices. Emphasizing the need to distinguish between the good and bad in the report and the totally negative White Paper, he also cautioned against a blanket condemnation of the report or its author. Hope Simpson enjoyed a good reputation in diplomatic circles, and Hexter believed that he would probably advise London on future policy in Palestine.[37]

Still persona grata with the English, Hexter repeated some of his objections to the White Paper in two meetings with Sir John Chancellor. There he sounded harsher than he had before: "I stated that did the White Paper contain anything genuinely constructive we would have perhaps been in position, despite its general critical and cynical tone, to persuade people to accept the whole. I pointed out that the document almost studiedly avoided the good parts of Hope Simpson's report and had included the bad points." He went on to criticize the White Paper's interpretation of the labor market as well as the proposal for a development department. Doubtless to pacify the non-Zionists, Chancellor told the American to see Passfield, but Hexter answered that he first had to consult with Weizmann.[38] Clearly, London had missed its chance to drive a wedge between the Zionists and non-Zionists. Hexter was prepared to continue as a go-between, but the English realized that he, and Warburg as well, were more pro-*yishuv* than they had anticipated.

Sixty years later, when he wrote his autobiography, Hexter was convinced of England's duplicity. The story of his negotiations with Hope Simpson in Athens is far different from his original report:

> I had to try to reason with a man who had already made up his mind. As far as he was concerned there just was "no room to swing a cat" in Palestine. I had facts and figures ready to show how every investment by world Jewry in Palestine served to provide new jobs for immigrants; how we had successfully uncovered and drilled for new water sources that made more agricultural colonies possible . . . and on and on. He wouldn't be budged. Worse, he now began arguing that in all justice the Jewish money should go to unemployed Arabs. I said we had Jewish unemployed to care for, and added with emphasis that a number were unemployed because of the Arab rioting, looting, and burning. He was anxious for my approval of his document, but . . . I told him with some severity that we were miles apart. That in no way could I approve his report. . . . Obviously Sir John had hoped to inveigle me, a non-Zionist, into accepting his report, which *might* lull

the Jewish community into accepting it. His obstinate mind set, his inability to see that it couldn't be acceptable, made it all too clear that we were in for a lengthy battle with the British government.[39]

In defense of Hexter we can add that he wasn't the only one to be taken in by Hope Simpson; Weizmann and Brandeis had been hopeful too. The American had set out to salvage what he could for the *yishuv*'s benefit, and in pursuance of that objective he overrated Hope Simpson's fairness and his influence with HMG.

Attempts at Compromise

Despite their resignations Weizmann and Warburg continued to work at their usual tasks. Hexter too was occupied with issues that he had faced before—the unfinished work of the Emergency Fund, the internal problems of the Agency, visits to members and supporters of the Agency on the Continent. But in certain ways the earlier picture was significantly altered. New difficulties in fundraising had arisen; the worldwide depression and, as Warburg put it, "disgust" with England because of the White Paper[40] were drying up the necessary flow of monies from Jews outside Palestine. On a personal level relationships too had changed. The problems with the mandatory had ended much of the bickering between Warburg and Weizmann, and the two men enjoyed a warmer rapport. Hexter also benefited thereby, since he was now able to draw much closer to the Zionist leader.[41]

The White Paper had upset England's customary juggling act between the demands of the *yishuv* and those of the Arabs, and after handing the Arabs a major victory in the Passfield White Paper, the government felt obliged to restore a more equitable balance. A few days after the appearance of the White Paper, England suggested negotiations between the government and the Jewish Agency for resolving the differences caused by the new statement of policy. Troubled by the American Jewish outcry against the White Paper, particularly the charge that the document was incompatible with British obligations under the mandate, London also desired to avoid criticism by the League of Nations. (The Permanent Mandates Commission of the League had only recently found fault with England's handling of Palestine.)[42] Its strategy of wedge-driving had failed, and despite rumblings from radical Zionists against Weizmann's Anglophile leanings, it now confronted a more united Agency.

Prime Minister MacDonald proceeded to set up a special cabinet committee to handle the matter, one in which Passfield was only an observer. Although the government would not rescind the White Paper, it was prepared to "interpret" it after hearing the Agency's objections. Weizmann liked the idea of negotiations, and Warburg also approved.[43] The Jews were well aware of England's

The Americanization of Zionism, 1897–1948

discomfort, and since the invitation for bilateral negotiations came from the government and not from them, the Agency was in a stronger position vis-à-vis England than it had been at any time after the riots. The meetings of several Agency representatives with a small cabinet committee began in November and lasted for three months. Warburg was unable to attend, but he insisted that Hexter participate.[44] The latter, who had long pressed for the Magnes/Warburg idea of roundtable conferences involving the three parties—the Agency, the Arabs, and England—loyally complied. He lived in London for a good deal of the time, where he actively contributed to deliberations and helped to draft opinions that the Agency prepared for submission to the other side. In the course of the sessions he established close working relationships with one participant, Professor Harold Laski, the intellectual mentor of the Labor party, as well as with Malcolm MacDonald, the prime minister's son, who acted as an intermediary between the Agency and the government and as a willing source of information on government opinion. Aside from their pragmatic value, those associations enhanced Hexter's reputation in official circles.[45] The American still called himself a non-Zionist, but his year in Palestine appears to have made him more sympathetic to the *yishuv* and its development. Since Weizmann some months earlier had termed a Jewish state "unrealizable" at least for the present, and had denounced Zionist propaganda for a state as "foolish and harmful,"[46] Hexter felt quite at ease with Zionist strategy and its defense of a Jewish national *home*. Enjoying the full confidence and trust of both Warburg and Weizmann, he increasingly relied on his own initiative, and although he often asked for Warburg's advice, in many instances he no longer waited for explicit instructions.

Sessions with the cabinet committee were closed and participants were obligated to keep deliberations under wraps, but a steady stream of phone calls, cables, and special messengers flowed back and forth between Agency men in London and New York. It was a circuitous route that started and ended with Hexter: 1) He informed Warburg of each step in the deliberations and added his own suggestions. 2) Warburg circulated the information among Brandeis and the ZOA as well as the non-Zionists. 3) They in turn reviewed the draft articles sentence by sentence and comma by comma. 4) Warburg reported their conclusions back to Hexter, who then labored to incorporate the American opinions into the Agency's position. Breaking the seal of confidentiality might have been improper, but the government well knew that the Agency representatives would not commit themselves to any decision without prior consultation with the Americans.[47]

In an atmosphere markedly different from the hostility of Chancellor's administration in Palestine and Passfield's Colonial Office in London, the Agency boldly put forth its grievances and demands. The same issues that had been raised by the Shaw and the Hope Simpson reports—the obligations of the mandatory towards the Jews, land acquisition and settlement, immigration and the labor market—were uppermost. The Agency's agenda also included the desirability of a new British administration in Palestine and the use of Transjordan for the resettlement of landless Arabs and/or the settlement of Jews.

From the written sources, it is impossible to define precisely what part Hexter played at the meetings. Behind the scenes at least, his task of incorporating the American suggestions was critical in the formulation of the Agency's position. He did report that Weizmann had left the issues of the labor market and unemployment for him to present. It is evident too that he pressed the matter of "tone," i.e., the need of a document in which a Jewish national home in Palestine was reaffirmed without the bias and hostility that suffused the White Paper. As he cabled to New York, "Since they obviously want to do right thing they should do it in right manner." Hexter and Laski also insisted that the last paragraph of the new document, which would take the form of a letter of interpretation by the prime minister, specifically state that the letter was as legally binding as the White Paper. For his part Weizmann had only praise for the American: "His presence here is of the greatest possible use. He is efficient, has excellent judgment, is devoted and pleasant."[48]

The cabinet committee concluded its business at the beginning of February, and MacDonald's letter of interpretation of the White Paper appeared a few days later. It began by protesting the loyalty of the government to the obligations imposed by the mandate. Written in a considerate tone (almost "ingratiating," one journal commented), it appeared to recant, if not apologize for, all the criticisms brought by the Agency. England still stressed its duties to the Arabs and its need to maintain a balance until the two sides themselves reached an agreement, but it disclaimed any intention of permanently ending Jewish immigration, freezing Jewish settlements, giving Arabs preference over Jews in land resettlement, or insulting Jewish labor institutions. In a positive vein it promised to consider the establishment of a development agency to facilitate both Jewish and Arab land settlement.[49]

Hexter was pleased with the substance of the letter,[50] and he defended the work of the cabinet committee to the high commissioner. When Chancellor said that the negotiations had been unwise, Hexter sharply retorted that it was difficult for the Jews to take the White Paper lying down. Much like a Zionist, he said that the Jews were in Palestine by right and not sufferance, and they "could not always be expected to swallow things of this sort." At the same time, Hexter continued to stress recognition of the rights of the Arabs and the need for roundtable conferences. Warning the Jews of the dangers inherent in ignoring the Arabs, he cautioned against "putting in the foreground only those obligations of the Mandate which are in our favour and neglecting the others. Some day these 'others' come to life and become very nasty realities."[51]

In March 1931 the government announced the establishment of a development department. Zionist acceptance of the scheme, which was mentioned in the White Paper and the MacDonald letter, was debated in another series of meetings between the Agency and the government in the spring of that year. Participants considered allocation of lands to Jews and Arabs for intensive cultivation, payments for such projects, and the personnel to head the department. Although England aimed primarily at land benefits for the Arabs, Warburg and Hexter were most concerned that Jews receive an equal share. Fully immersed in the deliberations, Hexter hoped for a short while that Hope Simpson himself might yet influence the government to return to his more palatable version of a development commission.[52]

Meanwhile, during the fall of 1930, Hexter and Sir John Hope Simpson had renewed their ties. Hexter explained that "all of us" (i.e., leaders of the Jewish Agency in London) "are convinced that he will exert great influence, not alone in the present administration in the Colonial Office, but in successive Governments as well. And, his influence in Geneva [seat of the League of Nations] is very strong." Banking on Hope Simpson's "honesty" and his readiness to accept demonstrable facts, as well as on his criticism of the MacDonald administration, Hexter thought the Englishman might yet become an ally of the Agency or at least a strong protagonist of an evenhanded development commission. He may also have hoped that if he succeeded in convincing Hope Simpson of the justice of the Agency's case, prior judgments of how he, Hexter, had been duped would be erased. Hope Simpson stood to benefit too. Angling for a post in Palestine, either as head of the development commission or as high commissioner, he may have thought of bolstering his chances by gaining the support of the American non-Zionists and even of the *yishuv*.[53]

In this, the third round of Hexter's personal diplomacy with Hope Simpson, both men spoke more frankly. This time no Zionist whispers of a British conspiracy or wedge-driving were heard; rather, it was Cyrus Adler, a prominent American non-Zionist and close associate of Warburg, who cautioned Hexter to be wary of committing himself to Hope Simpson's personal ambitions.[54] Weizmann agreed to Hexter's strategy, and although the choice of subjects and the formulation were Hexter's, he was shown the exchange of letters.

It was a new Hope Simpson who met with Hexter. At first he defended the White Paper; he regretted that his concept of a development commission was not adopted, but he did not agree that the document, or Passfield himself, meant to express hostility on the part of London. More defensive of his own report, he claimed that it had aroused less criticism than the White Paper, and that no one had impugned his impartiality. When Hexter stressed the points in the report that had been criticized, such as its treatment of the land question and unemployment, Hope Simpson was not convinced. No longer the accredited representative of the Colonial Office, he made no effort to sound impartial or for that matter even diplomatic. He repeated his criticisms of Zionist exclusion of Arab labor and of Jewish land practices that displaced the Arabs; again and again he found fault with the Jews for ignoring Arab needs and interests. The deliberations of the cabinet committee were useless and unwise so long as

Arab representatives were excluded. If he, Hope Simpson, had been invited to participate, he could have spoken on their behalf.

Overall, Hexter was far less eager to come to a meeting of minds with the Englishman than before. He maintained that roundtable conferences were necessary to settle the friction in Palestine, and indeed the Agency had told that to the government. The Jews had shown "a strong consideration for the Arab side," he added. "The Government could have gotten us to agree to any reasonable approach to this problem if they had sat down and reasoned the thing out with us, taking into account our own needs and position as well as the needs and interests of the Arabs." Hexter remained calm and softspoken despite Hope Simpson's impassioned words. His only positive request of the Englishman, on a matter that Hope Simpson had hinted at during the summer, was to help make Transjordan available for Palestinian settlement.

On at least two subjects Hope Simpson sounded downright antisemitic. One time he hinted broadly at Jewish international power. Whereas Arabs lacked the ability to present their case effectively, "the Jewish side is powerfully represented everywhere. I suppose there is no more complete and efficient system of propaganda in the world than the Zionist system." Another time he picked up the myth of Jew = Communist. On the subject of the *kibbutz* he asserted that control of the land by the Jewish National Fund was bad enough, but the use of the land for collectives was even worse. "It is intolerable that under the aegis of the Mandate and the funds provided in large measure by American Jews who I am sure do not approve . . . a revolutionary system of social organization should be set up in Palestine. The [*kibbutzim*] seem to me to be little nuclei of the Russian social and political system transported into Palestine."

Hexter made no comment on "Jewish power," but he rallied to the defense of the *kibbutzim*. All Jews did not agree on the wisdom of collectives, he countered, but the Agency believed that only time would prove or disprove their underlying philosophy. "One thing, however, is certain, that is, that they have nothing in common with the Bolsheviks." Moreover, their existence had nothing to do with the mandate. "You and I probably see eye to eye with respect to the capitalist system and yet, I do not go with you to the extent of saying that the system that we think is right must be created in Palestine. In addition, don't you think it is an interesting commentary on the genuine liberality of outlook on the part of the Jews who contribute to the upbuilding of Palestine, to promote the subsidy of forms of social organization with which they are utterly out of sympathy?" Neither man would have spoken so candidly before, nor did either pretend that he was convinced by the other's opinions.[55]

When Hope Simpson returned from his post in Athens, he met with Hexter in London in January 1931. At that time the Englishman distinctly tried to distance himself from Passfield and the White Paper, but Hexter's prodding kept him on the defensive with respect to his own report. According to Hexter's account of the meeting:

H.S. stated that he and a large number of the C.O. [Colonial Office] felt that Passfield had bungled the job. . . . He stated that Passfield was tired of his job and never wanted it, and wanted to get out. . . . He told me that he regretted that the C.O. had not carried out his original suggestion, namely to publish his report as a feeler to determine where the attacks would most likely be made. . . . But this is in line with their usual stupidity, and they are unusually weak in the Near East Division. . . . He . . . realized, as I had written to him, that the relative silence of Jews [on] certain of his findings was the result of the focussing of all attention upon the White Paper. I told him that I was disappointed in a number of places, . . . that I had the feeling that either the C.O. had cut out a good deal of what he sent, or he had cut out much before sending. He told me that two days before transmitting it he had received . . . a letter from Passfield asking him not to embarrass the Government with his report or his recommendations. He stated that he had sent a hot letter in exchange, and said he would not consent to this at all.

His grumbling notwithstanding, Hope Simpson did not dare publicly to criticize Passfield or the White Paper.

The Englishman and the American talked in general terms about the development commission, but they came to no agreement on the major issues— who would finance it and to whom it would be responsible. Hope Simpson was prepared to accept the chairmanship, but only if he were given independent power free of the high commissioner's jurisdiction. When he asked Hexter if the Agency had any ideas about the development commission, Hexter said that they couldn't discuss it without knowing the details. He made clear, however, that "the commission had potentialities for either good or evil from our point of view; that we would have to pay dearly for it in money [a reference to the idea that the *yishuv* would be taxed to help cover the commission's expenses] and in liberty of action." Again suggesting Transjordan as an outlet for resettling Arabs, Hexter added that "the obligation to the fellahin was governmental in origin and nature, while the obligation to the Jews was mandatory in origin; that certainly to put the case mildly, the latter was not inferior to the former, and the Jews had a right to expect the . . . Government . . . to seek an alternative way [i.e., Transjordan] of discharging its obligations."[56]

Hexter reported the gist of the conversation to Chaim Weizmann, admitting that he didn't totally support Hope Simpson's candidacy as chairman of development, but that he had no better alternative. Weizmann, however, had finally met Hope Simpson and had taken a liking to him. Noting the Englishman's overriding concern for the Arabs (as well as Hexter's importance in the negotiations), he said: "You [Hexter] will have to put him right." Discussions on the development commission, including another talk between Hexter and Hope Simpson, dragged on, and Hexter continued to press for Transjordan. In May it became apparent that Hope Simpson's influence with the government on Palestine was rapidly fading. Nonetheless, he and Hexter corresponded sporadically until the former left England on another assignment. By mid-1931, however, Hexter had become convinced that Hope Simpson harbored an anti-Jewish bias of which, in light of his contradictory statements over the year, the Englishman was genuinely unconscious.[57] In the end, neither of the two men emerged victorious. Hope Simpson failed to incite the non-Zionists through Hexter, and Hexter failed to influence the Colonial Office through Hope Simpson.

Despite England's desire to appease the Arabs after the riots of 1929, the *yishuv* refused to yield to a new interpretation of the Balfour Declaration. To be sure, MacDonald's letter "explaining" the White Paper enraged the Arabs and presaged renewed violence in the immediate years to come. But Zionism had scored at least one lasting gain. Just as non-Zionists had joined Zionists in protesting restrictions on Jewish immigration during the year after the riots, so did they line up in the 1930s. When German Jews hounded by the Nazis turned their eyes to Palestine, non-Zionists too were untroubled by the fact that increased Jewish immigration was contributing to the infrastructure of an eventual Jewish state.

Hexter remained in Palestine as a member of the Jewish Agency and for several years as head of its colonization department. (One friend explained that Hexter had been infected with "Palestinitis or Zionitis."[58]) The most able representative of the non-Zionists in Agency affairs during the mandate era, he returned to the United States shortly after Warburg's death in 1937. From then until 1948 the influence of the American non-Zionists in Palestine grew weaker.

Hexter resumed his successful career in social work, and he served in the prestigious post of co-executive vice president of the New York Federation from 1948 to 1967. His reputation in Israel was assured too, and a chair in international relations was established in his name at the Hebrew University. A more telling tribute to his abilities came when Prime Minister David Ben-Gurion offered Hexter, despite his non-Zionism, the cabinet post of minister of welfare.[59]

CHAPTER 6

Jewish Immigration to Palestine:
The Zionists and the State Department

During the 1930s, when the Nazis embarked on their anti-Jewish crusade, the right of unrestricted Jewish immigration into British-ruled Palestine assumed a critical urgency. Since the United States and other Western countries had closed their doors to new immigrants, Palestine was considered the most likely haven for refugees. As the need intensified, free immigration loomed as *the* irreconcilable issue dividing Jews and Arabs and laying bare the deeper conflict over the legitimacy of the Balfour Declaration's promise of a Jewish national home. The two issues, immigration and a national home, were in reality one and the same—free immigration flowed from the right to a Jewish homeland, and a Jewish homeland could not be developed without free immigration.

American Zionists worked to enlist the support of their country in the three-way dispute, which involved the Arabs, the Jews, and England. In so doing, they focused on what increasingly became the major point of their brief for immigration, the right of America to intervene in the Palestine mandate. Positing the country's commitment to Zionism since the days of Woodrow Wilson, the Zionists reasoned that if their attempts failed to keep England from reneging on the Balfour Declaration, the United States could and should lend them its support. In the 1930s, while tension and violence in the mandate reached new heights, the American Zionists fought an uphill battle for an active American role on behalf of Jewish claims.

It was quite natural for Zionists to seek America's aid. The League of Nations, the official guardian of the mandates, was but a caricature of Wilson's grand design. During those same years it chalked up repeated failures: it could neither protect the minority rights written into the peace treaties with the eastern European states, nor could it halt the aggression of Japan, Italy, and Germany. The United States, a longtime ally of England, was the only major power in a position to impress upon His Majesty's Government (HMG) its responsibilities toward the Jews. The United States too had accepted the idea of a Jewish homeland in Palestine in the Lodge-Fish congressional resolution of 1922 and the Anglo-American treaty of 1924. Furthermore, the Zionists had proved their good faith as Americans by Americanizing their movement. They had tailored their ideology to suit American tastes, and they followed the broad guidelines of American foreign policy. Claiming after World War I that they were building an American-like democracy in Palestine, they were now propelled by concern over immigration. Were they to successfully engage the United States on their side during the 1930s, a Jewish homeland in Palestine would become—much like the Wilsonian wartime aim of a free Poland—an *American* goal. What could be a more glorious climax to the process of Americanizing Zionism! Nevertheless, the Zionists were handicapped from the start. Since Jewish love for Franklin Roosevelt was paramount, they never used the threat of the Jewish vote against the president and his administration.

The State Department's position on Zionist demands in the years leading up to World War II traces the interaction of the department and the Zionists with respect to the entry of refugees into Palestine, the Arab riots of 1936, the Peel Commission and the British proposal of partition, and the immediate events culminating in the White Paper of 1939. Based exclusively on the unpublished and published records of the State Department, the following analysis reveals two fixed mind sets, that of the Zionists and that of the State Department. On one side it shows how the Jews, a frightened and vulnerable minority in a period of economic depression and ugly antisemitism, attempted to pressure the government. It also shows how Zionists were slowly learning the ways of American pressure groups—in effect they were Americanizing their tactics as they had their ideology—and lobbying in Washington more intensely than ever before. On the other side it considers the actions of the State Department, isolationist, Anglophile, and anti-Jewish, which, despite the condition of the Jews under Hitler, kept it on the same anti-Zionist track that it had followed before the 1930s. Not until 1938, a grim year for the Jews of Europe and the *yishuv*, did the department give serious consideration to Jewish pressure.

The Issue

Control of Jewish immigration to Palestine had shifted after the World War from Turkey to England. As the mandatory power over Palestine, England was pledged to the goal of a Jewish national home by the text of the mandate, which incorporated the Balfour Declaration. But since England's expectation of a large influx of Jews into Palestine immediately after the war never materialized, it had few compunctions about tilting toward the Arab side. Arab resentment of Zionist settlement flared up in the riots of 1920 and 1921, and among other things the Arabs called for a cessation to Jewish immigration. The colonial secretary, Winston Churchill, reaffirmed the Balfour Declaration and its implicit guarantee of unrestricted immigration, but nonetheless the Colonial Office adopted the principle of "economic absorptive capacity" to regulate Jewish immigration. The number of immigrant certificates doled out through the Jewish Agency was to be limited thereby to the ability of the land to absorb new arrivals. Since the Zionist response to that emendation was too mild to alarm England, the latter continued comfortably on the road of Arab appeasement.

As the decade wore on, agitation by the Arabs, invoking the wartime promises they too had received from England, persisted. Immigration was again a key issue in the bloody riots of 1929, and again England's recommendations, resulting in the Passfield White Paper of 1930, whittled down the mandatory's commitments to the Jews. This time Zionists and their friends protested loudly. To quiet the opposition Prime Minister Ramsay MacDonald reassured Chaim Weizmann, head of the Jewish Agency, in February 1931 that England recognized its obligation to facilitate Jewish immigration. MacDonald's letter, which was declared to be the official interpretation of the White Paper and which the Arabs called the "Black Paper," temporarily halted total repudiation of the Balfour Declaration.[1] Nevertheless, in light of Nazi persecution, immigration remained a serious point of contention.

The American State Department was little more than an observer of these events. Its hostility toward Zionism carried on a tradition fixed by Secretary of State Robert Lansing during Wilson's administration. In the 1920s the department supported England's rule of the mandate, and in Arab-Jewish clashes it sided with the Arabs. Internal files reveal that its officials both in Washington and Jerusalem were antisemitic to boot. Adhering to a noninterventionist position, the department limited its concern to the rights of America and American nationals. Under the Anglo-American treaty of 1924 the mandatory guaranteed the protection of American citizens and their rights—a category that encompassed the investments and institutions of non-Jewish businessmen and Christian missionaries as well as American Zionist holdings—but the State Department interpreted those clauses narrowly. Zionism, called a "private enterprise" by Secretary of State Frank Kellogg in 1926, was in no way an American interest. The department turned a deaf ear to American Zionist appeals in the immediate aftermath of the 1929 riots for government support, especially since comparatively few Americans had settled in Palestine. As it said then, it had no reason to urge unrestricted Jewish immigration on England. At all times, however, Zionist activities bearing on American foreign relations were closely monitored. The chief of the Near Eastern division acknowledged in 1932 that the "Jewish aspect of Anglo-American relations is a delicate one which merits careful watching."[2]

It may have been unrealistic to expect a change in departmental policy, but Zionists worked toward that end. The path was a familiar one. Ever since the Damascus affair of 1840 American Jews had turned to Washington on behalf of persecuted or needy Jews abroad, and on some occasions the administration complied, but those precedents failed to sway the postwar American government from its path of nonintervention. It proved equally futile to couch Jewish appeals in terms of the country's tradition of humanitarian diplomacy, the base on which American Jews had rested most of their earlier requests, since the State Department had quietly buried humanitarian diplomacy with World War I. The situation of German Jewry offered a most opportune moment to resurrect that cardinal tenet of the American creed, but the department turned a deaf ear. (When Secretary of the Interior Harold Ickes asked the department in 1936 to read a speech he had prepared for a Jewish audience, he was advised to delete his examples of humanitarian diplomacy.)[3] Although neither the United States nor England responded seriously to the plight of the Jews under Hitler, the Zionists did. Self-interest, or an awareness that increased settlement in Palestine would aid the nationalist cause, doubtless contributed to Zionist thinking, but it led to the same result, namely the publicization of the European Jewish plight. Claiming now that they were speaking in the name of all American Jews on behalf of the refugees, the Zionists clamored repeatedly for government intervention on the immigration issue. But only when non-Zionists added their voice did the department feel obliged to give serious attention to Jewish pressure.

An unfriendly department and its refusal to forward Jewish requests to London drove the Zionists to a variety of methods, including direct protests to England and efforts to bypass the executive by appeals to congressmen. Additional obstacles impeded their action. The problems spawned by the Great Depression left little time or energy for extra-American affairs, and a rash of Nazi-inspired antisemitic organizations inhibited both Jews and Christians from lending their names to activities under Zionist sponsorship. America's Jews were fast becoming the largest, wealthiest, and most influential community in Jewish history, but the decade of the 1930s dictated that Jews maintain a low profile.

The consuls in Jerusalem fed the State Department frequent reports of developments within the Zionist and Arab communities after the MacDonald letter. They felt that they, like the State Department, were under constant scrutiny because of worldwide Jewish interest in Zionism. As one member of the consular staff put it, Zionism, an example of an international Jewish network, had a "megaphonelike" quality: "The slightest whisper is heard from Shanghai to New York. The least incident can set telephone wires buzzing from London to San Francisco."[4] American officials were most concerned about the animosity toward England and the resultant political agitation from both the Arab and Jewish sides. Paul Knabenshue, the consul general during the 1929 riots and a firm anti-Zionist, continued to prophesy doom and destruction from his posts in the Near East. Nor had his animosity toward "our Jewish friends," who, he said, wielded extraordinary power in the United States, abated. Knabenshue's successors in Jerusalem were usually less vitriolic, but none sided with the Jews.[5]

Early in the 1930s the department asked the consulate to report on the issue of communism in Palestine. In response, despatches from Jerusalem assigned Jewish Communists a major part in causing the 1929 riots and in fomenting continued unrest. They said that Palestine was important to the Communist mission and that settlers from Russia were potential Bolsheviks. Jews, bearers of the "revolutionary germ" and builders of secret international organizations, were actively or passively spreading Communist propaganda under directives from Moscow. Admittedly, many Russian Jews opposed Bolshevism, but the "prominent Bolsheviks . . . are preponderantly Jewish," and "Jewry as a whole has consciously or unconsciously worked for and promoted an international economic, material despotism which . . . has tended in an ever-increasing degree to crush national and spiritual values out of existence."[6]

The reports had serious implications. They reinforced familiar stereotypes of the international Bolshevik Jew feared and hated by all proper Americans. Evidence from the *yishuv*, be it the Socialist *kibbutzim* or the threat of a "class war" provoked by powerful Jewish labor unions, confirmed the department's image of "Jew = Communist" and compounded their distaste for Zionist activities. Moreover, although communism contradicted Jewish nationalism, Russian Jews appeared to be among the most dedicated supporters of each movement. Hence, it was difficult to separate Zionists from Communists, would-be Communists, or Communist sympathizers in the *yishuv*. Whether or not a firm distinction was made, both the words "Zionist" and "Bolshevik" suggested a Jewish conspiracy to undercut Western values. It followed that Jewish immigration in general was hardly desirable.

Despatches from Jerusalem to Washington focused increasingly on immigration after Hitler came to power. Pushed by persecution and pulled by a country that was one of the few enjoying economic prosperity,[7] the flow of Jewish immigrants intensified. In 1933 Jews from Germany and Poland accounted for more than 50 percent of new arrivals and with other immigrants raised the number of Jews to 20 percent of the Palestinian population. By the end of 1938 the ratio of Jews to Arabs was estimated at 30 to 70.[8] Not only did the new immigrants make important contributions to the economy of the *yishuv*, but the potential inherent in their numbers compounded Arab suspicions.

In 1933 Jewish officials in Jerusalem and London claimed that some 600,000 German Jews could be settled in Palestine in the next fifteen years. While the Jewish National Council, the executive body in Palestine that administered Jewish affairs under the mandate, called on Jews to support immigration and build up the *yishuv* as a refuge for the persecuted, American Consul Alexander Sloan reported on Arab dissatisfaction with "excessive" numbers of Jews. He charged that the Jewish Agency, determined to increase the Jewish population dramatically, played on the sympathy for the German Jews and inflated the need for immigration certificates. According to Sloan, British officials agreed with the Arabs. One said that in light of the formation of several large companies by German Jews who were out to make Palestine a world center of capitalism, the Arabs deserved protection against the Jews. But as Sloan explained, officials in the region were not heeded by London, because the Colonial Office "bows" to Jewish capitalists.[9]

The number of German Jews who entered Palestine in 1933 was put at 6805, and roughly one-half of those were counted as capitalists. Another survey estimated that half of those new arrivals were potential birds of passage, anti- or non-Zionists who were prepared to return to Germany if circumstances permitted.[10] The numbers of refugees continued to rise, but the State Department refused to act on Jewish appeals for a permanent or temporary refuge in Palestine. It held fast to the position taken by Secretary of State Charles Evans Hughes. An opponent of American intervention in the matter of Palestinian immigration, Hughes had said in 1923 that since Americans constituted but a very small fraction of that immigration, and since Congress was then busily writing America's own restrictive immigration laws, the United States was hardly in a position to challenge England. Ironically, one early report from Jerusalem favored German Jewish immigration as a defense *against* communism. It said that the "steady stream of Jewish immigrants and capital is the best possible insurance against Communism in Palestine Jewry."[11] The department, however, was won over neither to the side of unrestricted immigration nor to the side of "capitalist" immigration.

In 1934 illegal Jewish immigration from Europe began to complicate the already thorny problem. Consul General Ely Palmer reported that illegal entries numbered about one hundred weekly; one consular report counted some twelve hundred illegal immigrants from the United States as well. England immediately cracked down—police raids and arrests, tighter security on the borders, and, most painful to the Jews, reduction of the number of immigration certificates—and the Arabs demanded restrictions harsher than the British principle of economic absorptive capacity. Not even a plan financed by Americans Mary Fels and Louis Brandeis to settle Arab villagers on household plots in the Jewish city of Netanya assuaged Arab wrath. Illegal immigration continued. Palmer reported that some two thousand Jews who had entered Palestine for the 1935 Maccabiah (international sports events) stayed on as illegal immigrants, and he blamed the *yishuv:* "Concealing 'illegals' is an activity in which Jewish colonists excel." By the summer of 1934 he predicted darkly that immigration would be the catalyst for another round of Arab violence.[12] In succeeding years the numbers of illegal immigrants multiplied despite British efforts until 1948 to stamp out the traffic.

Palmer's animus against the Zionists and Jewish immigration was reflected in his despatches. He lumped the *c halutzim* together with "other irresponsible elements," and he charged that Jews who faulted Arabs for unrest in Palestine either "whine[d] their lamentations" or reacted with blatantly false "injured innocence." The *haganah*, the Jewish defense force, operated clandestinely and, as one British policeman said, would soon constitute an "attack" group. Claiming that Jews arbitrarily wanted a population equal to that of the Arabs, Palmer and the State Department doubted that England could resolve the matter in a manner satisfactory to both sides.[13]

Immigration both legal and illegal continued to swell the Jewish population. The consul in 1934 put the number of Jews in Palestine at 250,000; a year and a half later, Wallace Murray, chief of the State Department's Near Eastern division, claimed that the influx from Germany had raised the figure to 350,000. Since the *yishuv* had been strengthened thereby, the British became more favorably disposed to the Arabs, but when the Arabs demanded a total stoppage to Jewish immigration, the colonial secretary turned them down. Meantime, the American consul in Jerusalem reported that the Jews had grown more bellicose toward both the Arabs and England and were prepared to fight any suspension of immigration.[14]

Arab Riots, British Commissions, and Zionist Lobbying

In April 1936 the powder keg that was the mandate finally exploded. Angry Arabs expressed their grievances in riots and in a general strike that lasted six months. Their primary demand was a ban on immigration; as one Arab spokesman said, let England find room for the immigrants elsewhere, perhaps in the United States. A consular report blamed "Jewish intrigue" for inciting the Arabs, but bias notwithstanding, the State Department immediately urged full protection of American nationals in Palestine by both the consulate and England.[15] The number of Americans in Palestine was then put at eight to twelve thousand and the amount of American investments at $40 million. Doubtless because of the influx of European refugees, the proportion of Americans in the population had dropped from 3 percent in 1922–35 to 1 percent in 1936.[16] Unlike the situation in 1929, no Americans were killed and American property suffered only slight damage, thus enabling the department to adhere to its policy of nonintervention.[17]

In May 1936, a month after the riots and general strike began, Rabbi Stephen S. Wise, chairman of the United Palestine Appeal, sent a personal letter to Roosevelt. Ardent Zionist and loyal follower of FDR, Wise asked the president to call for a report on the Palestinian situation from the British ambassador. On the surface the request looked insignificant, but if the ambassador were summoned to the White House, England would understand that Roosevelt had an interest in Zionist affairs. Wise's letter reminded the president of Wilson's support of the Balfour Declaration and of sympathetic comments by Roosevelt himself on Zionism. In addition to those American Jews who had settled or invested in Palestine, the rabbi emphasized American Jewish emotional support for the *yishuv*. Wise's suggestion, however, was ignored. His letter went from Roosevelt to Secretary of State Cordell Hull to Wallace Murray. Murray, a confirmed anti-Zionist, drafted a reply to Wise that mentioned merely the steps taken for the protection of American nationals. But the request had some effect. A day later the department saw fit to remind the consul general in Jerusalem to act "vigorously and promptly" with local British authorities for the protection of Americans: "You are, of course, aware of the widespread interest in Jewish circles in this country in the Palestine situation." Hull also instructed the ambassador to England to ask the Foreign Office for any information on the safety of Americans.[18]

In that episode the department set a pattern that was often repeated. A Zionist request was first rejected, but the State Department was moved to act on related matters—for example, the protection of American citizens in Palestine, or the American Jewish mood, or departmental reexamination of the American interpretation of the Anglo-American treaty of 1924.

American Christians became involved too. The *Palestine Post* of June 1 printed a petition to the State Department from the Pro-Palestine Federation of Americans, a group of prominent clergymen and other public figures cultivated by American Zionist Emanuel Neumann. The latter hoped that the Christian group would generate sympathy for Zionism on the part of American officials abroad. (Murray, however, sneered at the group's importance, saying that it did not reflect any spontaneous expression of Christian sentiment.) Asking for free immigration and for the removal of obstacles to the establishment of a Jewish national home, the petition called forth a counterstatement against immigration from heads of Christian denominations and churches in Palestine, who candidly warned against Jewish domination of the Arabs.[19]

When England announced plans for a Royal Commission of Inquiry on the Palestine situation, rumors circulated that immigration would be suspended at least temporarily while the commission conducted its investigation. American Zionists, now supported by non-Zionists, again turned to Roosevelt. Word from London, where Wise and Felix Frankfurter, both friends of the president, were working with Weizmann, urged that FDR be alerted. Stressing the critical needs of German Jewry, the message asked that Roosevelt, who was "much more warm-hearted than . . . some of his official family," inform England that suspension of immigration would hurt Anglo-American relations. The message reached Samuel Rosenman, a close associate of the president, and he forwarded it to the White House with the comment "Naturally a great deal seems to be involved, . . . so that I am much interested." Roosevelt, however, refused to bypass the State Department. Murray formulated a reply in the form of instructions from Hull to Ambassador Robert Bingham in London that reflected

Murray's position rather than the Zionists' plea. Bingham was told to apprise Foreign Secretary Anthony Eden of the request on immigration from "influential Jewish groups." Any strength in that message was immediately undercut, however, by the directive that Bingham make clear that neither was he speaking for the American government nor would he presume to interfere in England's affairs. In sum, he was to say only that he thought England would want the information. The ambassador followed orders, reporting that Eden had thanked him but had revealed nothing of England's intentions. Nor was Eden's office more forthcoming when it was questioned in the House of Commons. Stating that the cabinet still had not reached a decision on the temporary suspension of immigration, the Foreign Office added that it would not be swayed by force or intimidation.[20]

The Royal Commission of Inquiry, headed by Lord Robert Peel, was appointed at the end of July 1936, and Arabs and Jews squared off on the matter of immigration. American Jews—Zionist organizations, fraternal orders, landsmanshaftn, rabbinical groups, labor unions—registered their concern in letters to Hull or their congressmen. (Only a few reached the secretary of state; Murray and associates Paul Alling and R. Walton Moore handled most.) All mustered the same arguments on behalf of Jewish immigration—England's obligations under the Balfour Declaration and the terms of the mandate, and the needs of persecuted Jews in Europe. Some warned against yielding to Arab terrorism, and a few mentioned American Jewish financial investments. Junior Hadassah told how its services benefited both Arabs and Jews, and the Order Sons of Zion claimed that were England to close "the gates of Zion in face of the return of her children," it would constitute a crime against civilization. The State Department gave its standard reply: England would act on immigration only after the Royal Commission submitted its report. It reassured the more powerful organizations that HMG was aware of American Jewish opinion, but it refused to transmit the messages to London. Like the petitioners, it understood that transmission alone indicated some degree of concern.[21]

Pressure on the department increased when three members of the Senate planned a two-week visit to Palestine to investigate the situation. George Wadsworth, now consul general in Jerusalem and the least outspoken of the consuls against Zionism, learned that the junket was organized and funded by newspaper mogul William Randolph Hearst. Some speculated that in anticipation of the presidential elections in November, Hearst sought to appeal to Jewish voters by neutralizing his former "Naziphilia"; others explained that the circulation of Hearst papers had declined because of their weak stand on the murder of Jews by Arabs. Wadsworth went on to report that prominent American Jews in the *yishuv*, like Rabbi Judah Magnes, now president of the Hebrew University, were actively cooperating with the visitors and that "propaganda visits" to Jewish colonies had been arranged. That same week, the ZOA forwarded a message to the State Department from the three senators that very possibly was drafted by the organization. Dismayed at events in Palestine that threatened to destroy Zionist achievements, and mindful of American Jewish contributions to Palestine, the senators called on England to fulfill its obligations. They said that they, like Congress and the president, sympathized with efforts to find a haven for the refugees, and therefore they protested any restriction of immigration. On their arrival in Palestine the senators stated publicly that they as well as Hearst were unbiased. Nevertheless, since Hearst was now pro-Zionist, and knowing that he was no friend of England, the department faced a challenge to its own anti-Zionist and Anglophile leanings.[22]

As the months passed the Zionists and their friends were shifting their concentration from immigration to the more inclusive issue of American intervention. They claimed that under the Anglo-American convention of 1924 the United States had the right to review changes by England concerning the mandate. When one of the senators who had visited Palestine, Royal Copeland of New York, met with Hull to report on his trip, he harshly criticized England's administration of Palestine, and he said that Hull would be justified in "reminding" England of its duties as mandatory. At that meeting Hull, who had been fully briefed by Murray, had the upper hand. He announced categorically that he was pleased with British policy and that American intervention was ill advised. Avoiding the technicalities of the 1924 treaty, he cited the congressional resolution of 1922 in favor of a Jewish national home in Palestine. He reminded Copeland that on the advice of Secretary of State Hughes, Congress then had purposely watered down any American commitment to the Zionist goal.[23]

The anti-British and pro-Jewish statements by the three senators gathered support on Capitol Hill, and from the White House came FDR's warm endorsement of "the rebuilding of the ancient Jewish homeland." Officially, however, the government kept silent.[24] The United States had done enough, Murray insisted, by demanding the protection of American nationals in Palestine.[25] To be sure, the department could not discount the influence of Jews and their allies at the polls. Murray's staff, therefore, reminded the Foreign Office in London more than once of American Jewish interests in Palestine, but it refused to assert the right of formal intervention.

As soon as the Peel Commission took up its work in the fall of 1936, England acted on immigration. Although claiming to adhere to the principle of economic absorptive capacity, it curtailed the monthly certificates for Jewish laborers from eight thousand to 1850. (Quotas did not apply to nonlaborers.) It also deducted the number of illegal arrivals from the allotted certificates. The State Department, which considered the move a fair compromise between Arabs and Jews, prepared for heavy pressure from dissatisfied Jews. The Arabs kept up their demands too. One Arab reportedly said, "If 65,000,000 Germans could not stomach 600,000 Jews," why expect 900,000 Arabs to accept 400,000 Jews? An internal memorandum of the department concluded: "Under the circumstances it would seem desirable for us to refrain from intervening in any way. . . . Since we ourselves strictly limit our own immigration we are scarcely in a strong position to insist that other countries adjust their immigration laws and regulations to suit the desires of . . . a portion of our population."[26]

A few days later another letter came to Roosevelt from Wise. It told of a document that Wise, then president of the ZOA, and other representative American Jews planned to send to England through the State Department. Having failed to elicit America's commitment to the right of intervention should the mandatory change the rules of governance, the Zionists hoped to reach the same end by pressuring England to recognize that right. The signers were not asking for Roosevelt's endorsement but only for his help in transmitting their message. Wise counted on the president's friendship and sympathy, but the message was referred to the State Department without ever reaching Roosevelt. Even for the president's friend the standard answer—that the department did not function as a channel of communication—applied. Murray countered that the Zionists had their own machinery, the Jewish Agency, to deal with immigration and the transmission of messages.

Wise tried again when he and a fellow Zionist leader, Robert Szold, met with Acting Secretary of State R. Walton Moore. The rabbi brought with him the document in question, but now behaving more obsequiously, he raised no objection when Moore again refused to transmit it to England. Szold, however, seemed less easily cowed. Positing that the United States could act if England limited immigration for any *political* motive, he warned that the Zionists would renew their pressure.[27] The document itself was a 36-page printed booklet addressed to the Royal Commission and signed by seven American Zionist organizations.[28] Its purpose, it stated, was to ensure the continuity of mutual confidence between England and the United States. Called a "Memorandum . . . on American Interest in the Administration of the Palestine Mandate," it gave a well-researched and mildly worded account of Anglo-American relations with respect to Palestine since 1917. It showed how England had desired and obtained American approval of the Balfour Declaration and the terms of the mandate, and how the United States insisted on and received England's pledges on the recognition of American rights and privileges within Palestine. Arguing that America had shown its interest in a Jewish national home, it quoted sympathetic statements on Zionism by all presidents from Wilson to Roosevelt. It also claimed, and this became central to subsequent appeals, that England was enjoined by diplomatic notes exchanged with America and by Article 7 of the Anglo-American convention of 1924 from altering the administration of the mandate without American consent.

The document recalled how American Jews, now called upon to lead in the development of Palestine and in providing thereby a haven for persecuted European Jews, had supported the choice of England as mandatory and how they had cooperated with England during World War I. The Zionists did not elaborate on the plight of Jews under the Nazis, but they did present detailed information on the money American Jews had poured into Palestine. Their investments in the mandate came to some $42 million and their gifts to $35.5 million—i.e., significant American interests that England cavalierly disregarded. The Zionists concluded that since England and the United States were both committed to the establishment of a Jewish national home, they were required to cooperate with appropriate Jewish agencies on matters of Jewish immigration and settlement.

The State Department summarily dismissed the Zionist brief. Murray wrote a detailed critique for circulation within the department. Citing chapter and verse, he maintained that the Zionists had misused or omitted relevant material and that their statement was utterly deceptive. Nevertheless, the State Department made three moves in response. First, it again instructed Bingham in London to inform the foreign minister unofficially of American Jewish concern. Second and more important to the department's anti-Zionist calculations, it began collecting anti-Zionist statements by influential American Jews to prove that many in the community agreed neither with Wise nor with the Zionists. Third, it felt constrained to consider anew the government's official commitment to the Balfour Declaration and a Jewish national home, and to American rights and obligations under the treaty of 1924. Repeatedly reassuring England that it had no intention of intervening,[29] the department worried, however, lest Zionist insistence on American intervention force it into an "untenable" position.[30]

While the Arabs and their sympathizers lobbied in Washington against Jewish immigration and the "imperialist and materialist" aims of the Zionists, the Peel Commission in Jerusalem heard testimony on the Palestine situation. A statement by one witness, Chaim Weizmann, who spoke impassionedly of the plight of six million European Jews facing persecution and death, was called brilliant even by the American consul. In Washington the State Department closely monitored the hearings, and to stay on top of new developments it despatched Paul Alling, assistant chief of the Near Eastern division, to London to serve as its special emissary.[31]

Partition and Divisiveness

From the time that the Peel Commission finished its work in January 1937 until the publication of its report in July, rumors circulated about the conclusions it had reached. In the *yishuv* the mood was one of anxiety, as Jews gloomily expected further curtailment of immigration. Meanwhile, the Arabs feared the success of Jewish efforts for American intervention against the Arabs' "rightful" demands. Although the department turned down a Zionist suggestion that it ascertain the contents of the report before publication and discuss them with

American Zionist leaders, it seriously weighed the speculations of allegedly knowledgeable parties. Murray reported that Jewish circles in London predicted intense Jewish pressure in both England and the United States, but that at the same time heavy pressure in either country could trigger an antisemitic backlash. He was also told that American Jewish organizations had demanded of their British counterparts the right to participate in the formulation of any Palestinian solution. Finally, the department heard—and this rumor turned out to be true—that the Peel Commission would recommend the partition of Palestine, a decision that both Arabs and Jews would very likely oppose.[32]

Talk of partition had been heard before in Palestine. Advanced by a Jewish newspaper editor in 1930, it became a serious topic of conversation for a while in 1933–34.[33] In 1937 the talk grew louder, and before the appearance of the Peel report, the State Department learned of Zionist and anti-Zionist opposition to such a plan. Consul General Wadsworth reported that Jews in Palestine considered a truncated area of settlement to be a return to the ghetto or a new Pale of Settlement. The Jewish Agency in London came out against partition and any alteration of the mandate; the annual convention of American Zionists followed suit, voting unanimously against partition or cantonization; and the Christian Pro-Palestine Federation also registered its disapproval. For their part, Arab leaders brooked no compromise with the Zionists.[34]

The idea of partition, tantamount to an admission of England's failure to balance the claims of Arabs and Jews satisfactorily, worried the State Department. Until then the Palestine situation had a quality of déjà vu. From the riots of 1929 until the Passfield White Paper of 1930 the department had also been subjected to American Jewish requests that it "do something." Then too, in response to Jewish pressure, it had considered at length whether the Anglo-American convention of 1924 committed the government to intervention if England altered the terms of the mandate.[35] But partition differed qualitatively from the usual issues of immigration and land settlement. Now the question was: Did England unilaterally have the right to make *structural changes* in a mandate it had received from the League of Nations? For all practical purposes the League in 1937 counted for little, and the United States was not even a member, but American action could have been crucial.

The arguments of American Jews in 1937 were also different because of the Nazi menace. Hull, who seemed more sympathetic to the refugee problem than did the Near Eastern division, informed the British Foreign Office that American Jewish groups feared a solution to the Palestine problem that would stymie the possible exodus of persecuted Jews from Europe. Jewish thinking was quite reasonable, the secretary admitted: "In the opinion of large sections of the Jews of this country, the Jews of the world as a whole, by reason of their experience at the hands of certain European governments, have come to be the logical supporters of democratic institutions and naturally look to the democratic governments of the world to accord them fair and equitable treatment."[36]

Publicly the department remained impassive to most Zionist protests, but it was sufficiently concerned to keep London abreast of the substance of Jewish demands. Ambassador Bingham and special envoy Alling, as well as department officials in Washington, repeatedly albeit informally raised the matter of Jewish protests with their British counterparts. When stripped of diplomatic jargon the Anglo-American exchange was straightforward:

The American concerns: 1. Financial and sentimental interests of influential American Jews might make it necessary for the State Department to register a protest upon publication of the Peel report. 2. How exactly did England interpret American rights under the 1924 treaty?[37]

The British response: 1. Jews in England were similarly concerned. 2. Because of Arab claims England could not permit unlimited numbers into Palestine: "To turn the country entirely over to the Jews would be much like asking the present inhabitants of Long Island to withdraw from their homes in order that another population might move in." 3. In the interest of finding a compromise fair to both Arabs and Jews, England was considering a "radical solution." 4. Although the consent of the League of Nations would be required for any change in the mandate, England was not obligated to consult the United States. When the House of Commons had asked whether, because of the 1924 treaty, the United States would be consulted on modifications in mandate policy, the colonial secretary admitted only that England would keep American interests in mind. Like the United States, it interpreted the 1924 convention narrowly and considered American rights limited to those largely economic in nature.[38]

The American conclusions: 1. "Radical solution" most likely meant partition. 2. The department would need to weigh the reaction to partition in British circles, including Parliament and England's Jews. Either the information would confirm the noninvolvement stand of the department, or, less likely, it would force the department to reconsider its stand. The tenor of the despatches indicated, however, that Washington was prepared to yield the initiative for the maintenance of cordial relations with England.[39]

England's narrow interpretation of the 1924 convention bolstered the department's rejection of the Zionist argument. Simultaneously, however, it sought to arm itself with proof that it hadn't entirely ignored Jewish demands. Hours before the Peel report was to be released, it submitted a memorandum to Foreign Secretary Eden that sounded very much like a Zionist brief. It showed with specific examples how both the presidents and Congress, as well as American Jews (and even a British statesman), had manifested ongoing support of a Jewish national home. The statement made no demand that England consult the United States, but it insisted yet again that the British pay close attention to American interests.[40] Too little and too late to change England's mind, the document nevertheless protected Washington. Should American public opinion ever question its handling (or mishandling) of the Palestine situation, the department could show that it had in fact fully apprised England of the Zionists' case.

The Peel report was published in July 1937, and as expected the proposal of partition satisfied neither Arabs nor Jews. The former rejected the idea of any Jewish state and began new rounds of attacks—the State Department called them "political disturbances"—that lasted until World War II, and the latter opposed the suggested boundaries that severely constricted the desired Jewish state. England left room for negotiations with both sides before partition took effect, and it delegated the task of working out the technical matters to the newly appointed Woodhead Commission.

On the sensitive issue of Jewish immigration, the British government acted on a recommendation of the Peel Commission. Since the *yishuv* had proved that economic developments could support increased immigration, England jettisoned the principle of "economic absorptive capacity" (fixed in 1922) for that of "political high level." The numbers of new Jewish immigrants now depended on British determination to placate the Arabs by keeping the ratio of Jews to Arabs at about 30 to 70. Despite loud protests from Jews against the departure from the earlier guideline, England set a maximum of twelve thousand immigrants annually to apply at least through March 1938; subsequent action extended the restrictive policy, with only slight modifications, throughout that year.[41]

Consul General Wadsworth in Jerusalem approved the new guidelines, and he warned that if England yielded to Jewish pressure on behalf of the refugees, political problems in the mandate would be further complicated. The State Department agreed, fully aware that England could point to America's own policy of restricted immigration to counter any American insistence on lifting the barriers.[42] But the need of a haven was underscored in 1938 by the Nazi *Anschluss* of Austria and by *Kristallnacht* in Germany. Appeals to the department multiplied. One, a resolution by the House of Representatives, called on Hull to urge the relaxation of British policy. Observers pessimistically believed that the quotas would be slashed still further. Even Murray was forced to admit that "the situation in Palestine is not an encouraging one in relation to the refugee problem."[43]

The State Department carefully monitored reactions to the partition plan from American and other sources—Palestine and the rest of the Near East, the House of Commons and the British press, European capitals and the League of Nations. It also studied the economic conditions in Palestine and the impact of Arab-Jewish clashes on the economy. International developments—Nazi expansionism, Mussolini's activity in the Mediterranean, England's long-range policy in the Near East, and the worsening condition of European Jews-now colored assessments of the Palestine situation. Worrisome too was Arab "Americanophobia," generated by the belief that since Jews controlled the American press and government, the United States very likely would intervene in their favor. The department knew that if partition took effect, treaties safeguarding American interests would be required with the new Arab and Jewish states and with England, which would remain in control of certain areas.[44] But for the time being it saw no reason to become involved.

The department paid careful attention to the responses of American Jews as well. To be sure, as Murray told his superiors, the small number of American Zionists, only 207,000 shekel payers out of a Jewish population of some 4,500,000, didn't seem to warrant any concern,[45] but despite its biases the Near Eastern division could not ignore pressure that might arouse Congress or the White House to suggest intervention.

A few days after the appearance of the Peel report, Stephen Wise sent Hull a long Zionist memorandum against partition. It rehashed the usual points on American interests in Palestine and on the right of the United States to intervene if changes were made in the mandate. But this time, without any other options, it invoked humanitarianism. Stating that the partition plan, with many built-in flaws, would only increase Arab-Jewish tension and require additional armed force by the British, the Zionists demanded justice for the Jews. Humanitarian concern for the targets of Nazism dictated the need for American sympathy, and Palestine as a Jewish national home would remedy in some measure the persecution suffered by European Jews. Although Wise mentioned that the memorandum was approved by Justice Brandeis, an adviser to the president, the Zionist plea went unheeded.[46]

When Wise requested Hull to arrange an appointment for him with Foreign Secretary Eden through the embassy in London, the department reluctantly agreed. Bingham, however, was instructed to assure the Foreign Office that Wise's views were not necessarily those of the American government. An appointment was set, but Eden, claiming that he was too busy to intervene in a matter that rightly belonged to the Colonial Office, passed Wise on to a subordinate. The rabbi returned the snub with one of his own. He neither appeared for the appointment nor gave notice of a cancellation.[47]

At the World Zionist Congress that convened in mid-August 1937, the proceedings were marked by divisiveness within Zionist ranks. All factions agreed that the Peel report was unacceptable with respect to boundaries, but the Weizmann-led majority, mindful of the desperate need for a refuge, authorized negotiations with England that might lead to a Jewish state. Passions ran high, and Wise, a leading dissenter, challenged Weizmann. The rabbi objected to any dealings with England on the idea of partition, but he failed to carry the American delegates. The tally was: ZOA, sixteen in favor of partition and six, including Wise, opposed; Hadassah, three in favor and six opposed; Mizrachi (Religious Zionists), eighteen opposed; Labor Zionists, fifty-two in favor.[48] Meanwhile, a poll conducted in July by the New York Yiddish daily *Jewish Morning Journal* revealed that 4631 of 6774 respondents approved partition, if the proposed area of a Jewish state were enlarged, and that 1945 were opposed.[49]

A week later the vote in the council of the Jewish Agency, which included non-Zionists as well as Zionists, was also divided. Consul General Wadsworth reported that Maurice Hexter, an American non-Zionist on the council whom Wadsworth respected, had told him privately that "Western Jewry envisages with no little foreboding the setting-up of a Jewish State in which the preponderant majority must necessarily bear the stamp of long-persecuted, less culturally-developed Eastern European Jewry." A similar position was taken by the non-Zionist American Jewish Committee, and at a conference of the United Palestine Appeal one non-Zionist delegate enumerated twelve reasons for opposition to partition.[50] Although the department preferred the more as-similated non-Zionists over the Zionists, it was still not swayed to an antiparti-tion stand.

The lack of unity among the Jews eased the government's problem. How realistic was it to expect the department to side with a subgroup of a small minority? In Murray's words: "In view of this clear division of opinion among the representatives of American Jews it seems to me that we are in a strong position to request that they come to some agreement among themselves before they approach us with a view to our taking any particular line of action." But Jewish pressure continued to be an annoyance. Since the embassy in London was also bombarded with letters from America, Murray suggested that a member of the embassy staff, when in America, handle the petitioners. Not only would that lighten the ambassador's burden, but it would keep him better informed about the American scene. Furthermore, since the League of Nations had agreed to receive petitions from individuals and organizations, the Near Eastern division hoped that Jews and their friends would turn to Geneva instead of Washington.[51]

Murray was particularly pleased that Wise, the ever troublesome Zionist bent on forcing the government to intervene, and one who tried to circumvent the department by appeals to the White House, had suffered a major defeat. The chief of the Near Eastern division told his superiors that the votes in the Zionist Congress and the Jewish Agency proved that Wise spoke neither for the American Zionists nor for the non-Zionists: "We seem to be in a good position to ask Rabbi Wise to produce some proof that he speaks on behalf of all of American Jewry before we comply with any specific requests that he may make." Murray preferred the Jewish Agency to the ZOA if only because its makeup belied the Zionists' claim that they represented all Jews. His views were corroborated by a prominent Zionist and opponent of Wise who confided to Murray that the rabbi had prevented a debate on partition by the ZOA in order to conceal any dissension that might embarrass him. Murray concluded as well from the *Morning Journal*'s poll that the Jewish rank and file did not support Wise or other "extreme" leaders. Noting European opposition to Wise, he happily announced that "the Rabbi's position is an extreme attitude which is out of harmony with that of World Jewry."[52]

Alert as well to non-Jewish American opinion, the department tabulated newspaper editorials on partition, those favoring the Jews and those favoring the Arabs. It also noted the concerns of Arab Americans, pro-Arab missionary and educational institutions, and businessmen. The head of an oil company operating in Saudi Arabia, for example, warned that if the government supported Jewish claims on partition, American oil interests in the Persian Gulf would suffer. Members of Congress added their opinions, and the Senate passed a resolution asking the department for material on the situation. Roosevelt too showed an interest. Talk to me about the Palestine issue, he told Hull. Was it true that modification of the mandate required American approval? The department dutifully prepared a long report for the president; reviewing the evidence, it reasserted that the government was not obligated to support a Jewish national home.[53]

In October 1937 Murray and two associates conferred with Dr. Benjamin Akzin. A different type of Zionist, Akzin was a political scientist and constitutional lawyer who had received his academic training in Europe. Serving in 1937 as a professor of international law in the United States, he was a prominent member of the New Zionist Organization (NZO), the right-wing Revisionist party. Doubtless because of his cosmopolitan background and demeanor, his academic credentials, and his seemingly easy entrée into various European ministries, Akzin impressed Murray. Moreover, in opposition to Chaim Weizmann, his organization asked far less of the United States than mainstream Zionists. To be sure, Akzin like the American Zionists called for unrestricted Jewish immigration into Palestine, but his case rested not on the Balfour Declaration and the mandate but on the broader issue of world peace.

Akzin spoke confidently of 100,000 European Jews who could emigrate annually and reach Palestine. He said that the NZO looked to young men and women in their twenties, who would reduce the pressure of Jewish competition in the eastern European labor markets and simultaneously build up the *yishuv*. If Transjordan as well as Palestine were part of a Jewish national home, and this was a primary plank of the NZO platform, room would be had for about six million Jews. He added that the NZO, after inquiries in influential diplomatic circles, doubted that the Arab reaction would be as hostile as expected. Given the NZO's goals, partition was out of the question.

Different from the usual treatment accorded to Zionist petitioners, Murray himself brought Akzin's views to the attention of the British. The latter, however, contradicted the major points of the plan. More than ever before the British were resentful of American interference. The embassy in London reported that "it has been implied that the British Government would dislike and might even resent receiving from the United States or any country such informal comments as [Dr. Akzin] proposed." Hoping that the State Department would appreciate England's position, the Foreign Office asked that it "not press the British Government further." Murray was also told that the Jewish question was a world problem and one that England alone should not have to solve. A more reasonable approach, the British thought, would be for the United States to increase its own immigration quotas![54]

Murray showed a keen interest in the plan of another Zionist, American-born Judah Magnes of Jerusalem. Early in 1938 the chief of the Near Eastern division learned that Magnes had met with Nuri Said Pasha, a prominent Iraqi official, and discussed a possible Arab-Jewish settlement for Palestine. Following attempts by a few non-Zionists in the Jewish Agency to dismiss partition and seek a rapprochement with the Arabs, Magnes revived his proposal for a binational state that had first appeared in 1929, and he urged Zionists to initiate policies of compromise. He personally was ready to accept an annual limit on Jewish immigration that would consign the Jews to minority status in Palestine. (He later stated that he hadn't suggested *permanent* minority status but rather a temporary arrangement for ten years that would bring the number of Jews to 40 percent of the population.) Although Zionist leaders denounced the negotiations, and although the colonial secretary was harshly critical, Magnes announced that he and his Iraqi acquaintance spoke for the Jews of the United States, England, and Germany.

The claim was grossly exaggerated; at best it included some non-Zionists. In principle Magnes had the support of Felix Warburg, influential leader of the American non-Zionists in the Jewish Agency. But, after the riots of 1929, when Magnes had put forth a similar solution, Warburg had sided against him and with Weizmann. With Warburg's death, shortly before the negotiations with Nuri began, Magnes was handicapped from the start. The Magnes-Nuri talks collapsed, and the vast majority of Zionists remained committed, albeit conditionally, to partition. Since Murray, however, seemed impressed with Magnes, the Near Eastern division directed Wadsworth to stay in touch with the American rabbi on efforts for an Arab-Jewish compromise.[55]

On a trip to Palestine in October 1938 Murray met Magnes. The American official had great respect for the president of the Hebrew University—"Dr. Magnes is admitted, even by those Jewish leaders who differ with him, to be one of the most distinguished intellectuals in American, as well as international Jewry"—and he approved of Magnes' criticism of the Zionists. By then, however, Magnes admitted regretfully that a negotiated settlement like the one he had proposed was no longer possible.[56]

The Woodhead Commission on the implementation of partition gathered information from April until August 1938, five months marked by Arab violence. Informed of the commission's activity, the State Department also studied the threat of the Arab revolt to American citizens and property. But it kept silent on partition even when, for the first time during the disturbances that had escalated since 1936, an American was killed in an Arab massacre.[57]

The furor over partition steadily gave way in 1938 to concentration on the immigration issue. In Jewish calculations the plight of the refugees now transcended the aim of preserving the Balfour Declaration and the mandate. Nevertheless, the department studiously avoided any discussion of Palestine for the refugees. Although the *yishuv* applauded Roosevelt's suggestion in March 1938 for an international conference in Evian on the refugee problem, American delegates were instructed to resist any effort to put Palestine on the agenda. Fearing that the subject might wreck the conference's deliberations, the United States also promised that no country was expected to receive more immigrants than permitted by its existing legislation. When the conference created an Intergovernmental Committee on Political Refugees, the State Department resisted public attempts to press that committee on immigration to Palestine. It prepared a bland reply to such appeals, saying merely that both the committee and the department were considering all pertinent matters.[58]

In June 1938, Stephen Wise and four others, Zionists and non-Zionists, tried a new approach with the department. They raised what was seemingly an economic matter, but their underlying concern was immigration. Acting very possibly on a suggestion by British Jews, they asked Hull's cooperation in an attempt to obtain special trading privileges from England for Palestinian citrus growers. Such privileges would increase opportunities for labor, thereby enlarging the economic absorptive capacity of the land, which in turn, according to the guideline laid down by England in 1922, would permit additional immigrants. (They ignored the Peel Commission's "political high level" principle.) Citing the major American Jewish investments in Palestine, they explained that only the "appalling situation" of European Jews forced them to seek help with their burden. The delegation added that the plan accorded with American interests, but the department, now more fearful of compounding political issues, tabled the request.[59]

Under the shadow of the Munich Pact (September 1938), the situation of European Jews grew ever more desperate. The *yishuv* feared that HMG's policy of appeasing Hitler would be replicated in its approach to the Arabs; apprehensive Jews thought that the betrayal of Czechoslovakia "was a poignant augury of what Jewry might expect from . . . London." In the United States Rabbi Solomon Goldman, then president of the ZOA, told Hull: "The anxiety of American Jewry with respect to Palestine far surpasses that which has been exhibited . . . in this generation with regard to any other Jewish problem." Eyes trained on Washington, and the State Department, barraged by appeals for admitting refugees into Palestine, considered anew how far it could and should maneuver within the boundaries of nonintervention. It noted with surprise that twenty-two out of twenty-five newspaper editorials said that the United States had the duty and the right to intervene.[60]

The refugee problem, now linked inseverably with the Palestinian settlement, compounded the mounting tension in anticipation of the Woodhead report. In October the British were seriously considering the adoption of Arab proposals amounting to the virtual nullification of the Balfour Declaration and the end to more than token Jewish immigration. Murray, who was then in the Near East, heard from British officials that the Arabs refused to discuss a permanent settlement for Palestine unless Jewish immigration was first drastically curtailed. The implication was clear; British strategic interests left no choice but to appease the Arabs.[61]

Alerted by Chaim Weizmann, American Zionists set up an emergency committee, which organized a national letter-writing campaign to the State Department and White House. A new Zionist lobbying tactic, the campaign succeeded. By the middle of the month Western Union had handled thirty-four thousand telegrams from Jews and their sympathizers—with more still coming in—and the Postal Telegraph Company some 30,500. (Only at the time of Roosevelt's plan to revamp the Supreme Court in 1937 were those numbers surpassed.) The bulk of the mail protested the alleged intention of England "to curtail or eliminate Jewish immigration" by altering the terms of the mandate and repudiating the Balfour Declaration. Several congressmen took up that argument, as did a resolution from Pennsylvania's state legislature and a wire from American Federation of Labor chief William Green to labor leaders in London. European Jewish leaders, often at odds with American Zionists, commended the campaign and said that the Americans were doing their utmost.[62]

Meantime in Tel Aviv, three hundred representatives of the eight to nine thousand permanent American Jewish settlers added their protests. They contended that their faith in the Anglo-American treaty of 1924 had led them to invest their resources in the *yishuv*. Nevertheless, the department ruled that the argument didn't change the legal picture, because the United States had not assumed responsibility for the establishment of a Jewish national home and the treaty was not meant to encourage American settlement in Palestine.[63]

To counteract Jewish activity the Arabs intensified their own lobbying in Washington. As did the British authorities in Palestine, Arabs still suspected that America, under pressure from the Jews, was pressing England to a pro-Jewish settlement. Their charges incorporated anti-Jewish imagery; Jewish influence and wealth, one Arab said, "enslave America." In a rare show of unity they argued primarily against any American interference. A wave of intense anti-Americanism, the likes of which had not been seen before, swept Arab communities throughout the Near East. Denouncing the president and American Christian churches for succumbing to the Zionists, the Arabs were particularly incensed over a speech by New York's Senator Robert Wagner. The latter had stated that Roosevelt was doing all he could to prevent the curtailment of Jewish immigration, and that in sympathy with a Jewish national home in Palestine he was prepared to take more than "normal" action.[64]

Like England, the State Department was forced to juggle Arab and Jewish arguments. Both sides now appeared more formidable; the department was impressed by the degree of American Jewish solidarity and by Arab threats. More ominous were the international ramifications of the Palestinian situation. Hitler and Mussolini sided with the Arabs, and along with Muslim activism in the Near East and India, they posed a grave threat to England. Were the latter to yield to Jewish pressure on the refugee issue, it would exacerbate the situation. The department continued to speculate about the Woodhead report and to debate the question of whether the United States had ever assumed obligations for a Jewish national home. It found some relief in the thought that any policy announced by England would require time to be implemented, thereby allowing the United States to maintain its neutrality, at least for a period of transition. In response to public criticism and petitions, Hull directed Ambassador Joseph Kennedy in London to tell the foreign secretary informally of the reaction in the United States. Like Bingham before him, Kennedy was instructed to deny that the department harbored any desires to interfere in British policy.[65]

The sheer volume of public pressure forced the department to break its silence. In mid-October it issued a press release that cited examples of America's interest in a Jewish national home since the World War: "It is in light of this interest that the American Government and people have watched with the keenest sympathy the development in Palestine of the National Home, a project in which American intellect and capital have played a leading role." The statement told how the department had alerted England several times to the rights of America and its nationals. Those "rights" comprised "non-discriminatory treatment in matters of commerce, non-impairment of vested American property rights, permission for American nationals to establish and maintain educational, philanthropic and religious institutions in Palestine, safeguards with respect to the judiciary, and, in general, equality of treatment with all other foreign nationals." On the key point at issue with the Zionists and their sympathizers—the right of the United States, according to Article 7 of the 1924 treaty, to intervene if the terms of the mandate were changed—the department said that the government was *not* empowered "to prevent the modification of the terms of any of the mandates." It could only "decline to recognize the validity of the application to American interests of any modification . . . unless such modification has been assented to by the . . . United States." Since "interests" had been defined narrowly and limited for the most part to economic concerns, it was abundantly clear that changes in immigration regulations did not legitimate American intervention.[66]

At best an expression of neutrality, the news release was seen by some officials as a pro-Jewish gesture. Paul Alling of the Near Eastern division suggested that an advance copy be sent to England to "appease" American Jews. But, the statement had no or little impact on the Arabs. American officials in Jerusalem, Baghdad, and Cairo continued to report Arab fear of American support of the

Jews, and from a few cities came threats of anti-American reprisals if the "justice" of the Arab cause was ignored.[67]

The same day that the press release appeared, sixteen American Jewish leaders of national Jewish organizations, Zionist and non-Zionist, waited on Hull. Their written presentation elaborated the usual arguments, but more than before, the appeal was to American humanitarianism. If England defaulted on its obligations and limited or stopped immigration, the harm to refugees would be incalculable: "Such a situation would constitute . . . a cruel blow that would aggravate the indescribable plight of the refugees from lands of oppression. . . . Are they to be barred, in the hour of their most desperate need, from asylum in their ancient homeland, the historic connection with which is hallowed by a continuous tradition of thousands of years and which was made a keystone of the mandate for Palestine?" Although the department learned from the Zionist press that the ZOA also planned mass meetings and a mass petition to Roosevelt, it saw no reason to add to its press release. The assistant chief of the Near Eastern division cynically observed that the focus on humanitarianism showed that the Jews themselves recognized the weakness of their legal argument.[68]

Some weeks later, upon his return from a trip to the Near East, Wallace Murray prepared a long, confidential memorandum that aimed at justifying an anti-Zionist stand. His message to his superiors was twofold: Don't change course and don't be swayed by Zionist propaganda. Murray thought that American Zionist sentiment was overrated. Even if 100,000 Jews were Zionists, that amounted to fewer than 10 percent of Jewish families in the United States. It was beyond doubt, he maintained, that "many . . . hundreds of thousands of American Jews" disapproved of Zionism but feared to speak out because of Zionist power. Murray cited statements from Jews themselves on the sharp division between Zionists and non- or anti-Zionists. The latter accused Zionism—a "filthy racket," one critic charged—of intimidating the community. Powerful, well organized, and vociferous, the Zionists were responsible for the pressure brought on Congress and the state legislatures.

Murray also charged that Zionists were using the refugee crisis for their own advantage; they had sabotaged both the Evian conference as well as attempts to settle Jews in havens other than Palestine. Since the Roosevelt administration had proved its concern for refugees, whose needs in any case could not be met by Palestine, "it should be possible for this Government to give *less* [emphasis added] support than it has in the past to Zionist insistence [on] large-scale immigration." In light of the department's consistently negative record, one can only wonder what "less" support, other than an open alliance with the Arabs, meant!

On the basis of evidence gleaned since 1936, Murray explained why American national interests could not permit pressure on England. First, support of England meant support of democracy in the Near East, and England, poised against the Axis, could not afford to arouse Arab enmity. Second, both American oilmen and leaders of Christian philanthropic and educational institutions maintained that their operations would be jeopardized were the government to adopt a pro-Zionist position. Third, why undermine American prestige in an area that had developed since the World War? Finally, Palestine was not "our" problem, and the government had no cause to assume any responsibility for a resolution of the Arab-Jewish controversy.[69]

From the Woodhead Report to "Palestine's Munich"

Not surprisingly the report of the Woodhead Commission in November 1938 concluded that partition of Palestine would be impracticable and unworkable. Thereupon England invited the Jewish Agency and Arabs from Palestine and neighboring states to send representatives to London for conferences. If the two sides did not agree, the British would unilaterally determine a settlement. Mindful of Jewish pressure in England and the United States, London temporarily shelved the idea of an Arab state. That month in Germany the horrors of *Kristallnacht* (the night of the broken glass, when Nazis went on an anti-Jewish rampage) also dictated temporary silence on the issues of refugees and immigration. Observers thought that ultimately, if the conferences failed, England's declared policy would jibe with Arab demands.[70]

Chaim Weizmann called the Woodhead report "the most unjust report in twenty years." The *yishuv* was relieved that England had not announced its repudiation of the Balfour Declaration or alteration of the mandate, but Zionist apprehension deepened. The report was but a temporary holding device, and they despaired of the inattention to refugee needs. Again the State Department was deluged by petitions in various languages from Jews worldwide. Some officials in British and American diplomatic circles likened unyielding Jewish insistence on a national home in accordance with the Balfour Declaration to Shylock's demand for a pound of flesh. (The analogy came easily to those who equated Jews generally with Shylock.) They posited that the Jewish demand, as in *The Merchant of Venice*, would necessarily lead to Christian as well as Arab bloodshed.[71]

Arab arguments, now better developed and more polished, continued too. Insisting on noninterference, or that America live up to its own principles of self-determination and international justice, Arabs brandished the threat of anti-American reprisals. As for the refugees, well, Arabs were sympathetic, but the problem justified neither Jewish oppression of the Arabs nor the idea that they alone bore responsibility for the solution. Since the State Department agreed that Palestine, even with unrestricted immigration, could not solve the refugee crisis, the Near Eastern division recommended that the government take steps to allay Arab fears.[72]

Murray played the "oil card" when King Ibn Saud of Saudi Arabia sent a letter to Roosevelt. Calling the monarch the most outstanding Arab ruler and a friend of America and American oil interests, Murray counseled his superiors to treat Ibn Saud seriously. But in a short reply drafted by Undersecretary Sumner Welles and signed "Your Good Friend," Roosevelt merely assured the king of America's neutral position as expressed in the October news release.[73]

Until the London conferences opened in February 1939, the State Department monitored opinion on the chances of a settlement. To the numerous messages it received linking Palestine to the refugee problem, the department gave a stock reply: It was on top of the situation. Unmoved by reports that predicted a pro-Arab settlement, Murray privately agreed with the British high commissioner in Palestine that the Jews' incessant pleading about their rights and the needs of their persecuted brethren threatened an antisemitic backlash. As he had in the fall of 1938, he maintained to Hull and Welles that American national interests, including the country's identification with England's defense of democracy, dictated a policy of nonintervention. Now he added that if England collapsed under attack by the Axis allied with the Arabs, the Jews in Palestine would be massacred. Hence, involvement meant "a disservice to ourselves, to the British, to the cause of democracy, and in the end to the Zionist Jews themselves."[74]

During the winter and early spring of 1939, Wadsworth in Jerusalem reported several times on the yishuv's affection for the president. His statements after Kristallnacht and his expressed hope that increased numbers of refugees, especially children, would be allowed into Palestine lifted their spirits. The Near Eastern division worried, however, lest the president, on whom Jews were building their hopes, become a loose cannon and utter rash comments that could inflame anti-Americanism in Arab circles. Thus, even if the president's sympathy for the refugees was genuine, the State Department would have to restrain his impulses.[75]

Once the London negotiations began, Arabs grew more anxious lest Zionists lead the United States to intervene. A request for American inaction was made directly to the department by the Egyptian government. Since British officials in the Near East were saying that American pressure prevented a just settlement, the department believed that England had instigated Cairo's move. Nevertheless, Murray didn't question the equation of "just" with pro-Arab, and the department assured Cairo of the government's nonintervention.[76]

The American Zionists at the London conferences included three from the ZOA, Stephen Wise, Robert Szold, and Louis Lipsky, and one, Rose Jacobs, of Hadassah. Wise—who had seen Prime Minister Neville Chamberlain—and Szold reported in mid-February to the American embassy in London on a plan suggested by the Colonial Office to end Jewish immigration after a fixed number of years. By this time the Jewish representatives had exhausted their counterarguments. They could only maintain that a cessation of immigration contradicted the mandate and that they were opposed to any proposal making the Jews a permanent minority in Palestine. At the conferences the right of the

Americans to speak for the *yishuv* and the WZO was questioned by an Arab delegate. After all, he pointedly asked Wise, how many American Jews had settled in Palestine since the war?[77]

A few days later the Foreign Secretary confirmed the essence of the Wise-Szold report in a talk with Ambassador Kennedy. England planned to terminate the mandate, and by limiting Jewish immigration over five years to 100,000 to 150,000, create an Arab-dominated state. Shortly thereafter a British official deposited a copy of the plan at the State Department. If unacceptable to both sides, it would be imposed by England on the two peoples. At a time when many American Jews were pleading that England not abandon European Jewry to "moral extermination," the foreign secretary had decided that ethical considerations or justice for the Jews took second place to England's diplomatic agenda.[78] The as yet unannounced policy had the outspoken support of British officials in Palestine. Haven't we already met our obligations under the Balfour Declaration and the mandate, they asked? Clearly, as Chaim Weizmann put it to an American diplomat, "zero hour" for the *yishuv* had arrived. Meanwhile, at the State Department Murray admitted that the British plan jibed with the extremist Arab position, but he thought that the five-year grace period for immigration would do much to solve the refugee problem. The Near Eastern division took note of public indignation voiced in the press over England's move at a time when Nazi persecution was running rampant—"Haman to Hitler—and Chamberlain," one article read—but Murray's staff was surprised that editorials put hardly any blame on the Jews, who, the department added, were as obstinate as the Arabs.[79] Nevertheless, those who called for American intervention lacked the strength to influence official policy.

The conferences ended in failure in mid-March, and again waiting began, this time for official announcement of England's decision. The Arabs grew increasingly convinced of American sympathy with the Jewish cause. Doubtless they heard of the rising tide of support in Congress for the Balfour Declaration and for American interests in Palestine. They also believed the story that Ambassador Kennedy (who personally denied the report) had told Lord Halifax, the foreign secretary, that American public opinion would be outraged were England to modify the mandate or reduce immigration. Very possibly they were impressed too by a news release in Palestine that Zionist leaders Wise and Solomon Goldman met with FDR in March and elicited strong expressions of presidential sympathy. On this "evidence," some Arabs blamed the United States outright for the failure of the conferences. Washington, however, hardly ever replied to Arab criticism. Hull advised Kennedy confidentially that the department would resist efforts to embroil the United States in the Palestine problem at least until England published its final plans.[80]

Mixed signals emanated from London. Stories of Whitehall's intention to scrap the mandate and prepare for an independent (= Arab) state—in substance the same plan that had been conveyed to Washington in mid-March—

continued to circulate, and so did a report that American Jewish influence re-strained the British from completely ignoring the Jews.[81] A few weeks before the appearance of the White Paper in May 1939, Wadsworth described the bit-terness of the *yishuv* over the expected "betrayal" by England. He also re-counted at length his meeting with Chaim Weizmann. The troubled Zionist leader had considered a visit to America and a direct appeal to Roosevelt, but in light of the international situation and his fear that Jews would be charged with undermining Anglo-American friendship, he rejected the idea. A confirmed Anglophile, Weizmann felt personally betrayed. To argue as Halifax did that practical necessities transcended ethical values was, Weizmann said, "to place onesself [sic] on the same plane with Hitler." He warned that drastic action by England would alienate five million American Jews. Wadsworth reported fur-ther on a more bellicose mood in the *yishuv*. A leading American Zionist had told him: "One thing you can be sure of is that if the British let us down, we are d[amned] well not going to take it lying down."[82]

Weizmann, who had pleaded since March that England delay a final settle-ment, was supported on that point by Louis Brandeis. The two men were hardly close friends, but at this juncture they cooperated. The Supreme Court justice suggested to Roosevelt on May 4 that he request a postponement from England. Five days later he forwarded a cable from Weizmann asking the presi-dent to denounce as a "breach of international trust" any move by England that "liquidated" its commitment to a Jewish national home. Roosevelt, who kept Brandeis informed of developments, sought to reassure his friend that every-thing possible was being done. He wrote to Welles: "I still believe that any an-nouncement about Palestine at this time by the British Government is a mis-take, and I think we should tell them that. What can I say to Justice Brandeis?" Welles, however, balked at American interference. He advised that Brandeis be told only that "our point of view is put before England whenever possible."[83] What that point of view explicitly was, or whether it had changed since the news release of the previous October, he didn't say. The president may have been eager to do Brandeis a favor, but he didn't override his State Department.

Roosevelt read an advance copy of the White Paper two days before it was published. The statement called for an independent Palestine within ten years. Aiming to keep the Jews at no more than one-third of the population, it also provided for the immigration of seventy-five thousand for five years—ten thousand annually plus twenty-five thousand refugees. After five years no addi-tional Jewish immigrants would be allowed without Arab consent. In addition, new measures against illegal immigrants were also promised. Expressing his dismay, the president termed the statement "deceptive," because, as he said, the whole world had thought that the intent of the Balfour Declaration was to con-vert Palestine into a Jewish home. Nor were limitations on Jewish immigration in accord with the mandate. In sum, Roosevelt doubted that the United States could approve the British policy. His own rather mild suggestion was to keep the figure of seventy-five thousand for five years and to renew discussions. If the question of immigration was not resolved then, the provisions of the White Paper would be extended temporarily for another five years. The State Department, however, disagreed. Murray called England's new policy as reasonable a compromise as could be expected, and he saw no necessity for an official American response.[84]

The White Paper, or "Palestine's Munich" as Senator Robert Taft termed it, was issued on May 17. A crippling blow to Zionism and to the cause of the refugees, it marked a permanent parting of the ways between England and the *yishuv*. What had heretofore been a three-way struggle among Jews, Arabs, and England became essentially two conflicts, one a Jewish-British impasse and one a Jewish-Arab struggle. The outbreak of the Second World War some three and a half months later made Jews worldwide the captive allies of the powers fighting Hitler. England grew less sensitive to Jewish pressure, and Jews were forced to blunt their anti-British animosity. Where it could, the *yishuv* took matters into its own hands—resorting to violence, smuggling in illegal immigrants, and building up the *haganah*, the nucleus of its future army.

Nor did the United States budge from its decade-long policy on Palestine. Roosevelt's campaign against the isolationists from 1939 until Pearl Harbor gave his pro-British administration another powerful reason for maintaining silence. Why risk isolationist ill will by interference in a comparatively minor matter when the cultivation of an anti-Nazi consensus was the first priority? Not until the defeat of the Axis some three years later did the United States support the Zionist goal of Jewish statehood. And then, in 1948, it was an eleventh-hour move by Roosevelt's successor, Harry Truman, against the better judgment of the State Department.

Events during the war years spurred on American Zionists, like the *yishuv*, to develop an assertiveness of their own. Their experience with immigration in the 1930s taught them that appeals based on American precedents or American principles, like humanitarian diplomacy, were insufficient. They never forgot the need to defend, and indeed to parade, the American-like characteristics of their movement, but World War II and the desire to prevent the total extermination of European Jewry at the hands of the Nazis rapidly broadened their focus. Within a very short time, the Zionist drive for American Jewish solidarity on behalf of Jewish survival *by means of a Jewish state* became at least as important as the need for complete identification with America. The era of Palestinianism drew to a close, and American Zionism with all its Americanized features reverted to the Herzlian goal of Jewish statehood.

CHAPTER 7

The American Jewish Conference: A Zionist Experiment at Unity and Leadership

O n August 29, 1943, forty-six years to the day that Theodor Herzl opened the first Zionist congress, the American Jewish Conference, an organization of national Jewish organizations, was launched. The announced purpose of the Zionist-inspired, democratically elected, and communitywide conference was threefold: it would work for free immigration to Palestine, the rescue of European Jews, and the postwar resettlement of Jews in the war-ravaged countries.

Two paramount objectives underlay the Zionist plan, the mobilization of public sentiment on behalf of a Jewish state in Palestine and the unity of American Jews under Zionist leadership. Each of those goals, if reached, would radically change existing patterns of communal behavior. A Jewish state presaged the end of a long period of Palestinianism and a return to the first principles of political Zionism. A unified community under Zionist control meant first, that the old established organizations would accept a reduction of their powers, and second, that Zionists would replace the stewards of the entrenched and oligarchical Jewish Establishment. The obstacles to be overcome appeared virtually insurmountable, but Zionist determination to create a conference won out. Since the Anglo-Jewish and Yiddish press had discussed a conference for several months during the spring and summer, a mood of excitement and anticipation gripped the Jewish community.

The hour appeared right for major communal changes. After the Arab riots of 1929, the Zionists realized that their fight both for unrestricted immigration and America's lasting commitment to the Balfour Declaration required American Jewish solidarity and unremitting Jewish pressure on public opinion and on Washington. Zionist lobbying became more serious in 1938, and it continued to expand during the war years. Resembling other American pressure groups, Zionists Americanized their tactics as they had their ideology. Now, intensified Zionist resolve in light of the bleak situation of European Jewry set the stage for what historian Evyatar Friesel has termed an "extra-ordinary" period of American Zionist expansion.[1]

Yet, despite a dramatic shift in tactics, Zionists continued to insist on the compatibility of their aims with Americanism. They applauded the democratic and hence American-like character of the conference. At the same time they sought to impress upon the public that their purposes were equivalent to American wartime aims. Although the conference can be studied as a manifestation of Jewish particularism, the Zionists preferred to insist that they were acting as loyal Americans.

The achievements of the American Jewish Conference and its very viability were tested during the first year of its existence. All understood that the future of the conference would be decided at the second meeting of the elected delegates in the fall of 1944; either the organization would correct the shortcomings that had become apparent after it began and win the renewed confidence of the Jewish public, or it would admit failure and close up shop. At stake was the future of the American Zionist movement and American support of a Jewish state.

Preliminaries and Initial Victories

The immediate event that started the wheels turning for an American Jewish Conference was the special Zionist congress in the spring of 1942. At New York's Biltmore Hotel in May, close to six hundred delegates under a new and more militant leadership unanimously demanded unrestricted immigration into Palestine. They further resolved that "Palestine be established as a Jewish Commonwealth integrated in the structure of the new democratic world." Adding that "then and only then will the age-old wrong to the Jewish people be righted," the resolution resurrected Herzl's goal of a Jewish state.[2] (The words "Jewish commonwealth," originally used by Woodrow Wilson in 1919, became the popular term after Biltmore. Although many equated it with a state, it also signified an autonomous Jewish territory, like Canada and Australia, with a place in the British empire.) The fact that many different Zionist factions united in passing the resolution was a victory in itself, but the leaders wanted more than a firm endorsement by the delegates. They aimed rather at the mobilization of all American Jews who identified as Jews, or at least a majority of them, in support of statehood. In the immediate aftermath of Biltmore, the design of a conference for achieving that aim took shape.

Written accounts usually attribute the idea of a representative body of American Jews that would ratify the Biltmore program to Henry Monsky, the national president of B'nai B'rith. But a confidential memorandum in the conference's files indicates that Monsky was acting under instructions from Chaim Weizmann. On trips to the United States in 1941–42, Weizmann negotiated unofficially with the American Jewish Committee (AJC) in efforts to undo its antinationalist stand. Since attempts at compromise with the AJC failed, he turned to Monsky and suggested the organization of a democratic body to ascertain the attitude of American Jews as a whole toward Zionism. Although Monsky personally was a Zionist, B'nai B'rith was officially neutral on the issue of statehood. Weizmann believed, therefore, that a scheme broached by Monsky would not be dismissed merely as a tool of Zionist propaganda. Without the mandate of his organization, and under the seal of strict confidentiality, Monsky agreed.[3]

Leadership as well as Zionism was involved in those first tentative steps. Monsky had resented the Weizmann/AJC negotiations, and now Weizmann was giving him the opportunity to recoup B'nai B'rith's importance at the expense of the AJC. It is plausible too that Weizmann, frustrated by the unsuccessful negotiations, was ready to discredit the leadership of the stewards by an appeal for a *democratic* group. He had worked with two former AJC leaders, Louis Marshall and Felix Warburg, but he stood little chance with the organization dominated by the autocratic Joseph M. Proskauer, an anti-Zionist or at best a non-Zionist. Weizmann had never crusaded against elitist leadership *per se*, but his only recourse was to turn to the larger Jewish public. All three players—Monsky, Weizmann, and the AJC—understood that the vague suggestion of a forum to sound out American Jews on Zionism could well lead to an attempt at mobilizing widespread support for a Jewish state.

Monsky called for a conference of organizations to be held in Pittsburgh in January 1943. Its purpose was to initiate a communitywide forum, but it was fortuitously timed to throw a wrench into the workings of the newly launched and rabidly antinationalist American Council for Judaism. (L. B. Namier, English historian and Zionist member of the Jewish Agency, referred to the prominent assimilationist, anti-Zionist supporters of the council as "trembling amateur gentiles."[4]) Without the participation of the AJC, the delegates in Pittsburgh resolved to convene a larger conference (initially called an "assembly") of individuals and organizations to recommend action on the rescue of European Jewry, Jewish rights to Palestine, and Jewish status in the postwar world.[5] Nothing yet was decided about statehood, but with Biltmore in mind, an endorsement of a Jewish commonwealth appeared imminent.

Before the day-to-day operations of the new organization had begun, Zionists had emerged victorious on the issue of leadership. By merely organizing a conference under their auspices, they had taken a major step toward the permanent repudiation of elitist control over communal policy. The AJC, the elitist agency *par excellence* and the most powerful bastion of the Jewish Establishment, as well as other anti- or non-Zionist groups, were not shorn of their importance, but as discussed below in full, the establishment of a Zionist conference severely jolted and permanently scarred the AJC. Its virtual monopoly over the direction of communal policy was finally broken.

The struggle over leadership, long antedating the conference, was woven into the history of American Zionism ever since the *Maccabaean* had railed against the Jewish stewards. Logically the two matters, Zionism and communal leadership, were quite distinct, but in fact the American Zionist movement from its very inception stood *for* a Jewish community led by democratically elected representatives and *against* the largely self-selected and anti-Zionist leaders of the Establishment. Meanwhile, the growth and maturation of the newer immigrants, the eastern Europeans who constituted the rank and file of the Zionist movement, had bred a legacy of keen resentment. Time and again rifts over leadership colored events in the early decades of the twentieth century—the relief drives for the pogrom-stricken Russian Jews, the organization of the AJC, and the drive for an American Jewish Congress in 1918. In those instances the Zionists and other opponents of steward rule were usually one and the same.

The Zionist stand on leadership stood to gain popularity in democratic America just because it was harnessed to the democratic idea. As mentioned above, the sentiment was in keeping with the teachings of Herzl, the founder of political Zionism, who called for a democratic movement after he failed to secure the patronage of Barons Edmond de Rothschild and Maurice de Hirsch. The Zionist leader claimed that the masses, in opposition to the upper-class leaders, favored Zionism, and that by democratic procedures they had to assume communal leadership and mobilize public support for a Jewish *and democratic* state. American Zionists developed the argument further. They insisted that merely replacing the stewards with men of their own choice was not the point; they were battling rather for the principle of a democratically organized community led by democratically chosen representatives. Precisely because they stood for democratic leadership, the Zionists maintained that they and not the assimilationist anti-Zionists (who had the gall to charge them with un-Americanism!) were the better Americans.[6] In 1943, Zionists again challenged the established leaders, and seizing upon the conference as their American-like democratic instrument, they successfully fought the battle for the leadership of American Jewry.

Another major Zionist victory came during the opening sessions of the conference. In a dramatic and unanticipated episode, a resolution was passed in favor of a Jewish commonwealth in Palestine—in effect a ratification of the Biltmore program.[7] To be sure, differences of opinion among the Zionists still divided the statists, who sought an immediate commitment by the Allies to Jewish statehood, and the moderates, who relied on "quiet pressure" for wresting promises from London and Washington on eventual Jewish autonomy. Moreover, the conference had initially agreed to omit a clause on statehood in order not to alienate the non-Zionist groups whose very affiliation with the new organization and whose support of free immigration to Palestine were deemed crucial. Nevertheless, an unscheduled appeal for a Jewish state by the charismatic rabbi and gifted orator from Cleveland, Abba Hillel Silver, upset the plans. Silver's "electrifying" remarks captivated the entire assembly; in an emotional frenzy the delegates cheered and rose to their feet to sing the Zionist anthem, *Hatikvah*. When the resolution was presented to the plenum, only four of some five hundred delegates opposed the demand for a state.

The resolution on Palestine now included two parts, one calling for the control of immigration by the Jewish Agency and the abrogation of the White Paper of 1939, and the second demanding the "recreation of the Jewish commonwealth." Passage of the resolution brought the American Zionist dream to a climax. For the first time since Herzl, the majority of American Jews who identified as members of the Jewish community endorsed a Jewish state. Despite pockets of lingering dissent, the consensus they forged in 1943 set a lasting precedent. Recognized and deferred to by government officials and political candidates ever since, it proclaimed an indestructible bond between American Jewry and the Jewish state.

Silver, the man responsible for the statists' coup, had urged the Zionists a few months earlier to reshuffle priorities and to change tactics in order to break what was called the "conspiracy of silence" in Washington with respect to the Holocaust as well as to the status of the Jews in the postwar world. His overriding aim, however, was Jewish statehood. Instead of meek accommodationism he counseled forceful demands on the government to speak out in support of Jewish *political* rights in Palestine. Like David Ben-Gurion in *yishuv*, Silver represented the new breed of nationalist leaders who agitated for a return to Herzlian principles. Enjoining his fellow Zionists to fight their own battles, he scorned reliance on the oft-broken promises of England and America. Implicitly questioning Jewish adoration of FDR, he advised dramatically, "Put not your trust in princes" (Psalms 146.3).[8]

Even the new breed of Zionist leaders never suggested that their followers mount the barricades. Despite the brave talk and despite the moral injunctions unleashed by the Holocaust, Zionists never forgot that they were Americans first, and that the cause of America at war transcended all others. They couldn't very well do without the approval of Washington and London, especially if those governments based their opposition on strategic and military wartime needs. Conditioned by a tradition of accommodationism and by a rise of popular antisemitism in the 1930s and early 1940s both at home and abroad, they believed that the very small and vulnerable Jewish minority dared not challenge or defy American inaction. They understood, therefore, that appeals to the public for support had to be based not on Zionist ideology but on American patriotism. Despite Hitler's death camps and the urgent need of Palestine as a haven if not a state, they Americanized their objectives and depicted the Jewish nationalist cause as a wartime aim. A Zionist circular made it clear: "American Zionists are first, last, and all the time American citizens eager to spend all they have and all they are to insure the victory of America against her enemies. No other consideration can diminish by one iota their devotion to this goal. American Zionists continue to be interested in Palestine because Palestine is an important outpost in *this indivisible war.*" Silver's sincerity notwithstanding, his assertive approach also kept to the limits imposed by the customary restraints—principally the Zionist reading of government and public opinion. When he talked of Jewish political activity instead of moral exhortations, he meant little more than use of the Jewish vote.[9]

Leaders of the *yishuv* also commented on how the war had heightened the American Jewish mood of accommodationism. One veteran Zionist observed: "The American Jew thinks of himself first and foremost as an American citizen. This is a fact whether we like it or not. When the . . . Zionist goes to vote in American elections, it is not the candidate's attitude to Zionism which will determine his choice. . . . Loyalty to America is now the supreme watchword."[10]

Obstacles to Unity

The times desperately called for unified action. European Jews were being systematically annihilated according to Hitler's Final Solution; the British White Paper of 1939 that drastically restricted immigration into Palestine was still operative, barring even the small number who slipped through the clutches of the Nazis in an eleventh-hour search for a refuge; the State Department, like the British, appeared intent on paring down Zionist requests. Only sustained Jewish pressure on the governments of the United States and England and on the newly created United Nations held out any hope for the rescue and survival of a remnant of Jews in postwar Europe. The European Jewish defense organizations and the World Jewish Congress (WJC),weakened or torn apart by the war, were unable to meet the demands of the situation; neither were the American Zionists, acting alone and focused primarily on a Jewish state.[11] Far weaker than they had been during World War I, when they had a chance to bargain with both England and Germany, Jews in 1943 were the captive allies of the nations fighting the Axis. Zionists could rely only on their moral position, and as a memorandum of the American Jewish Conference bluntly put it, "Morality in political affairs is not a very marketable commodity."[12]

The outlook for effective responses from a united American Jewry was gloomy. The major organizations, frightened and inhibited by antisemitism in the United States, quarreled over policy and tactics more than they cooperated. True, leaders of communal agencies met frequently and pooled information, but attempts by major defense agencies to forge a common strategy through ad hoc bodies such as the Joint Consultative Council, the Committee on Cooperation, and the General Jewish Council failed miserably.[13] Concerned Jews grew impatient with the established organizations; wasting energy and resources in needless duplication of effort, they put the enhancement of their respective images above Jewish survival. A flurry of new organizations—often just names and post office boxes—committed to different aspects of the same problems only compounded the overall confusion and paralysis. Zionist leaders confidently referred to the short-lived American Jewish Congress of 1918 as a precedent for effective unity, but even that had failed to prove a resounding Zionist success.[14]

In preparation for the first meeting of the conference, organizers called upon the community at large to hold elections for delegates. The latter were chosen indirectly; local membership organizations in various regions that were engaged in Jewish activities, or branches of national organizations, voted according to prearranged ratios for electors, who in turn chose the delegates. Provision was made for a very small representation of federations and welfare funds, usually under elitist control, and for some unaffiliated persons as well. All told, at least 2,235,000 Jews were represented; of some five hundred seats to be allocated, 379 went to delegates chosen by elections and 125 to appointees of the participating national organizations. The Zionists campaigned strenuously for their side, and results showed that most elected delegates were affiliated with the ZOA or other Zionist groups. In control of the majority of votes, the Zionists set the procedures and formulated the platform for the first plenary session. From their midst came the luminaries of the conference—Monsky of B'nai B'rith, Louis Lipsky and Israel Goldstein of the ZOA, Stephen Wise of the American Jewish Congress, and Abba Hillel Silver of the American Zionist Emergency Council. The episode of the commonwealth resolution underscored the Zionists' overwhelming victory.[15]

Critics later charged that the conference was merely a Zionist front and that the "same old leaders" were interested primarily in their own organizations. Proskauer of the AJC explained to an American senator that Zionist control was the result of "an enormous propaganda, stemming from a zealotry that knows no bounds," and the president of Hebrew Union College described Zionist methods for assumimg power as "piratical." But none could deny that the Zionists had successfully engineered a shift of power.[16]

The euphoria that greeted the establishment of the conference dissipated rapidly. The Jewish press in particular was quick to find fault with the new organization. One question, "how democratic in fact was the conference," aroused comment throughout the first year. Some thought that true democracy was elusive as long as certain organizations were excluded, and a few suggested greater participatory democracy by making the conference an open forum. Most critics, however, challenged the leadership on other grounds. They charged that despite the procedures adopted by the founders for the airing of multiple points of view, the delegates were largely silent partners. Since they and the local constituencies they represented were uninformed about policy planning, and since important decisions and directives came from the unrepresentative Executive,

Administrative, and Interim Committees, the elected delegates had little input in the formulation of policy. As a result, minority opinions were often ignored.[17]

On the eve of the second annual meeting, an executive memorandum acknowledged the shortcomings of the organization: "The Conference was created as a people's instrumentality, and the people have a right to demand from its leaders an account of their action or inaction. A major error of the Interim Committee was its failure to keep in close personal contact with the delegates and the communities throughout the country, and to take the problems of the Conference to the people at frequent intervals." As a corrective, the conference amended the structure of the committees in 1944. It promised improved communication with the delegates and it urged the latter to meet regularly with their constituents.[18]

If the conference's claims of a democratic structure were exaggerated, its boasts of overall unity were even more unreal. To begin with, the absence of the prestigious AJC, which left the conference after two and a half months, was keenly felt. Other organizations had not appeared at all. Some, such as the Orthodox Agudath Israel and Agudas Harabbonim, which objected to the secularist nature of the major participants, refused to join. Others, including the Reconstructionist Foundation, the Federation of Palestinian Jews in America, and philanthropies like ORT and the Joint Distribution Committee, were not invited because they were not national *membership* organizations. Nor did invitations go to the militant New Zionist Organization (Revisionist) and other right-wing splinter groups; more than once the conference denounced the right-wingers for their "irresponsible" ideas, and for their plan for a Jewish army in particular. Certain Communist labor unions were similarly consigned at first to the ranks of the "unacceptables," groups whose ideologies sharply contradicted the views and practices of mainstream Zionism and Jewish labor.[19]

Two numerically strong organizations, the Union of American Hebrew Congregations (Reform) and the fraternal order B'nai B'rith, affiliated but qualified their participation. The union said that since their members included both Zionists and anti-Zionists, they could not be bound by the commonwealth resolution. Monsky, expaining why B'nai B'rith hadn't voted in favor of a state, insisted that each member had the right to determine his own stand. A similar position was taken by the Central Conference of American Rabbis (Reform) as well as by the National Council of Jewish Women. Finally, the influential Jewish Labor Committee, uncomfortable with the Communists and with nationalist objectives, flitted in and out of the conference.[20]

Although the conference, during its first year and with mixed results, wooed the AJC and other "tolerable" agencies—the anti-Zionist American Council for Judaism was totally intolerable—its unity was never absolute. Collaboration with unaffiliated groups, such as the Orthodox rabbis, the Joint Distribution Committee, and even the AJC, in matters pertaining to rescue and postwar planning compensated to some small degree for inadequacies in membership.

In other instances the conference insisted that joint action be taken under its name, but despite an awareness that greater strength lay in unity, the agencies concerned rarely acceded. Forced to comply, the conference often became merely one of several equal organizations, and its claim that it spoke for a united American Jewry was inaccurate.[21] Further complicating the lack of unity was the practical matter of funding. Even if the conference represented all American Zionists and their sympathizers, and even if all of the affiliates paid the amounts levied upon them, it was virtually unable to meet its budget without the financial support of the elitist federations—miffed because they were given only token representation—and the wealthy stewards of the AJC.[22]

Of all the reasons that bred disunity, the knottiest problem concerned the distribution of power between the conference and its affiliates. Which powers belonged exclusively to the central body and which to its member organizations? Was it reasonable to expect the old established defense agencies and federations, which had carved out roles for themselves in areas relating to foreign Jews—thereby duplicating or conflicting with the work of the conference on rescue, Palestine, and postwar problems—to permit the conference to preempt their independent activities? It was difficult enough for the national organizations to cope with power sharing within their own ranks. Meanwhile, the press kept up a steady commentary on the rivalries and jealousies among the agencies. As one rabbi commented, "The measure of [the conference's] failure is the measure of individualism run riot on the part of our national organizations." Questions of sovereignty were debated at length during the first year of the conference. The issue posed a no-win situation. Were the conference to take strong action that antagonized its affiliates, it would put at risk the degree of unity that had been won. On the other hand, the same or different affiliates could be similarly alienated by a show of weakness. Either way the conference stood to lose. No wonder that an officer of the organization likened it to the ineffectual League of Nations.[23]

The conference admitted the problem time and again, but it blamed outside factors: "Precisely because of the tragic circumstances of Jewish life, the established organizations were facing greater demands, laboring under greater excitement and strain, and more jealous than ever before of their . . . traditions and prestige." At the same time, it denied that it expected those agencies to suspend their activities or that it ever intended to supersede them: "On the contrary, the Conference is intended as a coordinating and unifying instrument, responsible and responsive to the whole of the Jewish people in America." What exactly that meant was not elaborated.[24]

The conflict over jurisdiction was well illustrated in connection with Jewish appeals to government officials and agencies. In some cases, individual organizations, including several of the conference's own affiliates, duplicated petitions or statements of the central body. The conference deplored such efforts, saying that duplication confused the public and weakened Jewish clout: "The spectacle of one delegation after another swooping down in Washington makes us not only ludicrous in the eyes of the public at large, but becomes positively harmful to the interest which these delegations are presumed to serve." Adding to the loss of prestige, members of the three important commissions established by the conference occasionally performed the work of those commissions through their individual agencies. Here too the claim to leadership of one united Jewry was undercut.[25]

The problem dragged on. Although the conference promised not to usurp the functions of the affiliates, it asked them in turn not to act independently. To be sure, it was easy for one group to tell another to yield its rights and position, but, to be effective, all groups had to yield at the same time. The conference took a firmer stand at the second annual meeting. Acknowledging the need to curtail the absolute sovereignty of the organizations, it resolved not to delegate its own rightful functions to them. It also insisted that a program of an affiliate that fell within the jurisdiction of the conference required the latter's consent.[26] This show of assertiveness did not generate any strong opposition, a fact that doubtless owed more to a sense of urgency pervading the community than to an abdication of rights on the part of the powerful national agencies.

Other divisions within the conference surfaced after the actual work had begun. One involved the duties of the three separate commissions to handle each area of concentration: Palestine, rescue of European Jewry, and postwar rehabilitation and reconstruction. The lines that divided the commissions often seemed arbitrary. For example, as Silver, the chairman of the Palestine Commission, explained, since free immigration into Palestine meant life or death for the refugees, the subjects of rescue and Palestine were "logically one and inseparable." A second and deeper issue was whether the conference was merely a deliberative and consultative forum, i.e., a sounding board and clearinghouse for ascertaining the consensus of the community, or whether it had the power to set policy as well. Since the conference never formally resolved the matter, criticism was heard from both sides. *The Reconstructionist* magazine put it bluntly: Either the conference was organized only to obtain a vote of confidence for certain national organizations, or it should have been authorized to replace those organizations.[27]

Still a third divisive question, and one that had become a crucial issue by the time the plenum met again in 1944, was whether the agency should concern itself with Jewish problems in the United States, particularly that of antisemitism. Wise, for example, was among those who demanded the inclusion of the American scene within the conference's jurisdiction, and only when Monsky explained that the organizers never had that in mind did he change his mind. Despite a strong popular current in favor of a more inclusive agenda, the second meeting of delegates (1944) decided not to broaden the scope of the conference. The Jewish press for the most part endorsed the decision, but some commentators added that it was only a matter of time until the conference would be ready for additional functions.[28] The decision was strategically sound. Since the central body had still not ironed out a satisfactory relationship with the affiliates, why add to its problems? Moreover, any effort to broaden its powers could well generate more active resentment on the part of both the affiliated and unaffiliated agencies. In that event, the Zionists' campaign for a shift in leadership would again be in jeopardy.

How far the conference could go in cooperating with foreign Jewish organizations and the WJC, with Christian groups, and with the government further complicated matters of jurisdiction. With regard to rescue, the conference worked with Christians, the War Refugee Board, and foreign Jewish agencies; on postwar reconstruction it turned to UNRRA and to the international meetings at Dumbarton Oaks. With respect to the WJC, it reached an arrangement whereby the two bodies would exchange information and cooperate on a joint planning commission for postwar affairs. The WJC retained the right to approach foreign governments on behalf of Jews, and the conference was designated to be the spokesman to the United States. The Americans hoped that the arrangement would be the first step in attaining "a Jewish representation which shall speak for the whole of world Jewry before the United Nations on post-war Jewish rehabilitation." On most other issues the conference plowed ahead on its own.[29]

Doubtless unified action was also made more difficult by the hyperbole that attended the organization of the conference. The initial enthusiasm that greeted it fostered the belief that it would resolve the problems of a divided community at one fell swoop. When the conference failed to live up to expectations, serious doubts were raised about its overall efficacy. Toward the end of its first year the young organization publicly discussed the lack of total unity: "It may not be representative of *every* segment of American Jewry," its newsletter stated, but it did represent "the *over-whelming majority* of Jews in this country." Reaching the goal of unity was a slow process, but the conference stuck by its principles. We well understand that we have no governmental power to enforce our decisions on our affiliates, one officer wrote: "We have to operate through moral enforcement, through persuasion, and this kind of operation . . . does not always yield the desired results." Some found comfort in the fact that the conference was still the closest thing to unity that American Jews had produced, but one Yiddish columnist was more pessimistic: "As far as unity of the American Jews is concerned, one may as well leave it quietly for the time when the Messiah will come."[30]

The Palestine Commission

Although the conference appointed separate commissions to deal with the three areas of concentration it had blocked out, all were informed by the commonwealth resolution. The critical issue of rescue worked in tandem with the Zionist hope that Jews able to escape the death camps would have the right of free entry into Palestine; postwar planning, dealing largely with the interests of the displaced persons of European nations, also banked on a Jewish state. As long as the leading democracies restricted the immigration of the war victims, Palestine was the surest option for survivors and for those stripped of their rights. At the same time, the immediate tasks of persuading the government and the United Nations of the legitimacy and merits of the Zionist objectives devolved upon the Palestine Commission (PC).

Statehood aside, Zionist leaders knew the obstacles they faced in winning government support on lifting the restrictions of the White Paper. Some congressmen were sympathetic, but the State Department was an implacable foe. A month before the conference convened Congressman Emanuel Celler of New York made public a long letter to the president accusing the department of purposely working to "nullify and destroy" the international promises that had been made regarding Jewish immigration to Palestine. Men in the department, Celler said, were guilty of "the betrayal of Palestine," and he specifically named Patrick Hurley and Halford Hoskins, pro-Arab envoys to the Middle East, and Wallace Murray, longtime chief of the department's Near Eastern division. A "cabal" was afoot, he charged: "There are those in the State Department with axes to grind, and they have been abetting this movement together with the Arab appeasers." Threatening a congressional inquiry into the department, he called for Roosevelt's immediate help. But the president, who had given verbal assurances to both the Zionists and the Arabs, took no action.[31]

The PC under the chairmanship of Abba Hillel Silver never budged from the end goals spelled out in the conference's resolution on the White Paper and statehood. Nor, like its parent body, did it serve as a forum for the deliberation of policy. Some pointed out that the Palestine resolution contradicted the avowed purpose of the conference to formulate a program acceptable to *all*—including those who were neutral or opposed—but the PC ignored the criticism. Ninety percent of the delegates had endorsed the resolution, and, as Zionist leaders candidly admitted, Zionism was the "motor" that drove the conference: "The American Jewish Conference was created as an instrument of Zionist policy. As [such] it must be activized [sic] and in course of time become the most potent body in American Jewish life. Any other course of action . . . would render us guilty of a crime against the movement, against Palestine and against all the things for which we have labored these many years." Were the conference to fail, the effort to win over American Jewry to Zionism would have to begin all over again.[32]

In a lengthy report of the PC's activities for 1943–44, Silver began by justifying the commonwealth resolution. Implicit in the resolution, he said, was the recognition that the conciliatory tactics of the past were ineffectual and that a more aggressive political approach to England and the United Nations was required. His views put him at odds with the leading moderate Zionists, men like Chaim Weizmann and Stephen Wise, but he was not deterred. Proud of the commonwealth resolution, which he said "marked the end of the[Zionist] retreat," he boasted that despite some dissent, the resolution drew "nation-wide affirmations of approval."[33]

The conference submitted the text of the resolution to Secretary Cordell Hull, and Silver, who spent much of his time lobbying in Washington, opened the fight for the abrogation of the White Paper. Along with the American Zionist Emergency Council (AZEC), the PC refused to separate the issue of statehood from that of immigration and the White Paper. It argued that whereas a commonwealth would in reality follow Jewish immigration, the right of Jewish immigration came first, since it was tantamount to acceptance of Palestine as the "Jewish National Home." In pursuance of its overall mandate to engage in "political and educational" work to mobilize American Jews on behalf of the resolution, and to press England to rescind the White Paper, the PC became the focal point of American Zionist public relations and lobbying.[34]

Silver's report discussed the highlights of the PC's operations. The bulk of its work went into propaganda, or efforts to sway the government and both Jewish and non-Jewish public opinion to the side of statehood. Meant for public consumption, it was understandably incomplete. It made no mention of the personal lobbying that was carried on simultaneously by Rabbis Silver and Wise. Silver had access to Republican officials after he left the Democrats in 1940, and Wise was a friend of Roosevelt and the Democratic administration. But even in the less sensitive area of public relations the report's account of day-to-day activities can be misleading. In reality, much of what the PC claimed to have achieved was done by or in tandem with the AZEC and the hundreds of local emergency committees under its control. The AZEC scored well in the campaign for public support, particularly in mobilizing Christian leaders and university professors, as well as the giant labor unions. Since it was in place and functioning efficiently before the establishment of the conference, a parallel apparatus constructed by the PC was needless. Moreover, Silver and Wise, despite a strong mutual dislike, served as cochairmen of the AZEC. Given their expertise and, especially in the case of Wise, long experience in presenting Zionist demands to the government, the conference saw no reason to substitute others to represent it in Washington. It was only natural, therefore, for the PC to urge the delegates of the conference to cooperate closely with the AZEC's local committees and any other agencies similarly involved.[35]

Although the conference never thought of the older Zionist organizations as competitors, it repeatedly denounced the Hebrew Committee of National Liberation, or what it called an "irresponsible adventurer." One of the right-wing Revisionist splinter groups and an offshoot of the Irgun Zvai Leumi (military organization) in the *yishuv*, the Hebrew Committee enjoyed a degree of popularity just because it appeared more aggressive and determined than mainstream

Zionists. Resentful of this flamboyant rival, the conference was especially irked by its proposal for emergency shelters for refugees in Palestine. Since the shelters were to be only temporary, the conference charged that the proposal weakened efforts for the rescission of the White Paper and insistence on the right of Jews to settle *permanently* in Palestine.[36] Doubtless to some observers, Jews and non-Jews, the rejection of temporary shelters suggested, however, that Zionists were sacrificing the immediate rescue of Jews for the sake of their own partisan purposes.

The high point of Zionist political activity centered on the bipartisan pro-Zionist congressional resolutions sponsored by the AZEC in January 1944. Given the attitude of the anti-Zionist State Department and its constant refrains about the danger of inciting the Arabs or compounding wartime problems for England, passage of the resolutions would have been a radical departure from the government's official silence on the White Paper. To some degree the resolution reflected a change in Washington. Historian Ben Halpern has written: "The atmosphere had . . . changed. Not only had Jewish anger been made widely and powerfully evident, and brought effectively to the attention of the public and of political officials, but the conscience of men in power was moved." The fact that 1944 was an election year helped too. Whatever the contributing factors, congressional action vindicated the pressure tactics of Zionist groups. Affirming America's endorsement of Zionist aims, the last words of the Wright-Compton resolutions were almost identical to the conference's resolution: "The United States shall use its good offices and take appropriate measures to the end that the doors of Palestine shall be opened for free entry of Jews . . . and that there shall be full opportunity for colonization so that the Jewish people may ultimately reconstitute Palestine as a free and democratic Jewish commonwealth."[37]

Before the hearings on the resolutions by the House Committee on Foreign Affairs, the PC swung into high gear. It worked on individuals, the press, and organizations, both Jewish and Christian, to express their support to committee members. The effort succeeded. Committee chairman Sol Bloom reported that letters and telegrams speaking for thousands of Jews favored the resolutions and only ten disapproved. Led by Silver, six officers of the conference, armed with reams of documents, spoke at the hearings. Among them they covered the major points of the Zionist brief: the history of modern Zionism; American Jewish interest and investments in Palestine; the legal obligations to Zionism spelled out in the Balfour Declaration and mandate; the pro-Zionist congressional resolution of 1922; and England's betrayal of the Zionists. Two points were repeatedly made: first, the primary loyalty of the speakers and of American Jews in general to the United States—Reform Rabbi James Heller casually mentioned that he was a member of the Sons of the American Revolution!—and second, the overwhelming support of Zionism on the part of the Jewish community. In response to testimony from members of the American

Council for Judaism, who yet again raised the charge of dual allegiance, the Zionist representatives said that the council spoke only for very few Jews.[38]

The Zionists could not have testified before a more sympathetic audience. Although the members listened politely to the views of the American Council for Judaism and the Arab sympathizers, their warmth and encouragement were reserved for the Zionists. According to an AZEC report, had Congress voted at that moment, the Wright-Compton resolutions would have garnered four hundred votes. In the end, however, after the War and State Departments indicated their opposition for reasons of military expediency, the resolutions were buried at least temporarily. Silver and others blamed political motives, i.e., the administration's desire not to alienate the Arab states that had protested to the American government. The episode further strained relations between Silver, who advocated a continued attack by the Zionists, and Wise, the moderate who preferred to play down the failure of the Roosevelt administration. Silver and his cohorts deplored the ongoing silence on the part of the government. "Silence itself," the Zionist leader said, "would become a political act and the forces which were urging it in the name of military expediency were, perhaps unwittingly, forging political policy." To be sure, the Zionists themselves were not totally blameless; a confidential memorandum in the conference's files faulted the organization for mishandling the political side of the campaign, doubtless a reference to the absence of sustained pressure on key officials immediately after the objections of the executive departments. A few weeks later, however, and to the delight of the conference, Roosevelt voiced his support of the Zionist objectives.[39]

At a meeting with Wise and Silver on March 9, 1944, the president authorized them to issue a statement expressing American "non-concurrence" with the White Paper as well as his own desire to see Palestine open to Jewish immigration. When peace settlements were reached, he hoped that "full justice will be done to those who seek a Jewish National Home, for which our Government and the American people have always had the deepest sympathy and today more than ever, in view of the tragic plight of hundreds of thousands of homeless Jewish refugees." The presidential message stopped short of backing a Jewish commonwealth; a Jewish National Home was a far cry from a state. It suggested, however, that even if Roosevelt had held negative feelings about Zionism, the facts of the Holocaust may have altered his thinking. Despite its shortcomings, and despite Silver's misgivings about Roosevelt's sincerity in an election year, the message injected a note of cheer into the otherwise gloomy situation. The official silence had been broken, and for the first time the American executive objected to the White Paper of 1939. Roosevelt's words also dispelled the notion spread by Arab propagandists that the United States had repudiated the congressional resolution of 1922. The president, however, had by no means become a supporter of Zionism, and before his death he continued to weigh various options on the future of Palestine.[40]

At a press conference that same month, the president denied that his message to Wise and Silver conflicted with the views of the War and State Departments. As if on cue, Secretary of War Henry Stimson stated a few months later that his department's objections to the Wright-Compton resolutions "are not as strong a factor now as they were." Nevertheless, the administration continued to find fault with congressional action. Although the two major political parties had adopted pro-Zionist planks in their platforms, and although Roosevelt finally pledged his aid for securing Palestine as a "free and democratic Commonwealth," a second attempt at congressional action in 1944 was stymied again by the president and the State Department. The conference resolved to continue its struggle for a favorable congressional statement, but not until December 1945, months after the war ended and almost three years after the Wright-Compton resolutions, did Congress by a concurrent resolution(not requiring presidential consent) endorse the Zionist objectives.[41]

During its first year of existence the PC chalked up failures as well as victories. First, it had neither coordinated all Zionist activity under its aegis nor functioned as the sole voice of American Zionism, and second, the lines of authority between the conference and other Zionist agencies, especially the AZEC, were still very blurred. At the hearings on Wright-Compton, not only did the speakers for the conference prefer to be identified with other organizations, but Zionists in addition to men from the conference also testified.[42] Clearly, the PC had failed thus far to unite American Zionists or put an end to the duplication of effort.

On the plus side, however, the PC's endorsement of the AZEC, or what in reality amounted to a quasi-merger with that organization, worked to bolster Zionism's appeal to the community. In the name of the conference the PC choreographed overall tactics with the AZEC, and it contributed important resources to the joint public relations campaign. Above all, the PC had changed the tone of American Zionism. Now more assertive than ever before, Zionists sent a message loud and clear that American Jewry was overwhelmingly committed to the establishment and protection of a Jewish state.

The AJC and the Conference

A major obstacle to unity and to the overall efficacy of the conference was the absence of the AJC. The latter's abrupt withdrawal from the new organization deprived the conference of an invaluable asset. The AJC may have had far fewer members than other national Jewish organizations, but the power that its self-selected officers wielded in the Jewish and non-Jewish worlds—a product of wealth and social status, close contacts with government officials, and almost forty years of experience in Jewish communal affairs—more than compensated for what it lacked in numbers. Proud of its position as *the* steward of American Jewish interests, the committee believed that precisely because of its elitist character and conservative behavior it was best fit to lead the community. Any populist challenge to its leadership, even if explained in democratic terms, would not be easily tolerated.

The AJC's rivalry with the conference was more than a Jewish communal squabble. In a larger sense its nonparticipation could even cast doubt on how American the Zionists and their new organization really were. Within non-Jewish society the committee had earned a name as a spokesman for American-ism. Since its inception in 1906 it had labored for the rapid acculturation of new immigrants and for full Jewish participation in the peacetime and wartime duties of American citizens. On the issue of Zionism the leaders of the AJC were at best non-Zionists if not anti-Zionists; members contributed to the *yishuv* but not to a state in the making. Since the members were all conservative men, the opinions, activities, and style of the AJC blended well with government policy and public tastes, and its reputation gave it a decided advantage over the Zionists and the conference. To the average American acquainted with Jewish matters, if the AJC opposed other American Jews, the former undoubtedly was correct.

In the preliminaries leading up to the conference, the AJC found many excuses for opposing the scheme. It objected among other things to the plans on representation, allocation of votes, and methods for electing delegates; those plans, it charged, worked for the benefit of the Zionists and thus belied the claim that the conference was a democratic forum. The committee learned too that the anti-Zionist State Department, attempting to prevent embarrassing public attacks on the administration and England during wartime, advised that the conference be postponed. Since the AJC, as was its customary behavior, also deplored diplomacy by popular agitation, it feared that the conference was likely to antagonize the government.[43]

Publicly the committee raised neither its claim to leadership nor its stand against political Zionism, the two reasons that underlay its opposition to the conference. It recalled its experience with the American Jewish Congress during World War I, when the Zionist-controlled congress aimed at destroying the elitist and antinationalist AJC.[44] In 1943 the threat appeared identical. If the conference of 1943 captured overall communal leadership, it would usurp the committee's long-established role as the representative of American Jews in foreign affairs. The intense power struggle with the Zionists was renewed, and again the prize at stake was the leadership of American Jewry. For that reason Morris Waldman, the executive vice president of the AJC, argued strongly from the start against the committee's participation in the conference. He called Monsky a Zionist "stooge" and the plan for a conference a Zionist ploy. Acting out of resentment against the self-assumed power of the "plutocrats" (= AJC), the Zionists had designed a conference to be a "tail" to the Zionist "kite." If the committee stayed out of the conference, he predicted that it would be able to build up an independent national following: "We would be afforded a grand opportunity to assert the leadership in Jewish life."[45]

During weeks of serious negotiations with Monsky and other conference sponsors, Proskauer insisted that he too favored unity but not according to the Zionist design, which trampled on the freedoms of non-Zionist minorities. Non-Zionists *could* cooperate with Zionists, he told Stephen Wise, but unity "cannot be achieved by majority vote." He preferred a strictly deliberative body that allowed all opinions to be aired and that guaranteed the right of dissent from majority decisions. Nevertheless, the committee realized that it could not very well fly in the face of an aroused Jewish public and isolate itself from the rest of the community. Thus, when the Zionists yielded on certain minor issues, the AJC agreed to join.[46]

The Zionists too were focused on the struggle over leadership even though they, like the AJC, did not debate the issue publicly. It was well understood, however, that their defense of a democratic, Zionist-controlled body was simultaneously an indictment of the AJC. In the bitter contest between the two, the conference had less to lose. Its existence did not depend solely on the displacement of the committee, whereas the future of the committee did depend on its retention of communal leadership. In the end, Proskauer advised his colleagues to agree to the conference but to keep to their convictions. He said with typical arrogance: "We are willing to collaborate but we must retain our full freedom of action. Otherwise the Committee will be sunk and Proskauer will be the follower—not the leader."[47]

With respect to the specific Zionist issues, the AJC distinguished between support of immigration to Palestine and statehood, a position consonant with its "Americanist" emphasis. Statehood was anathema; Jews were a religious group only, and Zionism conjured up the bogey that American Jews were a national group whose primary political allegiance was to a Jewish state. Moreover, statehood was undemocratic and hence also un-American just because it concerned a land where the majority of inhabitants were Arabs. Finally, if statehood conflicted in any way with Allied wartime aims, as some officials in Washington and London thought, it was beyond consideration. On the other hand, support of Jewish immigration into Palestine and other forms of nonpolitical aid to the *yishuv* did not contradict American values. The committee called the White Paper illegal because it violated the terms of the mandate and because it "constitutes an act of discrimination against one particular religious group." Much like the Zionists the AJC believed that the American commitment to humanitarian principles condoned immigration as the solution to the problem of war victims. Unlike the conference, however, it did not push for immediate abrogation of the White Paper, again on the grounds that it might interfere with the war effort, nor did it adopt Silver's reasoning on the indivisibility of immigration and statehood. Conviction as well as fear of public reaction led the AJC to retain the now-anachronistic label of "non-Zionist." In effect, its position gave the anti-Zionist State Department and British an edge for undermining the Jewish statists.[48]

Addressing the first plenary session of the conference, Proskauer again spoke of unity. The entire community yearned for unity, he said, but not at the expense of the individual's or the minority group's principles. He advised, therefore, that the conference concentrate not on competing ideologies but on areas of agreement, like the demand for a postwar world in which Jews were guaranteed their fundamental rights or the physical upbuilding of the *yishuv*. Proskauer sounded more conciliatory than usual, and he avoided all divisive issues. He stressed rather the "fundamental passion" that all shared: "the preservation of Jewry, and the preservation of the democratic way of life."[49] The Palestine resolution, however, shattered any hopes of keeping the AJC in the new organization. Since the Zionists had violated the preconference agreement not to raise the issue of statehood, Proskauer had no qualms about casting a dissenting vote.

The committee moved immediately to the question of withdrawing from the conference, and for seven weeks it debated the pros and cons. Proskauer, who led the case for withdrawal, received the overwhelming support of the committee's leaders. When the AJC's Adminstrative Committee voted in favor of withdrawal, only one member dissented. Shortly thereafter the organization submitted its formal resignation.[50]

The AJC's statement on withdrawal offered several reasons by way of explanation—the exclusion of some agencies from the conference and the preconference instructions from the Zionists to the delegates on how to vote. As for the Palestine resolution, they charged that it was railroaded through without prior attempts to work out a compromise with the non-Zionists. Moreover, the resolution contradicted the AJC's program, adopted in January 1943, on the agency's war and postwar aims. In that Statement of Views the committee had defined its own objectives, including postwar rehabilitation and full equality for Jews throughout the world. As for Palestine, although the committee took pride in the achievements of the *yishuv*—after all, its own leaders had worked with the Zionists in the Jewish Agency and in projects like the Hebrew University—it insisted that Diaspora Jews must not identify politically with any Jewish government established there. Instead the AJC advocated an international trusteeship to guard Jewish immigration into Palestine, which was to be limited only by the economic absorptive capacity of the land and Jewish settlement. The trustees would also safeguard the rights of all inhabitants and protect the holy places of all religions. Thereby guaranteeing the growth and development of the land, Palestine would be ready within "a reasonable period of years" to become a "self-governing Commonwealth." Note: a "Commonwealth," yes, but not necessarily a Jewish one.[51]

The statement on withdrawal was carefully constructed. To deflect critics in the Jewish community, it explained that the AJC was non-Zionist and not anti-Zionist like the much-abhorred American Council for Judaism. To win the support of the government and non-Jewish public, its message echoed American sentiments. Its emphasis on universalism rather than parochial Jewish nationalism, its patriotic concern for the Allied war effort (not to be disturbed by agitation for a Jewish state), its idea of a trusteeship that absolved the United States from responsibility for Palestine, and its insistence on fundamental human rights for all religions and peoples made it seemingly more patriotic than the conference's statist position.

The committee's statement did not even hint at the issue of leadership, but Proskauer admitted informally that it was an overriding concern: "It is just a simple fact to say that if we had not withdrawn, there would not have been any American Jewish Committee left." He refused to explain his motives to his numerous critics. Despite the abuse that was heaped upon him and the AJC, he said he would not wash Jewish dirty linen publicly. Nor did he want to leave the impression that he personally was playing for power.[52]

The AJC could not totally ignore the storm of protests that greeted its withdrawal from the conference. To be sure, it had some powerful defenders, like the heads of the Reform and Conservative rabbinical seminaries and the anti-Zionist *New York Times,* but statements by those supporters were vastly outnumbered by letters of protest and resignations of members. The Anglo-Jewish and Yiddish press for the most part bitterly condemned the AJC, accusing it primarily of destroying Jewish unity. Some critics brought up the issue of leadership, and they usually dismissed the claim of achievements by the elitist committee. The ZOA termed the withdrawal a "willful sin against the Jewish people here and abroad," and the AZEC charged that the committee's philosophy was "rule or ruin."

A scathing rejoinder by the conference to what it called the AJC's "morally indefensible" action blamed the AJC for acting on considerations of leadership. Its decision to withdraw was "dictated by its determination to maintain an independent course of action without public responsibility to the organized Jewish community." The conference rejected out of hand the committee's intimation that the conference had shown by its resolutions that it was less than loyal to the United States. Abba Hillel Silver said that the committee believed in "domination or secession." Veteran Zionist B. G. Richards called Proskauer a "hoary-minded, die-hard reactionary and isolationist," and he recalled nostalgically how Louis Marshall had led the AJC into the congress of 1918. (Those like Richards who praised Marshall did not, or did not choose to, remember that the congress of 1918 had not converted Marshall into a Zionist or a believer in democratic leadership. Rather, his strategy, which ultimately succeeded, was to capture control of the congress by first agreeing to participate.)[53]

The committee quickly realized that it needed to mend its fences. Reporting on a trip around the country for precisely that purpose, Waldman noted the widespread Jewish view of the AJC as the archopponent of Jewish unity and democracy. The indictment of the AJC also emphasized the issue of leadership. The agency was charged, Waldman said, with being "oligarchic, dictatorial, and callous to the will of the masses, manifesting the superciliousness and arrogance of wealth"; in short, it was "a handful of self-appointed, self-anointed leaders." The prevalent notion held that the AJC was not only "out of sympathy with Jewish aspirations, but is actually consciously undermining these aspirations." Among the Zionists, Waldman added, he found "a general hatred of our group. . . . "I get the sense that they would rather see the Committee completely destroyed than have us re-enter the Conference." Waldman did not mince words. He called political Zionism a virtual religion that at times became a fanaticism. So despicable were the Zionists that he likened the implications of their extreme Jewish nationalism to the "race state" idea of the Nazis![54]

In addition to talks by Waldman and others, the AJC sought various ways of improving public relations. Most significant were its plans to restructure the organization and expand its membership by the creation of chapters in various cities. It seems obvious that the popular groundswell for democratic leadership embodied in the design for a conference contributed to those plans. Thus, despite its withdrawal, the elitist committee was changed permanently by the new organization it opposed.[55]

Because of the Holocaust, the committee lost control of the community to the conference. Zionists too always paraded their Americanism, but in 1943, with a focus on the Jewish condition in Europe, they elevated Jewish particularism to a higher level than ever before. The AJC shared their concern about Jewish survival, but they saw no reason as yet to support political Zionism and a Jewish state. Whereas the Zionists felt secure enough in their Americanism to campaign publicly for statehood, the AJC remained frozen in the time warp of Palestinianism.

The AJC continued its independent work on the rescue of European Jewry and on the rights of Jews in the postwar world. In some instances it cooperated with the conference, especially on postwar work, and in many others it did not. Inevitably there were glaring instances of duplication. (One example was the international declaration of human rights that both organizations formulated.) The committee never yielded its advantages in the non-Jewish world, which gave it a decided edge over the conference. Keeping the government informed of its major activities, it maintained its close contacts with officials in the State Department and the Roosevelt circle and with members of Congress. Shortly after it withdrew from the conference, Waldman proudly wrote Proskauer: "The State Department hailed our dissent and withdrawal from the Conference with the deepest satisfaction. Even though the Committee's position is not as anti-Zionist as the Department would like it to be, our separation from the Zionists, as reflected in our withdrawal from the Conference, gives us a preferred position in the Department." He neglected to add that the AJC's withdrawal helped the State Department's anti-Zionists, enabling them to resist Zionist pressure on the grounds that the Jewish community was hopelessly divided on the issue of statehood.[56]

Its "preferred position" notwithstanding, the AJC's influence with the State Department was less than significant. One official commented that it was easier to deal with the Zionists because their stand was clear. As for the committee, it was "always straddling the fence," making it "impossible to tell what their position is on any problem."[57]

During the first year of the conference, the AJC contributed little to the Zionist cause. Determined above all to remain in the good graces of the State Department, it paraded its "reasonable" opinions (as opposed to the "unreasonable" ones of the Zionists) to the government. In the episode of the Wright-Compton resolutions, the committee's determination to follow an independent course of action faced a dilemma. Proskauer told Congressman Sol Bloom of the House Committee that his organization thought it inappropriate to press the Zionist demands during wartime. But the primary reason for the AJC's disapproval was a partisan one. It realized that sending any non- or antinationalist witnesses might alienate the community still further and lead Jews to believe that the committee was in league with the American Council for Judaism. Still justifying a non-Zionist stand, Proskauer bemoaned the fact that members of Congress did not recognize "the distinction between being friendly to the Jews and advocating a political state in Palestine." The AJC would have preferred no hearings at all, but simply not to appear would have further tarnished its reputation as the spokesman of American Jewry. In the end, instead of testifying, the committee submitted a written memorandum of its views with only moderate criticisms of Zionist goals. Privately, however, it impugned the loyalty of the Zionists when it told the State Department that the commonwealth resolutions would harm the war effort and would lend credence to the antisemitic charge of dual allegiance.[58]

Summing Up

Historian David Wyman has written that except for the progress made toward winning popular and congressional support for Jewish statehood, the American Jewish Conference scored no substantive gains. The all-important need to concentrate resources on rescue attempts was totally eclipsed, he maintains, by the Zionist focus on Palestine. But although he brings evidence of the steady disintegration of the conference during its first year, the leaders of the organization were determined to persist.[59]

At the end of 1944 the conference convened the second meeting of the ple-

The Americanization of Zionism, 1897–1948

num. Less dramatic than the first sessions of August–September 1943, it was nonetheless at least as important. By their actions the assembled delegates were to decide whether the new organization had a viable future. Their answer was positive. Despite its flaws and unfulfilled promises, the continuation of the conference was endorsed by the delegates and affiliated agencies. With renewed determination the leaders of the conference drew up plans for correcting its weaknesses and intensifying its three-pronged program of rescue, postwar rights, and Jewish statehood. The organization may not have been (in the words of the Zionist periodical *New Palestine)* "a genuine and powerful and permanent expression of the will and temper of American Jewry," but it still filled a need of the Jewish community. When, a few months later, the AJC and the American Jewish Conference were the only Jewish organizations invited to serve as consultants to the American delegation at the international conference in San Francisco, the legitimacy of the conference was acknowledged by the American government.[60]

The reasons for perpetuating the conference were basically the same that had led to its creation in the first place. One reason, as the *Reconstructionist* pointed out, was the enduring "spirit of revolt" against the ineffectiveness of the major national organizations. Popular impatience with the narrow and selfish concerns of those agencies had not evaporated after the founding of the conference, and at least for the moment American Jews continued to support a centralized, and they hoped more successful, way of communitywide action. Nor, despite the progress made toward a Jewish state, could they deny that the problems of world Jewry were of a magnitude that still cried for a united response. As the war in Europe wound down, the state of the displaced persons and homeless survivors captured greater attention. The fight for statehood before the United Nations was still to come, but the needs of the refugees who successfully reached Palestine, legally or illegally, and who required aid for settlement and rehabilitation added to the responsibilities of their American brethren. Concerned American Jews may have also thought that through the conference they could vent their own feelings of frustration and rage over the Holocaust in a constructive fashion.

The first and most crucial year of the conference had set the lines along which the organization continued to operate, but the sense of urgency that had energized its program petered out after the collapse of the Axis powers. International committees and agencies handled the issues of displaced persons and postwar rights, and in November 1947 the United Nations voted the partition of Palestine into Arab and Jewish states. Accordingly, two main objectives of the conference were realized. The organization held annual conventions in 1946 and 1947, but early in 1949 the major affiliated agencies voted for dissolution.[61]

The legacy of the conference lasted longer, for it planted seeds that sprouted only later. On the subject of Palestine, for example, it had succeeded in stamping the vast majority of American Jews with the Zionist label, a crucial step that laid the foundation for American support of a Jewish state in 1948. In an entirely different area, the influence of the conference was significant in the revamping of the AJC. Not only did the committee become a warm supporter of the Jewish state within a few years, but it was forced both to adopt a more democratic structure and to relinquish its claim to the exclusive leadership of American Jewry. Elitism within the community lingered on, especially in the powerful philanthropic federations and in Jewish social clubs, but the conference had given the process of social levelling a significant boost.

More subtle but perhaps more important, the conference changed the tone of American Zionist activity. Instead of the customary timid approach, it substituted a confident and assertive posture that became entrenched in the postwar era. Like other American pressure groups after the war, the Zionist lobby of today openly presses its demands without apology as it works on the public and on political candidates and officeholders. It is therefore fair to say, as one journal did after the convention of 1944, that the conference marked "the political coming of age of the Jewish people of the United States."[62]

An equally important contribution of the conference was the impetus it gave for overall communal unity in the area of Zionism and Israel. Although the self-interest of the major national organizations brought the conference to a relatively quick end, the establishment within a few years of two organizations, the American Israel Public Affairs Committee (AIPAC) in 1954 and the Conference of Presidents of Major American Jewish Organizations in 1955, unifed Jewish policymaking with respect to the Jewish state. AIPAC, which became one of the most effective lobbies on Capitol Hill, took over the defense of Israel's political interests and the maintenance of a strong American-Israeli connection. The Conference of Presidents, which speaks today for more than fifty member agencies, represents the opinion of Jewish organizations to the American government on Israel and other international issues. Duplication of organizational operations has not been entirely eliminated, but, in the path marked out by the conference, the two postwar organizations have centralized American Jewish pro-Zionist and pro-Israel activities. They have thereby undone much of the rampant disunity of the preconference period.

For our purposes it is also important to note that aside from continuing Zionist pressure after the state of Israel was created, both AIPAC and the Conference of Presidents followed the long-established precedent of Americanizing their Zionism. Just as the Zionists of 1943 had called their cause an American wartime aim, so did the new organizations justify their postwar programs on the premise that a strong and secure Israel was in the interests of the United States. Whether as a bulwark against Soviet expansionism during the Cold War or as a democratic outpost in the troubled Near East of today, the interests of the Jewish state have been equated by Zionists with those of America.[63]

CHAPTER 8

Out of Step with the Times:
Rabbi Louis Finkelstein
of the Jewish Theological Seminary

The Setting

*F*or eight years preceding the establishment of the Jewish state (1940–48) the Jewish Theological Seminary (JTS), the fountainhead of the American Conservative movement, was headed by Rabbi Louis Finkelstein. The story of those years is that of a religious institution whose students and faculty had fully accepted an Americanized Zionism but who by the time of World War II were prepared without further debate to broaden their nationalist commitment to include the demand for a Jewish state. It is also an account of the fourth president of the institution, who turned his back on statehood at a time when the survival of world Jewry was in jeopardy. The result of conflicting pressures during the war and its immediate aftermath, Finkelstein's opposition to political Zionism was out of step with the growing conviction among his Conservative constituents and American Jewry at large that only a Jewish state would solve the problem of Jewish refugees and displaced persons.

The account of Finkelstein and the JTS continues the discussion of the war years and the American Jewish Conference. As shown in previous chapters, the Zionists had revived Herzlian Zionism and had energized an organized Jewish community in support of a Jewish state. The AJC was a notable exception to the agencies allied in the Zionist-led conference, and Finkelstein too was among the last holdouts. The Reform movement, except for the small American Council for Judaism, was by then on the side of the Zionists; the AJC first fell into line in 1946. By then the subcategories of Zionism—religious Zionism, cultural Zionism, and even non-Zionism—had lost their meaning. A person who contributed in any fashion to the building of the *yishuv*, which as most now understood was the preparation for a Jewish state, was *ipso facto* a Zionist.

But Finkelstein, although a card-carrying Zionist, lagged behind. The Conservative leader was guided by his emphasis on religious Zionism to the exclusion of political aims, and his determination to develop a meaningful Judeo-Christian program in the United States. Those fixed principles in tandem with the financial needs of the Seminary distanced him from the political, and now mainstream, Zionist movement.

The Finkelstein era is testimony to the overwhelming public acceptance, non-Jewish as well as Jewish, of a Jewish home/center/state in Palestine. Within the Jewish community Zionist successes were particularly dramatic. Membership in the ZOA climbed from 43,000 in 1940 to more than 250,000 in 1948; American Jews raised less than $3 million for Palestine in 1940 but more than $70 million in 1948. The records of the United Jewish Appeal (UJA) also show that the UJA raised $14 million in 1941 and $148 million in 1948.[1] Except for small pockets of opponents (Arab sympathizers, antisemites, the American Council for Judaism), the war years and their immediate aftermath made talk of dual allegiance or the compatibility of Zionism and Americanism secondary at best. In terms of the sheer number of supporters, American Zionism had succeeded.

If only tangentially, the war years furthered the Americanization of Zionism. This time, however, conditions in Europe rather than Zionist efforts were the cause. Precisely because wartime Zionism was bound up with the rescue and survival of European Jews, it tapped into American humanitarian instincts. As a giant wartime humanitarian crusade, Zionism could be interpreted as a noble, American-like cause. Many Jews and Christians who had held serious reservations about the prospect of a Jewish homeland or state were moved by the needs of the survivors. True, the State Department still kept humanitarianism out of diplomacy, but concerned Americans allowed its importance. The changed climate of opinion made the approach of the Zionists less defensive. More than before, they boldly injected themselves into the political arena, and, under strong leadership and with the help of influential Christian organizations, effectively disseminated their propaganda. No longer peddling an alien or outlandish product, they presented a Zionism acceptable to Americans and suited to American endorsement. In that setting, Finkelstein's voice was conspicuously silent.

Finkelstein's spiritual Zionism replicated that of one of his predecessors, Solomon Schechter, whose views on a Jewish center in Palestine had encouraged the development of a distinctly American Zionism. Schechter's religious and cultural Zionism satisfied the ethnic needs of America's Jews. Positing an unconditional commitment to the United States alongside a devotion to Eretz Yisrael, it demanded neither a shift in political loyalties nor personal sacrifices like *aliyah*. Schechter affiliated with the Federation of American Zionists in 1905 even though he opposed the political nationalism of the secular Zionists. He bequeathed to his students a belief that a vibrant Jewish center in Palestine, even without a state, would nurture Judaism throughout the world. After his death his views continued to inspire the graduates of the Seminary and through them hundreds of Conservative synagogues. Schechter's successor, American-born Cyrus Adler, was a non-Zionist whose traditionalism underlay his belief in divinely ordained roles for Judaism and Palestine in the messianic scheme of restoration. More concerned about Judaism than about Jews, Adler opposed political Zionism or any form of Jewish nationalism in the Diaspora. Like Schechter, he never discussed or advocated *aliyah* from America.[2] Louis Finkelstein, who followed Adler, sounded at times much like his predecessors. He too dreamed of a Jewish spiritual and religious center, and like most American Zionists of his generation he assumed consciously or unconsciously that the values taught by that center would mirror those of post–World War I American liberalism.

On a more profound level, however, Finkelstein's communal agenda broke new ground in the linkage between Americanism and Zionism. The rabbi stood for the regeneration of religious values in America at the same time that he worked to reinvigorate the vibrancy of Judaism both in Palestine and in the United States. He believed that an America sensitive to values embodied in the Judeo-Christian tradition would be no different in kind from an Eretz Yisrael acting in accordance with Jewish religio-ethical values. Positing a religious core in Americanism and Judaism, he stressed the resultant commonality. If the two countries shared the same religious consciousness and moral commitment, not only would each exemplify the highest form of living, be it American or Jewish, but each would closely resemble the other. By adding the American connection to the religious-cultural Zionism of Schechter, Finkelstein Americanized Zionism in a way that had not been done before. Nevertheless, the onrush of world events, particularly the Nazi threat to Jewish survival, called for a different response.

The JTS and Zionism Before the War

It has long been commonplace in scholarly accounts to note the special bond between Conservative Judaism and Zionism. In *The Political World of American Zionism*, for example, Samuel Halperin wrote some forty years ago: "The American Zionist movement derived its most unanimously enthusiastic and dedicated supporters from the ranks of Conservative Judaism."[3] Yet the role played by the JTS, the acknowledged head of the movement, in forging the Conservative-Zionist nexus is less obvious. A study of the Seminary and Zionism until the establishment of the state of Israel reveals neither unanimity nor ongoing consensus. Among the components that made up the school—administration, faculty and students, board of directors—different views of Zionism, reflecting a variety of backgrounds, religious beliefs, and political values, pre-vailed. At times the subject of Zionism exposed serious differences between the Seminary's administration and the affiliated arms of the Conservative move-ment—the Rabbinical Assembly (RA), the organization of Conservative rabbis and the United Synagogue, the organization of Conservative congregations—which usually outpaced the school in support of Jewish nationalist activities. The overall picture differed markedly from that at the Seminary's older counterpart, Reform's Hebrew Union College (HUC). There, despite sporadic manifestations of Zionist sympathies from students and faculty, a tighter insti-tutional structure (HUC was directly controlled by Reform's Union of Ameri-can Hebrew Congregations) allowed the first presidents to steer the college along an official anti-Zionist course in tandem with Reform's rabbinical and congregational organizations.[4]

Before 1948 the Seminary never sought or mandated conformity on Zionism. Sabato Morais, who headed the school from its inception in 1886 until his death in 1897, broke with his fellow rabbis by speaking out against a manmade resto-ration of Jews to Eretz Yisrael. In his case, an upbringing in a home of fervent Italian nationalists dedicated to Italian unification failed to elicit his support for modern Jewish nationalism.[5] Unconstrained by those views, Solomon Schech-ter, who followed Morais, allied himself with the Zionist movement. Neverthe-less, he insisted that his action in no way bound the Seminary: "I should like it to be distinctly understood that this allegiance [to the Zionist movement] can-not be predicated of the Institution over which I have the honor to preside, and which has never committed itself to the Movement, leaving this to the individ-ual inclination of the students and Faculty, composed of Zionists, anti-Zionists, and indifferentists." Since the chairman of Schechter's board of direc-tors agreed that each director as well as student and faculty member was free to take his own stand, Zionism early on became an extra-institutional matter and, within the walls of the Seminary, a subject that rarely aroused heated debate.[6]

In large measure differences over Zionism stemmed from variant readings of the Seminary's mission. The religious founding fathers, the generations of Morais and Schechter, envisioned a school for the propagation of historical Ju-daism in accommodation with modernity. With an emphasis on scholarship, the Seminary would train rabbis committed to *halakhah*, or Jewish religious law, but conversant and comfortable with modern intellectual trends and scholarly methods. Aiming for "conservative progress" that would safeguard the future of Judaism against the inroads of Reform and assimilation, the Seminary was pledged to defend the cardinal principles of normative Judaism: the synagogue, *kashrut* (dietary laws), the Sabbath, and Eretz Yisrael. Jewish peoplehood was axiomatic, and a divinely sanctioned return to Palestine was nonnegotiable. All of the Seminary's academic heads before 1948—Morais, Schechter, Cyrus Adler, Finkelstein—subscribed to that mission despite differ-ences in interpretation and differences over political Zionism.

Unlike the religionists, the laymen, who reorganized the Seminary at the turn of the century and set the pattern for the first and for succeeding boards of directors, stressed an American agenda. The patrician circle led in 1902 by Jacob H. Schiff and Louis Marshall were not averse to Jewish tradition in modern dress, but most refused to countenance the idea of a discrete Jewish nationality. They saw the Seminary primarily as an Americanizing agency, one that would produce modern rabbis and teachers to hasten the acculturation of the eastern European immigrant masses and, equally important, to guard them against the nefarious "un-American" doctrines of secularism and radicalism. More than another philanthropic organization created by the German Jewish Establishment, the Seminary took on a practical urgency. It would teach the eastern Europeans how to retain their religion in a form both respectable and acceptable to Americans. Zionists sat alongside non-Zionists and anti-Zionists on the first boards, but all agreed that Zionism as well as Palestine, a land significant chiefly as a possible haven for persecuted European Jews, was extraneous to the Seminary's program.

Although one vision emphasized the preservation of *Judaism* and the other focused on shoring up the security of *Jews,* the two converged on a critical point: neither one negated the American Diaspora. Until 1948 the lay leaders for the most part summarily rejected the notion that America was *galut.* The one homeland for America's Jews, the United States alone held out the promise of permanent Jewish survival, and it alone demanded undivided Jewish loyalty. The religionists followed a two-centered approach. Nationalists at least in the traditional religious sense, they prayed for a return to Zion, but they deemed the ongoing exilic experience essential to the unfolding of modern Zionism.[7] At the same time, they dedicated themselves to service the religious needs of an American Jewry and to perpetuate the Jewish heritage in the United States. A genuine love of the country also underlay their insistence that Judaism and Americanism were eminently compatible. Thus, however justified, acceptance of Diaspora survivalism united both groups and allowed each to invest in the future of the Seminary.

The outlook of the students reinforced the two-centered vision. They took pride in their Americanism and were grateful for the country's bounties. Moreover, their education and professional ambitions were predicated on an American future. Like the lay founders of the institution, and like American Jews in general, including Zionists, they emended Herzl's laws with respect to the United States. The virulent antisemitism that menaced European Jewish wellbeing and physical security, the base on which Herzl rested his case, did not obtain in America. But although the students agreed that America was different, their highly developed sense of Jewish ethnicity was virtually ineradicable. Overwhelmingly of eastern European origin, they bore a cultural baggage steeped in both traditional religious and modern secular concepts of Jewish peoplehood and nationality. A few of the early ones recalled the Zionist influences that touched them as youngsters in the Old World or in American immigrant homes.[8] Since Zionism was neither taught nor officially sanctioned in the rabbinical school, it became a popular extracurricular activity. Not every rabbi ordained by the Seminary was an ardent Zionist—a member of the class of 1904 preached rabid anti-Zionist views when he went on to edit the Chicago-based *Reform Advocate*—but in a pattern set by the first graduate, England's Chief Rabbi Joseph Hertz,[9] Seminary men developed their Zionist leanings more fully during their pulpit careers.

Actual clashes within the Seminary between defenders of the one-centered and two-centered approaches were avoided so long as Zionism was little more than a pious dream or exercise in philanthropy. Tensions mounted, however, whenever Zionism as a secular political movement appeared to threaten the directors' image of American Jews, which the Jewish Establishment had so assiduously cultivated. What in each instance determined the administration's position, or its response to conflicting Zionist and anti-Zionist pressures from within the Seminary and from the larger Jewish and American communities, depended on diverse factors ranging from the needs of American and European Jewry to the school's financial state. During Finkelstein's administration the balance between the one-centered and two-centered visions collapsed. Forced by his priorities to choose between the two, the president opted to focus his attention primarily on the American center. Controversy ended only with the establishment of Israel in 1948. Then, the Seminary and the organizational affiliates of the Conservative movement united in forging ever closer ties with the Jewish state.

A Spiritual Zionist

The succession of Louis Finkelstein to the presidency upon the death of Adler came as no surprise to the Seminary family. Finkelstein had risen through the ranks; ordained in 1919, he left his congregation in 1931 to teach at the Seminary and to serve as Cyrus Adler's assistant and provost. Recognized unofficially as heir apparent, he enjoyed a warm and congenial relationship with his chief. The two men shared a commitment to scientific scholarship and to traditional observance both as a personal and as an institutional norm.[10] Even the sensitive issue of Zionism, which had aroused considerable anti-Adler sentiment among Finkelstein's rabbinical colleagues, did not strain the bonds of mutual trust and respect. Unlike the non-Zionist Adler, Finkelstein was a dues-paying member of the Zionist Organization, but, since he was a staunch opponent of political as well as secular nationalism, his Zionism was purely of a spiritual nature. An early statement of his—"We want to see Palestine rebuilt; we have for it . . . an intuitional, unreasoning, and mystic love"[11]—could very well have been made by any religious Zionist or the non-Zionist Adler.

Finkelstein's stand on a Jewish Palestine presaged no significant change in Seminary policy, and, had critical events between 1940 and 1948 not intervened, it would hardly have aroused debate. The new president had a passion for study and scholarship. By 1940 he had produced major works on the Pharisees and Rabbi Akiba, but, so different from his oldest friend, Rabbi Solomon Goldman of Chicago, he took little interest in the politics or strategy of modern Jewish state-building. Unlike Schechter and Adler, Finkelstein neither engaged in public polemics on Zionist policies and personalities nor did he campaign actively, the way Adler had, for building up the *yishuv*. He followed Adler into the executive councils of the AJC but not into the Jewish Agency. His popular writings that touched on Zionism reveal how he concentrated on fitting modern Zionism into the religious chain welded by his heroes, the Prophets and the spiritual leaders of the Second Commonwealth. Seeking to apply his scholarship to this-worldly activities, he viewed the establishment of a Jewish Palestine through an historical-religious lens.[12]

Finkelstein began with two premises. One affirmed the need of Palestine for the religious Jew: "I believe that every Jew has a religious duty to strive to live in Palestine as the Holy Land of Israel; that because of the association of prayer and ceremonial with the Holy Land, he can worship God in Palestine in a manner in which he cannot worship Him anywhere else in the world." The second underscored the place of Palestine in a vibrant Judaism, in his words, "Judaism without Palestine is spiritually retarded." The land, he maintained, was necessary for the development of the prophetic teachings of peace, equality, and social justice. His objective was a Jewish community in Palestine dedicated to the observance of the Torah, the living word of God, and one that would, as the spiritual center of Israel, spark Jewish cultural creativity. He spoke vaguely at times of a predominantly Jewish Palestine,[13] or of an autonomous community, but religious content always took precedence over political form.

A religious community in Palestine had a larger purpose as well. Citing the views of Rabbi Akiba, Finkelstein insisted that nationhood had meaning only if Israel existed for an ideal outside itself. Upon a Jewish Palestine lay the responsibility of contributing to the survival of civilization by making God's reality manifest to the world and by transmitting the message of the fatherhood of God and brotherhood of man. He liked to think of a restored Palestine as the "third commonwealth," infused with the same spiritual vitality that inspired the deeds of the leaders of the Second Commonwealth—Ezra, the Chasideans, and the Pharisees—and that molded the spiritual life of both Israelites and non-Israelites. If the world cherished the prophetic ideals taught by the Jews, it would help in the rebuilding of Palestine.

Finkelstein's form of spiritual Zionism emphasized the universalist role of Judaism but did not delimit it, as classical Reform had, to religious contributions. Israel as the kingdom of priests had more to impart than a message of monotheism. Positing the ongoing creativity of Israel, he affirmed in an early talk that the people's historical contributions to civilization through prophecy, religious law, philosophy, and poetry had not exhausted their potential: "What future creations lie latent in the still growing mind of Israel we do not know." All attempts at creativity deserved encouragement, be they in "Jewish art, Jewish music, the renaissance of the Hebrew language as the medium of daily intercourse, and above all the rebuilding of the Jewish homeland." The Hebrew University, for example, to which he promised Seminary support early on, illustrated his point.[14] Zionism was therefore a good; itself a product of Jewish creativity, it held out the promise of ongoing creativity for the benefit of mankind through a religion-based Jewish center.

Finkelstein's emphasis on universalism and on spiritual rather than political Zionism bore distinct traces of the American liberal creed. Coming to maturity during the Great War, his generation repudiated the militarism and hypernationalism that in their opinion had precipitated the world conflict. Their faith in a new postwar world was rudely shaken by the failure of the League of Nations and the rise of totalitarianism, but they held fast to the twin beliefs of universalism and pacifism. In the case of Finkelstein, who found reinforcement for those precepts in rabbinic teachings, they assumed even greater significance.[15] They fed his aversion to power politics in general and to the politics of Jewish state-building in particular.

Palestine as the spiritual hub of Judaism—and Finkelstein usually used the term "Judaism" in preference to "Jews"—never negated the viability or desirability of the American Diaspora. Like the earlier religious and cultural Zionists, he neither challenged the validity of a "comfortable" or "Americanized" Zionism nor did he urge American Jews to plan on *aliyah*. Jews had found spiritual as well as material well-being in America, he said, for the ethical values of the Founding Fathers of the United States were identical to those of the Pharisees. American Jews too were called upon to render service to God, Torah, and mankind, and the Seminary in particular, which Finkelstein likened to the academy at Yavneh of Roman times, had a universal mission. Just as the spiritual influence of Yavneh had transcended the material glories of the Hellenistic world, so might the Seminary similarly serve mankind. Finkelstein may have agonized privately that he, an observant Jew, could not live a full religious life outside Eretz Yisrael,[16] but he chose to build up the primacy of Judaism's spiritual mission in America.

The president's refusal to make Jewish political sovereignty a Seminary objective never seriously undermined his control over the students and faculty. The more nationalistically minded grumbled, but since the Seminary did not mandate conformity, they were free to act out their Zionist sentiments independently. Besides, Finkelstein had a singular ability to keep his institution in line. A forceful and charismatic leader, charming and hospitable, worldly but unassuming, he could reason, cajole, conciliate, and, above all, inspire loyalty. Unlike his immediate predecessor he was a "hands-on" president, a respected teacher as well as astute administrator, whose single-minded dedication to the Seminary was exemplary and whose scholarship earned universal admiration. Students and faculty neither rebelled against his determination to keep the Seminary more traditionalist than Conservative, nor force his hand on Zionism.

The RA and United Synagogue, despite disaffection with Finkelstein's approach to Zionism as well as some of his administrative policies, were similarly captivated by the personality and achievements of their classmate and colleague. When the Seminary launched a fund-raising campaign with the RA and the United Synagogue, which gave the school the power to allocate funds to the arms of the movement, their submission to the president and the Seminary was virtually total.[17] In fact as well as in theory the school now spoke for a centralized movement. And, just as the Seminary was the fount of Conservative Judaism, Louis Finkelstein was the Seminary.

The board of directors of the Seminary also accepted Finkelstein's religious Zionism. No more representative of Conservative Judaism than their predecessors, the non-Zionist and anti-Zionist members, however, lacked the deep Jewish attachments of a Schiff or a Marshall. Although they opposed any sign of Jewish nationalism within the school, they could empathize with the principles of universalism and mission that suffused the president's ideology and rhetoric. They genuinely revered Finkelstein for his piety and his learning,[18] and (his New York accent notwithstanding!) they too were captivated by his charm. To this author's knowledge, he functioned for some as personal counselor and spiritual guide.

Zionism became a disruptive force in the smooth administration of the Seminary only when demands for an independent Palestine resurfaced in the 1940s. British intransigence with respect to Jewish immigration to Palestine, compounding the horrors of Hitler's war against the Jews, testified to the inadequacies of a passive Palestinianism or gradualist Zionism. The crisis demanded an immediate refuge for European Jewish survivors. Since refugees had long been a drug on the international market, Zionists fixed on Jewish political autonomy as the one solution for keeping open the doors of Palestine. Under the leadership of a new generation, David Ben-Gurion in Palestine and Reform Rabbi Abba Hillel Silver in the United States, they assumed a more militant approach. At a Zionist conference at New York's Biltmore Hotel in May 1942, more than six hundred delegates, calling for unity within the movement, demanded free entry into Palestine, control over immigration and land development by the Jewish Agency, and the establishment of Palestine as a "Jewish commonwealth." To make support of a commonwealth coextensive with the Jewish community, the Zionists orchestrated the organization of an American Jewish Conference, where, in September 1943, the delegates endorsed the Biltmore program. One Seminary professor predicted that the action of the conference "will probably figure prominently in the annals of the modern Jewish renaissance."[19]

Herzlian Zionism was thus resurrected, forcing Finkelstein to confront the issue of Jewish political nationalism and somehow to reconcile four factors: his personal convictions, his American agenda, his dependence on anti-Zionist board members, and the Zionist loyalties of the students, faculty, and Conservative movement at large. He soon learned that spiritual Zionism was no longer a viable category. According to the new rules of the game, one was either for a Jewish state in Palestine or against it. As President Maurice Wertheim of the AJC explained at the beginning of the war, there were only Zionists and anti-Zionists. Predicting that the *yishuv*, with its own agenda for independence, would take matters into its own hands, he claimed that any financial help to Palestine, heretofore condoned by the non-Zionists, only strengthened the political position and aspirations of the *yishuv*.[20] Since Wertheim's conclusions were correct, Finkelstein's options were constricted; he had to decide whether to join the movement for a political state or to wear the label of anti-Zionist.

For a fuller understanding of the pressures on Finkelstein, a recognition of what one scholar has called his "central vision" is critical. The pet project of the Seminary's president throughout his administration was the development of interreligious and intergroup activities under the aegis of the JTS. Through various types of academic programs—lectures, seminars, institutes, and conferences—scholars from different disciplines and of different faiths would hammer out a "synthesis of traditional religious truth with modern scientific knowledge" and arrive at "inclusive universal ethics that would incorporate the best of the various religious and philosophical traditions."[21]

The idea sprouted with the outbreak of World War II. Then, in response to totalitarianism, Americans took a greater interest in religion, reasoning that a healthy democracy was sustained by religion. Finkelstein was in full accord: "The real difficulty we must face . . . is the . . . heathenization or paganization of such a large part of the population both Jewish and Christian. . . . I do not know of anything we can do more important than to make some contribution to the preservation of religion as a vital force in America."[22] Many Christians as well as Jews agreed. For their part, rabbis welcomed the opportunity to reassert the centrality of faith within the Jewish community—to emphasize the role of religion in the prosecution of the war and in the blueprints for peace. They saw an opportunity to teach the essential compatibility of Judaism with democracy and of Jewish with American values.[23]

Finkelstein wanted more. Besides disseminating an overall framework of morality forged by an ongoing intergroup dialogue of committed scholars, he sought to raise the status of Judaism within the United States to that of American Protestantism and Catholicism. Jews constituted only a small minority, but their religion, he taught, ranked on a par with Christianity. Both lay at the core of the American faith, and both were joined in the religious struggle against totalitarianism. By his efforts for the proper recognition of Judaism, Finkelstein stamped the importance of the Jewish faith on the religious map of the United States, and he was the one who did the most to gain respectability among Christian leaders for the "Judeo" component of the "Judeo-Christian tradition."

By positing the foundations of Americanism on a *Judeo*-Christian tradition, Finkelstein injected a radically new dimension into the Americanization of *Judaism*. Zionism fit his central vision of an aroused religious consciousness in America but only in an indirect fashion: if the ancient religious center in Palestine had been responsible for shaping the nation's moral values and ethical tradition, a restored Jewish center—enriching Judaism, Christianity, and the very ethos of America—promised to nurture that tradition. Since a center like that could well appeal to Americans by showing them the untapped value of a Jewish Palestine, he was unwittingly adding to the Americanization of *Zionism*. But whether the implications of his vision could ultimately benefit the Zionist goal of statehood remained a moot point. Publicly the Conservative leader preferred neither to endorse nor reject a Jewish state, and he maintained his purist spiritual stance during the era of the Holocaust.

It is more than likely that Finkelstein's commitment to the intergroup program constrained him further on the subject of political Zionism. If for no other reason he faulted Zionist appeals for aid to the *yishuv*, since they drained financial resources away from religious institutions.[24] In no way could he afford to lose Christian goodwill or to alienate those affluent Jews, like the members of his board, who funded his projects. The board cheered on Finkelstein's intergroup activities, and they supported his major plans to broaden the institution's outreach to Christians, principally intellectuals, as well as to Jews. Their cooperation enabled him in turn to withstand the criticism of Jewish skeptics. In 1937 when Finkelstein, then provost, coordinated the Seminary's semicentennial celebration, which featured prominent Christian academics, he was chided by Solomon Goldman for "constantly running after the goyim." In response Finkelstein said that American Jews were obliged to educate others in Jewish values, for without a relationship with American Christians Judaism would survive only as a reaction to antisemitism. Nor did he find it inappropriate, the way Goldman had, for board member Lewis L. Strauss, a Reform Jew and anti-Zionist, to serve as chairman of the celebration.[25]

As his outreach program developed further, Finkelstein strengthened the board's pride in the JTS. Doubtless in their eyes he was transforming the institution from a parochial yeshivah geared to service eastern European immigrants into a creative intellectual center harnessed to the needs of the entire nation.[26] He may have felt impelled to yield on Zionism in order not to alienate the board, but that seemed a small price to pay when the effort to strengthen the Seminary and Judaism within American society was on the line.

Above the Contending Factions

Finkelstein's views of Zionism did not arouse public comment before he became president. His interest after the riots of 1929 in Jewish negotiations with
the Palestinian Arabs was a topic of conversation only among Seminary students; his opposition to England's suggestion in 1937 of partitioning Palestine
was voiced privately and merely to show his support of Cyrus Adler's antistatist
stand.[27] Less than a year after he assumed office, however, Zionists pounced
upon the man who now spoke for the Conservative movement.

In March 1941 Lord Halifax, British ambassador to the United States, invited
three rabbis—David de Sola Pool, Louis Finkelstein, and Israel Goldstein—to a
private conference on the issues facing American Jews. (Pool was Orthodox,
Goldstein like Finkelstein was Conservative.) Halifax raised the subject of
Zionism, and the rabbis assured him that although they differed on minor
points they were all Zionists. In the course of the conversation and without any
prompting, Finkelstein commented on the irreligiosity of the *yishuv*, a condition that shocked Christian leaders but that he, Finkelstein, was confident
would change. Immediately after the meeting, when Pool and Goldstein re-
buked him for those gratuitous remarks, he replied that he believed in being
honest about such matters, and besides, Halifax, a religious man, was probably
well aware of the facts. Finkelstein may have felt that an emphasis on religion in
the *yishuv* rather than on political Zionism would appeal to the ambassador,
but in Zionist eyes he had tarnished the image of a united Jewry in support of
the Jews in Palestine.

Although the proceedings of the conference were supposed to remain confidential, Goldstein leaked the substance to several leading Zionists, including
Chaim Weizmann and Stephen Wise, and Finkelstein became fair game for the
nationalists. A Zionist smear campaign ensued: Finkelstein had maligned the
yishuv, and, at a time when the British White Paper had cut the sole remaining
lifeline for Jews trapped by the Nazis, he was no better than a *moser* (informer
against the Jews to the non-Jews). Chaim Weizmann did not return
Finkelstein's call; Wise refused to shake Finkelstein's hand on a social occasion.
Furious with a now contrite Goldstein, who at once attempted to defend Finkelstein to Weizmann, the Seminary's president told his colleague that the "poi-
son" was rapidly spreading: "If unchecked, the trouble will spread to Palestine
. . . and will be told to Chief Rabbi [Isaac] Herzog." Claiming to be concerned
more for his institution than for his own good name, Finkelstein wanted to be,
and was, judged as the leader of the Seminary and the Conservative movement.
His office gave him public recognition and clout, but, as this episode taught, it
put constraints upon his speech and behavior.[28]

The new militancy on the part of the Zionists after the Biltmore conference
revitalized the diehard anti-Zionists. In the summer of 1942 a small group of
Reform rabbis initiated what shortly became the American Council for Judaism.

Embittered by the Zionist commitment to statehood and by the action of Reform's Central Conference of American Rabbis (CCAR) endorsing the creation of a Jewish army in Palestine to fight alongside the Allies, the dissidents published a statement in condemnation of political Zionism. It denied neither the plight of the refugees nor the admirable achievements of the *yishuv*, but it contended that a nationalistic and secularistic movement contradicted the cardinal tenets of Judaism. Still frightened by the charge of dual allegiance, the council worried lest Zionist demands cast doubts anew on the primary loyalty to America that Jews had so long protested. Since some Seminary board members sympathized with the council, Finkelstein was dragged into the Zionist/anti-Zionist dispute.[29]

A few months later Rabbi Philip Bernstein, a Reform rabbi and an active Zionist, consulted with several prominent rabbis, including the presidents of the RA, CCAR, and Rabbinical Council of America (Orthodox), and proceeded to draft a counterstatement to the council's. Arguing that Zionism was fully compatible with Judaism and its universalistic teachings, and that Jews like other peoples enjoyed the right to political self-determination, the statement lashed out at the anti-Zionists for their disservice to beleaguered Jews and for providing aid to the enemies of a Jewish homeland. Not to be outdone by the council's claims to unalloyed Americanism, the statement included a separate paragraph reaffirming Zionist loyalty to the country:

> We have not the least fear that our fellow Americans will be led to misconstrue the attitudes of American Jews to America because of their interest in Zionism. Every fair-minded American knows that American Jews have only one political allegiance—and that is to America. There is nothing in Zionism to impair this loyalty. Zionism has been endorsed in our generation by every President from Woodrow Wilson to Franklin Delano Roosevelt, and has been approved by the Congress of the United States.

Bernstein then called upon Finkelstein, along with twenty other leading rabbis, to sponsor a letter soliciting endorsement of the statement from fellow rabbis from all branches of American Judaism. Although members of the RA signed that letter, Finkelstein refused. He said that the statement was open to misinterpretation and that it could trigger a major controversy that might actually harm the Zionist cause. Disturbed, however, that his refusal was construed by some as anti-Zionist, he wrote Bernstein that he, as president of the JTS, had been advised not to sign. Since the advice came from a Zionist, indeed a sponsor of the counterstatement, he labored to prove that his decision in no way reflected any personal opposition to Zionism.[30]

Caught between Zionist pressure on the one hand and an unwillingness to ally himself with the statehood movement on the other, Finkelstein wrote Bernstein yet again, stating that he was well aware of the "whispering campaign" against him, even though no American Jew had cause to presume "that I am not deeply concerned about the future of our homeland in Palestine." He reiterated his fear of communal disunity generated by the statement and its adverse effect on a Jewish restoration to Palestine. He added that perhaps the American Council for Judaism was not totally in error, noting its influence on some of his Christian friends. Calling for Zionist patience and soul-searching, he urged above all the need to square Zionist thought with religious principles. Only a Zionism grounded fully in religion stood a chance of achieving unity among American Jews and of furthering Jewish aspirations in Palestine.[31] In no way did Finkelstein condone the council's activities, but clearly the principal culprit in his analysis was the Zionist movement.

The letters to Bernstein reveal how Finkelstein groped for a way out of the conflicting pressures that beset him. His validation of Zionism solely on religious grounds, now largely ignoring the themes of Jewish peoplehood and creativity, became the most expedient way for him to operate publicly. It involved no compromise of principle on his part, and neither Zionists nor anti-Zionists could very well dispute his vision of a Torah-true community in Palestine. Perhaps too, as he suggested, Jewish consensus on a religious homeland would more readily evoke a positive response in Christian circles, doubtless the same circles to which he turned in his outreach programs. As the spiritual guide who tried to stand above the contending factions and judge them according to religious norms, Finkelstein donned the mantle of arbiter, pleading for Jewish unity and chiding those whose communal in-fighting injured the cause of a legitimate, i.e., religious, Jewish homeland.

Zionists, however, were persuaded neither by appeals for a transcendent Jewish unity nor by what they regarded as pious platitudes. World Jewry in crisis could not afford the luxury of religious visions alone, and after Biltmore a true Zionist did not equivocate about statehood. In the flareup over the Council for Judaism, Bernstein never even acknowledged receipt of Finkelstein's letters. Although the Seminary's president genuinely believed that Zionist attacks on him were totally unwarranted, his attempts to appear as a principled religious Zionist ended in failure. Historian Moshe Davis, who for many years worked closely with Finkelstein, once explained: "He tried to straddle, . . . to stick to both sides of the issue. And . . . that's why there is to this day the recollection on the part of many students at the time . . . of his non-Zionism and anti-Zionism."[32]

The counterstatement of the Bernstein group eventually garnered more than eight hundred signatures. The RA soon followed, calling on Conservative rabbis to sign a statement repudiating the purposes of the American Council for Judaism. Rabbinical students at the JTS acted too; along with students from Orthodox and Reform seminaries, they unanimously endorsed a program advocating Jewish membership in the United Nations, a Jewish army, and the establishment of a Jewish state in Palestine.[33] Publicly, however, the Seminary's administration kept silent. Virtually the lone Conservative rabbi who refused to sign the RA statement, Finkelstein attempted to placate both sides. He explained to a Zionist colleague: "I, of course, agreed with my colleagues in their basic strictures against the Council. . . . On the other hand, I simply could not sign a statement which equated Judaism with American, British and French nationalism."[34] At the same time, when board member Arthur Hays Sulzberger of the *New York Times*, a rabid anti-Zionist, wondered suspiciously what the connection of the RA was to the Seminary, Finkelstein assured him that, although the RA "as a whole is very much under the influence of the Zionist Organization," it had no control over the policy of the school. He added that the statement of the students, who were caught up in a Zionist-fomented wave of hysteria, had been considerably stronger and "more foolish" before he convinced them that they had misunderstood the situation. Sulzberger's sympathies with the council notwithstanding, Finkelstein mildly criticized the anti-Zionists for their "injudicious" behavior, but conforming to his role as arbiter, he preferred to stay above the controversy. For resolving the impasse he suggested only renewed "educational effort."[35]

Where the Seminary stood on the fight between the Zionists and the American Council for Judaism became a public issue when the Independent Jewish News Service reported that several board members were associated with the council. Finkelstein called the report "unscrupulous propaganda," charging that it contained "misinterpretations" if not "actual falsities." He explained to the faculty that none of the board members under attack was, or intended to become, associated with the council. Moreover, the Seminary was not obligated to defend the statements of any individuals connected with it.[36]

The issue was not whether Finkelstein lied. That he felt impelled to offer an explanation suggests first, a widespread awareness of the positive interest in the council on the part of several Seminary directors (notably Sulzberger, Strauss, and Alan Stroock), and second, a fear on the part of the faculty that the council sympathizers would attempt to impose an anti-Zionist policy upon the Seminary. At this juncture the Seminary's respected Talmudist, Professor Louis Ginzberg, intervened. He called the incident "much ado about nothing"; he hoped at least that the Seminary's laissez-faire policy on Zionism would prevail and "that the members of the Board will . . . not object to any pro-Zionistic declarations by members of the Faculty expressed by them as individuals." He reminded Finkelstein of the public exchange of letters between Jacob Schiff and Solomon Schechter in 1907 on the dangers of Zionism to American Jewry. Schechter had not yielded to his most important board member, and Ginzberg hoped that Finkelstein would take similar action with respect to *his* board.[37]

A few months after that uproar, another crisis erupted, this one concerning the withdrawal of the AJC from the American Jewish Conference. The non-Zionist committee, a reluctant participant from the beginning, suffered a major defeat when the conference dismissed its pleas to defer the issue of Jewish statehood and proceeded to endorse the Biltmore program. The committee's executive voted in October 1943 to leave the conference, thereby damaging the impressive show of Jewish unity on the Palestine issue. The action called forth torrents of abuse, and 10 percent of the AJC's membership resigned in protest.[38] The arms of the Conservative movement stood in the forefront of the opposition; the RA, United Synagogue, and Women's League(affiliated with the United Synagogue) all dissociated themselves from the AJC. Cries came from Conservative rabbis and congregations for Louis Finkelstein, a member of the committee's executive, to follow suit. Milton Steinberg, rabbi of New York's prestigious Park Avenue Synagogue, called the committee's withdrawal "an expression of the most dejudaized and detraditionalized elements in American Jewish life"—which fed into the hands of the anti-Zionists. The president of a congregation in Pottsville, Pennsylvania, similarly inveighed against the AJC's action, "which flouts those very religious principles and democratic ideals to which we in our small way are dedicated." Both the prominent rabbi and the obscure layman, allied in the Conservative movement that had since Schechter's days linked Zionism with Judaism, asked Finkelstein to resign from the committee. As Steinberg diplomatically put it: "You do serve as spokesman for Conservative Judaism in this country. And, ideally, there ought not to be a sharp dichotomy between the leadership of a movement and the overwhelming sentiment of its following."[39]

Again Finkelstein was forced to balance institutional pressures and personal beliefs. He participated in the committee's debate on quitting the conference, and there too his guarded remarks revealed his distance from political Zionism. Like the AJC, he faulted the British White Paper of 1939, which drastically curtailed immigration to Palestine, but although he favored a refuge for Jews in Palestine, he spoke against statehood. For one thing, if the commonwealth resolution meant a less-than-equal political status for Christians and Muslims in Palestine (which he seemed to assume), it was unacceptable. Furthermore, it was bad statesmanship to ask for the unattainable: "There isn't one possibility in five hundred that there will be established in the course of the next twenty-five years what is called a Jewish state in Palestine." Age-old Jewish prayers did not ask for a Jewish president in Palestine: "What the Jews have been praying for two thousand years is that the Kingdom of God shall be restored in Palestine." The rabbi abstained on the committee's vote to withdraw from the conference, and for the sake of communal unity he called for further negotiations with the Zionists. If they refused to change the statehood resolution, only then was withdrawal in order.[40] Except for that qualification, which again put him above the contending parties, his spiritual Zionism and vague ecumenicism led to a conclusion identical to the committee's.

Seminary tradition also worked to keep Finkelstein loyal to the AJC. The school and the defense agency had been closely linked throughout their histories. In the days of Schechter and Adler the same prominent few who ran the committee sat on the Seminary's board; Cyrus Adler was a lynchpin of the committee while he headed the Seminary. During Finkelstein's administration traces of the interlocking directorate persisted. Finkelstein himself served on various committees of the AJC, and the AJC in turn helped fund the Seminary's intergroup Conference on Science, Philosophy, and Religion.[41] Were Finkelstein to sever the long-standing relationship, he could have triggered a major crisis with the board or forfeited funds for his outreach program.

Dissent within the Ranks

The president, however, could not ignore the pressures from the Seminary's rank and file. Milton Steinberg for one probed beyond the conference episode and asked for answers to a series of pointed questions: Did Finkelstein envision a Jewish Palestine solely as "a community of Saints such as that of Safed in the sixteenth century" or as a home for "many Jews even if not all of them are saints and scholars" (a takeoff on *Scholar, Saint and Martyr,* the subtitle of Finkelstein's biography of Rabbi Akiba)? On what basis did Jews have the right to demand free entry into Palestine? Was the Western world still bound by the promises of the Balfour Declaration and mandate? Did Finkelstein deny Jewish nationhood? Would he favor Jewish political self-determination if Jews constituted a majority in Palestine?

Finkelstein answered forthrightly: Palestine was not only for saints and scholars; the Balfour Declaration and mandate were permanent covenants; the right to enter Palestine stemmed primarily from the right of any Jew to fulfill a religious obligation: "The question of whether the Jew who comes to Palestine is himself religious in other respects, is not a relevant issue. . . . His desire to come to Palestine is a desire to perform a religious act." Yes, he believed in Jewish peoplehood—"nation" was too loose a term—but he did not regard Jews as a political group. Nor did present circumstances warrant statehood:

> I believe the interest of Palestine and the world requires that for the time being, it should remain under international control. If, at sometime in the future, the Jews constitute a majority of the land, and as such a majority desire that the land be reconstituted as the Republic of Eretz Israel (with guarantees of full and equal rights to all individuals and groups), I would regard it as the duty of the world to grant that request, insofar as it will grant similar requests to other small countries.

Although Steinberg the Zionist concluded that at least for the moment Finkelstein's response "leaves little to be desired," the question of why the president opposed the conference resolution and sided with the AJC remained. Finkelstein explained at length to the rabbi that since the committee's attempts at unity had been rebuffed, the fault for the rupture lay with the Zionists. He personally was dismayed by Zionist tactics at the conference, but more important he thought the Palestine resolution was intrinsically flawed. The word "commonwealth," which connoted an arrogation of political power on the part of Jews at the expense of non-Jews in Palestine, was morally and religiously indefensible as well as potentially harmful to Diaspora Jews. Long the universalist, he was also concerned lest the resolution, drawn along lines of narrow nationalism, cause Jews to forget their mission to the world at large. He, Finkelstein, had suggested that the word "homeland" be substituted for "commonwealth," but the Zionists had turned him down.[42]

Finkelstein's explanations jibed with his remarks at the AJC meeting and his most recent article for the New Palestine. But a private letter to Steinberg illuminated more clearly than before the essential distinction he drew between his spiritual Zionism and political Zionism: "The primary question is not one of political control of the land, but whether the Jews are given the opportunity to perform their religious duty, and to develop their spiritual and cultural life in the Holy Land, and whether they are there in such numbers and preponderance as to make the development of their religious and spiritual life basic elements in the civilization of the country." A Jewish majority in Palestine might be desirable, but the concept of a majority in a political sense carried no special merit.[43] Finkelstein held fast to his principles, but his dismissal of "political control" hardly endeared him in 1943 to American Zionists.

The Seminary's president discussed the AJC/conference rupture with a handpicked committee that consisted of four board members, four alumni, and four faculty members. The group, of which he said "virtually everyone ... is an ardent Zionist," agreed that he should remain in the AJC with a view toward achieving collaboration between the committee and the Zionists. There the matter was dropped, and a letter of resignation from the AJC, which Finkelstein had drafted earlier, was never sent. Nevertheless, disaffection with his close ties to the committee lingered.[44]

By 1943, as thoughts turned to plans for a postwar world, Finkelstein's universalist and antinationalist leanings grew more pronounced. In articles that appeared in the New Palestine he ranked national sovereignty well below internationalism: "The creation of an enduring peace presupposes an active cooperative relationship among nations and peoples, which makes the question of statehood less and less relevant; while emphasis on national sovereignty anywhere must be fatal to civilization." He spoke on the need for a restored Jewish homeland—never did he use the word "state" or "commonwealth"—but again he depicted a center through which a revitalized Judaism (not Jews)would effectively disseminate the spiritual values required for the survival of civilization. The political contours of that center remained fuzzy. In favor of a postwar association of nations committed to the prophetic ideals of peace and justice, he envisioned a Jewish homeland under the supervision of the United Nations.

A restored Palestine and a new world order were interlocked. The former was both "indispensable to a reformation of world culture as well as one of the major expressions of that reformation itself." Since he decried secular Jewish nationalism, the editor of the *New Palestine* pressed him for a similar denunciation of anti-Zionism. All Finkelstein agreed to, however, was one narrowly worded sentence in keeping with his religious focus: "To oppose this effort to restore the Jewish settlement of the Holy Land," he added, "is to repudiate a cardinal tradition of Judaism."[45]

Zionists who looked for a positive endorsement from the leader of Conservative Jewry remained dissatisfied. They had drawn the line between Zionist and anti-Zionist on the issue of Jewish political autonomy, and a "homeland" or "settlement" under international control fell short of that objective. Yet, out of principle as well as a healthy fear of antagonizing his board, Finkelstein would venture no further. Sulzberger's behavior, for example, proved that anti-nationalists were at least as uncompromising as the political Zionists. Moving from non-Zionism to anti-Zionism in response to nationalist militancy,[46] the publisher aired his bias publicly through the *New York Times*. Privately he needled Finkelstein repeatedly whenever he suspected Seminary identification with Jewish nationalism. On one occasion he mistakenly detected a Jewish flag in a *Times* photograph of a Seminary convocation, and he protested that the display of a flag "which is not my national emblem again raises the issue which has so much disturbed me."[47]

The president trod warily with the board. As early as 1941 he began to clear with them any matter—even as inconsequential as signing a statement in support of the Hebrew University—that smacked of Seminary involvement with Palestine or Zionism.[48] At one faculty meeting he described his difficulties with individual board members and the countless hours he was forced to spend on placating them. Since financial pressures fostered a dependence on the goodwill of Sulzberger and Lewis Strauss, the two most likely to expand the Seminary's circle of large donors, it was politic to keep Zionist sentiments in check. Professor Mordecai Kaplan reported that the president agreed to certain conditions that Sulzberger thought would help the chances of reaching the "big money": The Seminary would not limit itself to servicing Conservative Judaism; the Seminary would continue its interfaith work; and the Seminary would not commit itself to political Zionism. The cynical Kaplan suspected that Finkelstein himself and not Sulzberger or Strauss had formulated those conditions.[49]

Finkelstein loyally sprang to Sulzberger's defense in a dispute between the publisher and Abba Hillel Silver. In the wake of the American Jewish Conference, the Reform rabbi, now the recognized voice of an aggressive Zionism, publicly denounced "the spirit of Arthur Hays Sulzberger," which had turned the *Times* into "the channel for anti-Zionist propaganda." Finkelstein, who claimed both men as his friends but deplored the injurious effect of such quarrels on the causes of both Jews and Judaism, blamed the Zionist leader.

He told Sulzberger that Silver had chosen a path of "violence and vehemence." Perhaps recalling that Silver was most responsible for the passage of the Palestine resolution at the American Jewish Conference, and hence for Finkelstein's own difficulties after the AJC/conference rupture, he may have unconsciously identified with him: "It is obviously the fate of the men who try to civilize the world to be misinterpreted and maligned by their contemporaries who resist being civilized." Nothing from "our hysterical friends," he assured his board member, could undermine "your place in American religious life and in Judaism, and your magnificent contributions to civilization in our time." Finkelstein wrote Silver at the same time, calling Sulzberger "a loyal and devout Jew trying to serve his faith and his people" whose outlook on Jewish life was, indeed, not that different from Silver's. He didn't neglect, however, to lavish equally high praise on the Zionist leader; there were few whose abilities he admired more and whose devotion "to the service of God and the Jewish faith, I have greater certainty."[50]

Again, as in the episodes of the Bernstein letter and the AJC's withdrawal from the American Jewish Conference, the Seminary's president attempted to juggle conflicting pressures—in this case his own principles, his dependence on the board, and the need to appease his Conservative constituency. Professing simultaneously a loyalty to both Zionists and anti-Zionists, he sought a way out of the maze by shifting the focus from political Zionism to Jewish unity. Finkelstein failed, however, to defuse the Sulzberger/Silver controversy, and the publisher and the rabbi exchanged heated letters replete with *ad hominem* attacks. A near-hysterical Sulzberger even charged that the Zionists, who perverted and distorted facts, were employing "Goebbels' tactics."[51]

When in 1945 the board officially considered the president's views on Zionism, it showed how sensitive all members, and not just Sulzberger and Strauss, were on the subject. A frank statement of his position, drafted by Finkelstein himself, appeared in the minutes of the board:

> He [Finkelstein] described his attitude toward the reestablishment of a Jewish settlement in Palestine as being precisely that of Doctor Schechter, and wholly within the Jewish tradition. He stated that it was his conviction that in this sense, every member of the Faculty, every alumnus of the Seminary, and he believed also, every member of the Board, was a Zionist. On the other hand, while he did not wish to make a public statement on the subject, . . . he wished the Board to know what he had believed had been made obvious from all his writings over many years, . . . namely, that he does not regard the Jews of the world as a political unit. He considers that the effort to describe them that way is extremely dangerous, not only to the Jews, but to democracy, generally, and that, though he hopes that events will prove him wrong, the concentration of the Zionist effort on the conception of Palestine as a "Jewish Commonwealth," rather than on widespread immigration will have a harmful effect on the future of the [*yishuv*].

The board accepted the president's statement. They may have thought that his spiritual Zionism posed no immediate challenge, or they may well have assumed, as did some faculty members, that he was not a Zionist.[52]

Meanwhile, Conservative Jews waited in vain for Finkelstein to endorse the Zionist demand for statehood. A cover story featuring Finkelstein that appeared in *Time* a few years later reported that at least one large contributor to the Seminary "tore up his usual check." Within the RA rumblings of discontent with Finkelstein's attempts to keep one foot in both the Zionist and anti-Zionist camps were also heard. As Milton Steinberg put it, "I want Dr. Finkelstein . . . to stop pussyfooting on Zionism."[53] The opposition came to a head in 1944–45 when several prominent Conservative rabbis, led by Steinberg and Solomon Goldman, prepared a list of grievances against the Seminary's president.[54] Their lengthy indictment criticized Finkelstein for initiating new programs of an interfaith or public relations nature that had little relevance to the Seminary as a seat of learning, for ignoring the need to formulate a Conservative theology, and for wielding too much power over the RA and United Synagogue. Furthermore, and this was the heart of their complaint, they charged that Finkelstein's board was a body unrepresentative of, and unsympathetic to, Conservative Judaism. Although Finkelstein's stand on Zionism was not specifically included as a grievance, it was implicit in the bill of particulars. One could well deduce from the rabbis' brief that if the Seminary stayed on a proper course—committed to the interests and spirit of Conservative Judaism, and heedful of its rabbis and congregations—it would emerge as an active supporter of the Zionist program. Finkelstein understood the linkage between the rabbis' complaints, which simultaneously fueled student resentment, and Zionism.

Steinberg and Goldman presented harsh criticisms to Finkelstein privately. Steinberg, who cancelled the annual appeal for the Seminary at his wealthy congregation, also aired the charges publicly in three sermons titled "Crises in Conservative Judaism." Not only did he pointedly question Finkelstein's power, but he lashed out against the board, men "who are anti-traditionalist, anti-Zionist, even assimilationist" and "flagrantly out of harmony with everything the Seminary represents." Finkelstein handled the dissidents with consummate skill. He patiently answered them individually; he arranged meetings where he, flanked by senior members of the faculty, entertained their complaints; and he flattered them with friendly invitations. In the end, his strategy wore them down. That plus a genuine loyalty to their teacher and friend on the part of the rabbis broke the back of the "Steinberg-Goldman revolt." In the long run not all was lost. The administrative organization of the Seminary was modified to include a larger board of overseers, representative of Conservative Jewry, that would share some authority with the board of directors. Finkelstein also promised that as long as he was president no one would be appointed a director without the endorsement of the RA's executive.

For the time being, however, the president and the board of directors reigned supreme with respect to political Zionism. At the very moment that he was negotiating with the rabbis, Finkelstein again refused to sign a Zionist statement responding to charges from the American Council for Judaism. This time he explained that if the text of the statement were properly altered, he might be able to induce Lessing Rosenwald, president and strong financial backer of the council, to withdraw his support of that organization. He did meet with Rosenwald, but his attempt at peacemaking between Zionists and anti-Zionists failed.[55] Whether in the interest of Jewish unity, or merely "pussy-footing" as Steinberg had called it, Finkelstein refused to burn his bridges to either group.

Within the walls of the Seminary, faculty and student anger also smoldered. Finkelstein's approach to Zionism was never debated publicly; in Moshe Davis's words, it generated only "corridor, cafeteria and house talk."[56] Much like Steinberg and Goldman, students linked their support of Zionism with scorn for the interfaith program. According to one quip that circulated at the time, Dr. Finkelstein even signed his letters "Interfaithfully yours!"

On several occasions, however, the opposition surfaced. In 1944 the Seminary awarded an honorary degree to Zionist leader Chaim Weizmann,[57] but to the consternation of the students the citation made no mention of Zionism. It referred only to Weizmann's scientific contributions to the cause of the Allies in World War I and his lifelong struggle to alleviate the sufferings of Jews and the world at large. A mirror of Finkelstein's own views, the citation commended Weizmann's efforts through the founding of the Hebrew University to further the "development of the spiritual values of Israel." "His pursuit of the prophetic vision," the text concluded, "is motivated by an earnest conviction that a Jewish community, reestablished in the Holy Land, can once more be a source of inspiration and moral strength to all mankind." In the eyes of the students, "spiritual values," "prophetic vision," and "Jewish community" ignored Weizmann's herculean tasks on behalf of Jewish nationhood. More important, the citation could hardly be construed as a message of encouragement to a *yishuv* bent on political independence. Several students complained jointly to the administration, but Finkelstein offered no explanation. Student bitterness mounted when the class of 1945 requested and was denied permission to sing the Zionist anthem, *Hatikvah*, at their commencement.[58]

Aside from his sensitivity to the board's outlook, Finkelstein's own opposition to Jewish statehood had not changed as the war wound down. He confided to board member Frieda Warburg in October 1944 that "I sympathize greatly" with the scheme to make Palestine a binationalist state. (Binationalism at that time would have meant permanent minority status for the Jews.) Moreover, he thought that the "temporary difficulties" in Palestine were overshadowed by larger issues—such as "seeing that the Jews shall be the best kind of people possible"—to which the Seminary was committed.[59] The letter coincided in time with student reaction to the Weizmann degree and the onset of the confrontation with Goldman and Steinberg. In spite of, or perhaps in answer to, the challenges from colleagues and students, Finkelstein stiffened both his resistance to a Jewish state and his determination to launch projects beyond the conventional parameters of a rabbinical school.

Nor did Finkelstein amend his position in the final months before the state of Israel came into being. The UN had voted for partition in November 1947, but diplomatic shifts until the very last days threatened to jettison international approval of a Jewish state. Meanwhile the *yishuv* was caught in a stranglehold between Arab guerrilla warfare and British restrictions on Jewish self-defense. On all levels—political, material, and moral—it desperately needed American Jewish support. Finkelstein, the confirmed pacifist, recoiled, however, at the thought of a Jewish-Arab war. Like others, he believed the warnings from high American officials that the establishment of a state might actually lead to the military destruction of a Jewish Palestine.[60] If a state was not viable at that time, he saw no imperative for altering his course.

On the eve of Israel's independence in 1948 Zionist members of the faculty stood up to the president. A dispute over a seemingly trivial issue, an honorary degree to be awarded at commencement, captured the bitterness that had built up over the years between the Zionists and Finkelstein. At a meeting in January, the president's nomination of Joseph Proskauer, president of the AJC, drew opposition because of the latter's opposition to statehood, and a compromise was reached whereby an award would also go to Moshe Shertok, head of the political department of the Jewish Agency and a leading force for a Jewish state. Unhappy with Shertok, Finkelstein tried a month later to substitute Paul Baerwald of the Joint Distribution Committee, also an antinationalist. Although the president promised a special convocation to honor Zionist leaders if and when partition was favorably resolved, Professors Hillel Bavli and Shalom Spiegel argued that it was the Seminary's duty to take an immediate public stand on the side of the *yishuv*. Mordecai Kaplan's diary provides a detailed description of the stormy meeting: "Both Bavli and Spiegel spoke sharply and bitterly of the ivory tower attitude of the Seminary, an attitude that is responsible for the tendency on the part of the Jewish masses to ignore the Seminary. At one point Finkelstein screamed at Bavli, and Bavli paled with anger." When Shertok's name was brought up once more in April, Finkelstein again lost his temper. Maintaining that it was a matter of conscience, he said that "he had no faith in the Zionist leaders who have made the issue of Jewish statehood paramount." In the end, honorary degrees went to both Zionists and anti-Zionists but not to Shertok.[61]

Barely a month after the birth of Israel, the Seminary held its graduation. On that day the students rebelled. As one popular story goes, they draped an Israeli flag on the Seminary tower only to have it whisked away by the administration before the ceremonies began. Since their request for *Hatikvah*, in which

Professor Bavli joined, was also turned down (a foreign anthem, nonreligious to boot!), they arranged with the carillonist at neighboring Union Theological Seminary to play the melody during commencement. Elated and triumphant, the students heard the bells formally announce the Seminary's identification with the new Jewish state.[62]

The birth of Israel brought a dramatic shift in Finkelstein's policy. Like its affiliated branches, the JTS now stood proudly behind the Jewish state. In 1952 the Seminary in conjunction with the Jewish Agency launched the Seminary Israel Institute, and that same year it awarded an honorary degree to Israel's prime minister, David Ben-Gurion. Ten years later the Seminary opened a student dormitory in Jerusalem, thereby establishing a permanent presence in the land.[63]

Finkelstein, still very much the spiritual Zionist, warmly endorsed the ties of active cooperation. The very existence of a state recharged his vision of a third commonwealth committed to the universal ideals and mission of Judaism, a vision in which American Jews also played a part. The latter, he said, like Babylonian Jewry of old (those who had been exiled when the first temple was destroyed), "who brought the vision of Judaism to bear upon the practical affairs of the world," were fully prepared to help their Israeli brethren in the service of God: "If we can labor with them toward a solution of the vast human problem, that in itself will be a privilege."[64] At Finkelstein's suggestion Chaim Weizmann, then Israel's first president, presented President Truman with a Torah scroll as a token of gratitude from the people of Israel for his efforts on behalf of an independent Jewish state.[65] No other object could have better conveyed Finkelstein's unchanged view of Israel's *raison d'être*.

Finkelstein openly altered his position after 1948 in one significant respect. Now, for the first time, he articulated a belief in a special bonding between Conservative Judaism and Zionism. Reverting to the theme of Jewish creativity, which he had raised before the RA in 1927, he explained that a common basis of self-confidence generated by that creativity underlay both ideologies. The self-confidence born of Zionism, he said, had allowed Conservative Judaism to take root and flourish in the United States: "That enormous faith in ourselves and in our tradition—which has enabled us, like our predecessors, to assert that . . . we can participate fully in the life of America and yet hold fast to the traditions of our fathers; the faith that convinced Solomon Schechter that the Seminary . . . was at once a Jewish Seminary and an American Seminary. . . . This faith and self-confidence were, in my opinion, by-products of the vast effort which had already begun to lay the foundations of a resurrected Jewish commonwealth in *Eretz Yisrael.*" He concluded: "In a certain sense, it may be said that Conservative Judaism is itself the first-born child of the marriage of Zionism and Americanism."[66] By "marrying" Zionism to Americanism, Finkelstein was also showing how American-like the Zionist movement in the United States had been all along.

Afterword

Without the Americanization of its ideology and politics, Zionism in the United States would have made little headway. The many ways in which Herzl's teachings were tailored to conform to American beliefs and public behavior may have watered down the classical Zionist definitions of *galut* and *aliyah*, but they ensured a hearing on the part of American Jews. Jews believed in American exceptionalism, and their Zionism followed suit.

The American factor continued to figure in American Jewish support of the new state of Israel. Only a few days after the birth of the Jewish state, the *New Palestine*, the newspaper of the ZOA, confidently declared: "We American Zionists know that Zionism is good Americanism."[1] When, almost immediately after the conclusion of World War II, the United States became entangled in the Cold War, Zionists argued that Israel, precisely because it held the same ideals and diplomatic objectives as the United States, deserved American friendship. Although American government officials resisted Zionist pressure by citing the nation's need of oil and strategic bases, the Zionists fought appeasement of the Arab states. Their answer emphasized the American-like character of the new state and the coincidence of Israeli and American interests: Both countries supported collective security and the United Nations; unlike the Arabs who had sided with the Axis during the war, Jewish loyalty to the United States and its allies was indisputable; Israel, different from despotic Arab emirates or monarchies, boasted a Western-like democratic government that would resist Soviet expansion in the Near East. Thus, just as American Jews were ever an accommodationist minority, so were American Zionists bent on accommodating Israel's policies to America's international image.

The emphasis on the identical objectives of the United States and Israel was echoed in the Jewish state by leaders like David Ben-Gurion. In 1950, Israel's first prime minister stated that the secret of his country's success was its vision. He added: "That was the secret of America's greatness. The oppressed of the Old World fled there, but they brought a vision with them, as do our immigrants today—a vision of a new life in freedom. They did wonderful things, and so can we."[2] That theme, invoked repeatedly to justify extensive American aid to its young partner, has persisted. It is hardly surprising, for example, that today Israel equates its struggle against Arab terrorism with America's war on Osama bin Laden. Differences between the two states on matters of foreign policy may and do arise, but in the end, since American goals and directives generally prevail, Israel's course of action is Americanized still further.

Yet, statehood raised new questions about the American Jewish–Israeli nexus. First, Israel was now a foreign state, a fact that automatically delimited the right of either side to interfere in the affairs of the other even in the name of protection. Was it appropriate, therefore, for Americans, supporters of the Jewish state or not, to demand an active role in shaping Israel's foreign policy or to agitate publicly on the internal problems of Israeli politics? On the other hand, was it proper for Israel's government to pass judgment on antisemitic incidents in the United States or to propagandize for *aliyah* from America?

Some American Jews worried that unless distinct boundaries were drawn between the two communities, the charge of dual allegiance might again arise. The AJC, for example, began studying the impact of a Jewish state on the position of American Jewry as early as 1947. To ward off any popular criticism Joseph Proskauer wrote in a letter to the press on the eve of Israel's independence: "We are told by the antisemite . . . and by some small small sections of American Jewry that [the UN's decision for a Jewish state] has created a problem of possible inconsistency between our obligations as Americans and as Jews. There is no such problem. . . . The Jews in America suffer from no political schizophrenia. . . . In faith and in conduct we shall continue to demonstrate . . . that we are bone of the bone and flesh of the flesh of America." Under pressure from the committee, Prime Minister Ben-Gurion was compelled to promise that Israel would not presume to speak for Jews of other countries. Recognizing American exceptionalism, he undercut the case for *aliyah* by agreeing that American Jews were not in exile. Israel sorely needed a strong Jewish community in the United States, Ben-Gurion said, and it would neither say nor do anything that might "undermine the sense of security and stability of American Jewry."[3] Given Israel's subordinate position in the alliance, the obverse of the coin, or the limits on American Jewish interference in Israeli affairs, was largely ignored.

Israel was more troubled by a second question of the post-1948 period. Could the country count on American Jews to come to its aid in times of crisis? Would the intensity of their response match that of 1943–48? Despite the outpouring of support during the Six-Day War (1967), recent decades have witnessed signs of slippage. The stand of the liberal churches, whose support of the Palestinian Arabs intensified after 1967, has troubled American Jewish leaders. Jewish communal agencies, fearing the loss of major Christian groups who had been their usual postwar allies on domestic matters, had to choose between their Christian friends and Israel. At the same time, those agencies were shifting their focus to American Jewish concerns such as intermarriage and Jewish continuity, and Israel was increasingly dislodged from center stage. Moreover, as analysts of the contemporary American Jewish scene point out, Jews like other Americans now forge their ties to religion and community on the basis of individual rather than collective needs. In the case of the Jews, that has meant less of a commitment to communal philanthropic causes or struggles against antisemitism, and more of a separation from Israel and Israelis.[4]

A third question concerned the relevance of American Zionist organizations after the goal of Jewish statehood was reached. To be sure, from the establishment of Israel in 1948 until the present, American Zionists have continued to fill two essential tasks on behalf of Israel, fund-raising and diplomatic lobbying. Never losing sight of the limits set by non-Jewish public opinion and the stand of the American government, they have contributed to the economic development of Israel, its ability to absorb Jewish refugees from Europe and other continents, and its military might. As long as Israel continues to seek a secure peace, its dependence on American agencies will not diminish. But, since most concerned American Jews took on those tasks through their synagogues or their defense and fraternal organizations, one could well ask if there was anything left to justify the continued existence of the prestate Zionist movement. Although some leaders considered a reorientation of their priorities, none could deny that American Zionism had failed to reach several of its goals. Their boasts notwithstanding, Zionists had not created meaningful forms of Jewish education in America, and only belatedly did they admit the importance of "cultural bridges," or the essential need to foster mutual understanding between American Jews and Israelis. Nor had they constructed an effective public relations network. They had lost liberal support in two public debates before Israel's independence, and after 1948 the need to win American public opinion steadily increased. If only to work on those matters, to which they are presently dedicated, Zionist organizations still have much to do.[5]

An exclusive focus on how Americanization nurtured a belief in the Jewish nationalist idea and sustained its growth within the community tells only part of the story. From its inception in 1897, American Zionism developed into a reciprocal relationship. More than the recipient of American Jewish largesse, Zionism and then the Jewish state have *given to,* while they simultaneously have *taken from,* American Jewry. The benefits of Zionism, although often understated or totally ignored, took various forms. One example: The concern that the community at large consistently exhibited for the persecuted Jews in foreign lands became less burdensome precisely because Zionism provided for a real refuge. England's control of the Palestine mandate during the 1930s and the war had blocked Jewish immigration, but once Israel declared its independence, oppressed Jews in the Soviet Union, Middle East, and South Africa had an avenue of escape. For those American Jews who took seriously the traditional obligation to "redeem the captives," a Zionist state lightened the task.

Another benefit of Zionism was to American Judaism. Whether active Zionists or not, American Jews cannot deny that Zionism added content to their religion. For those affiliated with synagogues, Zionism came to occupy a major place in their houses of worship, enriching prayer and ritual as well as extrareligious synagogal activities. Judaism as well as Zionism were strengthened thereby. The design of the religious and cultural Zionists for a center in Palestine that would revitalize Judaism in the Diaspora fell short of its mark, but it was never discarded. Today it takes the modified form of bringing synagogue youth, grandchildren of the Holocaust generation, to Israel to awaken and stimulate their commitment to the ethos of a Jewish state and to a living and creative Jewry. Although Zionism without religion preserved the ties of secularist and unaffiliated Jews to the Jewish past and present, the history of American Zionism proves that it worked more effectively in tandem with the synagogues.

Perhaps Zionism best served American Jewish interests because it offered a meaning to Jewish "groupness" or a reason for a Jewish collectivity. Built on the philosophy of cultural pluralism as expounded by Kallen, Brandeis, and others, it confronted and eased the tensions of the individual Jew caught between the pulls of the larger society and his feelings, often unconscious or visceral, of belonging to a Jewish people. Modern Jews—Reform as well as Orthodox, religious as well as secular—carried a cultural baggage of peoplehood over and above the bonds of religion even after Emancipation. Zionism revivified that baggage and provided emancipated Jews with links to the premodern culture of the Jews and ties to the scattered Jewish people of the present. Even before cultural pluralism was popularly acclaimed, American Zionism offered a new dimension to Jewish ethnicity at the same time that it strove for popular acceptance.

Admittedly, American Jews were content to enjoy the *yishuv* vicariously; only a very few contributed to the new Jewish normality by embarking on *aliyah*. But influenced in part by Zionism and by Israel—which has long disparaged the timid and insecure Diaspora Jew—Jews in the United States have slowly grown more comfortable with their Jewishness. Some random examples: a non-Orthodox undergraduate student who explains that he wears a *kippah* (skullcap) on campus not out of religious reasons but because it identifies him as a member of the Jewish people; Jewish lobbyists on Capitol Hill who approach the American government on behalf of Israel without fear of being charged with dual loyalty; American Jews and their children who sing Israeli songs, dance Israeli dances, and march in the Israel Day parades.

Zionism in action, i.e., the very evolution of the *yishuv* and the state of Israel, enhanced the Jewish self-image. Although American Jews greatly feared eruptions of antisemitism, particularly in the 1920s and 1930s, Zionism fed a counter force that redounded to their benefit. Its very goal, the creation of a restored Jewish state wherein Jews independently wielded the power to carve out their destiny, boosted their pride. Zionist idealists, both workers and even small businessmen and capitalists, also took pleasure in the Zionist dream of a democratic socialist or welfare state that would eliminate the category of have-nots. On a more tangible level, since the development of the *yishuv* proved that Jews could be farmers and pilots, American Jews could readily adopt the images of the pioneers in Palestine, which contradicted the age-old negative stereotypes consigning Jews to the class of "old-clothes men" and petty traders. Before and after 1948, Zionism also disproved the popular opinions that Jews were unsuited for self-government or for armed service. American Jews in turn basked in the light of Israel's military exploits. (The story goes that Diaspora Jews held their heads a bit higher when, after the Suez campaign of 1956, Israel offered to exchange fifty-eight hundred Egyptian prisoners for four captured Israelis.) Creating the counterimages of "the Jew as *goy*"[6] and the Jewish state like "all the nations," Zionism imbued American Jews with greater self-confidence and optimism.

The results of Zionist activity in the United States ultimately served to modify the identity of the Jewish community. No longer merely another religious denomination, Judaism enriched by Zionism made Jews, synagogue affiliated or not, into a recognizable ethnic group. When a wave of ethnicity swept America in the last third of the twentieth century, early Zionist efforts at instilling a national consciousness laid the groundwork that permitted Jewish ethnic loyalties to emerge full blown, now recognized as perfectly legitimate, in their American setting. What Zionism had always taught, that Jews worldwide constituted a distinct people who shared a common destiny as well as a common past, has become a strong belief of American Jews.

All told, American Jews made use of Zionism to balance their identities as Americans and Jews. There would have been an American Jewry without Zionism, doubtless one smaller in number and one where the divide between the synagogue affiliated and unaffiliated would have been more pronounced. But Zionism even in a secularist form contributed to the cohesiveness of the community and put American Jews squarely within the larger frame of modern Jewish history.

Notes

Introduction *(Pages 1-14)*

1. Quoted in the *Maccabaean* 7 (Nov. 1904): 292.
2. Saul Bellow, *Ravelstein* (New York, 2000), p. 23.
3. Professor Allon Gal, for one, emphasizes the mission motif, or the belief of American Zionism that its mission was to propagate universal, and distinctly American, values like democracy and social justice. For example, Allon Gal, "The Mission Motif in American Zionism," *American Jewish History* 75 (June 1986): 363-85. Other scholars who analyzed the American dimension of American Zionism include Melvin Urofsky, Ben Halpern, and Evyatar Friesel.
4. Hans Kohn, *The Idea of Nationalism* (New York, 1946), pp. 35, 47.
5. For a brief examination of the two sources feeding American Zionism, one immigrant and one native, see Ben Halpern, "The Americanization of Zionism," *American Jewish History* 69 (Sept. 1979): 15-33.
6. Quotations from Brandeis in Arthur Hertzberg, ed., *The Zionist Idea* (New York and Philadelphia, 1960), pp. 519-20.
7. It has been shown elsewhere that even Jewish liberals in Palestine were then seriously questioning the tenets of political Zionism. Yoram Hazony, *The Jewish State* (New York, 2000), part III.
8. Melvin I. Urofsky, *American Zionism from Herzl to the Holocaust* (Garden City, NY, 1975), p. 426.
9. Doreen Bierbrier, "The American Zionist Emergency Council," *American Jewish Historical Quarterly* 60 (Sept. 1970): 83-84.
10. J. Proskauer to B. Crum, 14 Oct. 1946, AJC archives—Proskauer.

1. Forging an American Zionism: The Maccabaean *(Pages 15-38)*

1. *Encyclopedia of Zionism and Israel,* 2:913-14, 1087, 1265.
2. *Maccabaean* 1 (Oct. 1901, supplement): xv; 14 (Feb. 1908): 66, 75. Unless otherwise noted, all references are to the *Maccabaean,* henceforth designated simply as "M."
3. Eric F. Goldman, *Rendezvous with Destiny* (New York, 1952), p. 185.
4. M 22 (Nov. 1912): 135.
5. M 16 (Mar. 1909): 113.
6. M 1 (Dec. 1901): 134.
7. M 1 (Oct. 1901): 9-11.

8. M 2 (Feb., Apr. 1902): 93, 206; 4 (May 1903): 288; 6 (Jan. 1904): 41; 8 (Mar. 1905): 118; 11 (Aug. 1906): 70; 15 (Dec. 1908): 252; 23 (Aug. 1913): 229.

9. M 14 (Feb. 1908): 64.

10. M 1 (Nov. 1901): 76; 11 (Aug. 1906): 61–71; 13 (Sept. 1907): 113; 14 (Jan. 1908): 31; 20 (June 1911): 181–82.

11. M 1 (Oct. 1901): 3–4; 2 (Jan. 1902): 2, 21; 6 (Apr. 1904): 185f.; 23 (June 1913): 161.

12. M 1 (Nov. 1901): 57–61; 6 (Feb. 1904): 85; 18 (Apr. 1910): 135; 21 (May 1912): 293; 22 (Aug. 1912): 39–40.

13. M 12 (Mar. 1907): 100–102.

14. M 23 (Aug., Nov. 1913): 230, 326.

15. M 3 (Aug. 1902): 104; 8 (Feb. 1905): 62f.; 12 (Mar., May 1907): 108, 191–92; 17 (Nov. 1909): 177; 21 (Mar. 1912): 236; 23 (Mar., May 1913): 67, 132.

16. M 23 (Feb. 1913): 34.

17. M 2 (May 1902): 262; 6 (Apr. 1904): 185; 19 (July 1910): 38.

18. M 7 (Dec. 1904): 271; 16 (May 1909): 228; 23 (Nov. 1913): 308.

19. M 2 (May 1902): 243; 5 (July 1903): 51–53; 21 (Jan. 1912): 195; 23 (Aug. 1913): 228.

20. For this and the next paragraph see M 7 (July 1904): 27; 8 (Mar. 1905): 112–15; 9 (July 1905): 29; 11 (July 1906): 11–12; 13 (Aug., Sept. 1907): 80, 121; 15 (July 1908): 64–65; 19 (Aug. 1910): 38; 22 (July 1912): 1–3.

21. M 12 (June 1907): 207–11.

22. M 15 (Nov. 1908): 187; 18 (Mar., June 1910): 79, 208; 19 (Dec. 1910): 195–98; 23 (Jan. 1913): 12–15; 25 (Nov.–Dec. 1914), 180–81.

23. M 15 (Aug. 1908): 64–65; 16 (Feb., May 1909): 45, 50ff., 160; 18 (June 1910): 200.

24. M 2 (Jan. 1902): 4; 14 (June 1908): 239; 17 (Nov. 1909): 101; 21 (June 1912): 322; 22 (July 1912): 6; 25 (Sept. 1914): 101.

25. M 9 (Nov. 1905): 243.

26. M 6 (Feb., Mar. 1904): 83–84, 133; 8 (May 1905): 198–204.

27. M 6 (Apr., June 1904): 185–87, 291.

28. For example, M 6 (Jan. 1904): 20; 10 (June 1906): 214–21.

29. M 16 (Mar. 1909): 113.

30. M 4 (Jan., Mar. 1903): 38, 177; 5 (July 1903): 11, 35; 9 (July 1905): 29; 16 (Jan., Feb. 1909): 3, 41–46.

31. M 4 (Feb. 1903): 102; 23 (Apr. 1913): 100.

32. M 2 (June 1902): 310; 14 (June 1908): 239; 15 (Dec. 1908): 254.

33. M 3 (Sept. 1902): 153; 4 (Jan. 1903): 46; 7 (Oct. 1904): 174; 23 (Mar. 1913): 66–67.

34. See, for example, Michael A. Meyer, "American Reform Judaism and Zionism," in *Studies in Zionism* No. 7 (Spring 1983), pp. 49–64; Jonathan D. Sarna, "Converts to Zionism in the American Reform Movement," in *Zionism and Religion,* ed. Shmuel Almog, Jehuda Reinharz, and Anita Shapira (Hanover, N.H., 1998) pp. 188–203.

35. M 2 (Jan., May 1902): 21, 243; 3 (Aug. 1902): 104; 4 (Mar. 1903): 131–38; 5 (Sept. 1903): 188; 20 (Jan. 1911): 255.

36. M 2 (Jan. 1902): 3; 3 (Dec. 1902): 324; 14 (Feb. 1908): 75; 15 (Dec. 1908): 230; 17 (Dec. 1909): 210–11; 19 (Jan. 1911): 255; 22 (Dec. 1912): 183.

37. M 13 (Oct. 1907): 168; 18 (Jan. 1910): 31–32; 25 (July 1914): 37–38.

38. M 6 (June 1904): 239; 15 (Oct. 1908): 139–40, 150; 16 (Mar. 1909): 111–12.

39. For example, M 23 (Apr. 1913): 98.

40. M 3 (Aug., Oct. 1902): 103–4, 216; 4 (Feb., June 1903): 100, 327–28, 339; 5 (July–Oct. 1903): 40, 51–52, 79, 120, 186; 9 (Aug., Sept. 1905): 70, 161–62.

41. For example, M 9 (Dec. 1905): 318.

42. M 16 (Jan. 1909): 14; 19 (Oct. 1910): 175; 20 (1911): 74; 21 (Aug., Oct., Dec. 1911): 44–45, 139, 166; 23 (Jan. 1913): 20.

43. M 12 (June 1907): 239; 13 (Dec. 1907): 254.

44. M 2 (Feb., Apr. 1902): 89, 212; 3 (Nov., Dec. 1902), 275, 325; 4 (Feb., May 1903): 100, 283; 13 (Dec. 1907): 254; 21 (Apr. 1912): 264.

45. M 2 (Jan. 1902): 16, 23–24; 13 (Dec. 1907): 253–54; 15 (Sept., Oct. 1908): 111–12, 171; 16 (June 1909): 228.

46. M 1 (Dec. 1901): 127.

47. M 1 (Mar. 1912): 236; 22 (Dec. 1912): 182; 30 (Mar. 1917): 170.

48. For example, M 8 (Feb. 1905): 69.

49. M 17 (July 1909): 42; 18 (Jan. 1910): 1–7; 23 (Nov. 1913): 306; 24 (June 1914): 168; 25 (Sept. 1914): 83. Most issues of the journal in 1908–1909 discuss the Young Turk revolt.

50. M 1 (Nov. 1901): 57ff.; 16 (Apr. 1909): 122; 24 (Feb. 1914): 37.

51. M 2 (June 1902): 307ff.

52. The book was printed in Leipzig in the fall of 1902 and was immediately translated into English by Jacob De Haas. Copyrighted by the FAZ, installments began in the *Maccabaean* in October 1902. I used the edition that was published in Haifa in 1960. See also Alex Bein, Theodore Herzl (New York, 1970), ch. 12, p. 532.

53. M 25 (Aug., Nov.–Dec. 1914): 54, 154–55; 26 (Feb. 1915): 29.

54. M 28 (Jan. 1916): 4–5; 30 (Mar., May, Sept., Nov. 1917): 169, 221–22, 336–37, 385.

55. M 25 (Sept. 1914): 83; 28 (June 1916): 121; 29 (Oct. 1916): 59–61.

56. Melvin I. Urofsky, *American Zionism from Herzl to the Holocaust* (Garden City, N.Y., 1975), p. 158; M 25 (Nov.–Dec. 1905): 156–57; 26 (Feb., Mar., May, June 1915.): 26, 29–31, 49, 93–94, 102; 27 (Oct. 1915): 92–96; 28 (Apr. 1916): 74; 29 (Sept. 1916): 25–26.

57. M 29 (Nov. 1916): 74, 86–88.

58. M 27 (July 1915): 9.

59. See, for example, Naomi W. Cohen, *Not Free to Desist* (Philadelphia, 1972), pp. 90–98; Urofsky, *American Zionism*, ch. 5.

60. M 26 (Apr., May, June 1915): 58, 81, 89, 101 103, 107–8.

61. M 29 (Aug. 1916): 1–2.

62. M 28 (Jan., Feb., Apr. 1916): 1–2, 4–5, 26, 73; 30 (May, Sept. 1917): 221, 335.

63. M 30, entire issue of Dec. 1917.

64. M 18 (Mar. 1910): 97.

65. Urofsky, *American Zionism*, p. 118; M 21 (Sept., Nov. 1911): 70, 138, 140–43; 22 (Nov. 1912): 135.

66. M 20 (Mar.–Apr. 1911): 102.

2. A Clash of Ideologies: Reform Judaism vs. Zionism (Pages 39–63)

The following abbreviations have been used in the Notes:

AH   American Hebrew
AI   American Israelite

CCARY   Central Conference of American Rabbis *Yearbook*
UAHCP   *Proceedings of the Union of American Hebrew Congregations*

1. On the significance of the Reform Zionists, see Michael A. Meyer, "American Reform Judaism and Zionism," *Studies in Zionism* No. 7 (Spring 1983), pp. 49–64; Jonathan D. Sarna, "Converts to Zionism in the American Reform Movement," in *Zionism and Religion*, ed. Shmuel Almog, Jehuda Reinharz, and Anita Shapira (Hanover, N.H., 1998), pp. 188–203.

2. Solomon B. Freehof, "Reform Judaism and Zionism," *Menorah Journal* 32 (Apr.–June 1944): 37–38; see, for example, Howard R. Greenstein, *Turning Point* (Brown University Judaic Studies No. 12, 1981), ch. 3.

3. Michael A. Meyer, *Response to Modernity* (New York, 1988), chs. 1–3; David Philipson, *The Reform Movement in Judaism* (New York, 1967), pp. xv, 19–20, 37, 77, 81–84, 151, 173–80, ch. 7.

4. Meyer, *Response to Modernity*, esp. pp. 240, 248.

5. For this and the next paragraph see Meyer, *Response to Modernity*, ch. 6 and Philipson, *Reform Movement*, ch. 12.

6. Philipson, *Reform Movement*, pp. 354–57.

7. Meyer, *Response to Modernity*, pp. 320–21; *CCARY* 1 (1891): 80–125.

8. Meyer, *Response to Modernity*, p. 282; Uriah Z. Engelman, "Jewish Statistics in the U.S. Census of Religious Bodies," *Jewish Social Studies* 9 (Apr. 1947): 136.

9. *CCARY* 8 (1897): xii; 16 (1906): 213; 27 (1917): 137, 139–40; *AI*, 16 Sept. 1897, 20 Oct. 1898, 22 Sept. 1904, 13 May 1909, 9 Sept. 1915, 27 June 1918; *AH*, 6 Dec. 1901, 28 Oct. 1904, 10 Dec. 1915, 26 Sept. 1919; Kaufmann Kohler, *Studies, Addresses, and Personal Papers* (New York, 1936), p. 454.

10. *CCARY* 8 (1897): 41.

11. Philipson, *Reform Movement*, p. 61. For explanations of the mission idea by Reform leaders, see, for example, Kaufmann Kohler, *Jewish Theology* (New York, 1918), p. 8; Kohler, *Studies*, p. 458; Emil G. Hirsch, "Reform Judaism from the Point of View of the Reform Jew," *Jewish Encyclopedia* 10: 348; David Philipson, *Centenary Papers and Others* (Cincinnati, 1919), pp. 58–59; *AI*, 17 Mar., 3 Nov. 1898, 16 Mar. 1916. For a brief study of the differences between the traditional and modern views of mission see Max Wiener, "The Conception of Mission in Traditional and Modern Judaism," *YIVO Annual of Jewish Social Science* 2–3 (1947–48): 9–24.

12. Kaufmann Kohler, "The Faith of Reform Judaism," *Menorah Journal* 2 (Feb. 1916): 12; Kohler, *Studies*, p. 461; *CCARY* 13 (1903): 371; 27 (1917): 137, 140–41; *UAHCP*, 1919, p. 8476; *AI*, 27 Dec. 1900, 23 Mar. 1916.

13. *CCARY* 1 (1891): 118; Emil G. Hirsch, *Reform Judaism* (Philadelphia, 1885), p. 9.

14. See, for example, *UAHCP*, 1909, p. 6347; 1919, p. 8470; Hirsch, "Reform Judaism," p. 345; Emil G. Hirsch, "The Reform Prayer Book," *Journal of Jewish Lore and Philosophy* 1 (Jan.–Apr. 1919): 216–17; Philipson, *Reform Movement*, pp. 84, 174, 179; David Philipson, *My Life as an American Jew* (Cincinnati, 1941), pp. 125–26; *AI*, 13 May 1909; Beryl H. Levy, *Reform Judaism in America* (New York, 1933), pp. 55–56; *Reform Advocate*, 18 July 1896; Kaufmann Kohler, "A Biographical Essay," *David Einhorn Memorial Volume* (New York, 1911), pp. 437–38.

15. Philipson, *Reform Movement*, p. 331; see debates at rabbinical conferences in Germany in *CCARY* 1.

16. Philipson, *Reform Movement*, p. 5; *CCARY* 12 (1902): 236; 17 (1907): 183; *UAHCP*, 1898, p. 4002; *AI*, 13 May 1909; Philipson, *Centenary Papers*, p. 171; Kohler, "Faith of Reform Judaism," p. 15; Kohler, *Studies*, pp. 229–30; *AI*, 23 Jan. 1913; *AH*, 14 May 1897.

17. Philipson, *Centenary Papers*, pp. 75–76.

18. Kohler, *Studies*, p. 232; Jerold S. Auerbach, *Rabbis and Lawyers* (Bloomington, 1990), ch. 1; Oscar S. Straus, *The Origin of Republican Form of Government in the United States of America* (New York, 1885).

19. Franklin quoted in Halvdan Koht, *The American Spirit in Europe* (Philadelphia, 1949), p. 14; *AH*, 21 Sept. 1900; Kohler, *Studies*, p. 230.

20. *UAHCP* 1898, p. 4002.

21. *AI*, 13 Jan. 1898, 19 Oct. 1899, 7 July 1904, 10 Aug. 1905, 29 Aug. 1909, 27 June 1918; Lee M. Franklin, "A Danger and a Duty Suggested by the Zionistic Agitation," *Hebrew Union College Journal* 2 (Mar. 1898): 147; *CCARY* 14 (1904): 183; Isaac M. Wise, *Reminiscences* (Cincinnati, 1901), pp. 49, 85–86, 331.

22. Adams quoted in Moses Rischin, ed., *Immigration and the American Tradition* (Indianapolis, 1976), p. 47; Kohler, *Studies*, pp. 455–57.

23. *CCARY* 8 (1897): 174; Kohler, "Faith of Reform Judaism," p. 15; Kohler, *Studies*, p. 232; *Reform Advocate*, 18 July 1896; *AI*, 16 Sept. 1915.

24. *UAHCP*, 1905, pp. 5314–15; 1909, p. 6548; Franklin, "A Danger and a Duty," pp. 144–45; Kohler, "Faith of Reform Judaism," p. 13; Kohler, *Studies*, pp. 458–59; *CCARY* 11 (1901): 82; 25 (1915): 166; *AI*, 11 Sept. 1902, 17 Jan. 1907, 9 Mar. 1916; *Reform Advocate*, 15 Dec. 1917.

25. *AI*, 10 Feb. 1898, 18 June 1903, 5 Mar. 1908, 28 July 1910, 27 Feb. 1913, 23 Mar., 4 May 1916; *AH*, 14 May 1897.

26. *AI*, 8 May 1897, 31 Dec. 1903, 25 Aug. 1898, 20 Apr. 1911, 27 Feb. 1913, 4 May 1918; *CCARY* 16 (1906): 231; 25 (1915): 166; *AH*, 14 May 1897, 20 Nov. 1903, 10 Dec. 1915, 23 Nov. 1917; *Reform Advocate*, 8 May, 25 Sept. 1897; Isaac M. Wise, "Zionism," *Hebrew Union College Journal* 4 (Dec. 1899): 47.

27. Wise, "Zionism," pp. 46–47; Samuel Schulman, "The Searching of the Jewish Heart," *Menorah Journal* 4 (Apr. 1918): 90; Philipson, *Centenary Papers*, p. 178.

28. Naomi W. Cohen, *Not Free to Desist* (Philadelphia, 1972), p. 315.

29. For example, Nathan Glazer, *American Judaism* (Chicago, 1957), pp. 53–54.

30. For this and the next three paragraphs see Naomi W. Cohen, "The Challenges of Darwinism and Biblical Criticism to American Judaism," *Modern Judaism* 4 (May 1984): 121–51.

31. Emma Felsenthal, *Bernhard Felsenthal* (New York, 1924), ch. 6; Bernhard Felsenthal, *Fundamental Principles of Judaism* (New York, 1918), pp. 3–5; Felsenthal in *Maccabaean* 4 (Mar. 1903): 131–38.

32. Gottheil quoted in Melvin I. Urofsky, *American Zionism from Herzl to the Holocaust* (Garden City, N.Y., 1975), p. 92.

33. The paragraphs on Gottheil are drawn from Richard Gottheil, *The Aims of Zionism* (New York, 1899), Gottheil, *Zionism* (Philadelphia, 1914), esp. pp. 200 and seq. Excerpts from *The Aims of Zionism* are reprinted in Arthur Hertzberg, ed., *The Zionist Idea* (New York, 1960), pp. 495–500. See also *Jewish Criterion*, 27 Nov. 1903.

34. Gottheil, "Aims," p. 19; Marnin Feinstein, *American Zionism, 1884–1904* (New York, 1965), pp. 172–73.

35. Stephen S. Wise, "The Beginnings of American Zionism," *Jewish Frontier* 14 (Aug. 1947): 7.

36. Melvin I. Urofsky, *A Voice That Spoke for Justice* (Albany, 1984), ch. 4; Carl Hermann Voss, ed., *Stephen S. Wise* (Philadelphia, 1969), pp. 25–34.

37. Unless otherwise noted, the section on HUC is reworked from my article "The Reaction of Reform Judaism in America to Political Zionism," *Publications* of the American Jewish Historical Society 40 (June 1951): pp. 372–82. Full citations are given there; manuscript material used for that article (unless otherwise indicated) is from the files of the American Jewish Archives. See also Herbert Parzen, "The Purge of the Dissidents," *Jewish Social Studies* 37 (Summer–Fall 1975): 291–322. An echo of the 1907 affair was heard at HUC in 1915 when a student was denied permission to deliver a sermon on Zionism.

38. An attempt, albeit unconvincing, to "revise" Kohler is Yaakov Ariel, "Kaufmann Kohler and His Attitude Towards Zionism," *American Jewish Archives* 43 (Fall–Winter 1991).

39. Naomi W. Cohen, *Encounters with Emancipation* (Philadelphia, 1984), pp. 295–96.

40. *AI* 9 May 1907; *Maccabaean* 12 (May, June 1907): 193–94, 240, 243.

41. Moshe Davis, *The Emergence of Conservative Judaism* (Philadelphia, 1963), pp. 87–88, 212ff., 268–74.

42. For this and the next two paragraphs see Hertzberg, *The Zionist Idea*, pp. 503–13 and Naomi W. Cohen, "'Diaspora Plus Palestine, Religion Plus Nationalism,'" in Jack Wertheimer, ed., *Tradition Renewed* (New York, 1997), 2: 118–27; Norman Bentwich, *Solomon Schechter* (New York, 1938), ch. 12.

43. Jonathan D. Sarna, "A Projection of America as It Ought to Be," in Allon Gal, ed., *Envisioning Israel* (Jerusalem and Detroit, 1996), pp. 41–42.

44. Allon Gal, *Brandeis of Boston* (Cambridge, Mass., 1980), passim.

45. Hertzberg, *The Zionist Idea*, pp. 517–23.

46. Urofsky, *American Zionism*, ch. 4; Melvin I. Urofsky, "Zionism: An American Experience," *Publication of the American Jewish Historical Society* 63 (Mar. 1974): 215–230, and "The Enduring Brandeis," *Midstream* 33 (Aug.–Sept. 1987): 28–31. Urofsky notes (p. 145 in *American Zionism*) that the number of members in the FAZ rose from some 12,000 in 1914 to 176,000 in 1919.

47. *CCARY* 28 (1918): 133–34.

48. *UAHCP*, 1919, pp. 8520–21.

49. *CCARY* 28 (1918): 141–44; Isaac W. Bernheim, *The Reform Church of American Israelites* (Buffalo, 1921); *Conference on the Advisability of Calling a Conference for the Purpose of Combating Zionism* (New York, 1918), p. 3. In another plan similar to Bernheim's, some Reformers refused to be associated with Zionists even as coworshipers. They were prepared, therefore, to drop the very label "Jew." *American Hebrew*, 24 Jan., 28 Mar. 1919.

50. *CCARY* 28 (1918): 133–34; 33 (1923): 92; 34 (1924): 106; *AI*, 6 May, 10 June 1920, 17 Feb. 1921; *AH*, 25 Oct., 1 Nov. 1918.

51. *CCARY* 45 (1935): 103; 47 (1937): 98; 52 (1942): 250–51; *UAHCP*, 1922, pp. 9129, 9333.

3. Zionism in the Public Square (Pages 64–94)

The following abbreviations have been used in the Notes:
AAJ Cong Archives of the American Jewish Congress
AAJC Archives of the American Jewish Committee
CWP Chaim Weizmann Papers (Rechoboth, Israel)
CZA Central Zionist Archives (Jerusalem, Israel)

FWP   Felix Warburg Papers, American Jewish Archives
JDB   *Jewish Daily Bulletin*
JMP   Judah Magnes Papers (Central Archives for the History of the Jewish People, Jerusalem, Israel)
NP   *New Palestine*
NYT   *New York Times*
ZAL   Zionist Archives and Library (I used this collection when it was located in New York. It is now part of the CZA.)

Page numbers are not given for articles that appeared in daily or weekly newspapers.

1. Antisemitic bigots from the radical fringe, like Henry Ford and his journal, the *Dearborn Independent,* joined the anti-Zionists. But Ford aimed primarily at exposing the conspiracy of the "international Jew" bent on destroying Christian civilization, and Zionism was only part of his overall crusade. Naomi W. Cohen, "The Specter of Zionism," in *Essays in American Zionism,* ed. Melvin I. Urofsky, *Herzl Year Book,* vol. 8 (New York, 1978): 107–11.

2. See, for example, *Jewish Messenger,* 9 Feb. 1877, 13 Mar. 1891, 24 July 1896, 18 Aug. 1899; Joseph Krauskopf, *Prejudice, Its Genesis and Exodus* (New York, 1909), p. 86.

3. Morris Jastrow, Jr., "The Objections to a Jewish State," *Menorah Journal* 4 (June 1918): 136; Morris Jastrow, Jr., *Zionism and the Future of Palestine* (New York, 1919), pp. 120–21; *American Hebrew,* 15 Nov. 1918, 7 Feb. 1919.

4. *NYT,* 6, 16 Feb. 1919.

5. Morgenthau reprinted the article in his autobiography, *All in a Life-Time* (Garden City, N.Y., 1925), ch. 12; Charles Goldblatt, "The Impact of the Balfour Declaration in America," *American Jewish Historical Quarterly* 57 (June 1968): 467.

6. Morris Raphael Cohen, "Zionism: Tribalism or Liberalism," *New Republic,* 8 Mar. 1919, 182–83; Stuart Knee, "Vision and Judgment" (Ph.D. diss., New York University, 1974), p. 105.

7. The text of the petition is found in Jastrow, *Zionism,* appendix; see also *NYT,* 5 Mar. 1919. When Wilson endorsed the Balfour Declaration, he received numerous letters from Reform Jews begging him not to deprive American Jews of their true homeland, the United States. Selig Adler, "The Palestine Question in the Wilson Era," *Jewish Social Studies* 10 (Oct. 1948): 312.

8. *Establishment of a National Home in Palestine,* 67 Cong. 2 Sess., Hearings before the Committee on Foreign Affairs on H. Con. Res. 52, pp. 85–87, 99–116; *American Hebrew,* 28 Apr., 5, 12 May 1922.

9. Morgenthau, *All in a Life-Time,* p. 392.

10. *American Hebrew,* 1 Feb. 1918.

11. Thomas Nixon Carver, "The Choice Before Jewry," *Menorah Journal* 5 (Feb. 1919): 10–11.

12. Paul Mowrer, "The Assimilation of Israel," *Atlantic Monthly* 128 (July 1921): 103–10.

13. Philip Marshall Brown, "Zionism and Antisemitism," *North American Review* 210 (Nov. 1919): 656–62.

14. For example, Philip Cowen, *Prejudice Against the Jew* (New York, 1928), pp. 46, 75, 83, 86, 93, 97, 104–5, 116, 117, 127, 132.

15. For example, H. N. MacCracken, "A University Problem," *Menorah Journal* 9

(Oct. 1921): 128; Reuben Fink, *The American War Congress and Zionism* (New York, 1919), p. 165.

16. John P. Peters, "Zionism and the Jewish Problem," *Sewanee Review* 19 (July 1921): 268, 294; Horace J. Bridges, *Jew-Baiting* (New York, 1923), pp. 5–6, 73–75.

17. Herbert Adams Gibbons, "The Jewish Problem—Its Relation to American Ideals and Interests," *Century Magazine* 102 (Sept. 1921): 787–92.

18. *Independent,* 19 Apr. 1919, p. 85.

19. Herbert Adams Gibbons, "Zionism and the World Peace," *Century Magazine* 92 (Jan. 1919): 370–78; Edward Bliss Reed, "The Injustice of Zionism," *Yale Review* 9 (Apr. 1920): 522–28; Albert T. Clay, "Political Zionism," *Atlantic Monthly* 127 (Feb. 1921): 268–79; Anstruther Mackay, "Zionist Aspirations in Palestine," *Atlantic Monthly* 126 (July 1920): 123–27; Peters, "Zionism and the Jewish Problem," pp. 282–93; Brown, "Zionism and Antisemitism," pp. 660–61.

20. See n. 19 for references to Reed, Clay, Gibbons, Mackay, and Peters; *Establishment of a National Home in Palestine,* pp. 21–35, 42, 69–74, 80, 83; Goldblatt, "Impact of the Balfour Declaration," pp. 473–74; *Literary Digest,* July 31, 1920, pp. 30–31; Selig Adler, "Backgrounds of American Policy Toward Zion," in Moshe Davis, ed., *Israel: Its Role in Civilization* (New York, 1956), p. 276; Frank E. Manuel, *The Realities of American-Palestine Relations* (Washington, 1949), pp. 199–200, 222, 291–93.

21. Clay, "Political Zionism," p. 272; Mackay, "Zionist Aspirations," pp. 125, 127; Gibbons, "Zionism and the World Peace," pp. 375–78; *Establishment of a National Home in Palestine,* pp. 22–34, 70, 83; letter of Reed to *NYT,* 16 Apr. 1922.

22. Rabbi Stephen S. Wise spoke bitterly of "the most tragic symptom of Jewish life in the world today—a panicky, sickening, tragi-comic nervousness of Jews in the light of any attempt to bring Jews together." *Jewish Antisemitism—A Tragi-Comedy,* address before the Free Synagogue, 1 Jan. 1928.

23. Some Zionists tried. Professor Israel Friedlaender answered Gibbons's articles in "Zionism and the World Peace—A Rejoinder," *Century Magazine* 97 (Apr. 1919): 803–10, and the *NP* (Apr. 28, 1922) responded to Reed's pro-Arab arguments. For Gottheil see *American Hebrew,* 2 Feb. 1906.

24. *Maccabaean* 31 (June, Oct. 1918): 143, 287–88; 32 (Feb., Mar. 1919): 31–32, 66–67, 69–70; *American Hebrew,* 14, 21 Feb. 1919; *NP,* 1 July, 5 Aug., 21 Oct. 1921, 13 Jan., 28 Apr., 5, 12 May, 2 June, 14 July, 1922; Samuel Untermyer, "Zionism—A Just Cause," *Forum* 66 (Sept. 1921): 214–27; David Amram, "Answering Professor Jastrow," *Menorah Journal* 4 (June 1918): 147–48.

25. Julian W. Mack, "Jewish Hopes at the Peace Table," *Menorah Journal* 5 (Feb. 1919): 1–7; Felix Frankfurter, "The Statesmanship of the Balfour Declaration," *Menorah Journal* 4 (Aug. 1918): 201–2.

26. Elisha M. Friedman, "In the Wake of Zionism," *Menorah Journal* 4 (Apr. 1918): 100–10; Horace M. Kallen, "The Issues of War and the Jewish Position," *Nation,* 29 Nov. 1917; "Democracy, Nationality and Zionism," *Maccabaean* 31 (July 1918): 175; Friedman in *American Hebrew,* 29 June 1917, 4 Jan. 1918; Naomi W. Cohen, *Jacob H. Schiff* (Hanover, N.H., 1999), pp. 226, 238, 232.

27. Amram in *Menorah Journal* 4 (June 1918); Untermyer in *NP,* 5 Aug. 1921; Lipsky in *Establishment of a National Home in Palestine;* Goldblatt, "Impact of the Balfour Declaration," pp. 498–99.

28. Cohen, "Zionism: Tribalism or Liberalism"; Horace M. Kallen, "Zionism: Democracy or Prussianism," *New Republic*, 5 Apr. 1919.

29. *NP*, 2 Sept. 1921, 14 Apr., 12 May, 2 June 1922; *NYT*, 28 May 1922.

30. Cf. Yonathan Shapiro, *Leadership of the American Zionist Organization* (Urbana, 1971), pp. 118, 127, 129, 131–32, 185–86, 251. For other Zionist arguments see Amram in *Menorah Journal* 4 (June 1918): 147–48; *Maccabaean* 34 (July 1920): 21–23; H. Dannenbaum in *NP*, 23 Dec. 1921; Friedman, "In the Wake of Zionism," p. 107, and "Anti-semitism," *Menorah Journal* 8 (Feb. 1922): 1–6.

31. Goldblatt, "Impact of the Balfour Declaration," passim; Samuel Halperin, *The Political World of American Zionism* (Detroit, 1961), p. 327.

32. Naomi W. Cohen, *The Year after the Riots* (Detroit, 1988), pp. 11–49.

33. On the makeup of the three groups and their inability to cooperate see Cohen, *Riots*, ch. 2.

34. L. Namier to T. Jones, 30 Aug. 1929, CWP; *JDB*, 29 Aug. 1929; *The Letters and Papers of Chaim Weizmann*, v. 14, ed. Camillo Dresner (New Brunswick, N.J., and Jerusalem, 1978), pp. 7–8, 15. On Weizmann's relations with England see Leonard Stein, *Weizmann and England* (London, 1964); N. A. Rose, *The Gentile Zionists* (London, 1973), pp. 223–27.

35. Minutes of ZOA National Executive Committee meeting, 15 Sept. 1929, CZA-A243/21; Simha Berkowitz, "Felix Frankfurter's Zionist Activities" (D.H.L. diss., Jewish Theological Seminary, 1971), pp. 360–62; *JDB*, 30 Aug. 1929; M. Waldman to H. Lehman, 29 Aug. 1929, AAJC-Palestine/Disturbances 1929; for Louis Lipsky's initial opposition see *JDB*, 3 Sept. 1929, *NP*, 20 Sept. 1929.

36. How England compromised its honor was a central theme of a book by Stephen S. Wise and Jacob De Haas, *The Great Betrayal* (New York, 1930).

37. *JDB*, 30 Aug. 1929; Louis Berg, "American Public Opinion on Palestine," *Menorah Journal* 17 (Oct. 1929): 78–79; Berkowitz, "Frankfurter's Zionist Activities," pp. 365–66; A. Tulin to S. Wise, 27 Aug. 1929, Stephen S. Wise Papers-Box 121, American Jewish Historical Society; Herbert Solow, "The Realities of Zionism," *Menorah Journal* 19 (Nov.–Dec. 1930): 92–127; Elinor Grumet, "The Apprenticeship of Lionel Trilling," *Prooftexts* 4 (May 1984): 163.

38. Berg, "American Public Opinion," pp. 71, 74–75; Judd L. Teller, *Strangers and Natives* (New York, 1968), p. 108; Julius Haber, *The Odyssey of an American Zionist* (New York, 1956), p. 224; *JDB*, 29 Oct. 1929.

39. Halperin, *Political World of American Zionism*, pp. 159–60; Stuart E. Knee, *The Concept of Zionist Dissent in the American Mind* (New York, 1979), p. 163; *NP*, 27 Sept., 4 Oct. 1929.

40. *New Leader*, 31 Aug., 14 Sept. 1929.

41. B. Deutsch to F. Warburg, 19, 27 Sept. 1929, F. Warburg to B. Deutsch, 20 Sept. 1929, AAJCong-Box 2; C. Weizmann to S. Wise, 24 Sept. 1929, CWP.

42. A fuller annotated discussion of the Magnes plan and the reaction it triggered, which is considered in this and the next five paragraphs, is found in Cohen, *Riots*, pp. 72–83, 97–98.

43. *NP*, 6, 20 Sept. 1929; Berg, "American Public Opinion," p. 70; *JDB*, 5, 6,8, 9 Sept. 1929; minutes of ZOA National Executive Committee meeting, 15 Sept. 1929, CZA-A243/21.

44. *Literary Digest*, 5 Oct. 1929; *Current History* 31 (Nov. 1929): 406; Berg, "American Public Opinion," p. 68; Louis Berg, "The American Press on Palestine," *NP*, 15 Nov. 1929.

45. Berg, "American Public Opinion," p. 67; minutes of ZOA National Executive Committee meeting, 29 Sept. 1929, ZAL.

46. J. Levy to Grand Mufti, 3 Nov. 1929, Joseph Levy Papers, Israel State Archives; *NYT*, 4, 24 Nov. 1929; G. Agronsky to J. Magnes, 10 Dec. 1929, JMP-2106.

47. Vincent Sheean, *Personal History* (Boston, 1969), pp. 337–41, 354–57, 374–75, 381–82; Meyer W. Weisgal, *So Far* (New York, 1971), pp. 65–66; *JDB*, 15, 19 Nov. 1929, 5 Jan. 1930; V. Sheean to G. Antonius, 21 Jan., 2 Apr. 1930, to M. Weisgal, 15 Jan. 1930, George Antonius Papers, Israel State Archives.

48. Goldblatt, "Impact of the Balfour Declaration," pp. 465–66; *Nation*, 11 Sept., 16 Oct., 4 Dec. 1929, 8 Jan., 30 July 1930; *New Republic*, 11 Sept., 23 Oct. 1929, 30 July 1930; *NP*, 11–18 Oct. 1929.

49. *Nation*, 11 Sept., 2, 23 Oct. 1929, 8 Jan. 1930; *New Republic*, 7 May 1930; S. Wise to J. Klausner, 3 Jan. 1930, J. Magnes to S. Wise, 6 Feb. 1930, JMP-2407; H. Mussey to J. Magnes, 4 Dec. 1929, JMP-2403.

50. J. Holmes to H. Kohn, 3 Dec. 1929, JMP-2408; R. Baldwin to J. Magnes, 4 Dec. 1920, C. Pickett to J. Magnes, 29 Nov. 1929, H. Mussey to J. Magnes, 24 Jan. 1930, JMP-2403.

51. *NP* 11–18 Oct., 13 Dec. 1929, 7 Feb., 11 Apr. 1930.

52. *NP*, 10 Jan. 1930.

53. *Letters and Papers of Weizmann*, pp. 181–82.

54. Except for quotations, which are documented separately, the composite of articles discussed in the next eight paragraphs is drawn from the following sources: William E. Hocking, "Palestine—An Impasse?" *Atlantic Monthly* 146 (July 1930): 121–32; Hallen Viney, "Jerusalem in Ferment," *Atlantic Monthly* 144 (Dec. 1929): 829–38; Owen Tweedy, "Zionism in Palestine," *Atlantic Monthly* 146 (Oct. 1930): 548–56; Pierre Crabites, "A Jewish Political State in Palestine," *Current History* 31 (Jan. 1930): 749–54; H. N. Brailsford, "British Policy in Palestine," *Current History* 31 (Jan. 1930): 754–57; H. N. Brailsford, "The Future in Palestine," *New Republic*, 30 July 1930; John Gunther, "The Realities of Zionism," *Harper's Magazine* 161 (July 1930): 202–12; William Martin, "The Position in Palestine," *Living Age*, 1 Feb. 1930; George C. Young, "The Labor Government and the Near East," *New Republic*, 23 Oct. 1929; Marion Weinstein, "The Paradox in Palestine," *Outlook*, 2 Oct. 1929; William Zukerman, "Myths in Palestine," *Nation*, 16 Oct. 1929; Victor Yarros, "What Next in Palestine?" *Nation*, 7 July 1929; John P. Gavit, "Parliaments of Persuasion," *Survey*, 1 Jan. 1930; Vincent Sheean, "The Palestine Report," *Commonweal*, 30 Apr. 1930; other articles by Sheean in *Asia* : 29 (Dec. 1929), 30 (Jan., Aug. 1930); *Nation*, 4 Dec. 1929; *New Republic*, 11 Sept. 1929; excerpts from *New York Herald-Tribune* in Berg, "American Public Opinion," p. 79, and Berg, "American Press on Palestine," p. 410.

55. Cited in Gunther, "Realities of Zionism," p. 204.

56. Gunther, "Realities of Zionism," p. 211.

57. Tweedy, "Zionism in Palestine," pp. 550, 554. William Hocking, professor of philosophy at Harvard, wrote that Christians too took offense at Zionist modernization and secularization of the Holy Land. They preferred a primitive Palestine, closer in spirit to the days of Jesus, where no motorcar would bump the camel. Hocking, "Palestine—An Impasse?" p. 131.

58. Gunther, "Realities of Zionism," p. 212.

59. Viney, "Jerusalem in Ferment," p. 837.

60. Viney, "Jerusalem in Ferment," p. 837.

61. *Nation*, 8 Jan. 1930; Viney, "Jerusalem in Ferment," p. 837.

62. Clare Kohavi-Finkelman, "The Eternal Jew in the American Christian Mind" (tutorial paper, Hunter College, 1984), pp. 16–17, 20–21, 24–27, 29–30; material from the *Christian Century:* W. Dewood David, "Whose 'Home' Is Palestine?" 23 Oct. 1929; letter from J. Wise, 13 Nov. 1929; Al Ghazali, "Human Nature in Palestine," 27 Nov. 1929; editorial, 11 Dec. 1929; Sherwood Eddy, "The Grand Mufti on Palestine's Problems," 18 Dec. 1929; Berg, "American Press on Palestine," p. 410; Esther Y. Feldblum, *The American Catholic Press and the Jewish State* (New York, 1977), pp. 39–43.

63. Kohavi-Finkelman, "Eternal Jew," pp. 10–12, 19–22; Hertzel Fishman, *American Protestantism and a Jewish State* (Detroit, 1973), ch. 1; memo by assistant chief of treaty division of State Department, 30 Oct. 1929, Records of the Department of State Relating to the Internal Affairs of Turkey, 1910–1929 (RDST), National Archives.

64. Kohavi-Finkelman, "Eternal Jew," pp. 14–17, 20, 31; Feldblum, *American Catholic Press*, p. 42; *Christian Century*, 11 Dec. 1929; David, "Whose 'Home' Is Palestine?" *Christian Century*, 23 Oct. 1929.

65. Kohavi-Finkelman, "Eternal Jew," pp. 28, 38–39; S. Wise to G. Agronsky, 30 Dec. 1929, CZA-A243/21; John Haynes Holmes, *Palestine Today and To-Morrow* (New York, 1929), pp. xiv, 81–83; J. Holmes to J. Magnes, 20 Nov. 1929, JMP-2408.

66. *NP*, 6, 20 Sept., 11–18 Oct. 1929; *JDB*, 16, 20 Sept. 1929.

67. Minutes of ZOA National Executive Committee meeting, 15 Sept. 1929, CZA-A243/21.

68. *JDB*, 30 Dec. 1929; Berkowitz, "Frankfurter's Zionist Activities," pp. 368–69, 392; memo from J. Mack, 9 Sept. 1929, CZA-A342/79; minutes of CPI meeting, 20 Sept. 1929, ZAL; J. Mack to L. Brandeis, 5, 19, 21 Oct. 1929, ZAL-Brandeis Papers; J. De Haas to J. Mack, n.d., ZAL-Brandeis Papers; Elizabeth P. MacCallum, *The Palestine Conflict*, FPA Information Service 5, no. 16, 16 Oct. 1929.

69. Berkowitz, "Frankfurter's Zionist Activities," pp. 367–69; memo of Mack-Lippmann telephone conversation, 23 Oct. 1929, ZAL-Brandeis Papers; L. Brandeis to J. Mack, 4 Oct. 1929, CZA-A342/82; Melvin I. Urofsky and David W. Levy, eds., *Letters of Louis D. Brandeis* (Albany, 1978), 5: 397–98, 408; Faisal-Frankfurter correspondence reprinted in *NP*, 17 Jan. 1930.

70. Berkowitz, "Frankfurter's Zionist Activities," pp. 358, 363, 367; *Letters of Brandeis*, 5: 413, 425; reprint of Faisal-Frankfurter correspondence in *NP*, 17 Jan. 1930. The authenticity of the correspondence was challenged by American Arabs in the same issue of the *NP*. Felix Frankfurter, "The Palestine Situation Restated," *Foreign Affairs* 9 (Apr. 1931): 409–34.

71. Berkowitz, "Frankfurter's Zionist Activities," p. 360.

72. Frankfurter rebutted one item in Hocking's article in a letter to the *Atlantic Monthly* 146 (Dec. 1930): 50.

73. Editorials in *American Hebrew*, 1929–30; I. Landman to F. Warburg, 14 Sept. 1929, FWP-Box 251; Jerome M. Kutnick, "Non-Zionist Leadership: Felix M. Warburg, 1929–37" (Ph.D. diss., Brandeis University, 1983), pp. 193–94.

74. Minutes of CPI meeting, 20, 25 Sept., 2 Oct. 1929, ZAL.

75. H. Montor to L. Barth, 21 Oct. 1929, ZOA General Correspondence, ZAL.

76. Minutes of CPI meeting, 2 Oct. 1929, ZAL; J. Mack to L. Brandeis, 13 Sept. 1929, ZAL-Brandeis Papers; L. Lipsky to S. Brodetsky, 16 Oct. 1929, CZA-S25/357; L. Lipsky to F. Warburg, 30 Oct. 1929, FWP-Box 259; Meyer W. Weisgal, "Zionism as a Spiritual Ideal and a Blessing to Palestine," *Current History* 31 (Nov. 1929): 279–85.

77. For example, Bernard Flexner, "The Rights to a Jewish Home Land," *Nation,* 2 Oct. 1929; Harold Loeb, "The Future of Zion," *New Republic,* 10 Sept. 1930; John Haynes Holmes, "New Pilgrims in Israel," *Survey,* 1 Oct. 1929.

78. Christopher Sykes, *Crossroads to Israel* (Cleveland, 1965), pp. 94–95; Bernard Wasserstein, *The British in Palestine* (London, 1978), ch. 6.

79. *JDB,* 3, 12, 19, 20 Jan. 1930; *NYT,* 10, 18, 22 Jan. 1930; *NP,* 6, 20 Sept., 11–18 Oct., 15 Nov., 6 Dec. 1929, 17, 24 Jan., 11 Apr., 6, 20 June 1930.

80. Knee, *Zionist Dissent,* pp. 198–214; *JDB,* 8 Sept., 30 Dec. 1929; letters to State Department from Arab committees, RDST-867 n.404 WW/Alphabetical File. Lipsky suggested that the American partners in the Agency launch an Arabic newspaper, friendly to the Jews, that would counteract the influence of the American Arabic press. Minutes of American members of Administrative Committee meeting, 26 Sept. 1929, CWP.

81. *JDB,* 30 Apr. 1930.

82. MacCallum, "An Arab Voice," pp. 130–34; Knee, *Zionist Dissent,* pp. 211–12; minutes of CPI meeting, 7 Oct. 1929, ZAL; articles by Rihani: "Zionism and the Peace of the World," *Nation,* 2 Oct. 1929, "Palestine Arabs Claim to Be Fighting for National Existence," *Current History* 31 (Nov. 1929): 272–28.

83. *JDB,* 30 Oct., 5, 30 Dec. 1930; Berkowitz, "Frankfurter's Zionist Activities," pp. 369–70; Knee, *Zionist Dissent,* p. 213; J. Hyman to F. Warburg, 21 Jan. 1930, FWP-Box 272.

84. A. Tulin to S. Wise, 9 Sept. 1930, Wise Papers-Box 121.

85. P. Van Paassen to S. Wise, 29 Aug. 1930, CZA-A243/92.

4. A Modern Synagogue in Jerusalem *(Pages 95–112)*

1. This essay is dedicated to the memory of Rabbi Moshe Davis, a pioneer in the study and teaching of American Jewish history. About thirty years ago Professor Davis collected some materials on the subject of an early attempt to establish a modern synagogue in Jerusalem, and after his death his notes were given to me by his wife, Mrs. Lottie K. Davis. I am grateful to Mrs. Davis for her interest. I alone, however, am responsible for the enlarged scope of the research and for the writing. The material from the Moshe Davis Papers is designated by the abbreviation MDP.

2. Arthur A. Goren, ed., *Dissenter in Zion* (Cambridge, Mass., 1982), p. 206; unpublished "Diary of Simon Greenberg, Trip to Palestine, Sept. 10, 1924–May 15, 1925," p. 2 (courtesy of Professor Moshe Greenberg). *Cook's Traveller's Handbook for Palestine and Syria,* written for Christian visitors, offers a full description of Jerusalem in its 1924 edition.

3. "Jerusalem," *Encyclopaedia Judaica,* 9: 1461–74.

4. *United Synagogue Recorder,* 5 (Oct. 1925): 6.

5. I am grateful to Professor Jonathan Sarna for letting me read a draft of his latest book on the history of American Judaism.

6. For this and the next two paragraphs I used Goren, *Dissenter in Zion,* and Norman Bentwich, *For Zion's Sake* (Philadelphia, 1954).

7. On the Szold-Magnes friendship in Jerusalem see Joan Dash, *Summoned to Jerusalem* (New York and Philadelphia, 1979), pp. 181–82.

8. Michael Brown, *The Israeli-American Connection* (Detroit, 1996), p. 138.

9. Irving Fineman, *Woman of Valor* (New York, 1961), p. 311.

10. M. Davis, Conversations with A. Dushkin, 11, 26 Nov. 1973, MDP; Marvin Lowenthal, *Henrietta Szold* (Westport, Conn., 1975), p. 160.

11. J. Magnes to F. Warburg, 14 Mar. 1923, MDP.

12. See n.11 and Bentwich, *For Zion's Sake*, p. 133.

13. Goren, *Dissenter in Zion*, p. 62; *Proceedings* of the Rabbinical Assembly, 1928, p. 53; 1929, p. 97.

14. Jerome M. Kutnick, "Non-Zionist Leadership: Felix M. Warburg" (Ph.D. diss., Brandeis University, 1983), pp. 147–49; C. Adler to F. Warburg, 13 May, 1924, Cyrus Adler Papers, Jewish Theological Seminary (JTS).

15. Magnes journal for Sept. 12, 13, 15, 19, 20, 1923, MDP; Goren, *Dissenter in Zion*, p. 219.

16. A first draft of the documents in Magnes's handwriting and a second typed draft with amendments are in MDP.

17. Goren, *Dissenter in Zion*, pp. 219–20.

18. Magnes journal for Sept. 15, 1923, N. Bentwich to J. Magnes, 2 Oct. 1923, MDP; Goren, *Dissenter in Zion*, p. 219.

19. Lober returned to the United States in 1926 and was appointed a director for MGM in Egypt, where he worked for ten years. On the young Lober, see Greenberg "Diary," pp. 88–89; M. Davis, lists of people in the *yishuv* connected to Magnes and the *Chevra*, MDP; M. Davis, Conversations with Lober, 18 and 22 Nov. 1973, MDP; Louis Lober, "Yeshurun" (memoir), MDP.

20. Lober, "Yeshurun," MDP; N. Bentwich to J. Magnes, 2 Oct. 1923, MDP.

21. M. Davis, Conversations with Lober, 18 and 22 Nov. 1973, MDP; Lober, "Yeshurun," MDP.

22. Lober, "Yeshurun," MDP.

23. Lober, "Yeshurun," MDP.

24. Greenberg, "Diary," pp. 34, 38–39, 60, 97.

25. Magnes journal for Sept. 15, 1923, MDP; Bentwich, *For Zion's Sake*, p. 134.

26. *United Synagogue Recorder*, 3 (Oct. 1923): 1.

27. *Proceedings* of the Rabbinical Assembly of America, 1927, p. 22.

28. Sarah Kussy, "Religious Life in Palestine," *United Synagogue Recorder*, 4 (Apr. 1924): 11.

29. The number 2000 was calculated by the State Department in 1929, Naomi W. Cohen, *The Year After the Riots* (Detroit, 1988), p. 24.

30. *Women's League Outlook*, 2 (Dec. 1931): 1; see also *Jewish Daily Bulletin*, 19 Oct. 1925; *United Synagogue Recorder*, 6 (Jan. 1926): 29; 7 (July 1927): 6.

31. Cyrus Adler, *I Have Considered the Days* (Philadelphia, 1941), p. 378.

32. *The Herald of the United Synagogue Recorder*, 1 Mar. 1925, p. 4, 1 May 1925, pp. 4–5.

33. *United Synagogue Recorder*, 5 (July 1925): 16; 5 (Oct. 1925): 7–8; Greenberg, "Diary," p. 174.

34. *United Synagogue Recorder*, 5 (Oct. 1925): 6; 7 (July 1927): 5 ("The Site of United Synagogue Centre in Jerusalem," by Elias Epstein).

35. *Jewish Daily Bulletin*, 19 Oct. 1925; *New Palestine*, 20 Nov. 1925.

36. *United Synagogue Recorder*, 5 (Oct. 1925): 6–8; Minutes of the Executive Council, 25 Nov. 1936, Women's League Archives (WLA).

37. Minutes of the Executive Council, 27 Sept. 1933, WLA.

38. *Jewish Daily Bulletin*, 19 Oct. 1925; United Synagogue of America and Women's League of the United Synagogue, *Annual Reports*, 1926, p. 35; *United Synagogue*

Recorder, 6 (Jan. 1926): 7–9, 28–29; 6 (June 1926): 15; Minutes of the Women's League Executive Council, 21 Sept. 1925, WLA.

39. I. Levinthal to N. Hecker and E. Yellin, 8 July 1925, WLA; *United Synagogue Recorder*, 6 (Mar. 1926): 6.

40. Minutes of the Women's League Executive Council, 16 Nov. 1925, WLA; *United Synagogue Recorder*, 6 (Mar. 1926): 8.

41. United Synagogue, *Annual Reports*, 1926, p. 35.

42. One piece of encouraging news about the synagogue-center momentarily relieved the gloomy outlook of the 1930s. In October 1935 a member of the Women's League received a personal letter reporting on the High Holiday services that were held in the yet unfinished building. Despite makeshift provisions compensating for the lack of flooring, pulpit, chairs, and permanent lighting, three hundred tickets were sold. Services on Rosh ha-Shanah were so impressive that the demand for seats on Yom Kippur soared. Every seat was filled for Yom Kippur eve, and between five to six hundred people stood in the back. Minutes of the Women's League Executive Council, 23 Oct. 1935, WLA; *Women's League Outlook*, 6 (Dec. 1935): 6.

43. Minutes of the Women's League Executive Council, especially 9 Oct., 27 Nov. 1929, 27 Sept., 25 Oct., 22 Nov. 1933, 21 Apr., 17 June, 25 Nov. 1936, 27 Dec. 1937, WLA; A. Neuman to Mrs. Kass, 4 June 1936, D. Spiegel to S. Cohen, 11 June 1936, to A. Neuman, 11 June 1938, to I. Levinthal, 11 June 1936, to L. Hoffman, 12 Apr. 1937, WLA Correspondence; Meeting of the Executive Council of the United Synagogue, 1 Apr., 21 May, 18 June 1936, JTS-General Files, Box 27, Series A; Adler, *I Have Considered the Days*, p. 378.

44. Abraham J. Karp, *A History of the United Synagogue of America* (New York, 1964), pp. 63, 73; *Proceedings* of the Rabbinical Assembly of America, 1948, p. 257. Negotiations on the cession of the land to the Jewish National Fund were carried on since the mid-1930s. Meeting of the Executive Council of the United Synagogue, 21 May 1936, JTS-General Files, Box 27, Series A. A popular article on Yeshurun entitled "Air of Distinction," with no mention of United Synagogue sponsorship in the interwar period, appeared in the supplementary section of the *Jerusalem Post*, 12 Jan. 2001.

5. The Social Worker and the Diplomat: Maurice B. Hexter and Sir John Hope Simpson (Pages 113–136)

The following abbreviations have been used in the Notes:

CWP   Chaim Weizmann Papers (Rechoboth, Israel)
CZA   Central Zionist Archives (Jerusalem, Israel)
FWP   Felix Warburg Papers, American Jewish Archives
JMP   Judah Magnes Papers (Central Archives for the History of the Jewish People, Jerusalem, Israel)
MHP   Maurice Hexter Papers, American Jewish Archives
RDS-JCC   Records of the Department of State, Consular Post Records (Jerusalem [National Archives], Israel)
RDST   Records of the Department of State Relating to the Internal Affairs of Turkey (National Archives)
ZAL   Zionist Archives and Library (I used this collection when it was located in New York. It is now part of the CZA.)

1. Naomi W. Cohen, "An Uneasy Alliance," in Bertram W. Korn, ed., *A Bicentennial Festschrift for Jacob Rader Marcus* (Waltham, Mass., and New York), pp. 114–18. Criticism of Weizmann, the Agency, and the ZOA pervades most of Warburg's correspondence on the Palestinian question for 1929–30.

2. Jerome M. Kutnick, "Non-Zionist Leadership: Felix M. Warburg, 1929–1937" (Ph.D. diss., Brandeis University, 1983), pp. 149, 184, 189, 193–94; F. Warburg to C. Weizmann, 11 Oct. 1929, FWP-Box 256.

3. See especially Warburg-Goldstein letters for September–October in FWP-Box 258; Maurice B. Hexter, *Life Size* (West Kennebunk, Maine, 1990), pp. 60, 75–76.

4. P. Knabenshue to G. H. Shaw, 6 Nov. 1929, RDS-JCC, pt. 5, to H. Stimson, 26 Oct. 1929, RDST-867n.404 WW/250; H. Stimson to P. Knabenshue, 19 Sept. 1929, RDS-JCC, pt. 8; J. Magnes to F. Warburg, 21 Sept. 1929, FWP-256; F. Warburg to J. Goldstein, 15, 16 Oct. 1929, J. Goldstein to F. Warburg, 16, 18 Oct. 1929, E. Mohl to B. Flexner, 15 Oct. 1929, FWP-Box 258; B. Flexner to F. Warburg, 25 Sept., 28 Oct. 1929, FWP-253; F. Kisch to F. Warburg, 26 Oct. 1929, FWP-Box256; J. Magnes to F. Warburg, 29 Sept. 1929, JMP-2396; F. Warburg to D. Brown, 23 Oct. 1929, MHP.

5. F. Warburg to J. Magnes, 9 Oct. 1929, FWP-Box 252; to O. d'Avigdor-Goldsmid, 26 Dec. 1929, FWP-258.

6. F. Warburg to Passfield, 18 Nov. 1930, FWP-Box 270.

7. The information for this and the next paragraph comes from Hexter's autobiography, *Life Size*.

8. Hexter, *Life Size*, pp. 2, 64, 81; see for example F. Warburg to J. de Rothschild, 8 Nov. 1929, MHP.

9. F. Warburg to C. Weizmann, 4 Nov. 1929, to M. Hexter, 13 Feb. 1930, MHP; Hexter, *Life Size*, pp. 64–65; *The Letters and Papers of Chaim Weizmann*, v. 14, ed. Camillo Dresner (New Brunswick, N.J., and Jerusalem, 1978), p. 103n.

10. F. Warburg to C. Weizmann, 28 Oct. 1929, MHP; *Letters and Papers of Weizmann*, pp. 87, 228n.

11. M. Hexter to F. Warburg, 13, 20 Dec. 1929, FWP-Box 258; Hexter, *Life Size*, pp. 65, 72–76, 87, 90.

12. Hexter's memorandum of a conference with Justice Brandeis, 3 Nov. 1929, FWP-Box 253; Hexter, *Life Size*, pp. 61–62, 65.

13. J. Mack to F. Frankfurter, 28 Aug. 1930, ZAL-Julian W. Mack 1930 trip, ZOA Personal Files; report by F. Warburg to Administrative Committee, Aug. 1930, FWP-Box 271.

14. Flexner, an American lawyer, served on the council of the Agency; Wasserman, a German banker, chaired the Agency's Finance and Budget Committee.

15. M. Hexter to F. Warburg, 27 Dec. 1929, MHP; M. Hexter to J. Hyman, 7 Jan. 1930, CWP.

16. The Shaw Commission, which had been sent to Palestine with the purpose of investigating the causes of the riots, had gone beyond its instructions and had dealt with matters of policy like immigration and land acquisitions.

17. Minutes of Meeting of Political Committee, June 23 and 24, 1930 in London, CZA-Z4/10073; Memorandum of our talk with the Prime Minister, 6 Apr. 1930, FWP-Box 270; C. Weizmann to F. Warburg, 15 May 1930, MHP; Hexter, *Life Size*, p. 78.

18. Kenneth W. Stein, *The Land Question in Palestine* (Chapel Hill, 1984), pp. 90, 104–5; F. H. Kisch, *Palestine Diary* (London, 1938), p. 300.

19. F. Warburg to R. Lindsay, 21 May 1930, FWP-Box 271, to C. Weizmann, 15,21, 28

May 1930, FWP-Box 268; J. Magnes to F. Warburg, 16 May 1930, FWP-Box 263; M. Hexter to F. Warburg, 6, 15, 20, 21 May 1930, C. Weizmann to M. MacDonald, 21 May 1930, MHP; Minutes of Meeting of Political Committee, June 23–24 1930, CZA-Z4/10073.

20. M. Hexter to F. Warburg, 4, 5 June 1930, FWP-Box 272; Stein, *Land Question in Palestine*, pp. 103–5.

21. Minutes of Meeting of Political Committee, June 23–24, 1930, CZA-Z4/10073.

22. M. Hexter to F. Warburg, 6, 7, 9 June 1930, FWP-Box 272.

23. Minutes of Meeting of Political Committee, June 23–24, 1930, CZA-Z4/10073; P. Rutenberg to L. Brandeis, 26 June 1930, CZA-S25/357; F. Warburg to J. Magnes, 28 July 1930, to B. Flexner, 1 Aug. 1930, FWP-Box 263.

24. Pinchas Ofer, "The Hope Simpson Report, Its Foundation and the Objectives of Its Framers to Influence the Internal Jewish Arena" (Hebrew), in *Proceedings of the Sixth World Congress of Jewish Studies* (Jerusalem, 1975),2:383–90.

25. Ofer, "Hope Simpson Report," n.19.

26. F. Warburg to C. Weizmann, 12 June 1930, CWP; M. Hexter to Admin Comm, undated [Sept. or Oct. 1930], MHP.

27. C. Weizmann to F. Warburg, 27 June 1930, MHP; F. Warburg to Admin Comm, 25 July 1930, FWP-Box 268; W. Senator to F. Warburg, 13 July 1930, P. Rutenberg to F. Warburg, 21 Aug. 1930, FWP-Box 270.

28. M. Hexter to L. Brandeis, 5 Aug. 1930, J. Hyman to M. Hexter, 18 July 1930, MHP.

29. Hexter's report on Hope Simpson meetings, 15–16 Aug. 1930, in MHP and FWP-Box 272; see also Stein, *Land Question in Palestine*, pp. 111–12.

30. J. Hope Simpson to F. Warburg, 16 Sept. 1930, M. Hexter to F. Warburg, 7 Sept. 1930, MHP; *Letters and Papers of Weizmann*, p. 377n.

31. M. Hexter to C. Weizmann, 20 Aug. 1930, CWP; *Letters and Papers of Weizmann*, p. 376; L. Brandeis to M. Hexter 29 Aug. 1930, M. Hexter to F. Warburg, 7 Sept. 1930, MHP.

32. *Report of the Chairman of the Administrative Committee of the Jewish Agency* (Berlin, 1929), p. 12, CZA-A264/70; memorandum by Warburg on meeting with Passfield, 25 Aug. 1930, ZAL-Julian W. Mack 1930 trip, ZOA Personal Files; Verbatim Notes of Meeting of Administrative Committee in New York, 18 Sept. 1930, J. Hope Simpson to F. Warburg, 3 Oct. 1930, FWP-Box 272.

33. C. Weizmann to F. Warburg, 6, 17, 24 Oct. 1930, to Passfield, 13 Oct. 1930, memo of conversation at Colonial Office, 15 Oct. 1930, MHP; *Letters and Papers of Weizmann*, p. 376.

34. M. Hexter to F. Warburg, 7 Sept., 14 Oct. 1930, MHP.

35. Melchett to F. Warburg, 1 Nov. 1930, MHP.

36. ESCO Foundation, *Palestine*, 2 vols. (New Haven, 1947), 2: 636–59; Passfield to F. Warburg, 30 Oct. 1930, FWP-Box 270; C. Weizmann to F. Warburg, 24 Oct. 1930, F. Warburg to C. Weizmann, 31 Oct. 1930, memo of 15 Nov. 1930: Differences between the White Paper and the Hope Simpson Document, MHP.

37. M. Hexter to J. de Rothschild, 13 Nov. 1930, to F. Warburg, 1 Nov. 1930, MHP; Stein, *Land Question in Palestine*, pp. 113–14.

38. M. Hexter to F. Warburg, 1 Nov. 1930, MHP.

39. Hexter, *Life Size*, pp. 81–83.

40. F. Warburg to F. Kisch, 5 Dec. 1930, MHP.

41. For example, F. Warburg to C. Weizmann, 22 Dec. 1930, MHP.

42. League of Nations Permanent Mandates Commission, *Minutes of the Seventeenth*

(Extraordinary) Session (Geneva, 1930); a summary of the Commission's report appeared in the *New Palestine*, 5 Sept. 1930; M. Hexter to F. Warburg, 7 Sept. 1930, to Admin Comm, 26 Nov. 1930, MHP.

43. F. Warburg to M. Hexter, 15 Dec. 1930, MHP; Kutnick, "Non-Zionist Leadership," pp. 303–9.

44. The general account in this paragraph has been pieced together from many letters and cables too numerous to cite in the Warburg and Hexter Papers.

45. F. Warburg to C. Weizmann, 23 Oct. 1930, M. Hexter to Admin Comm, 9 Jan. 1931, MHP; O. d'Avigdor-Goldsmid to F. Warburg, 25 June 1930, M. MacDonald to M. Hexter, 21 Jan. 1931, F. Warburg to C. Weizmann, 2 Jan. 1931, FWP-Box 272.

46. C. Weizmann to F. Warburg, 16 Jan. 1930, CZA-S25/1422.

47. Kutnick, "Non-Zionist Leadership," p. 312; book of cables from M. Hexter to F. Warburg, p. 29 (undated), p. 30 (22 Nov. 1930), cables from F. Warburg to M. Hexter, p. 22, #97, MHP.

48. H. Laski to Admin Comm, undated, M. Hexter to J. Hyman, 22 Nov., 1 Dec. 1930, 12 Jan. 1931, cables from Hexter to Admin Comm, 2 Dec. 1930 and #121(undated), to J. Hyman, 22 Nov. 1930, cable from J. Hyman to M. Hexter #97, MHP; Stein, *Land Question in Palestine*, p. 128; *The Letters and Papers of Chaim Weizmann*, v. 15, ed. Camillo Dresner (New Brunswick, N.J., and Jerusalem, 1978), p. 63.

49. ESCO Foundation, *Palestine*, 2: 656–60.

50. For example, M. Hexter cable to Admin Comm, 8 Jan. 1931, MHP.

51. Memo of conversation with the High Commissioner, 6 Feb. 1931, MHP; M. Hexter to J. Hyman, 22 Apr. 1931, FWP-Box 272.

52. See numerous cables between Hexter and Warburg's office for April and May 1931, MHP; ESCO Foundation, *Palestine*, 2:658; Stein, *Land Question in Palestine*, pp. 134–41; *Letters and Papers of Weizmann*, v. 15, pp. 165–69; editorial in *New Palestine*, 22 May 1931.

53. M. Hexter to F. Warburg, 27 Nov. 1930, MHP; Stein, *Land Question in Palestine*, pp. 111–14.

54. C. Adler to M. Hexter, 30 Jan. 1931, FWP-Box 272.

55. J. Hope Simpson to M. Hexter, 6, 18, 26 Nov. 1930, M. Hexter to J. Hope Simpson, 20, 26 Nov., 2 Dec. 1930, MHP; M. Hexter to J. Hyman, 2 Jan. 1931, FWP-Box 272.

56. Note of conversation with Sir John Hope Simpson, London, 10 Jan. 1931, FWP-Box 272.

57. M. Hexter to C. Weizmann, 21 Jan. 1931, C. Weizmann to M. Hexter, 27 Feb. 1931, note of conversation with Hope Simpson, 10 Mar. 1931, J. Hope Simpson to M. Hexter, 9 May 1931, M. Hexter to J. Hope Simpson, 11 May 1931, MHP; M. Hexter to F. Warburg, 22 June 1931, FWP-Box 272.

58. Address by I. B. Berkson at Philadelphia, 13 May 1932, Berkson Papers, CZA-A348/9.

59. *American Jewish Year Book* 92 (1992): 597–98; Hexter, *Life Size*, p. 133.

6. Jewish Immigration to Palestine: The Zionists and the State Department (Pages 137–164)

Unless otherwise indicated all references are to the Records of the Department of State Relating to the Internal Affairs of Palestine, 1930–1944. The documents cited often include enclosures and replies to letters received.

1. 867n.00/124, P. Knabenshue to H. Stimson, 2 Oct. 1931; 867n.55/38, R.Atherton to H. Stimson, 16 Feb. 1931.

2. 867n.01/522, W. Murray to solicitor, 19 Mar. 1930; /524, memorandum by P. Alling, 10 Mar. 1930; /525, P. Alling to solicitor, 19 Mar. 1930; /526, solicitor to W. Murray, 15 Apr. 1930; /616, W. Murray to J. Rogers, 5 Feb. 1932; /674 1/2, W. Murray to C. Hull, 8 Sept. 1933; /727 1/2, W. Murray to R. Moore, 18 Nov. 1936.

3. 867n.01/709, W. Phillips to H. Ickes, 18 May 1936.

4. 867.n00B/25, report by J. Simon, 14 July 1932.

5. On Paul Knabenshue see Naomi W. Cohen, *The Year After the Riots* (Detroit, 1988), ch. 1.

6. 867n.00B/5–27, especially /7, report by R. McGregor, 5 July 1930 and /25, report by J. Simon, 14 July 1932.

7. See, for example, the survey by Vice-Consul H. Minnigerode, 867n.50/3, 15 July 1932.

8. 867n.55/66, report by A. Richards, 27 Oct. 1934; *Foreign Relations of the United States (FRUS)*, 1938, II, 991.

9. 867n.55/51, A. Sloan to C. Hull, 26 Apr. 1933, /54, 28 Oct. 1933, /56, 7 Nov. 1933, /70, 14 Dec. 1934; 867n.00/164, A. Sloan to C. Hull, 1 Mar. 1933,/180, 4 Oct. 1933, /183, 16 Oct. 1933.

10. 867n.00/217, E. Palmer to C. Hull, 26 Sept. 1934, /227, 9 Jan. 1935.

11. 867n.55/27, W. Murray to J. Cotton, 20 June 1930; 867n.00B/25, report by J. Simon, 14 July 1932.

12. 867n.55/49, A. Sloan to C. Hull, 22 Apr. 1933, /51, 26 Apr. 1933; /66, report by A. Richards, 27 Oct. 1934; 867n.00/174, A. Sloan to C. Hull, 1 May 1933; /205, E. Palmer to C. Hull, 15 Aug. 1934, /213, 21 Sept. 1934, /214, 21 Sept. 1934, /230, 5 Jan. 1935, /251, 3 Aug. 1935.

13. 867n.00/237, E. Palmer to C. Hull, 9 Mar. 1935, /256, 7 Sept. 1935, /263, 25 Nov. 1935; /241, W. Murray to E. Palmer, 7 May 1935.

14. 867n.00/217, E. Palmer to C. Hull, 26 Sept. 1934, /263, 25 Nov. 1935; /273, L. Morris to C. Hull, 6 Mar. 1936, /311, 6 June 1936.

15. 867n.00/276, L. Morris to C. Hull, 20 Apr. 1936; /311, 6 June 1936; /305,A. Kirk to C. Hull, 4 June 1936; /316, R. Atherton to C. Hull, 22 June 1936; *FRUS*, 1936, III, 434–41.

16. 867n.00/338, G. Wadsworth to C. Hull, 13 July 1936; 867n.55/100, report by H. Minor, 5 May 1937. The figures for the number of American Jews were little more than estimates. Despite that small number, Jews in America contributed one-half to two-thirds of the monies collected worldwide 1920–32 by the Jewish National Fund and the Palestine Foundation Fund. 867n.01/633, report by T. Hickok, 10 June 1932.

17. 867n.00/334, W. Murray to C. Hull, 25 July 1936; /338, G. Wadsworth to C. Hull, 13 July 1936. Wallace Murray added that were England to adopt a course of action suggested by the United States, it could then disclaim any responsibility for American interests.

18. 867n.00/288, S. Wise to F. Roosevelt, 18 May 1936; *FRUS*, 1936, II, 442–43.

19. 867n.00/154, W. Murray to J. Rogers, 6 May 1932; /331, L. Morris to C. Hull, 23 July 1936; 867n.01/616, E. Neumann to J. Rogers, 29 Jan. 1932; /622, R. Atherton to J. Rogers, 10 Mar. 1932.

20. 867n.00/334, S. Rosenman to F. Roosevelt, 16 July 1936; /337, R. Bingham to C. Hull, 5 Aug. 1936; *FRUS*, 1936, II, 444–45, 453.

21. For example, 867n.00/352, P. Englander to C. Hull, 20 Aug. 1936; /353, J. Kraemer to C. Hull, 20 Aug. 1936. Most of the letters arrived in August.

22. 867n.00/362, *Washington Herald* of 26 Aug. 1936; /369, ZOA to C. Hull, 28 Aug. 1936; /370, C. DuBois to C. Hull, 18 Aug. 1936; /473, G. Wadsworth to C. Hull, 15 May 1937; *FRUS*, 1936, III, 446–47.

23. 867n.00/392, W. Murray to C. Hull, 19 Sept. 1936; *FRUS*, 1936, III, 450–51.

24. 867n.00/376, A. Lonergan to C. Hull, 2 Sept. 1936; /378, W. King to C. Hull, 1 Sept. 1936; /379, W. Hocking to C. Hull, 7 Sept. 1936; /383, G. Kheirallah to F. Roosevelt, 8 Sept. 1936; newspaper clipping probably enclosed in /383.

25. 867n.01/744 1/2, W. Murray to R. Moore, 26 Mar. 1937.

26. 867n.00/488, G. Wadsworth to C. Hull, 12 June 1937; *FRUS*, 1936, III, 452–54.

27. 867n.00/420, memo of conversation (and copy of Zionist document), 2 Dec. 1936; 867n.01/725 1/2, S. Wise to M. McIntyre, 13 Nov. 1936; /727 1/2, W. Murray to R. Moore, 18 Nov. 1936; *FRUS*, 1936, III, 454–59.

28. See /420 cited in n.27 and memo added to the Zionist document, W. Murray to R. Moore, 2 Dec. 1936; *FRUS*, 1936, III, 455–58.

29. For example, 867n.01/742, State Department's wire to embassy in London, 27 Apr. 1937.

30. 867n.01/744, W. Murray to R. Moore, 23 Jan. 1937, /469 1/2 (original number of document is inaccurate), 28 May 1937; /743 1/2, W. Murray to S. Welles, 30 Apr. 1937. The department prepared several substantive memoranda that defended the narrow interpretation of the 1924 treaty against the Zionist brief. 867n.01/744, memo by F. Ward; memos by J. Cotton, /758, 9 June 1937, on "The American Government and the Balfour Declaration," /760, 14 June 1937, on American public opinion and the Balfour Declaration (with an emphasis on anti-Zionist opinion), /779, 8 July 1937; /758 1/2, memo by W. Murray, 22 June 1937.

31. 867n.00/431, memo of conversation of Arabs with C. Hull, 1 Feb. 1937; /438, G. Wadsworth to C. Hull, 4 Feb. 1937; /439, 5 Feb. 1937; /458, W. Murray to W. Carr, 12 May 1937.

32. 867n.00/438, G. Wadsworth to C. Hull, 4 Feb. 1937; /445, S. Wise to R. Moore, 5 Apr. 1937; /453, memo by W. Murray, 3 May 1937; /465–/466, S. Wise to C. Hull, 4, 18 June 1937 (Wise, who also spoke for Louis Brandeis, noted the "warm interest" of both Roosevelt and Hull); /471, wire from Arabs to F. Roosevelt, 21 June 1937.

33. 867n.00/189, C. Thiel to C. Hull, 20 Jan. 1934.

34. 867n.00/434, memo by W. Murray, 27 Jan. 1937; /457 G. Wadsworth to C. Hull, 17 Apr. 1937, /461, 30 Apr. 1937; /480, S. Wise to C. Hull, 2 July 1937; 867n.01/769, A. Elias to R. Wagner, 2 July 1937; *FRUS*, 1937, II, 881.

35. For example, 867n.01/524, report by W. Murray, 10 Mar. 1930; /539 1/2, W. Murray to H. Stimson, 23 Oct. 1930.

36. 1937, II, 882.

37. 1937, II, 887–89.

38. 1937, II, 884–87.

39. 1937, II, 884–93.

40. 867n.01/769, C. Hull to R. Wagner, 14 July 1937; *FRUS*, 1937, II, 888–90.

41. 867n.01/962, H. Johnson to C. Hull, 5 Nov. 1937; /1076, G. Wadsworth to C. Hull, 2 May 1938; 867n.55/100, report by H. Minor, 5 May 1937; /109, G. Wadsworth to C. Hull, / 109, 10 Nov. 1937, /110, 17 Nov. 1937, /111, 30 Oct. 1937, /137, 14 July 1938, /154, 14 Dec. 1937; /149, memo by P. Alling, 22 Nov. 1937; *FRUS*, 1937, II, 914–20, 1938, II, 991–92.

42. 867n.55/109, G. Wadsworth to C. Hull, 10 Nov. 1937, /129, 28 May 1938; /113, H. Johnson to C. Hull, 24 Nov. 1937; /122, W. Murray to C. Hull, 13 Apr. 1938.

43. 867n.55/122, W. Murray to C. Hull, 13 Apr. 1938; 867n.01/1077, 75 Cong. 3 Sess., H. Con. Res. 50, 12 May 1938; /1092, G. Wadsworth to C. Hull, 14 May 1938; *FRUS*, 1938, II, 918, 993–94.

44. 867n.01/919, G. Wadsworth to C. Hull, 31 Aug. 1937; /1048, W. Murray to A. Berle, 2 Apr. 1938; /1085, G. Wadsworth to W. Murray, 16 May 1938; 867n.50/17, A. Scott to C. Hull, 17 Sept. 1937; /19, G. Wadsworth to C. Hull, 10 July 1939.

45. 867n.01/907 1/2, W. Murray to C. Hull, 11 Aug. 1937.

46. 867n.01/806, S. Wise to C. Hull, 21 July 1937.

47. 867n.01/791A, W. Murray to London embassy, 12 July 1937; /851, H. Johnson to C. Hull, 5 Aug. 1937.

48. 867n.01/873, A. Frost to C. Hull, 13 Aug. 1937; /904, G. Wadsworth to C.Hull, 20 Aug. 1937, /928, 17 Sept. 1937; /907 1/2, W. Murray to C. Hull, 11 Aug. 1937; *FRUS*, 1937, II, 904.

49. 867n.01/750 1/2, P. Alling to C. Hull, 7 Aug. 1937; /813, W. Murray to C. Hull, 19 July 1937, /946, W. Murray to C. Hull et al., 24 July 1937.

50. 867n.01/751 1/2, P. Alling to C. Hull, 17 Aug. 1937; /752 1/2, W. Murray to C. Hull, 20 Aug. 1937; /920, G. Wadsworth to C. Hull, 3 Sept. 1937, /1068,19 Feb. 1938; /1012, C. Adler to C. Hull, 21 Jan. 1938; *FRUS*, 1938, II, 899–901.

51. 867n.01/809, W. Murray to C. Hull, 23 July 1937; /826, memo by W. Murray on London despatch of 30 July 1937; /959, memo of conversation, 27 Oct. 1937; *FRUS*, 1937, II, 909.

52. 867n.01/743 1/2, W. Murray to S. Welles, 20 Apr. 1937; /469 1/2 (original number of document is inaccurate), W. Murray to R. Moore, 28 May 1937; /825, memo by W. Murray, 20 July 1937, /982, 2 Dec. 1937; /907 1/2, W. Murray to C. Hull, 11 Aug. 1937, /946, 24 July 1937; *FRUS*, 1937, II, 908–9, 921–22.

53. 867n.01/780 1/2, F. Roosevelt to C. Hull, 7 July 1937; /807, W. Murray to C. Hull, 19 July 1937, /811, 23 July 1937, /814, 19 July 1937, /947, 28 July 1937; /812, Near Eastern Affairs memo, 17 July 1937; /847, K. Pittman to C. Hull, 17 Aug. 1937; *FRUS*, 1937, II, 893–94.

54. 867n.01/958, W. Murray to B. Akzin, 28 Oct. 1937; /959, W. Murray to C. Hull, 16 Nov. 1937, /988, 14 Dec. 1937; /981, H. Johnson to C. Hull, 7 Dec. 1937; *FRUS*, 1937, II, 921–22. Murray learned shortly thereafter that Akzin had spoken to the American minister in Prague on the situation of American Jewry. He thought that a "latent antipathy" to Jews in the United States might well be converted into active antisemitism. 867n.01/1015 1/2, B. Akzin to W. Murray, 19 Jan. 1938; /1026, P. Alling to C. Hull and S. Welles, 25 Aug. 1938; /1048, W. Murray to A. Berle, 2 Apr. 1938; /1132, H. Johnson to W. Murray, 6 Aug. 1938; *FRUS*, 1938, II, 889, 896–99.

55. 867n.01/752 1/2, W. Murray to C. Hull, 20 Aug. 1937; /1076, G. Wadsworthto C. Hull, 2 May 1938; /1113, G. Wadsworth to W. Murray, 9 June 1938, and W. Murray to G. Wadsworth, 18 July 1938; *FRUS*, 1938, II, 903–13, 916–17, 920–27.

56. *FRUS*, 1938, II, 989–90.

57. *FRUS*, 1938, II, 929, 934, 943–50; 867n.01/1105, J. Epstein to W. Murray, 9 June 1938; /1113, G. Wadsworth to W. Murray, 9 June 1938.

58. 867n.01/1089, G. Wadsworth to C. Hull, 28 May 1938; /1106, W. Murray to G. Wadsworth, 2 July 1938; 867n.55/122, W. Murray to C. Hull, 13 Apr. 1938; /124 W. Murray to E. Khourie, 14 May 1938; *FRUS*, 1938, II, 928.

59. 867n.01/1094, S. Wise to C. Hull, 24 June 1938. That same month Hull met with a delegation from the (Christian) Pro-Palestine Federation which now pressed for in-

creased immigration. The delegates subsequently reported that Hull had "heartily endorsed" their position, but the secretary denied the claim. He had not yet read their written statement, but in customary fashion he said that all matters relating to foreign affairs received the government's attention. *FRUS*, 1938, II, 927–29.

60. 867n.01/1172, S. Goldman to C. Hull, 11 Oct. 1938; /1208 1/2, Near Eastern division memo, 22 Oct. 1938; /1257, G. Wadsworth to C. Hull, 17 Oct. 1938.

61. 867n.01/1156, W. Green to C. Hull, 7 Oct. 1938; /1185, P. Alling to J. Morlock, 24 Oct. 1938; /1219, P. Alling to C. Hull, 24 Oct. 1938; *FRUS*, 1938, II, 960, 965–66; 1939, IV, 699.

62. 867n.01/1257, G. Wadsworth to C. Hull, 17 Oct. 1938, /1296, 29 Oct. 1938; /1296, P. Alling to G. Messersmith, 22 Nov. 1938.

63. 867n.01/1321, G. Wadsworth to C. Hull, 31 Oct. 1938, /1371, 25 Oct. 1938; memo by F. Ward, 6 Mar. 1939 (incorrectly filed); *FRUS*, 1938, II, 966–68;1939, IV, 725–29.

64. 867n.01/893, G. Wadsworth to C. Hull, 5 Aug. 1937, /1296, 29 Oct. 1938, /1297, 1 Nov. 1938; /1252, G. Merriam to C. Hull, 25 Oct. 1938; /1287, memo by P. Alling, 2 Nov. 1938; /1304, E. Palmer to C. Hull, 9 Nov. 1938; /1346, W. Murray to S. Welles, 23 Nov. 1938; /1426, W. Murray to C. Hull, 27 Jan. 1939; *FRUS*, 1938, II, 962, 964, 966–69, 975–76, 981.

65. *FRUS*, 1938, II, 952–53, 962–63, 988; P. Alling to C. Hull, 5 Nov. 1938, /1329, 867n.01/1265, 21 Oct. 1938; /1270, P. Alling to P. Knabenshue, 7 Nov. 1938; 867n.55/129, G. Wadsworth to C. Hull, 28 May 1938. The department noted with some satisfaction that American editorial opinion was less insistent than it had been on the country's duty to intervene. 867n.01/1267, P. Alling to C.Hull, 7 Nov. 1938.

66. *FRUS*, 1938, II, 954–55.

67. 867n.01/1220, P. Alling to C. Hull, 14 Oct. 1938; *FRUS*, 1938, II, 968–70,975–76, 980–84, 994–98.

68. *FRUS*, 1938, II, 956–59; 867n.01/1219, P. Alling to C. Hull, 24 Oct. 1938.

69. 867n.01/1560 1/2, W. Murray to R. Moore, 19 May 1939.

70. *FRUS*, 1938, II, 982–83, 985, 988.

71. *FRUS*, 1938, II, 984; 867n.01/1321, G. Wadsworth to C. Hull, 14 Nov. 1938,/1421, 21 Jan. 1939 (with report of the Jewish Agency council meeting, 11–16 Nov. 1938); /1334, P. Knabenshue to W. Murray, 13 Nov. 1938.

72. 867n.01/1252, G. Merriam to C. Hull, 25 Oct. 1938; /1297, P. Alling to C. Hull, 22 Nov. 1938; /1298, J. Erwin to C. Hull, 15 Nov. 1938; /1349, E. Palmer to C. Hull, 17 Dec. 1938; /1353, W. Murray to S. Welles and G. Messersmith, 1 Dec. 1938; /1378, W. Murray to S. Welles, 16 Jan. 1939; /1402, State Dept. memo of conversation, 20 Jan. 1939; /1560 1/2, W. Murray to R. Moore, 19 May 1939; *FRUS*, 1938, II, 981–82; 1939, IV, 702.

73. *FRUS*, 1938, II, 994–98; 1939, IV, 694–96; 867n.01/1333, G. Merriam to C. Hull, 8 Dec. 1939.

74. See, for example, 867n.01/1373, W. Murray to S. Welles, 16 Jan. 1939, and /1399, W. Murray to H. Montor, 3 Feb. 1939; /1397, W. Murray to C. Hull and S. Welles, 28 Jan. 1939, /1431 1/2, 9 Feb. 1939.

75. 867n.01/1317, P. Alling to S. Welles, 23 Nov. 1938; /1380, W. Murray to S. Welles, 6 Jan. 1939; /1400, W. Murray to A. Ordman, 3 Feb. 1939; /1415, G. Wadsworth to C. Hull, 28 Nov. 1938.

76. 867n.01/1431 1/2, W. Murray to C. Hull and S. Welles, 9 Feb. 1939, /14461/2, 25 Feb. 1939; *FRUS*, 1939, IV, 713–14, 717, 719–20.

77. 867n.01/1450, J. Kennedy to C. Hull, 28 Feb. 1939; /1518, P. Knabenshue to C. Hull, 16 Mar. 1939; *FRUS*, 1939, IV, 714–16.

78. *FRUS*, 1939, IV, 718, 732–37; 867n.01/1452, W. Murray to C. Hull and S. Welles, 28 Feb. 1939; /1455, J. Schlossberg to C. Hull, 3 Mar. 1939; /1457, J. Kennedy to C. Hull, 3 Mar. 1939.

79. *FRUS*, 1939, IV, 731; 867n.01/1472 1/2, W. Murray to C. Hull and S. Welles, 2 Mar. 1939; /1474, G. Wadsworth to C. Hull, 25 Feb. 1939; /1507 1/2, Near Eastern division memo, 13 Mar. 1939.

80. 867n.01/1529, G. Wadsworth to C. Hull, 3 Apr. 1939; /1534, W. Murray to A. Berle, 22 Apr. 1939; /1545, W. Murray to S. Welles and C. Hull, 12 May 1939; *FRUS*, 1939, IV, 718, 722.

81. 867n.01/1535, G. Wadsworth to C. Hull, 19 Apr. 1939; *FRUS*, 1939, IV 742.

82. 867n.01/1550, G. Wadsworth to C. Hull, 3 May 1939; 867n.55/163, [P.Alling] to J. Kennedy, 4 Apr. 1939.

83. 867n.01/1542A, S. Welles to G. Tully, 10 May 1939; /1542B, F. Roosevelt to C. Hull and S. Welles, 10 May 1939; /1548, S. Welles to W. Murray, 6 May 1939; *FRUS*, 1939, IV, 731–32, 748–50.

84. *FRUS*, 1939, IV, 751–58.

7. The American Jewish Conference: A Zionist Experiment at Unity and Leadership (Pages 165–184)

1. Evyatar Friesel, "The Influence of Zionism on the American Jewish Community," *American Jewish History* 75 (Dec. 1985): 140–42.

2. Melvin I. Urofsky, *American Zionism from Herzl to the Holocaust* (Garden City, N.Y., 1975), pp. 422–25.

3. Central Zionist Archives (CZA)-Z 5/774, undated confidential memorandum by M. Weisgal; Samuel Halperin, *The Political World of American Zionism* (Detroit, 1981), pp. 121–27, 223–24; cf. Isaac Neustadt-Noy, "Toward Unity: Zionist and Non-Zionist Cooperation," *Essays in American Zionism* (= *Herzl Year Book*, vol.8. New York, 1978), pp. 149–65.

4. On the council see Thomas A. Kolsky, *Jews Against Zionism* (Philadelphia,1990); Namier is quoted in Michael Ignatieff, *Isaiah Berlin* (London, 2000), p. 105.

5. Halperin, *Political World of American Zionism*, pp. 223–25.

6. Halperin, *Political World of American Zionism*, pp. 219–20.

7. For this and the following two paragraphs see Urofsky, *American Zionism*, pp. 421–27; American Jewish Conference (AJ Conf), *A Statement of the Organization of the Conference and a Summary of Resolutions, . . .* Aug. 29-Sept.2 (New York, 1943), pp. 22–24; Halperin, *Political World of American Zionism, pp.* 233–42; Menahem Kaufman, *An Ambiguous Partnership* (Jerusalem, 1991), pp. 139–45; *Vision and Victory: A Collection of Addresses by Dr. Abba Hillel Silver* (New York, 1949), pp. 13–21; Marc L. Raphael, *Abba Hillel Silver* (New York, 1989), pp. 87–89.

8. *Vision and Victory*, pp. 1–13; Kaufman, *Ambiguous Partnership*, pp. 139–45.

9. Doreen Bierbrier, "The American Zionist Emergency Council," *American Jewish Historical Quarterly* 60 (Sept. 1970): 83–84; Raphael, *Silver*, pp. 97–98.

10. Quoted in Urofsky, *American Zionism*, p. 420.

11. Professor David Wyman has harshly criticized the conference for its concentration on statehood at the expense of rescue efforts. David S. Wyman, *The Abandonment of the Jews* (New York, 1984), ch. 9.

12. Halperin, *Political World of American Zionism*, p. 221; Ben Halpern, Introduction to *The Jewish National Home in Palestine, Hearings before the Committee on Foreign Affairs, House of Representatives, 78th Congress 2nd Session on H. Res. 418 and H. Res. 419, Feb. 1944* (Reprinted in New York, 1970); AJ Conf, American Zionist Political Tactics [1944], CZA-Z 5/772.

13. Memo by M. Waldman, 4 Dec. 1940, American Jewish Committee Archives and Library (AJCA)—Records of the General Jewish Council.

14. Halperin, *Political World of American Zionism*, pp. 220–21; Henry Monsky, *Toward a Common Program of Action* (Washington, 1943), p. 9; AJ Conf, Bulletin, 16 June 1944, CZA-Z 5/774; on the congress episode see Urofsky, *American Zionism*, ch. 5, and Naomi W. Cohen, *Not Free to Desist* (Philadelphia, 1972), pp. 90–98.

15. Halperin, *Political World of American Zionism*, pp. 223–33.

16. AJ Conf, Bulletin, 23 June *(Forward)*, 1 Aug. *(Jewish Press Service)*, 22 Sept. *(Jewish Review)*, 29 Sept. 1944 *(Forward)*, CZA-Z 5/773; J. Proskauer to R. Brewster, 1 Aug. 1944, J. Morgenstern to J. Proskauer, 11 May 1944, AJCA-Proskauer Papers (PP) Box 5.

17. For example, AJ Conf, Minutes of Executive Committee, 31 Oct. 1943, Bulletin, 20 Oct. 1944 *(Day)*, CZA-Z 5/763; Minutes of Interim Committee, 1 Aug. 1944, CZA-Z5/773.

18. AJ Conf, AJ Conf in Retrospect and Prospect [1944], Memorandum on Future Activities [1944], CZA-Z 5/772; Minutes of Interim Committee, 21 Mar. 1944, CZA-Z 5/747; Minutes of Executive Committee, 31 Oct. 1943, CZA-Z 5/763; Bulletin, 4 Aug., 12 Oct., 20 Oct. 1944, Minutes of Interim Committee, 29 June 1944, CZA-Z 5/773; Bulletin, 23 June 1944, Memorandum on the Functions of the Conference [1944], CZA-Z 5/774. Where local meetings were convened, the participants urged a more democratic structure.

19. AJ Conf, Minutes of Interim Committee, 12 Sept. 1944, CZA-Z 5/774; for comments on Revisionists, see for example, draft of statement denouncing Emergency Committee to Save Jewish People, 10 Dec. 1943, I. Kenen to delegates, 27 Mar. 1944, CZA-Z 5/747; Halperin, *Political World of American Zionism*, p. 228.

20. AJ Conf, Minutes of Interim Committee, 25 Jan. 1944, CZA-Z 5/747; Maurice N. Eisendrath, "The Union of American Hebrew Congregations," *American Jewish Historical Quarterly* 63 (Dec. 1973): 143–44; *Conference Record* 1 (June 1944); *Report of the Commission on Palestine*, in AJ Conf, *Report of the Interim Committee*, Nov. 1944, p. 65, AJCA-AJ Conf/Report; Halperin, *Political World of American Zionism*, pp. 166–67.

21. AJ Conf, Minutes of Interim Committee, 25 Jan., 21 Mar. 1944, I. Kenen to delegates, 27 Mar. 1944, CZA-Z 5/747; Minutes of Special Meeting of Rescue Actions Committee, 4 Sept. 1944, CZA-Z 5/772; Bulletin, 25 Aug., 29 Sept. 1944, Minutes of Interim Committee, 1 Aug., 12 Sept. 1944, CZA-Z 5/773.

22. AJ Conf, Report of the Budget Committee, 20 Mar. 1944, CZA-Z 5/761.

23. AJ Conf, AJ Conf in Retrospect and Prospect [1944], Bulletin, 6 Oct. 1944, CZA-Z5/772; press comments in Bulletin, 21 July, 11 Aug., 25 Aug., 1 Sept. 1944, CZA-Z 5/773.

24. AJ Conf, Undated memorandum, draft of statement denouncing Emergency Committee to Save Jewish People, CZA-Z 5/747; address by L. Lipsky in *Conference Record* 1(June 1944), CZA-Z 5/773; undated confidential memorandum by M. Weisgal on the AJC, CZA-Z 5/774.

25. See, for example, AJ Conf, Bulletin, 29 Sept. 1944, CZA-Z 5/773; Memorandum on AJ Conf, Bulletin, 6 Oct. 1944 *(Reconstructionist)*, Memorandum on Future Activities, CZA-Z 5/772.

26. AJ Conf, Bulletin, 29 Sept. 1944, CZA-Z 5/773; AJ Conf in Retrospect and Prospect [1944], Bulletin, 8 Dec. 1944, CZA-Z 5/772.

27. AJ Conf, Minutes of the Interim Committee, 23 Nov. 1943, Bulletin, 1 Sept., 6 Oct. 1944 *(Reconstructionist)*, CZA-Z 5/772.

28. AJ Conf, undated memorandum, CZA-Z 5/747; report of Budget Committee, 20 Mar. 1944, CZA-Z 5/761; Bulletin, 16 June *(Jewish Morning Journal)*, 23 June (with digest of press), 21 July 1944, CZA-Z 5/774; Bulletin, 21 July 1944 *(Jewish Post)*, CZA-Z 5/773; Bulletin, 8, 22, 29 Dec. 1944, 12 Jan. 1945 (digest of press), CZA-Z 5/772.

29. For instances of contact with UNRRA see, for example, AJ Conf, Bulletin, 29 Sept. 1944, CZA-Z 5/773; on WJC see Bulletin, 27 Oct. 1944, Proposal for Collaboration with WJC, 11 Sept. 1944, CZA-Z 5/772.

30. AJ Conf, Bulletin, 27 Oct. 1944 (also *Day, Forward)*, AJ Conf in Retrospect and Prospect, CZA-Z 5/772; *Conference Record* 1 (Jan. 1944): *Morning Freiheit*, CZA-Z 5/774.

31. E. Celler to F. Roosevelt, 18 Aug. 1943, AJCA-unsorted files; Raphael, *Silver*, pp. 97–98, 101; Melvin I. Urofsky, *We Are One!* (Garden City, N.Y., 1978), pp. 59–63.

32. AJ Conf, Bulletin, 16 June *(Jewish Morning Journal)*, 23 June 1944 *(Recontructionist)*, undated confidential memorandum by M. Weisgal, CZA-Z5/774.

33. AJ Conf, *Report of Commission on Palestine* (full citation in n. 20), p. 64; *Conference Record* 1 (Mar. 1944).

34. AJ Conf, *Conference Record* 1 (Jan., Oct. 1944); memorandum of 23 Jan. 1944, CZA-Z5/file 1945–46; *Report of PC*, pp. 66–67, 71. The *Conference Record* for October 1944 contains the text of an appeal to the British ambassador, Lord Halifax, on immigration.

35. AJ Conf, *Report of PC*, pp. 75–77; Memorandum on the Functions of the Conference [1943], CZA-Z 5/774; *Conference Record* 1 (Jan. 1944); Bierbrier, "American Zionist Emergency Council," *passim.*

36. AJ Conf, *Report of PC*, pp. 77–79; Minutes of the Interim Committee, 12 Sept. 1944, CZA-Z 5/773; *Conference Record* 1 (Oct. 1944).

37. Edward E. Grusd, "What the Conference Has Done," from B'nai B'rith's *National Jewish Monthly*, CZA-Z 5/772; Halpern, Introduction to *The Jewish National Home*, p. xxii; Joseph B. Schechtman, *The United States and the Jewish State Movement* (New York, 1966), pp. 64–80.

38. AJ Conf, *Report of PC*, pp. 68–69; *The Jewish National Home*, Hearings, pp. 24–95, 110–47, 159–71, 197–230, 271–75, 327–43, 356–88.

39. AJ Conf, *Report of PC*, pp. 72–73, 75; draft of report of PC, pp. 13–15, American Zionist Political Tactics [1944], CZA-Z 5/772; Halpern, Introduction to *The Jewish National Home*, pp. xxiv–xxv; J. Slawson to Executive Committee, 19 Jan. 1945, AJCA-unsorted files; Schechtman, *The US and the Jewish State Movement*, pp. 84–89; Urofsky, *We Are One!*, pp. 89–93.

40. AJ Conf, *Conference Record* 1 (Oct. 1944); Raphael, *Silver*, p. 101; Schechtman, *US and the Jewish State Movement*, ch. 4. Early in 1945 Roosevelt told the AJC that he had changed his mind about a Jewish state and that extremist Zionist propaganda was ill advised. Cohen, *Not Free to Desist*, pp. 295–96.

41. AJ Conf, *Report of PC*, pp. 73–75, 84–85; Bulletin, 22 Dec. 1945, CZA-Z 5/772; Schechtman, *US and the Jewish State Movement*, pp. 80–92.

42. See references in n. 38 to *The Jewish National Home,* Hearings.

43. Minutes of AJC Administrative Committee, 4 Oct. 1943, J. Proskauer to H. Monsky, 26 Mar. 1943 (same file), AJCA; J. Proskauer to R. Goldman, 28 July 1943, M. Waldman to J. Proskauer, 13 July 1943, Third Suggested Draft of Statement—13 Oct. 1943, AJCA-PP Box 1; Kaufman, *Ambiguous Partnership,* pp. 131–33; Nathan Schachner, *The Price of Liberty* (New York, 1946), pp. 143–48.

44. Cohen, *Not Free to Desist,* pp. 90–98.

45. Morris D. Waldman, *Nor By Power* (New York, 1953), p. 276, chs. 19–23; M. Waldman to J. Proskauer, 30 June 1943, AJCA-Waldman Papers.

46. Minutes of AJC Administrative Committee, Resolution Authorizing Participation in the American Jewish Conference—9 Apr. 1943, Proskauer-Monsky correspondence of 1943, AJCA-Admin Comm; Third Suggested Draft of Statement, 11 Oct. 1943, J. Proskauer to S. Wise, 28 July 1943, to M. Edelbaum, 20 May 1943, to E. Kaufman, 20 May 1943, I. Lehman and others to H. Monsky, 31 Mar. 1943, AJCA-PP Box 1; Kaufman, *Ambiguous Partnership,* p. 122; Waldman, *Nor By Power,* chs. 22–23.

47. Waldman, *Nor By Power,* p. 254.

48. The organization outlined its position on Zionism in a long letter from Proskauer to Roosevelt that called again for an international trusteeship. On the issue of the White Paper, see Kaufman, *Ambiguous Partnership,* p. 149. Waldman maintained publicly, however, that the AJC did support the abrogation of the White Paper. J. Proskauer to F. Roosevelt, 8 Nov. 1943, speech by M. Waldman, 28 Jan. 1944, AJCA-unsorted files; J. Proskauer to G. Cohen, 14 Apr. 1944, AJCA-PP Box 5; J. Proskauer to S. Bloom, 2 Dec. 1943, AJCA-PP Box 6. On the committee's protest to Lord Halifax on the White Paper see Joseph M. Proskauer, *A Segment of My Times* (New York, 1950), pp. 233–36.

49. Address by Proskauer at Meeting of American Jewish Conference, 29 Aug. 1943, AJCA-PP Box 1.

50. Minutes of AJC Administrative Committee, 4 Oct. 1943, AJCA; Waldman wrote later that withdrawal was largely *"in response to pressure conveyed from the White House and the State Department."* *Nor By Power,* p. 275.

51. Cohen, *Not Free to Desist,* pp. 253–55; *Statement of the American Jewish Committee on Withdrawal from the American Jewish Conference* (printed), AJCA-Resolutions and Statements.

52. J. Proskauer to R. Goldman, 13 Mar. 1944, to P. Haber, 28 Mar. 1944, AJCA-PP Box 6.

53. For example, see AJCA-Pamphlet Collection, press comments on withdrawal from conference—including statements by conference, ZOA, AZEC, and article by B. G. Richards, "American Committee Deserts Marshall"; letters in support of withdrawal, AJCA-PP Box 1; J. Proskauer–J. Morgenstern correspondence, AJCA-PP Box 5; AJ Conf, press conference, 17 Nov. 1943, CZA-Z 5/747; editorial in *Jewish Morning Journal,* 26 Oct. 1943, CZA-Z 5/766; digests of press in Bulletin, Oct.–Nov. 1943, CZA-Z 5/772; address by A. Silver, CZA-Z 5/773; undated confidential memorandum by M. Weisgal on AJC, CZA-Z 5/774; Cohen, *Not Free to Desist,* pp. 112–16.

54. Minutes of AJC Adminstrative Committee, 13 Oct., 9, 24 Nov., 8 Dec. 1943, AJCA; speech by M. Waldman, 28 Jan. 1944, AJCA-unsorted files.

55. *Jewish Morning Journal,* 23 July 1944, AJCA-PP Box 5; Minutes of AJC Administrative Committee, 13 Oct. 1943, AJCA.

56. On the two bills of rights, see AJ Conf, Bulletin, 25 Aug. (digest of press), 15 Sept. 1944, Minutes of Interim Committee, 12 Sept. 1944, CZA-Z 5/773; M. Waldman to J. Proskauer, 9 Nov. 1943, AJCA-unsorted files.

57. Cohen, *Not Free to Desist*, p. 296.

58. J. Proskauer to J. Slawson, 18 May 1944, AJCA-PP Box 5; J. Proskauer to S. Bloom, 3 Dec. 1943, AJCA-PP Box 6; *The Jewish National Home*, Hearings, pp. 276–77; Kaufman, *Ambiguous Partnership*, pp. 168–69.

59. Wyman, *Abandonment of the Jews*, pp. 172–77.

60. AJ Conf, Memorandum on Future Activities, Bulletins for Dec. 1944 and Jan. 1945, CZA-Z 5/772; Confidential Minutes of Executive Committee, 10 Apr. 1945, CZA-Z5/1945–46.

61. *Encyclopedia of Zionism and Israel*, 1:30–31.

62. AJ Conf, Bulletin, 29 Dec. 1944 *(New Palestine)*, CZA-Z 5/772.

63. For brief notes on AIPAC and the Conference of Presidents see annual *American Jewish Year Book* and Jerome A. Chanes, *A Primer on the American Jewish Community* (New York, 1999).

8. Out of Step with the Times: Rabbi Louis Finkelstein of the Jewish Theological Seminary *(Pages 189–212)*

Unless otherwise noted, all manuscript material is in the archives of the JTS. The abbreviation *NP* is used for *New Palestine*.

1. Samuel Halperin, *The Political World of American Zionism* (Detroit, 1961),p. 212; Melvin I. Urofsky, *We Are One!* (Garden City, N.Y., 1978), p. 125.

2. For brief summaries of the opinions of Schechter and Adler see Abraham J. Karp, "Reaction to Zionism and to the State of Israel in the American Jewish Religious Community," *Jewish Journal of Sociology* 8 (Sept. 1966): 118–47.

3. P. 101.

4. Michael A. Meyer, "A Centennial History," in *Hebrew Union College—Jewish Institute of Religion at One Hundred Years*, ed. Samuel E. Karff (Cincinnati, 1976), pp. 44–46, 62–69.

5. Moshe Davis, *The Emergence of Conservative Judaism* (Philadelphia, 1963), pp. 214–16, 271, 354; David G. Dalin, "Cyrus Adler, Non-Zionism, and the Zionist Movement," *AJS Review* 10 (Spring 1985): 68.

6. Solomon Schechter, *Seminary Addresses and Other Papers* (New York, 1959), pp. xxiii–xxiv; *American Hebrew*, 30 Sept. 1907.

7. For a recent analysis see Allon Gal, "The Historical Continuity Motif in Conservative Judaism's Concept of Israel," *Journal of Jewish Thought and Philosophy* 2 (1993): 157–83.

8. See, for example, Herman H. and Mignon L. Rubenovitz, *The Waking Heart* (Cambridge, 1967), pp. 1–7; Israel Goldstein, *My World As a Jew*, 2 vols. (New York, 1984), 1:32; Jacob Kohn, Memoirs, Kohn Papers.

9. Karp, "Reaction to Zionism," p. 153.

10. Herbert Parzen, *Architects of Conservative Judaism* (New York, 1964), pp. 207–9.

11. Louis Finkelstein, "The Things that Unite Us," *Proceedings* of the Rabbinical Assembly, 1927, p. 51.

12. Unless otherwise noted, the material in the next five paragraphs has been culled from the following pre-1948 articles and speeches by Finkelstein: "The Things that Unite Us"; "Jewish Nationalism and the Hebrew Language," *Avukah Annual* (1925–1930); "Some Aspects of Rabbinic Nationalism," *Brandeis Avukah Annual*, ed. J. S. Shubow (Boston, 1932); "Need for Land to Develop Teachings," *NP*, 25 Jan. 1935; "Address," *NP*, 17 July 1936; "A Program for Positive Judaism," *American Hebrew*, 11 Mar. 1938; "Tradition in the Making," in *Jewish Theological Seminary of American Semi-Centennial Volume;* "The Duty of the Jew," *Jewish Exponent*, 4 Oct. 1940; "Reflections on Judaism, Zionism and Enduring Peace," *NP*, 21 May 1943; "Zionism and World Culture," *NP*, 15 Sept. 1944; draft of radio address, 17 June 1938, RG 1A-Zionist Organization of America. See also Menahem Schmelzer's sensitive analysis in "Rabbi Louis Finkelstein" (Hebrew) *Mada'ei ha-Yahadut* 32 (1992); Moshe Davis, "To Our Teacher, Rabbi Louis Finkelstein, on the First Anniversary of His Death,"(Hebrew) *Hadoar*, 1 Jan. 1993.

13. L. Finkelstein to M. Steinberg, 9 Nov. 1943, RG 1B-AJC.

14. L. Finkelstein to J. Kahn, 28 Dec. 1931, to J. Magnes, 17 June 1940, RG 1A-Hebrew University.

15. In 1937, in reference to the heated disputes generated by the Arab riots and the Palestine partition proposal, Finkelstein recalled the words of Rabbi Joshua ben Hananiah urging his brethren to always resolve their problems peaceably. L. Finkelstein to Felix Warburg, 3 Sept. 1937, RG 1A-Warburg.

16. M. Davis to author, 27 Sept. 1992.

17. Pamela S. Nadell, *Conservative Judaism in America* (New York, 1988), pp. 86, 279–80.

18. Moshe Davis oral history interview, 15 Apr. 1990, Davis Papers—Ratner Archives.

19. Urofsky, *We Are One!* pp. 3–30; Mordecai M. Kaplan, Diary, 2 Sept. 1943.

20. Naomi W. Cohen, *Not Free to Desist* (Philadelphia, 1972), p. 251.

21. Unless otherwise noted, all material on Finkelstein's intergroup activities is from Fred W. Beuttler, "For the World at Large," in Jack Wertheimer, ed., *Tradition Renewed*, 2 vols. (New York, 1997), 2:669–730.

22. Michael Greenbaum, "The Finkelstein Era," in Wertheimer, *Tradition Renewed*, 1: 165–70.

23. Naomi W. Cohen, *Jews in Christian America* (New York, 1992), p. 120.

24. Baila R. Shargel, "The Texture of Seminary Life during the Finkelstein Era," in Wertheimer, *Tradition Renewed*, 1:534.

25. Cyrus Adler, *I Have Considered the Days* (Philadelphia, 1945), pp. 422–24; S. Goldman to L. Finkelstein, 12 Nov. 1936, L. Finkelstein to S. Goldman, 27 Nov. 1936, RG 1A-Goldman.

26. See, for example, *American Jewish Year Book* 43 (1941–42): 29, 45 (1943–44):138–39; Louis Finkelstein, "Hope as Well as Despair," *American Hebrew*, 27 Sept. 1940, "The Duty of the Jew," *Jewish Exponent*, 4 Oct. 1940, "For a Complete Democracy," *Atlantic Monthly* 168 (Sept. 1941), "America and a World of Darkness," *Jewish Forum* 24 (Sept. 1941). Finkelstein spoke of the Judeo-Christian tradition as early as the semicentennial. Finkelstein, "Tradition in the Making," p. 27; Schmelzer, "Rabbi Louis Finkelstein," p. 41.

27. Kaplan, Diary, 14 Sept. 1929; L. Finkelstein to Frieda Warburg, 1 Sept. 1937, RG 1A-Warburg.

28. Memorandum of conference with Lord Halifax, 27 Mar. 1941, L. Finkelstein's memorandum of telephone conversation with I. Goldstein, 9 Apr. 1941, I. Goldstein to S. Wise, 11 Apr. 1941, to C. Weizmann, 11 Apr. 1941, RG 1A-Goldstein; Finkelstein memorandum, 27 Mar. 1941, RG 1A-Minutes of a Meeting.

29. Thomas A. Kolsky, *Jews Against Zionism* (Philadelphia, 1990), ch. 2.

30. Halperin, *Political World of American Zionism,* pp. 333–34; P. Bernstein to L. Finkelstein, 6, 8 Oct. 1942, L. Finkelstein to P. Bernstein, 9, 16 Oct. 1942, RG 1A-Bernstein; L. Finkelstein to L. Levinthal, 22 Oct. 1942, RG 1A-Levinthal; *NP,* 20 Nov. 1942; Howard R. Greenstein, *Turning Point* (Brown Judaic Studies 12, 1981), p. 144.

31. L. Finkelstein to P. Bernstein, 30 Dec. 1942, RG 1A-Bernstein; L. Finkelstein to A. Lelyveld, 24 Apr. 1946, RG 1B-responses to Finkelstein's RA address.

32. Moshe Davis oral history interview, 15 Apr. 1990, Davis Papers, Ratner archives.

33. Urofsky, *We Are One!,* p. 67; *New York Times,* 23 Jan. 1943; *Reconstructionist,* 5 Feb. 1943; *NP,* 19 Feb. 1943.

34. L. Finkelstein to M. Steinberg, 9 Nov. 1943, RG 1B-Steinberg.

35. A. Sulzberger to L. Finkelstein, 25 Jan. 1943, L. Finkelstein to A.Sulzberger, 27 Jan. 1943, RG 1B-Sulzberger. On Sulzberger's anti-Zionism see *NP,* 20 Nov. 1942, 7 Jan. 1944; Kolsky, *Jews Against Zionism,* pp. 55, 58; Gay Talese, *The Kingdom and the Power* (New York, 1969), pp. 90–91.

36. *NP,* 8 Jan. 1943; L. Finkelstein to H. Bavli, 20 Jan. 1943, RG 1A-Bavli; L. Finkelstein to A. Sulzberger, 27 Jan. 1943, RG 1B-Sulzberger.

37. Kolsky, *Jews Against Zionism,* pp. 42, 46, 58, 79; L. Ginzberg to L. Finkelstein, 2 Feb. 1943, RG 1A-Ginzberg.

38. Cohen, *Not Free to Desist,* pp. 249–60; Morris D. Waldman, *Nor by Power* (New York, 1953), ch. 22.

39. *American Jewish Year Book* 46 (1944–45): 557; M. Steinberg to L. Finkelstein, 29 Oct. 1943, RG 1B-Steinberg; M. Hanin to L. Finkelstein, 5 Nov. 1943, RG 1B-AJC.

40. Waldman, *Nor by Power,* pp. 280–81; S. Schulman to L. Finkelstein, 28 Oct. 1943, L. Finkelstein to S. Schulman, 1 Nov. 1943, RG 1B-Schulman; L. Finkelstein to M. Steinberg, 9 Nov. 1943, RG 1B-AJC.

41. S. Wallach to L. Finkelstein, 15 Aug. 1941, RG 1A-AJC; for a view of Finkelstein's participation in the AJC see AJC files in RG 1.

42. M. Steinberg to L. Finkelstein, 11, 18 Nov. 1943, L. Finkelstein to M. Steinberg, 12, 24 Nov. 1943, RG 1B-Steinberg; L. Finkelstein to M. Steinberg, 9 Nov. 1943, RG 1B-AJC.

43. Louis Finkelstein, "Reflections on Judaism, Zionism and Enduring Peace," *NP,* 21 May 1943; L. Finkelstein to M. Steinberg, 9 Nov. 1943, RG 1B-AJC.

44. L. Finkelstein to "Dear Colleague," 28 Dec. 1943, RG 1B-AJC; L. Finkelstein to J. Proskauer, 20 Oct. 1943, RG 1B-Proskauer; Jacob J.Weinstein, *Solomon Goldman* (New York, 1973), p. 44.

45. Articles by Finkelstein: "Reflections on Judaism, Zionism and Enduring Peace"; "Zionism and World Culture," *NP,* 15 Sept. 1944; see also C. Alpert to L. Finkelstein, 22 Apr. 1943, L. Finkelstein to C. Alpert,30 Apr. 1943, RG-1B *NP.*

46. Talk by Sulzberger to a Baltimore temple group, 5 Nov. 1942, RG 1A-Sulzberger; A. Sulzberger to L. Finkelstein, 21 May 1945, 12 Aug. 1946, RG 1C-Sulzberger; Kaplan, Diary, 17 Mar. 1948; Sulzberger's letter to Abba Hillel Silver, *NP,* 7 Jan. 1944. On Milton Steinberg's interchange with Sulzberger, see Simon Noveck, *Milton Steinberg* (New York, 1978), pp. 134–36.

47. A. Sulzberger to L. Finkelstein, 16 Sept, 1946, RG 1C-Sulzberger.

48. L. Finkelstein to S. Stroock, 1 July 1941, RG 1A-Stroock; note on C. Weizmann to L. Finkelstein, 2 May 1941, RG 1A-Weizmann.

49. Kaplan, Diary, 26 Mar., 24 Sept. 1945.

50. *New York Times,* 29 Oct. 1943; L. Finkelstein to A. Silver, 3 Nov. 1945, RG 1B-Silver; L. Finkelstein to A. Sulzberger, 5 Nov. 1943, RG 1B-Sulzberger.

51. *NP,* 7 Jan. 1944.

52. Minutes, JTS Board of Directors, 17 Apr. [1945]; Kaplan, Diary, 17 Apr. 1945.

53. *Time,* 15 Oct. 1951; Weinstein, *Solomon Goldman,* p. 44.

54. For this and the next paragraph see Steinberg's sermons, "Crises in Conservative Judaism," in RG 1B-Steinberg; Weinstein, *Solomon Goldman,* pp. 42–49, 259–70; Noveck, *Milton Steinberg,* pp. 171–79; Kaplan, Diary, 20 Nov. 1944, 23 Jan., 17 June 1945; unsorted Steinberg papers: Finkelstein-Steinberg correspondence for January–July 1945; Shargel, "Texture of Seminary Life," p. 534.

55. Kaplan, Diary, 29 June 1945.

56. M. Davis to author, 28 Oct. 1992.

57. A degree was first considered in 1942. At that time the only one to question it, on the grounds that Weizmann was a secularist, was Zionist Simon Greenberg. Kaplan, Diary, 23 Oct. 1942.

58. Copy of citation and JTS news release 8 Dec. 1944, RG 11C-Communications; A. Karp to author, 4 Dec. 1992; Arthur Hertzberg, "The Changing Rabbinate," *Proceedings of the Rabbinical Assembly,* 1975, p. 67.

59. L. Finkelstein to Frieda Warburg, 27 Oct. 1944, RG 1B-Warburg; L.Finkelstein to J. Magnes, 31 Mar. 1947, RG 1D-Magnes; Arthur A. Goren, ed., *Dissenter in Zion* (Cambridge, 1982), p. 483.

60. S. Greenberg to author, 18 Aug. 1992.

61. Kaplan, Diary, 7 Jan., 22, 28 Feb., 17 Mar., 27 Apr. 1948; *New York Times,* 7 June 1948. In protest against the Seminary's attitude, Bavli published a bitter poem, "Gayim v'Aririm," that appeared in his *Aderet Ha-shanim* (Hebrew; Jerusalem, 1955), pp. 72–73. My thanks to Professor Alan Mintz for calling the poem to my attention.

62. M. Leifman to author, 30 Aug. 1992; Y. Rosenberg to author, 7 Nov. 1992. Moshe Davis disputes the story of *Hatikvah* at the 1948 graduation, claiming that the carillonist played a melody that only sounded like the Jewish anthem. Moshe Davis oral history interview, 20 Nov. 1990, Davis Papers, Ratner archives.

63. Moshe Davis, ed., *Israel: Its Role in Civilization* (New York, 1956),introduction; Moshe Davis, ed., "Our Share in Eretz Yisrael," symposium in *Conservative Judaism* 11 (Spring 1957): 26–36; *New York Times,* 29 Apr. 1952.

64. Finkelstein's address at a dinner in honor of Maxwell Abbell, 31 Oct. 1948, RG 1E-Abbell; Louis Finkelstein, "The State of Israel as a Spiritual Force," in *Israel: Its Role in Civilization,* p. 16.

65. *Board of Directors Newsletter,* 17 June 1948, RG 1E-JTS Board of Directors.

66. Finkelstein, "State of Israel as a Spiritual Force," p. 6.

Afterword (Pages 213–217)

1. *New Palestine,* 18 May 1948.

2. David Ben-Gurion, *Rebirth and Destiny of Israel,* edited and translated from the Hebrew under the supervision of M. Nurock (New York, 1954), p. 539.

3. Naomi W. Cohen, *Not Free to Desist* (Philadelphia, 1972), pp. 305–6, 312.

4. See, for example, Steven M. Cohen and Arnold M. Eisen, *The Jew Within* (Bloomington, 2000), esp. pp. 142–52.

5. The impact of statehood on organized American Zionism and the search for a redefinition of Zionism in the decade after 1948 are treated in Melvin I. Urofsky, "A Cause in Search of Itself," *American Jewish History* 69 (Sept. 1979): 79–91.

6. Robert Alter, "Israel and the Intellectuals," *A Commentary Report* (New York, 1967), p. 7.

Index

Aaronsohn, Aaron, 60

Abbott, Lyman, 16

academic freedom and Reform heretics at HUC, 55–58

acculturation: AJC support for, 181; Conservative version, 193; eastern European desire for, 4, 15; and Reform Judaism, 27; Zionism as measure of, 2; vs. Zionist message, 15–16. *See also* assimilation

Adler, Cyrus: contributions to AJC, 205; and Finkelstein, 194; and Hexter, 133; in leadership struggles with Zionists, 36; and non-Zionists' lack of initiative, 90; spiritual-cultural Zionism of, 191; and synagogue plans for Palestine, 101, 107

agricultural development in Palestine, 121–22, 126

The Aims of Zionism (Gottheil, R.), 53, 54

AIPAC (American Israel Public Affairs Committee), 188

AJC (American Jewish Committee). *See* American Jewish Committee (AJC)

Akzin, Benjamin, 154

aliyah and American Jews, 6, 24, 139, 162, 216. *See also* immigration into Palestine

Alling, Paul, 148, 150, 158

Altneuland (Herzl), 33–34

America as permanent home for most Jews, 6, 18, 20, 193, 214

American Council for Judaism: as anti-Zionist holdout, 13, 63, 167, 179, 189; exclusion from American Jewish Conference, 172; Zionist pressure for repudiation of, 200–201, 202, 210

American Hebrew, 90

Americanism: intensity of post-WWI, 65–66; vs. Jewish state, 21; of Reform Judaism, 39–40, 45–49; and Zionism, 23–25, 31–32, 60, 166

American Israelite, 47, 62

American Israel Public Affairs Committee (AIPAC), 188

Americanization of Zionism: and abandonment by State Department, 138; and America as Jewish cultural center, 26; in American Jewish Conference, 188; and Finkelstein, 199; Gottheil's contribution, 54; and humanitarianism, 190; international role of, 34; as key to survival and progress, 213–17; lack of synagogue fit in Jerusalem, 96; *Maccabaean*'s contribution, 18, 38; and public response to Balfour, 64; reduction of Zionism to philanthropy, 75; and spiritual-cultural Zionism, 191; support of WWII aims, 169–70; tactical application of, 165–66; tailoring of to American values, 18–23, 28–32, 113

American Jewish Committee (AJC): and American Jewish Conference, 170, 172, 180–86, 203–4; Finkelstein's loyalty to, 204–6; and focus of Zionism on politics, 198; post-WWII loss of influence, 13; Zionist attempt to convert, 167; vs. Zionist campaign for democratic congress, 36; Zionist criticism of, 28–30

American Jewish Conference: conflicts with AJC, 180–86, 203–4; establishment of, 165–66; legacy of, 186–88; obstacles to unity, 170–75; Palestine

Index

Reform opposition, 61– 62; public response to, 64– 75, 78– 81; State Department neglect of, 10; vs. statehood, 84

Bavli, Hillel, 211

Beilis, Mendel, 20

Bellow, Saul, 2

Ben-Gurion, David, 12, 49, 136, 169, 213–14

Bentwich, Norman, 96, 103, 104

Berkowitz, Henry, 67

Bernheim, Isaac W., 61

Bernstein, Philip, 201, 202

Biltmore program, 166, 168, 200

binational state thesis, 79– 81, 83, 86, 88, 98

Bingham, Robert, 144, 150

Blaustein, Jacob, 49

Bloom, Sol, 178

B'nai B'rith, 167, 172

Boas, Ralph, 66

Bolsheviks, accusation of Jews as, 65, 71, 134

Borah, William, 81

Brandeis, Louis: Arab village settlement plan, 142; and British policy in Palestine, 126; championing of Zionism, 59– 61; and Establishment vs. Zionists, 36; leadership role, 6– 7, 34, 37; support for Weizmann's efforts, 163; Zionist sharing of American ideals, 35

Brandeis group, 77, 80, 89

Britain, Great: and American right to intervene in mandate, 138– 48, 156– 64; conflicting promises in Palestine, 8, 75– 76; cultivation of non-Zionists, 115; Hope Simpson report, 119– 28; and imperialist impressions of Zionism, 83; Jewish Agency attempts at compromise, 130– 36; Jewish refugees and immigration issue, 11– 12, 137–38, 156– 64; partition proposal and Peel Commission, 148– 55; Passfield White Paper, 128– 30; Socialist support for, 79; Zionist reluctance to criticize, 77–78. See also Balfour Declaration

Brown, Philip Marshall, 69

Carver, Thomas Nixon, 68

Cavert, Samuel, 88

Celler, Emanuel, 176

Central Conference of American Rabbis (CCAR), 39– 40, 42– 43, 61, 62– 63, 172, 201

Chancellor, Sir John, 120, 123, 127, 129, 132

charities, Jewish, 29–31, 38

chasidic sects, 95, 98

Chevra group in Jerusalem, 97–107

Christians: and biblical roots of Zionism, 2–3; and Finkelstein's ecumenism, 191, 199; loss of support for Israel after 1967, 214; opposition to political Zionism, 8, 68–71, 72, 87–88, 160, 228n57; on partition of Palestine, 149; pro-Zionist groups, 144; Reform concerns about alienation of, 27; response to Balfour, 67; and spiritual-cultural Zionism, 202; support for Arabs in Palestine, 65, 92, 154; support for Jewish refugees, 190

Churchill, Winston, 138

class issues among Jews, 16, 30, 54– 55

Cohen, Morris Raphael, 67, 73

Cold War, Israel's role in, 213

collectivism in kibbutzim, 85, 134

commonwealth, Palestine as Jewish, 166, 168– 69, 177, 178, 206

communal leadership: democratic campaign, 35–36; Establishment vs. Zionists, 68; Maccabaean's contribution, 38; Zionist role in struggle, 1, 5– 6, 28–32. See also American Jewish Conference; unity vs. disunity of American Jewry

Communists: accusation of Jews as, 65, 71, 134, 141; anti-Zionism of Jewish, 78– 79; Cold War role of Israel, 213; and labor movement, 172

Congress, U.S., sympathy for Zionist cause, 145– 46, 176, 178, 179, 180, 186

Conservative Jewry: Finkelstein and JTS, 189– 212; support for Zionism, 58– 59; synagogue project in Jerusalem, 95– 97, 106, 107–12, 232n42. See also American Jewish Committee (AJC)

Copeland, Royal, 146

cultural pluralism, 7, 23–25, 53– 54, 74, 97, 216

cultural Zionism. *See* spiritual-cultural Zionism

d'Avigdor-Goldsmid, Sir Osmond, 115
Davis, Moshe, 202, 210, 230*n*1
defense force, Jewish, 143, 164
De Haas, Jacob, 18, 93
democracy: ability of Arabs to participate in, 84; and American Jewish Conference, 170–71, 188; and American Jewish Congress, 35–36; Arab Palestinian rights vs. Zionists, 67; and changes in AJC, 185; and criticism of Zionists as imperialistic, 70, 71, 82, 83, 84–85, 87; and Israel's position in Middle East, 213; Jewish leadership structures, 5–6, 7, 13, 167, 168; *Maccabaean's* contribution, 38; Magnes's support for, 97; majority rule vs. Jewish hegemony in Palestine, 91; non-Zionist loyalty to, 115; preservation as goal of WWI, 34; Zionist commitment to, 24–25, 28–32, 60
Depression, Great, 8, 140
development commission for Palestine, 125, 128, 132–33, 135
Diaspora: as abnormality for Jews, 19–20; Conservative support for, 193, 196; legitimate functions of, 22; in partnership with Palestine, 9; Reform's support for, 43–44; and survival dangers for Jews, 53
discrimination against Jews. *See* antisemitism
disunity vs. unity of American Jewry. *See* unity vs. disunity of American Jewry
Drob, Max, 107–8
dual allegiance problem: and American relations to Israel, 214; Brandeis's dismissal of, 60–61; Conservative Judaism's avoidance of, 59; and opposition to Zionism, 5, 48–49, 67–68, 186, 201; and public response to Balfour, 66; Zionist avoidance of, 9, 13, 23, 53–54, 73
Dushkin, Alexander, 99

eastern European Jews: acculturation of, 4, 15, 192; appeal of Conservative Judaism for, 58; increased influence in America, 62; nationalism of, 49, 193–94; and Reform Jews, 42, 47; resentment of Establishment by, 168; support for Zionism, 27; WWI relief efforts, 35; Zionist targeting of, 6, 17
economic considerations in Palestine: absorptive capacity for immigration, 138, 156; British economic betrayal, 128; cooperativism in utopian Jewish state, 34; employment situation, 125, 126, 133; land transfer issue, 121–22, 124, 125, 128, 132–33; needs and plans, 107, 119, 121–22, 125; State Department study of, 151
Eden, Anthony, 145, 152
education, Jewish, 25–26, 38
Ehrlich, Emma, 105
elitist Jewish leadership structure. *See* Establishment, Jewish
employment situation in Palestine, 125, 126, 133
Enlightenment basis for Reform Judaism, 40, 45
Establishment, Jewish: accusations of unreasonable power, 85; and American Jewish Congress, 36; assimilationist attitude, 5; and Conservative Judaism, 193; loss of power for, 13, 62; Reform domination of, 42; as threatened by political Zionism, 68; WWI relief efforts, 35; Zionism as opposed to, 7, 28–32, 168, 194; Zionists within, 54. *See also* American Jewish Committee (AJC)
ethical leaders, Jews as, 59–60, 79–80, 170
ethnic identity: and criticism of Zionism, 69; cultural pluralism, 7, 23–25, 53–54, 74, 216; dangers in post-WWI America, 66; and Zionism as unifying force, 19, 23, 52. *See also* nationalism
European Jews. *See* eastern European Jews; German Jewry; refugees, Jewish
exile, America as refuge rather than, 193, 214. *See also* Diaspora

HUC (Hebrew Union College), 55–58, 170, 192
Hughes, Charles Evans, 142
Hull, Cordell, 144, 146, 162, 177, 238–39n59
humanitarianism, 35, 140, 152, 159, 182. *See also* refugees, Jewish
Hurley, Patrick, 176
Hyman, Joseph, 118

Ibn Saud, King of Saudi Arabia, 160–61
illegal immigration to Palestine, 14, 142, 143
immigrants to America: American barriers against, 72; drive to assimilate, 66; restrictions on, 31, 32, 146–47, 151, 155, 170; Zionism as bridge to, 55. *See also* eastern European Jews; German Jewry
immigration into Palestine: American Jewish Conference initiatives, 176; American Jews' lack of, 6, 24, 139, 162, 216; Arab-Jewish population balance, 150, 161–62; British restrictions on, 10, 11, 120, 122, 126, 132, 146–47, 151, 155, 170; call for Jewish control of, 169; Christian groups' support for, 144; and outsiders' fears of power of Jews, 141–43; and Peel Commission, 145; refugee issue in 1930s, 11–12, 137–38, 156–64; Roosevelt's support for, 179; State Department policies, 138–39, 143, 164; vs. statehood for AJC, 182–83; Zionist demand for, 12, 166, 177
imperialists, Zionists portrayed as, 70, 71, 82, 83, 84–85, 87
Independent, 70
individual freedom and criticism of Zionists in Palestine, 67
international Jewry concept, 70–71, 85, 140–41
international organizations' takeover of postwar resolution, 187. *See also* Jewish Agency
international supervision of Palestine, 183, 184, 205, 206
Irgun Zvai Leumi, 177
Israel, state of, 212–17. *See also* state, Jewish

Jastrow, Morris, 66, 67, 73
Jerusalem, 95–112, 232n42
Jewish Agency: anti-Zionist criticism of, 77; and Hope Simpson's report, 119–28; immigration to Palestine issues, 11, 12, 141–42, 169; loyalty of British members to Britain, 77–78; non-Zionists vs. Zionists in, 80–81; on partition, 149; Passfield White Paper, 128–36; refusal to support ZOA, 90; Warburg vs. Weizmann in, 113–19; Zionist/non-Zionist collaboration in, 8–9
Jewish center: Conservative support for, 191, 195–96; projects for Jerusalem, 99–100, 107, 108, 110–11
Jewish Labor Committee, 172
Jewish National Fund, 125, 127
Jewish Relief Committee, 35
Jewish Self-Defense Association, 29
Jewish Territorial Organization (ITO), 15
Jewish Theological Seminary (JTS), 22, 58–59, 189–212
Jewish Welfare Board, 99
Joseph, Jacob, 20
Judaism. *See* Conservative Jewry; Orthodox Jewry; Reform Jewry
Der Judenstaat (Herzl), 33, 42
Judeo-Christian tradition, Finkelstein's focus on, 191, 199
jurisdiction issues among Jewish national organizations, 173–74, 180

Kahn, Julius, 66
Kallen, Horace, 18, 73–74
Kaplan, Mordecai, 207, 211
Kellogg, Frank, 139
Kennedy, Joseph, 158, 162
kibbutzim, 85, 134
Kishinev petition, 29
Knabenshue, Paul, 140
Kohler, Kaufmann, 43, 46, 51–52, 55–58
Kohn, Hans, 3
Kook, Abraham Isaac, 104
Kussy, Sarah, 108

labor organizations, 5, 8–9, 60, 79, 172
Landman, Isaac, 68, 90

land transfers and cultivation in Palestine, 121–22, 124, 125, 128, 132–33
Lansing, Robert, 10, 139
Laski, Harold, 131, 132
Lazarus, Josephine, 24–25
Lazarus, Moritz, 51
leadership. *See* communal leadership
League of Nations, 130, 137, 150, 153
left, Jewish political: anti-Zionism in, 78–79; Socialists, 5, 79, 85, 134. *See also* liberals
Lehman, Arthur, 99
Levias, Caspar, 55
Levinthal, Israel, 109, 110–11
Levy, Joseph, 82
liberals: opposition to Zionism from, 8, 82, 84, 89; as original leaders of Jewish mission, 59–60; and origins of Zionism, 74; pro-Arab tendencies of, 11; response to Balfour, 66–68; support for binational state thesis, 83; sympathy for minority nationalism, 16. *See also* Reform Jewry
Lipsky, Louis: commitment to political Zionism, 18; on education, 25; and *galut* as doom of Jewry, 20; as head of ZOA, 77; on *Maccabaean* contributions, 37–38; and public opinion on Zionists in Palestine, 81–82; rebuttal of anti-Zionist critics, 73; Warburg's dislike of, 90
Littauer, Lucius, 29
lobbying: Arab efforts for Palestine, 92, 157, 160, 161; Jewish vs. Arab for U.S. support, 157–58; Zionist techniques, 138, 188
Lober, Louis, 103–4, 109–10
Lodge-Fish resolution, 68, 70–71, 72–73, 74, 138

Maccabaean: contributions of, 37–38; founding of, 15–17; national consciousness project of, 17–23; political Zionism for America, 28–32; religious/cultural issues, 25–28; WWI shift to international focus, 32–37; Zionist accommodations to Americanism, 23–25

MacCallum, Elizabeth, 89
MacDonald, Malcolm, 131
MacDonald, Ramsay, 78, 126, 128, 139
MacDonald White Paper, 10, 12. *See also* Passfield White Paper
Mack, Julian, 73, 89, 127
Magnes, Judah: binational state thesis, 79–81, 83; as divisive influence on Zionism, 118, 120; and Jewish-Arab rapprochement attempt, 155; modern synagogue project for Jerusalem, 96, 97–107; and political nature of Jewish homeland, 33; preservation of Jewish identity in America, 24; and senatorial visit to Palestine, 145–46; Zionism as bridge to new immigrants, 55
Malter, Henry, 55, 56
mandate of Palestine. *See* Palestine
Margolis, Max, 55, 56–57
Marshall, James, 83
Marshall, Louis, 36, 55, 99, 114, 184, 192
Melchett, Lord (Alfred Mond), 115
melting-pot theory vs. cultural pluralism, 15, 23
Menorah Journal, 73
military force as necessity in Palestine, 85, 91
military service and Jews, 34, 35
minority nationalism, liberal sympathy for, 16. *See also* cultural pluralism
missionaries, Christian, 65, 87, 108, 109
mission of Israel: criticism of Reform view, 52–53; moral nature of, 59–60, 79–80, 170; as national consciousness, 51; Reform view of, 43, 44, 45; and Zionism as proponent of American values, 219n3
Mond, Alfred, Lord Melchett, 115
Monsky, Henry, 166–67
Moore, R. Walton, 147
Morais, Sabato, 192
moral leaders, Jews as, 59–60, 79–80, 170
Morgenthau, Henry, 33, 66, 73
Mowrer, Paul, 68–69
Murray, Wallace: advantages of Zionist disunity for, 153; anti-Zionist stance, 159–60; on immigration levels in

Murray, Wallace *(cont'd.)*
  Palestine, 143, 164; nonintervention
  position on Palestine, 144– 45, 146, 147,
  148; and oil interests in Arab countries, 160– 61; placation of Wise, 144;
  press accusations of anti-Jewish sentiment, 176; support for Magnes, 155;
  treatment of Revisionists, 154
musaf, 102, 103, 106

Nation, 82– 83
national consciousness, 17–23, 51
National Council of Jewish Women, 172
nationalism: vs. assimilation, 17, 38; of
  eastern European Jews, 49, 193– 94;
  Holocaust as fuel for, 185; liberal sympathy for minority, 16; Reform's response to, 40, 43, 46, 53; vs. universalism, 19, 27; and Zionism's origins, 3;
  Zionist modification for American
  Jews, 7–10. *See also* dual allegiance
  problem; ethnic identity
nationalities, rights of, 74
national Jewish organizations. *See individual organizations*
Nazi persecution of Jews: dramatic in-
  creases in, 151; Final Solution and
  Zionist urgency, 170; increasingly desperate plight of Jews, 152, 156, 162; and
  partition issue in Palestine, 149; Zionist call for British/U.S. intervention,
  140. *See also* Holocaust
Neumann, Emanuel, 144
Nevinson, H. W., 85
New Palestine, 74, 83
New York Times, 74, 184, 207
New Zionist Organization (NZO), 154, 172
nonintervention in Palestine, U.S. *See*
  State Department, U.S.
non-Jews: and AJC, 181, 184; AZEC's work
  in mobilizing, 177; fears about dual
  allegiance issue, 49; Finkelstein's need
  for goodwill from, 199; Holocaust effect on, 13–14; indifference to Zionist
  cause, 16; initial sympathy after Arab
  riots, 81; religion as protection from
  totalitarianism, 198; Zionist accom-

modation of, 7– 8. *See also* Christians;
  public opinion
non-Zionists: in AJC, 184; on Arabs, 113;
  Britain's cultivation of, 115; differences
  with Zionists, 77– 78, 80– 81; Finkelstein, 189–212; in Jewish Agency, 77;
  opposition to Jewish state, 114, 153;
  overview, 5; reluctance to counter
  anti-Zionism, 90; State Department's
  preference for, 140; support for Zionists, 8– 9, 11; traditional American Jewish organizations as, 167; unity vs. disunity in American Jewry, 77– 78, 120,
  123, 128, 129, 130, 136; WWII loss of
  distinction, 183; Zionist conversion
  attempts, 73. *See also* Hexter, Maurice
  B.; Magnes, Judah; Warburg, Felix
Nordau, Max, 1, 17, 33
NZO (New Zionist Organization), 154, 172

Ochs, Adolph, 74
oil interests in Arab countries, 160– 61
*The Origin of Republican Form of Govern-
  ment in the United States of America*
  (Straus), 45
Orthodox Jewry: and American Jewish
  Conference, 172; entrenchment in
  Jerusalem, 101, 109, 111; vs. Magnes's
  attempt at modern synagogue, 95– 97;
  opposition to secularized Zionism, 5,
  26, 96; unequal treatment of women,
  108; and Yeshurun's success, 103–12;
  Zionism in, 201

Paassen, Pierre Van, 93– 94
Palestine: American Jewish Conference's
  initiatives, 174; American Jewish investment in, 6, 143, 148, 190, 236*n*16;
  Arab and British interests against Jews
  in, 143– 48; Christian criticism of
  Zionists in, 70– 71; and Hope Simpson's report, 119–28; international supervision of, 183, 184, 205, 206; modern synagogue project in Jerusalem,
  95–112, 232*n*42; partition proposal for,
  148–55, 160, 187; Passfield White Paper,
  76, 128–36, 177, 179, 182, 204; post-Arab

unrest debate on, 75–94; Reform's rejection of restoration to, 41, 44–45; refugee crisis of 1930s, 11–12, 137–38, 156–64; relief work in, 116–19; as spiritual-cultural center, 9, 22, 26, 53, 191, 195–96; State Department policies, 10, 138–43, 159–60, 176, 178; Zionist support for WWII Allied goals, 170. *See also* Arabs; Balfour Declaration; immigration; practical building of Palestine; state; *yishuv*

Palestine Commission (PC) of American Jewish Conference, 175–80

Palestinianism: American Jewish support for, 5; Reform acceptance of, 62; as response to Arab unrest in Palestine, 75; Zionism's shift to, 4, 7–10, 93. *See also* practical building of Palestine; spiritual-cultural Zionism

Palmer, Ely, 142–43

partition of Palestine, 148–55, 160, 187

Pasha, Nuri Said, 155

Passfield, Lord (Sidney Webb), 119, 124, 126–27, 135

Passfield White Paper, 76, 128–30, 177, 179, 182, 204

patriotism: Jewish claim of American, 169–70, 184; and post-WWI America, 65–66, 67; and Reform's criticism of Zionism, 48–49; during WWI, 34; and Zionism, 24, 168, 178

Peel Commission, 144–45, 146, 148–49, 151

Perry, Ralph Barton, 23

persecution of Jews. *See* antisemitism

philanthropy and Zionism's evolution, 9, 18, 75, 93

Philipson, David, 44–45, 62, 68, 73

The Political World of American Zionism (Halperin), 191

political Zionism: AJC stand against, 181; and Balfour Declaration, 37, 72–75; Christian opposition to, 8, 68–71, 72, 87–88, 160, 228*n*57; elements of post-WWI opposition to, 71–75; FAZ commitment to, 15; Finkelstein's opposition to, 189–212; Jewish criticism of, 66–68, 78–81; last stand against, 201;

overview of development, 3–4; public's apprehensions about, 65; Reform's opposition to, 44–45; WWII era resurrection of, 4, 165, 176–77, 188. *See also* Americanization of Zionism; nationalism; state

Pool, David de Sola, 200

practical building of Palestine: American Zionist role, 34; Conservative support for, 58; and disunity within Zionist camp, 77; economic issues, 107, 119, 121–22, 125, 128; and modern synagogue project, 96; post-Passfield White Paper funding problems, 130; vs. statehood, 15, 22, 182, 183. *See also* Palestinianism; *yishuv*

press role in Zionism, 74, 81–88, 156, 173, 184. *See also individual periodicals*

Progressive movement, 7, 16, 38, 60–61

The Promised Land (Antin), 20

Pro-Palestinian Federation of Americans, 144, 149

Proskauer, Joseph M.: on dual allegiance problem, 214; and Finkelstein's non-Zionist position, 211; role in American Jewish Conference, 167, 170, 182, 183, 185–86

Protocols of the Elders of Zion, 8, 65

Provisional Zionist Committee (PZC), 34–35

public opinion: Arab riots and Arab rights issue, 75–78, 122, 124; Christian criticism of political Zionism, 68–71; Holocaust effect on, 13–14; indifference to Zionist cause, 16; issues in post-Balfour debate, 64–66; Jewish opponents of political Zionism, 66–68, 78–81; press response to Jewish presence in Palestine, 74, 81–88; State Department's consideration of, 150–51, 154, 158; Zionist response to, 7–8, 71–75, 88–94, 165

PZC (Provisional Zionist Committee), 34–35

Rabbinical Assembly (RA), 192, 197, 202, 203, 204, 209

Rabbinical Council of America, 201

universalism, Jewish: AJC support for, 184; and binational state thesis, 81; Christian support for, 87; and Finkelstein's Zionism, 195–96, 198, 206–7; and Magnes's call for Jewish center in Jerusalem, 100; vs. nationalism, 19, 27; Reform's commitment to, 42–43, 51
Untermyer, Samuel, 73
Urofsky, Melvin, 35, 61

values, American: of Reform Judaism, 39–40, 45–49; Zionism's sharing of, 7, 24–25, 35, 191
Viney, Hallen, 87

Wadsworth, George, 145, 149, 151, 153, 161, 163
Wagner, Robert, 157
Waldman, Morris, 181, 185
Warburg, Felix: death of, 136; financial support for *yishuv*, 8; Jewish Agency relationships, 113–19; as leader of non-Zionist group, 77; meeting with Passfield, 126; post-White Paper negotiations, 130; reluctance to counter anti-Zionism, 90; response to British betrayal, 128; support for Magnes, 100–101, 155
Webb, Sidney, Lord Passfield, 119, 124, 126–27, 135
Weisgal, Meyer, 92
Weizmann, Chaim: and American Jewish Conference, 166–67; betrayal by Britain, 139, 163; and Finkelstein, 200, 210; and Hexter, 117, 124, 128, 132; on Hope Simpson, 128, 135–36; immigration to Palestine campaign, 11, 130, 148, 157, 160, 162; as Israel's first president, 212; on Jewish state, 131, 152; and liberal criticism of Zionism, 84; loyalty to Britain, 77–78; suspicions about British motives, 126; vs. Warburg, 113–19
Wertheim, Maurice, 198
western European Jews, 5, 17–18. *See also* German Jewry

Wilson, Woodrow, 34, 60
Wise, Isaac Mayer, 47, 55
Wise, Stephen S.: and antisemitism in America, 174; on binational state thesis, 88; campaign for U.S. government support, 143–44, 147, 156, 161; hostility toward Finkelstein, 200; influence in government, 177, 179; and Jewish fears of unified action, 226n22; on need for Jewish state, 152; on partition, 152, 153; response to Christian criticism, 89; Zionism as bridge to new immigrants, 55
Witte, Sergius, 29
WJC (World Jewish Congress), 170, 175
women, equal treatment in synagogues, 102, 104, 108
Women's League, 111, 204
Woodhead Commission, 151, 155, 157
World Jewish Congress (WJC), 170, 175
World War I, 32–37
World War II: AJC's claims to patriotism in, 184; Jewish support of war aims, 169–70; and resurrection of Zionism, 4, 165, 176–77, 188
World Zionist Organization (WZO), 4, 15, 34
Wright-Compton resolutions, 178, 179, 180, 186
Wyman, David, 186

Yellin, David, 95
Yeshurun congregation in Jerusalem, 103–12
yishuv: affection for Roosevelt, 161; AJC's support of, 183; and American Jewish patriotism in WWII, 170; Brandeis's view of, 60; British plan to undermine, 123–24; contributions to Arabs in Palestine, 80; *haganah*, 143, 164; hostility toward British, 120; internal independence agenda, 198; need for American institutional support, 23; outside fears of communism in, 141; radical military groups in, 177; rejection of Conservatism, 106–7; secularism in,

98, 200; violence during transition to statehood, 211; WWI relief efforts, 35. *See also* Palestine

Zangwill, Israel, 23
Zionism: overview of American, 1–14; post-statehood role of, 215; pre-WWII